WHAT KILLED DOWNTOWN?

Norristown, Pennsylvania, from Main Street to the Malls

Michael E. Tolle

ISBN: 978-0-615-72222-1

Front Cover: The Valley Forge Hotel (1930s) and during its demolition (1974).

Back Cover: The first block of East Main Street, c. 1930s. The Valley Forge Hotel
is at the center top.

Dedication

To my wife Barbara, whom I have loved since I first laid eyes on her almost half a century ago. She has tolerated and enabled my obsession with this topic for many years. Now, at last, I can tell her I am finished.

Acknowledgements

I owe a great deal to a great many people, many more than I can acknowledge here. For those I do not mention by name, please know that every act of assistance and support has not gone unnoticed nor unappreciated.

There were many important resources involved in compiling this book, and I am grateful to have had access to a number of excellent local historical records for the period. The R. L. Polk & Co. published a detailed directory of residences and businesses in the area centered on Norristown approximately every other year (the editions through 1953 were titled "Boyd's Norristown Area Directory"; the 1955 edition added the Polk name). Fifteen of these directories, between 1951 and 1978, yielded the database from which the statistics herein were drawn.

The *Times Herald*, published at Norristown, was a substantial newspaper with a decidedly local focus; it provided much of the material used as the basis of this narrative. These records, buttressed by the (rather less complete) records of the municipality of Norristown and interviews of many who lived through the period, allow the highly relevant story of downtown Norristown to be heard by broader audience. The official records of Norristown are in a deplorable condition. I was lucky to have the assistance of Sandra Grubb, Administrative Assistant at the Norristown Municipal headquarters, in sorting through the attic and making available the existing records.

The resources of the Historical Society of Montgomery County, Pennsylvania, were fundamental to the completion of this work. The Society had several executive directors during the period of my research; each aided immensely, and I thank them all. Jeff McGranahan, a figure of continuity during this time, was a great help. Since he left, Nancy Sullivan stepped in and helped in the selection of photographs for the book. The Society also provided several contacts for interviews. Among those who have passed away, I must make special mention of "Johnny" Young. An essential volunteer at the Society for decades, "Johnny" was a compendium of knowledge about Norristown and its people, all delivered with a biting wit; I was never in her presence but that I longed for a tape recorder.

Of all those interviewed, I owe the most to Hank Cisco. Still a bundle of energy, he was free with his time, his archives, and most of all, his memory. He escorted me down today's Main Street while locating and reminiscing about both the businesses and the individuals that had once prospered there, all by memory.

Turning the result of this research into a readable book, as well as finishing the cover, was my editor, Max Gordon (www.mizmaxgordon.com), to whom I am very grateful, for her inspiration as well as for her labors. I recommend her to all aspiring authors out there.

Inga Vesik (www.vesikphotography.com) created the basic cover, as well as the maps inside, which made all the difference.

It's a whole new world out there for marketing books, but I was fortunate to have Diane Loviglio as my guide.

Finally, I owe thanks to my son, Gilman, without whose aid and support this work would most likely not have been published.

—Michael E. Tolle

Contents

Preface

The Death of the Downtown

S hopping malls killed Main Street America. At least, that is what conventional wisdom says. As with most conventional wisdom, there is a kernel of truth there, and enough undeniable supporting facts to keep the story alive. The real truth, the full story, is much bigger, broader, and occasionally darker.

This book tells that story through a case study of the collapse of one traditional downtown center of retail commerce and services, the borough of Norristown, Pennsylvania. Established in colonial times, by 1950, Norristown boasted an established and dynamic downtown shopping area that centered the six core blocks of Main Street. Downtown Norristown offered the complete shopping experience, 1950s-style: a tightly packed business community with a mix of department stores, retail specialty stores, service businesses, professional offices, and auxiliary services such as banks and restaurants. Packed into those six blocks were 323 for profit businesses. A study of Norristown by the University of Pennsylvania called downtown Norristown "the economic, social and political center for an extensive hinterland,"[1] naming it as the shopping destination of choice for some 160,000 people living in the 220 square miles surrounding the borough.[2] In 1950, downtown merchants were thriving, and looked forward to even greater prosperity in the future.

It was not to be. By 1975, downtown Norristown had collapsed: 65% of its "for profit" businesses had moved away or closed, and 99 storefronts on Main Street's core blocks sat vacant and deteriorating. Main Street itself was pockmarked with the gaps of missing buildings, abandoned and then torn down. In 1984, historians Toll and Schwager, in *Montgomery County: The Second Hundred Years*, accurately described downtown Norristown "a scene of quiet desolation."[3]

What happened during those 25 years?

Many people, then and now, believe they can name the villain in this story: The Malls. In the Norristown area, that refers primarily to the King of Prussia Mall—at present either the largest or second-largest shopping mall in the United States, depending on the measurement used—and, to a lesser extent, the Plymouth Meeting Mall. Downtown Norristown, they say, was literally trapped between these two giant retail centers, could not compete. This is true, as far as it goes, but there is much more to the story.

There are other suspects. The Norristown merchants themselves always blamed their Borough Government for its lack of support. This too is true, as far as it goes. As Norristown is the seat of Montgomery County, this level of local government also had a hand in what transpired. And how about the Norristown merchants themselves? Did their parochial lack of vision itself doom them?

Unless you live near, came from, or plan to move to the borough of Norristown, you might think it's of no consequence what happened to that little patch of Montgomery County, Pennsylvania. In fact, the names and details may not ultimately matter in the greater scheme of things. However, what happened in Norristown happened in other pockets of America over and over during those same 25 years, and what's happening there and elsewhere now will affect the next 25 years. That makes Norristown a useful case study for analysis.

Norristown's qualifications for an analysis of widespread validity begin with what it was, and are solidified by what it was not. Norristown was and remains a medium-sized urban area with a population of around 30,000 people, not a classic "small town." Its size blessed it with a resiliency through redundancy that small towns lack. Norristown is not, however, a city. Though it had a sizeable downtown and a similar but smaller commercial center in its western section, Norristown never possessed the commercial redundancy that significantly larger and more well endowed cities possess. This renders the situation in Norristown considerably different from that of, say, Philadelphia. It also attests to the truth of Jane Jacobs' observation that "towns, suburbs and even little cities are totally different organisms from great cities."[4]

Of equal importance to what Norristown was, and therefore might symbolize, is what it was not. Norristown lacked the characteristics that define similar towns of sufficient size and influence that could readily explain the downtown's decline. For example, Norristown was never a one-company town. It was never dependent on single employer whose corporate fate might have led to a catastrophic domino effect; rather, Norristown's workforce has always been distributed among many workplaces. Nor was Norristown a one-industry town' its diverse employers spanned industries and technologies. The national or international forces that were sweeping over American industry during the period of this study were by no means absent; they were merely dispersed and diluted.

Downtown Norristown was a significant economic center in Montgomery County, Pennsylvania, since the latter part of the 19th century. Over that considerable span of time, businesses had come and gone, but downtown had prospered. Norristown weathered the Depression without a single bank failure. The cause—or causes—for a complete collapse within a quarter century had to be major, indeed.

Norristown's decline cannot be explained easily, either, by any simple changes in local or county governance. The borough grew around the location specified in the document that founded the new County of Montgomery in 1784, which made it an "imperial city," although its actual circumstances were anything but imperial. Governance has been both the founding and sustaining reason for Norristown's existence. County government had never been a major employer, although that would change somewhat over the decades, but its mere presence generated traffic into and within downtown Norristown. Government thus guaranteed a level of stability, a continuing presence upon which economic dreams might be built.

By the middle of the 19th century, many of those economic dreams in Norristown were built on commerce, giving birth to "Downtown Norristown," which grew into a shopping and service center for much of Montgomery County. (The county's eastern extremity, so close to Philadelphia, was largely excluded from this). In 1950, the economic heart of Norristown was commercial, with hundreds of small- to medium-sized merchants offering goods and services, primarily downtown, but also at the smaller West Marshall Street shopping center and other ventures scattered throughout the borough. Retail commerce and services had become dominant base of Norristown's economic foundation.

That foundation crumbled.

What follows is an account of what happened to the downtown of Norristown, Pennsylvania, between 1950 and 1975. Norristown's businesses, commercial organizations, and even individual shoppers found themselves cast in a drama that would soon play out in a great many towns across the country, as going shopping changed from going downtown to going to the mall. The fate of downtown Norristown would soon be shared nationwide by a great many other medium-sized urban areas, each with its own twist on what would become a familiar story. There are broad lessons to be learned from this story, because Norristown's characteristics—or rather its lack of any dominant characteristic—renders its experience pertinent to a critical and broader issue: the fundamental conflict between urban areas and the automobile. That conflict still resonates today.

The story of downtown Norristown is the story of downtown America.

Part I

Good Times

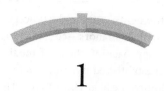

1

Settling Along the Schuylkill

In many ways, the geography of the area brought about both its inevitable growth—the very growth that led the surrounding areas to thrive…and the downtown to die. As William Penn strove to grasp the enormity of the lands in the new world he had been given by King Charles II, the waterways within his new realm occupied much of his attention. In Penn's time and for a long time after, the most expeditious way to transport both people and products for any distance was by river. Penn founded his new capital on the banks of the Delaware River, which would serve as his colony's outlet to the Atlantic, and thus to England. When his gaze and intentions turned westward, he looked again at the rivers, particularly the Schuylkill River, the geographical backbone of his vast holdings.

The Schuylkill was smaller than the Delaware, but as one writer observed, "The Schuylkill was a Penn river from source to mouth."[5] The Schuylkill begins as the joining of several small streams that descend from the first few of the many mountain ridges that would successively confront Pennsylvania's settlers migrating westward. These collectively mark the western perimeter of the Schuylkill Watershed, whose runs, streams, and creeks gradually combine to form the Schuylkill, which carries those waters to the Delaware and beyond to the Atlantic. The Schuylkill's two branches join just north of Schuylkill Haven and flow into what is now Schuylkill County, where the land it traverses, today known as Berks and Montgomery counties, becomes relatively flat and very fertile.[6]

Penn imagined that the Schuylkill River would carry an endless flow of immigrants to settle his lands, but this optimistic view foundered upon the rocks of reality. As a means of transportation, the Schuylkill River always seemed to promise more than it would ever be able to deliver. Depth of water, or rather the lack of it, was not the only obstacle. There was an even greater problem. While the Schuylkill is a placid river, periods of high rainfall can quickly swell the river to several times its normal size and flow rate. These surges, then known as *freshnets*, often sent the normally peaceful river onto a rampage. Following a heavy rain or large snowmelts, surging waters swept many of the structures from along its banks. Along with the natural detritus of branches, leaves, and silt, this debris steadily accumulated, collecting against and eventually destroying the fragile bridges that spanned the river. Penn's disposition of the lands along the Schuylkill are a testament to the river's immense value to

1

him as he established his settlements. Among the powers granted by Charles II's charter was the authority to establish manors—considerable tracts of land over which owners would have powers approaching those of medieval lords, including the administration of justice. Penn established five manors for himself and for members of his family. Four of these adjoined the Schuylkill River. The fifth, the Manor of Springfield, while comprising some 4,000 acres rather removed from the river, included a corridor three miles long and less than a mile wide that provided access to the Schuylkill.

In 1689, Penn directed a surveyor to lay out a manor, specifying that it consist of lands along "the canoeable part of the Schuylkill." This manor comprised some 7,500 acres on the north bank of the Schuylkill between two tributaries named Stony Creek and Saw Mill Run, although the precise acreage has been the subject of disagreement among historians. Penn granted this manor to his son, William Penn Jr., as the Manor of Williamstadt.[7] The Manor of Williamstadt did not prove attractive to Penn the younger. There is no record that he ever visited it after he arrived in the area in 1703. He clearly preferred Philadelphia, especially its inns and taverns, so much so that his behavior scandalized the Quakers of Philadelphia; after one such ruckus, the young Penn was indicted for disturbing the peace. He resolved to leave Pennsylvania as quickly as possible,[8] and decided to sell Williamstadt.

Unfortunately, his indifference to his manor had led to no warrant of ownership actually having been being issued. This dearth of paperwork threatened to delay his departure, but he was determined. He finally managed to obtain the necessary warrant on October 2, 1704,[9] and five day later sold the land to Isaac Norris and William Trent for £850 pounds.[10] Both Norris and Trent were prominent citizens of the colony of Pennsylvania. Isaac Norris was particularly well regarded. Born in London in 1671, Norris immigrated to Philadelphia in 1693 and rose to become one of its leading citizens, serving as a member of the Governor's Council, speaker of the Assembly, justice of the county, and eventually mayor of Philadelphia. In 1712, Isaac Norris bought out Trent's share in the Manor of Williamstadt, after which Trent removed himself to New Jersey and established Trent's Town (known today as Trenton). Norris then divided his manor into large farms, but for reasons left undocumented, laid out the portion surrounding Stony Creek and Saw Mill Run into smaller lots—an act both curious and prophetic.

Local Roads

The Schuylkill's inability to provide sufficient transport for the farmers within its watershed became more apparent as their numbers increased. One result was an increased emphasis on building up the area's road system. The network of existing Indian trails co-opted by the Europeans provided the original planning guide for this slow evolution. Indian trails invariably traversed the path of least resistance, which often meant along the beds of creeks and streams. The Europeans, while needing wider paths, initially lacked the numbers and the means to overcome even the relatively benign variations in the land immediately northwest of Philadelphia. Thus, they tended to follow quite literally in the footsteps of the Native Americans they were displacing.

The early roads spread out from Philadelphia in what 20th-century historian John T. Faris described as a "fan shape."[11] One spoke of the fan followed the eastern and northern bank of the Schuylkill: In 1706, the court in Philadelphia ordered that "a common cartway" be built to connect the Schuylkill's two primary tributaries in Philadelphia County, the Wissahickon and Perkiomen creeks.[12] This was the origin of a road that would, by sections and in fits and starts, gradually parallel the Schuylkill along its north bank. Since the road generally followed the high ground along the river's north ridge, it eventually came to be called the Ridge Pike.

It was by hardly a "pike" by today's standards. Like virtually all rural roads in America at that time, it was rough, rutted, and alternately dusty, muddy, slushy, or frozen. Construction proceeded sporadically and haphazardly; maintenance was even more problematical. At that time, the courts usually appointed local road supervisors to direct the necessary work. In theory, the actual labor was generally provided by the local taxpayers for a specific number of days each year, unless they could afford to either hire substitutes or pay a tax directly to the township; in reality, little actual work was ever done. The unwilling, equipped with the inadequate, and led by the unqualified produced only brief and insubstantial improvements in the local road conditions.

In forging their trails, the Native Americans had found the best locations to ford the Schuylkill and its larger tributaries. The Schuylkill could be forded, with varying degrees of difficulty, in several places, except during times of high flow. As European settlers moved into the area, these fording locations became focal points for the evolution of the area's primitive road system. A few of the area's earliest European arrivals—Swedish immigrants who were already established along the lower Delaware River by the time William Penn arrived—had moved again, settling on a tract near one of the most practical fording places, along the south bank of the river, just below Saw Mill Run. They received formal title to this land in 1712.[13] The area would become known as Swedeland, and the ford as Swedes Ford. When roads were laid out to approach it on both sides of the river, they would become jointly known as Swedesford Road, a name that survives to this day.

From Williamstadt to Norriton

In 1730, the Court of Quarter Sessions of Philadelphia County ordered that the land previously known as The Manor of Williamstadt be renamed Norriton Township after Isaac Norris. The new township's population at this time was identified as 20 people.[14] Isaac Norris died in either 1735 or 1736 (accounts differ).[15] His will appointed his wife Mary and his sons, Isaac, Charles, and Samuel, as joint executors. In 1741, upon the final division of the Norris estates, Charles Norris emerged as owner of the Norriton lands.[16] He sold several tracts of land to settlers, but resided in Philadelphia until his death. His widow, also named Mary, inherited the lands still in the Norris family, the core of the old Manor of Williamstadt, encompassing the land between Stony Creek and Saw Mill Run. On February 27, 1771, she offered up for public sale

The Norriton Plantation and Mill Tract, identified as 543½ acres, including Barbadoes Island (in the Schuylkill River), about 88 acres, most of which extended downriver from Stony Creek for about a mile.[17]

John Bull, a colonel in the Pennsylvania Militia, purchased the tract for £4,600. On October 30, 1776, he sold all of it except 40 acres on Barbadoes Island to Dr. William Smith for £6,000. Smith was acting on behalf of what was, by its confirmatory charter of 1755, the College, Academy and Charitable School of the Province of Pennsylvania; Smith transferred the land to the College, which immediately leased it back to Bull, who continued to occupy it. Whatever the College's plans for the Norriton Plantation and Mill Tract were when they purchased the property, those plans were disrupted by the inconvenient intrusion of the American Revolution.

A Test of Loyalty

The Norriton lands were caught up in the American Revolution as the focus of the war shifted south from New York to Philadelphia. Montgomery County was the scene of marches, counter-marches, picket lines and a few skirmishes, as the contending armies contested the Philadelphia area in 1777–1778. John Bull, despite his English name, was an ardent patriot who distinguished himself in the Continental Army. Between the Battle of Brandywine on September 11, 1777, and the arrival of Washington's colonial troops at Valley Forge on December 19, at various times both the Continental and the British forces (led by General William Howe) occupied the Norriton lands. General Howe expropriated John Bull's "Mansion House" just north of Egypt Road as his headquarters, and his troops burned down Bull's barn and his mills along the river before marching to Philadelphia. General Washington followed. The result was the Battle of Germantown, October 4, 1777. The Continental Army, fleeing the British after the battle, crossed the Schuylkill at Swedes' Ford on its approach to Valley Forge.[18]

Americans generally think of the American Revolution as a series of important battles between armies of men, with dramatic moments immortalized in earnest paintings and songs. As with any war, the reality was quite different. Among the forgotten battles were those fought on a personal, familial front as individual citizens were forced to choose sides. The question of loyalty also confronted organizations, and one such painful struggle that played itself out at the Academy. The trustees of the college, and Dr. Smith personally, were suspected of not supporting the revolutionary cause with sufficient patriotic fervor. In retaliation, the Pennsylvania Assembly passed an Act of Assembly on November 27, 1779, that created a new school, the University of the State of Pennsylvania, to be administered by a new Board of Trustees. The Act transferred all rights and property of the previous College, Academy and Charitable School of the Province of Pennsylvania—including the Norriton lands—to the new school. Smith was forced to retire from his post as provost.[19] In the coming years, the previous board of directors, along with Dr. Smith, lobbied relentlessly to have the decision reversed.[20] This conflict would bear directly on the formative years of Norristown.

A New County—And a New County Seat

In the years following the Revolution, the population of Philadelphia County increased steadily, with people moving out to the more distant reaches, farther and farther away from Philadelphia, the county seat. Travel from the western portions of the county to Philadelphia was difficult, and the residents of this area begrudged the fact that fulfillment of many legal obligations required such a journey.[21] Petitions arguing for the creation of a new county northwest of Philadelphia began to appear in the General Assembly in 1782.[22] More or less simultaneously, there arose agitation to carve a new county out of parts of Philadelphia, Berks, and Chester counties, with the county seat at Pottstown. By 1784 there were, broadly stated, two alternatives: the Pottstown Plan, and a coalescing proposal to carve the new county out of only Philadelphia County. The Pottstown proposal submitted to a committee of the Pennsylvania Assembly in January 1784 was rejected.

Another committee was appointed to study the matter of dividing Philadelphia County itself, which is where the University of the State of Pennsylvania and the the Norriton Plantation and Mill Tract entered the story (Barbadoes Island had been sold, and was no longer part of the University's lands). On March 3, 1784, trustees met at the University of Pennsylvania and read a letter from Jacob Rush, member of the Assembly from Philadelphia County, allegedly representing "the members of Philada [sic] county" asking on what terms the University would part with 20 acres in Norriton for the site of the county buildings. On March 11, the trustees announced that they had agreed to offer not 20 acres, but 4 acres "forever as a free gift," bolstered by a promise to lay out an additional 20 acres of land surrounding the 4 acres in small plots, and offer these at a public auction whenever the commissioners of the new county might request this. [23] The bill was submitted to a committee, which prepared the formal bill for consideration by the Assembly. After public scrutiny, committee wrangling, and some back-and-forth over boundaries, the Pennsylvania Assembly passed the proposal September 10, 1784. This carved out the new county, Montgomery, from land lopped off Philadelphia County, and named the county seat as "a piece of land, situated in some convenient place in the neighborhood of Stony Run, contiguous to the river Schuylkill, in Norriton township...."[24]

The final version of the Act appointed five individuals by name to obtain and hold title to the piece of land. These were not county commissioners. Their appointments were for life, and they had no governmental functions beyond ensuring that there would be suitable buildings available for county offices. Since there were no suitable buildings in the specified area, the five men met at Hannah Thompson's tavern, about a mile west of Stony Run, in what is now known as Jeffersonville.[25] County executives were appointed, county commissioners were elected, and by October 1784, the government of Montgomery County had begun to function. Determining the exact size and location of the lot for the county buildings thus became a priority. Negotiations with the University of Pennsylvania took some time; the deed transferring the property from the University to Montgomery County was not entered into the official record until December 7, 1785.

Curiously, the lot for the county seat had shrunk considerably, for reasons that were never fully documented. What the new county actually received for its public buildings was far less than the four acres originally offered by the trustees: a rectangular lot, 344 feet by 140 feet. The lot lay just up the hillside from the area's major road, Ridge Pike, which constituted the lot's southern boundary along its 140-foot length. Furthermore, this "gift" by now had a price: 5 shillings.[26]

The new county commissioners moved forward even before they had the formal agreement in hand. A November 10, 1784, notice in the *Pennsylvania Gazette* announced that the commissioners would meet, again at Hannah Thompson's inn, to accept proposals for construction of the county buildings. Records indicate that the work was initiated long before the date of deed transfer.[27] The commissioners contracted for and oversaw the construction of the two original county buildings, a courthouse and a jail. The courthouse, a small two-story stone structure, was built at the foot of the designated tract, facing Egypt Road. The jail was built just up the hill from the courthouse. Behind the jail stood the whipping post, though it seems that only four whippings ever took place there—two in 1785 and two in 1786—probably because the jail was not yet available.[28]

The Deed of December 7, 1785, which formally conveyed the land to the five commissioners, described the lot reserved for the county buildings as extending 344 feet south from Airy Street, specifying that after construction of the county buildings, the remainder to Egypt Road (Ridge Pike) was to be "a public square to remain open forever."[29] Thus, the center of the seat of Montgomery County, the intersection of Swede Street and Egypt Road (later Main Street) is an open park.

The selection of the Stony Creek site for the new county seat was clearly an attempt by the University of the State of Pennsylvania to curry favor with the state legislature and to profit thereby. It occurred in 1784, precisely halfway between the Act of 1779 that bestowed a new board of trustees and a new title on the previous Academy and School, and its partial repeal in 1789. By 1784, the Act of 1779 was increasingly being viewed as "a simple act of spoliation," although somewhat legitimized by the passions of war.[30] With public sentiment beginning to swing against them, the trustees of the University clearly saw in the letter from Jacob Rush an opportunity to advance their institution's cause. It cannot have escaped the notice of the embattled trustees that a land grant for the new county seat would both sit well with the Assembly and, in a larger context, reflect that the University was aligned with them—in contrast to the alleged inclinations of the Academy under Dr. Smith.

The offer to divide the surrounding land into small lots and offer them for sale at the wish of the county commissioners also demonstrated that the University hoped to reap some profit from the new county seat growing on its land. The trustees had, through their five-shilling "gift," ensured that the new county seat, as it grew and developed, would do so wholly on lands owned by the University. Unfortunately for them, the expectation of profit would prove to be a chimera.

The Town of Norris

The original Deed of Indenture of December 7, 1785, which formally conveyed the "county lot" to the five appointed commissioners, is in the possession of the Historical Society of Montgomery County. Accompanying the Indenture in the original deed book is a map that lays out "the Town of Norris" around the county lot. The map shows no existing structures within the new town, although the accuracy of that is disputed. The only structure referenced is John Bull's "Mansion House" west of the town along Egypt Road. The new town of Norris lay entirely within land belonging to the University of the State of Pennsylvania.[31]

Virtually all local sources claim that the central figure in the process of establishing the town of Norris was William Moore Smith, the son of Dr. William Smith. This seems highly unlikely. Dr. Smith, the Academy's former provost, had moved to Chestertown, Maryland, and was serving as president of a new institution, Washington College. His departure from Philadelphia had been acrimonious, and he retained a strong feeling that an injustice had been done.[32] In 1784–85, when the town plan was prepared, the dispute between the old Academy and the new University still festered. Though the younger Smith had graduated from the old Academy in 1775 and had not taken the openly loyalist approach of his father, there is no evidence of a breach between the two.[33] It seems improbable that William Moore Smith would have served the University trustees who had removed his father from his position as provost of his beloved Academy.

2

Roads, Rivers, & Railroads

The well situated spot that became Norristown was to Penn and the colonials merely "the canoeable part of the Schuylkill,"[34] but before long it had become much more, a real town, neatly arranged and nearly self-sufficient, tucked happily into the countryside 17 miles northwest of Philadelphia. Once inhabited solely by the Native Americans known as the Lenni Lenape (and called the Delawares by the white interlopers), the area slowly grew larger and more diverse as settlers trickled in—English, Welsh, Dutch, Welsh, Scottish, German, and Swedish. Soon that trickle would rival the flow of the Schuylkill itself as advances in transportation transformed the tiny town into an industrial boomtown.

For the initial layout as the town of Norris through its development into Norristown, the area that would become known as "downtown" followed what is known as the "Pennsylvania Town Model," an approach derived from William Penn's plan for Philadelphia. Streets intersected at right angles, forming rectangular lots. Alleys subdivided some blocks. Building footprints stretched nearly to the street to make maximum use of the space. Thus, the town of Norris (later the borough of Norristown) was a model Pennsylvania town of "sheer compactness and tightness."[35] This compactness served downtown merchants well during the 18th and 19th centuries; its maximization of structure space on each lot delivered the greatest possible square footage for the price. Given the modest population numbers and still-primitive transportation technology, the lack of any significant ability to expand the street network was of no importance at that time. As the 20th century progressed, however, this compactness and lack of room for expansion would complicate attempts to deal with the astonishing growth that choked the downtown streets. Streets designed for dense usage and primarily pedestrian travel were not well suited to a public increasingly enamored of the automobile and dismissive of public transportation.

The town of Norris incorporated the only two roads that existed at that time, Ridge Pike–Egypt Road and Swede Street. Their intersection at the southwest corner of the county plot became the geographic center of the town of Norris, and later the borough of Norristown. Egypt Road was a slightly straightened section of the already-existing Ridge Pike, known locally as "The Road to Egypt" for its destination, a fertile delta of the Perkiomen Creek. Swede Street was a shortcut to Swedes Ford on the Schuylkill, and not part of the also-existing Swedes Ford Road, which skirted the original town of

Norris, first on the west and then the south. In 1775, the Philadelphia County court had ordered the opening of a road along this route, from Egypt Road south to the river, then the site of the mill owned by John Bull. The portion of the shortcut north of Egypt Road and the "open" path south to the riverbank were joined and designated as Swede Street in the town of Norris.[36] The southern boundary of the town was a narrow alley that ran parallel to and south of Egypt Road and connected structures on the south side. North of and roughly parallel to Egypt Road along the actual ridge of the river valley was Airy Street, the northern boundary of Norris. The county tract was laid out from the intersection of Swede and Airy streets. The new courthouse faced Swede Street, while the jail up the hill faced Airy Street. Below both was the public square.

DeKalb Street, a north/south road that connected Airy and Egypt 500 feet east of the county plot, was apparently named after a general in the Revolutionary army, though he appears to have had no local connections. Perhaps someone simply liked the name. Two north/south alleys—Green Alley to the east of DeKalb Street and Cherry Alley to the west of Swede Street—formed the town's eastern and western boundaries respectively. A lane designated as Courthouse Alley followed the east side of the courthouse property between Egypt and Airy streets, beginning at Swede Street and extending eastward to Green Alley. The streets (Egypt, Airy, Swede, and DeKalb) were each 50 feet wide; the alleys (Green, Cherry, and Courthouse) were each 24 feet wide. The original town of Norris was neatly squared off into a compact, orderly layout, perfect for pedestrian, horse, and carriage travel.

In addition to the courthouse, 64 lots extended from the Egypt Road to Airy Street, and from Cherry Alley to Green Alley. The first 10 lots east of the public square, stretching along Egypt to DeKalb, set the standard for the lot size in Norris, 50 feet by 250 feet. They were offered for public sale on February 28, 1785; Lot #1, adjacent to the public square, sold for £77. Others went for varying, lesser prices.[37] Curiously, each of the deeds for the lots in the original block offered for sale revived the medieval concept of "quit rent": the purchaser of each was to pay annually to the University of Pennsylvania one acorn, if demanded. It is not known whether this was ever enforced.[38]

William J. Buck, who wrote the first history of Montgomery County in 1858, claimed that "the lots were soon all sold and a number of buildings commenced."[39] Initial sales were in fact quite slow. Only three lots were recorded as sold in February 1785,[40] and none in the second year. When the Town of Norris became the Borough of Norristown in 1812, the University still owned seven of the original lots.[41] The last of the original 64 lots finally sold in 1822.[42] William Moore Smith bought one of the lots, then two more adjacent lots in 1791, and built a house.[43]

Not only did the University of Pennsylvania not profit from the sale of its property subdivided as the town of Norris, a change in public opinion soon deprived the institution of the remaining portion of the original Norriton Plantation and Mill Tract. By 1789, residual ill-will toward the allegedly unpatriotic Dr. Smith and the Academy had waned sufficiently that the Pennsylvania Assembly partially abrogated the 1779 Act and restored the rights of the old Academy and College, including its remaining land in Norriton. In 1791, the two schools merged. Just prior to this, however, William Moore Smith purchased the remaining Norriton lands for £4,300; the deed was recorded on January 18, 1791. This property, some 484 acres, encircled the town, touching the Schuylkill both above and below it.[44]

Whatever his role or lack thereof in laying out the town in 1784, once William Moore Smith became the owner of the land around Norris, he attempted to profit from his investment. He became a strong supporter of the plans then being discussed to connect Philadelphia with the Susquehanna River in the west via a canal and the Schuylkill River. Sales, however, continued at a snail's pace.

By the turn of the century, with few of his lots sold, Smith sold the entire tract to local resident John Markley, effective September 30, 1802. He received £15,000, finally earning a profit above the £4,300 he had paid in 1791. Markley, who had purchased one of the original lots in the town of Norris, had in 1801 demonstrated his business acumen by purchasing from the University the three lots along Swede Street closest to Egypt Road, still unsold since the original offering in 1785. He realized that the Swede Street lots between Egypt and Airy had been laid out with the assumption that the property owners would wish to face the county courthouse, and that lagging sales had proven this incorrect. When he rearranged the Swede/Egypt lots so that the new lots fronted on Egypt Road from Swede Street west to Cherry Street, he quickly found buyers for them all.[45]

The First Turnpike Era

Growth continued to be slow. That the Town of Norris grew at all was due in part to its easy access to transportation routes, including the stagecoach trade. In 1781, William Coleman had begun to operate a stagecoach line between Philadelphia and Reading, using the Ridge Road and thus Egypt Road through what was still the Town of Norris. The trip took "one full long day" in good weather. In winter, the coach had to start from Philadelphia at two o'clock in the morning to make it to Reading by nightfall.[46] Norris benefited from being a stopover for travelers seeking refreshment or accommodations. The traffic along Egypt Road meant that the actual activity center of the town quickly gravitated one block south of the county buildings at Swede and Airy streets to the intersection of Swede and Egypt streets. Businesses catering to travelers began setting up along Egypt Road.

Egypt Road remained the main road, although by the time Norris became Norristown in 1812, a fundamental change had begun. Pennsylvania was in the middle of the First Turnpike Era, during which private companies constructed roads after receiving government approval. The first private company to receive a charter to build a road in Pennsylvania—and charge tolls for its use—had been the Lancaster Turnpike Company, organized in 1792. By 1821, there were 146 turnpike companies authorized by law in the state of Pennsylvania; by 1830, the number had increased to 220. The actual number of turnpikes begun was considerably fewer, and the number of those completed fewer still. The mileage of turnpikes steadily rose, but the record of achievement in Pennsylvania was mixed. One chronicler of Pennsylvania turnpikes wrote that after 1832, "abandonment of turnpikes more than offset construction."[47]

One early effort was the Ridge Turnpike Company, organized in 1804 to build a stone road beginning at the intersection of 8th and Vine streets in Philadelphia and extending through Norristown and on to Reading. As happened with so many other such companies, the Ridge Turnpike Company had problems raising capital, which led to a slow pace of construction. Despite its problems, the Ridge Turnpike Company did improve the road between Philadelphia and Norristown. In 1808, three stagecoaches per week left Norristown for Philadelphia, on Monday, Wednesday and Friday, returning on the alternate days. By 1813, the run was being made on a daily basis.[48]

The Ridge Turnpike reached Norristown in 1812. Within the borough, the turnpike company constructed a macadamized (compacted stones of differing sizes) path down the middle, with dirt on each side to the width of the street. While this work marked a fundamental improvement to Egypt Road, residents viewed it as a mixed blessing. On each side of the macadamized center strip, the road remained dirt. Over time, the dirt sections along each side would become known as the "summer road." In warm weather, people preferred to travel down the sides in the dirt, rather than the "loosely deposited" stones in the middle.[49]

Another improvement was the beginning of a north/south road connection for the borough. In 1830, the state legislature authorized a commission to lay out a road from New Hope, on the Pennsylvania side of the Delaware River not far from Trenton, New Jersey, through Bucks County, including the county seat at Doylestown, continuing south through Norristown and West Chester to the Maryland state line. The route was thus termed the "State Road," a name that would remain locally into the 20th century. No state funds were earmarked for the actual construction, however, and all subsequent costs were to be borne by the townships and boroughs through which the road would run. Thus, the road itself remained little more than an idea in many areas. In Norristown, it followed the planned route of DeKalb Street. Despite its supposed "state" status, DeKalb Street remained unpaved for decades, a major source of dust in the summer and mud in the winter.[50]

One reason the State Road followed DeKalb Street was the new bridge across the Schuylkill, the first such bridge at Norristown. Fording the Schuylkill had always been a chancy proposition, and as the population of Montgomery County increased, the need for a crossing at the county seat was becoming more obvious. By 1815 the state legislature had passed an act authorizing the formation of a Norristown Bridge Company, and in 1829 construction on a wooden covered bridge actually began at the foot of DeKalb Street. Toll collection began in January 1830.[51]

The Schuylkill Navigation

While William Penn's idea of channeling the commerce of his western lands to Philadelphia via the Schuylkill River remained just a dream during his lifetime, his vision would continue to tempt those who followed him. It was not until the Revolution had been fought and won and the state of Pennsylvania established that actual planning took place, however. Two attempts at the end of the 18th century to construct a canal system failed in their larger goal, and had virtually no effect on the new town of Norris, but in 1815, another attempt with a more limited goal would be more successful. The system contributed somewhat to Norristown's growth and development in the brief period—little more than ten years—before yet another new mode of transportation (the railroad) would render it redundant.

The Schuylkill Navigation Company was chartered in 1815. The project was to be a combination canal and "slack water" system. The slack water portions would be where dams could be constructed to render the Schuylkill deep enough to allow boats to travel; a lock at each dam would make it possible to raise and lower the boats. Along the Schuylkill's many stretches that were too shallow, sections of canal were to be built. A path was constructed along the side of each canal section; attached to each boat by ropes, mules pulled the boats from one slack-water section to the next.[52]

The Schuylkill Navigation system was completed in 1828, although because the occasional freshnets wreaked havoc, construction never actually ceased. The completed canal traversed a total of 108.59 miles, of which 62.07 miles were canals and 46.52 miles were slack-water systems.[53] Three round-trips per week between Philadelphia and Norristown were initially scheduled. Travel on the system, however, was almost entirely downstream, through Norristown to Philadelphia.

Despite the Schuylkill Navigation's promised advantages for communities through which it passed, Norristown residents were largely opposed to locating the canal on the borough's side of the river. Canal locks elsewhere were known to attract ruffians, troublemakers, and petty criminals, which meant more work for the police and courts. A local resident who owned considerable land along the river's south bank stepped in and offered the Schuylkill Navigation land along this bank for construction. The canal would thus contribute the "port" to the eventual borough of Bridgeport, Norristown's neighbor to the immediate south across the Schuylkill River.[54] Norristown Borough Council in 1819 did purchase a tract of land from John Markley along the river on the eastern bank of Stony Creek for $100. The land was to be "a public landing forever." The council eventually established "wharfage rates"—a landing toll that varied according to the items landed. There is little evidence that it was much used, although canal boats continued to occasionally land at the wharf into the late 1870s.[55]

While the Schuylkill Navigation's canal bypassed Norristown, a side benefit of the canal/slack water system proved to be of benefit to the borough. The company constructed a dam just upriver from Swede Street to create the slack water for what would become known as the "Norristown Pool," which extended upriver until the next dam, Catfish Dam, in the area later known as Betzwood. By providing a more consistent source of power, the dam launched industry in Norristown. Water-powered factories powered by the flow from the Norristown Dam soon dwarfed the small mills that had depended on Stony Creek and Saw Mill Run for power. With more—and more consistent—power now available, mills for dyeing, spinning, and weaving textiles sprang up just downriver from the Norristown Dam. These plants initially used the Schuylkill River for power (and for disposal of by-products). They did not use it to transport their raw materials or finished products: that task would be fulfilled by the railroad.

The Coming of the Railroad

Proximity to an intersection of local roads and to the Schuylkill River—in addition to the price—had made the plot of land offered by the University of Pennsylvania for the seat of the new county quite attractive. However, the limited capacity and periodic unavailability of both the roads and river limited their use for transporting both people and products. This slowed the initial growth of the town. That changed with the arrival of a revolutionary mode of transportation—the railroad. The rail system ushered in an era of rapid growth and increasing prosperity. Quickly relegating the Schuylkill Navigation to secondary status, the railroad made Norristown the locus of an increasingly vigorous transportation network.

The residents of Montgomery County, including Norristown, were among the earliest Americans to experience this revolutionary mode of transportation. In February 1831, the state granted a legal charter to the Philadelphia, Germantown and Norristown Railroad (PG&N) to connect Philadelphia to Germantown and proceed up the north bank of the Schuylkill to Norristown.[56] In 1832, the first "train" traveled along the first segment, a six-mile stretch from Philadelphia to Germantown: there were nine cars, each pulled by a horse. In November that same year, the first steam locomotive began service on the Philadelphia-Germantown section. This locomotive, "Old Ironsides," was the first produced at the works of Matthias W. Baldwin in Philadelphia, where steam power would continue to be developed and put into service well into the 20th century.[57]

On Saturday, August 15, 1835, the first PG&N Railroad train steamed into Norristown and was greeted by enthusiastic locals.[58] Thereafter, PG&N ran two trains between Philadelphia and Norristown in each direction every day. As with other early railroads in American cities, PG&N's train tracks shared the streets with the other vehicles and pedestrian traffic. The Norristown Borough Council granted PG&N rights for its line to enter the town on Washington Street.[59] The initial PG&N rail terminus was at DeKalb Street to meet the bridge across the Schuylkill. Although there was no station at the time, there was a ticket office and a small waiting room in a hotel at the northwest corner of DeKalb and Washington.

The location of the tracks began what would become a long tradition: trains blocking road traffic across the DeKalb Street bridge. PG&N eventually built a terminal in 1856 on Mill Street in the eastern end of Norristown. The Mill Street terminal was grand by the standards of the time, with a wide plaza fronting the street to accommodate the omnibuses, carriages, and cabs that flocked to meet the trains. Originally built in 1809 to access the Egypt Flour Mill, which used Saw Mill Run for its power, Mill Street had until then been only a minor road. After PG&N built the station with its elaborate entrance, Mill Street became the widest street in the borough for a time.[60]

In 1833, while the PG&N was still under construction, a new railroad corporation was organized to link Philadelphia to Reading and the anthracite fields to the north. Unlike the PG&N and other small railroad ventures, the new Philadelphia and Reading Railroad was underwritten by banking houses in New York and Philadelphia, giving it from the start an advantage in the ability to expend capital.[61] Construction began in

1835, but substantial engineering challenges faced the new line. While the PG&N had built its tracks along the eastern/northern bank of the Schuylkill, the P&R decided to build on the western/southern bank. That choice pitted the P&R against the same geographical challenges that would torment the designers of the Schuylkill Expressway more than 100 years later. Despite the company's large initial funding, financial difficulties further slowed the slow pace of work thanks in part to President Jackson's "war" with the Second Bank of the United States, and the depression that swept the country following his "victory."[62]

The track from Reading to Philadelphia opened in sections; the section that opened in 1838 established service between Reading and Bridgeport. By 1842, the P&R Railroad had freight and passenger service from Philadelphia all the way to Pottsville, 94 miles. The railroad's main concern was not passengers, however, but anthracite coal, the "black gold" that underlay its prosperity. Thus, P&R sought to gain monopoly control of transporting coal from the mines to Philadelphia, first squeezing out the Schuylkill Navigation, then gradually absorbing most of the area's smaller lines. For example, in 1870 P&R leased PG&N railroad for 999 years. Thereafter, though PG&N continued to operate, it did so as a component of the Reading system. In the same way, P&R gained control of other local railroads, and soon dominated Norristown's railroad connections until 1880. Then, an even larger and wealthier railroad, the Pennsylvania, intruded on its territory.

The Pennsylvania Comes to Town

By the final quarter of the 19th century, with a more mature technology and considerably greater financing, the by-now corporate giants of railroading were fully engaged in all-out high-stakes competition. The railroad wars of this era affected Norristown directly, as the Reading found itself challenged by the Pennsylvania Railroad. The physical results of this competition would extend and cement the sectioning of Norristown first introduced to the town by the PG&N when it arrived in the 1830s. Another such war in south-central Pennsylvania would have a much-delayed but enormous impact on Norristown in the 20th century.

By the latter decades of the 19th century, the Reading Railroad had grown into a large, multi-faceted corporate power known as the Reading System. While its power and financial clout had greatly increased, its growth had also brought it into conflict with other railroad corporations of equal or even greater resources. These corporations engaged in competition across a spectrum of possibilities, some of them of dubious legality. While the Reading engaged in several disputes with more than one railroad, by the latter 19th century its primary competitor was clearly the Pennsylvania Railroad. During the 1880s the Pennsylvania decided to challenge the Reading's near-monopoly of coal transport from the fields to Philadelphia.[63] In 1883, it began construction on a Schuylkill branch line, a new railroad connection between Pottstown and Philadelphia. The challenge could not have been more direct: the Pennsylvania built its tracks up the east bank of the Schuylkill, closely paralleling those of the PG&N (now the) Reading, which fought to prevent construction of the competing

14

rails, filing lawsuit after lawsuit. Fights frequently broke out between workers of the rival companies at points where the two lines came close to one another.[64]

The tracks of the Pennsylvania also closely paralleled those of the Reading as they approached Norristown. The PG&N tracks used by the Reading wended into town along Washington Street, and the Pennsylvania tracks entered Norristown directly adjacent, along Lafayette Street. The Pennsylvania opened its first passenger station at the corner of DeKalb and Lafayette streets on June 23, 1884, and began service between Philadelphia and Norristown that same day. The Pennsylvania ran 12 trains each way on weekdays and five on Sundays. Within 20 years, ridership increased to the point where the Pennsylvania needed a new station. Wisely recognizing that its first terminal location had added to the number of trains blocking DeKalb Street, they built the new terminal midway between DeKalb and Swede streets. This second station was opened to the public on February 21, 1904.[65]

The railroads not only underlay Norristown's growth, but they would fundamentally shape the nature of that growth. As the railroads in Norristown occupied the valleys of the Schuylkill River and Stony Creek, Norristown's industries largely cluster along their routes like magnets to steel. The industries could have raw materials delivered by rail to their front doors, and dispose of the waste generated by their processes out the back doors—directly into the Schuylkill. Over time, the railroads would broadly delineate an industrial zone in Norristown, occupying the flat land along the river from the south side of Lafayette Street to the riverbank, and along the easternmost stretch of Egypt Road. A narrower zone would follow the railroad tracks north along the valley of Stony Creek. Those lowest on the economic rung clung to a precarious existence here, but the great bulk of Norristown's population increase would settle nearby in areas of the borough little better than those clustered around the railroad tracks and factories.

During this period, the railroads permanently relegated the flat lands south of Main Street to secondary status, of little use to anything other than industry and the railroads themselves. While the coming of the PG&N had initially caused the population of this area to swell, with Mill Street becoming a heavily traveled street, the arrival of the Pennsylvania Railroad in the 1880s had the opposite effect. This second railroad necessitated the wholesale removal of buildings to accommodate the new route. The construction of the new station beginning in 1902 subtracted another 30 dwellings, which were purchased by the Pennsylvania and leveled.[66] This second coming of a railroad virtually eliminated what commercial or residential presence had located on Lafayette and Washington streets. Both streets were relegated to the status of arteries serving industry, and for Lafayette, offering rear access to shops and stores along the south side of Main Street.

Just as the Reading was at war with the larger, so too was the Pennsylvania competing with a much bigger foe. The Pennsylvania's long-distance focus had set it repeatedly against the New York Central, led by William H. Vanderbilt. Vanderbilt was the son of "the Commodore," and the living stereotype of a 19th-century tycoon. In 1882, Vanderbilt concluded, with good reason, that the Pennsylvania Railroad was scheming to build a line that would challenge his route up the Hudson River, and decided to reply in kind: he would build a railroad across southern Pennsylvania in direct competition with the Pennsylvania Railroad. Investors with Vanderbilt in this affair included Andrew Carnegie (the new railroad would pass directly through his steel plant in Homestead, Pennsylvania), the Rockefeller brothers, and others of similarly substantial means. Thus the South Pennsylvania Railroad was born (reborn, actually, as Vanderbilt had bought an existing corporation, a railroad in name only that had performed no work whatsoever).

The project faced the same obstacles every Pennsylvanian with a westward focus had confronted: the many low, parallel ridges that lie across the east/west path. While the Pennsylvania Railroad had decided to take a circuitous route around these obstacles, the South Pennsylvania proposed to tunnel right through them. The resulting route would be shorter, with lower grades than those traversed by the Pennsylvania's route. There were to be nine tunnels in all, along with a substantial new bridge across the Susquehanna River. The work proved to be hideously expensive, especially given the financial pressures applied by the Pennsylvania. The financial drain on the New York Central alarmed its large stockholders, who appealed to the one man who could prevail over such powerful contestants as the Carnegies and Rockefellers: banker J. P. Morgan. In July 1885, in one of the classic episodes of 19th-century capitalism, Morgan summoned representatives from both the New York Central and the Pennsylvania railroads to meet on his yacht. The parties resolved the matter during a long, leisurely cruise along the East River and Long Island Sound. Both projects, the provocation and the response, would be absorbed by their respective corporations. The New York Central would lease its Hudson River competitor, and the Pennsylvania would buy the South Pennsylvania, after the value of both had been heavily written down.

As it turned out, a court decision blocked the Pennsylvania's purchase of its interloper, and thereafter work ceased forever on the South Pennsylvania Railroad.[67] The half-finished tunnels began to fill with water and undergrowth, and slowly disappeared from the public's consciousness until 50 years later, when their existence would be the crucial factor in the state of Pennsylvania's decision to fight the Depression by building a limited-access road along the abandoned right of way: the Pennsylvania Turnpike.

Light Rail

While corporate giants with enormous amounts of money were sparring over properties that had become extensive networks crossing state lines, a much smaller network that featured competition among corporations of considerably smaller size and wealth began to spread through eastern Pennsylvania. This was the era of "light rail" construction. The more substantial engines and train cars on the rails for the most part linked the nation's cities and ports. Their smaller cousins were often known as "trolleys." The distinction between "the railroad" and "light rail" is easily blurred; several of the small local railroads built in southeastern Pennsylvania in the first flush of the railroad era were light indeed.

This evolution of light rail travel spawned something close to a repeat of the early railroad era, with many small, underfinanced companies proposing to build short lines of track to connect local destinations. The light rail companies also tended to underestimate the physical requirements traversing the numerous hills, valleys and watercourses, and found construction expenses ballooning. The low durability of the equipment, combined with the highly variable Pennsylvania weather, conspired to keep maintenance expenses at unacceptably high levels. As a result, light rail companies experienced frequent corporate "reorganizations" and consolidations.

As with the first railroad cars, the trolleys were pulled by horses. This meant that the first lines were confined to urban areas. In 1885, Norristown received the first trolley line in Montgomery County when the Citizens Passenger Railway Company began service down DeKalb Street as far as Main Street. With electrification during the 1890s, trolley lines began to spread out from Norristown, sometimes making use of existing roads, sometimes following their own separate rights-of-way, depending on topographic and legal constraints. These lines ran south to Bridgeport, east to Conshohocken and west to Collegeville, and eventually as far as Pottstown.[68]

Efforts at establishing light rail systems in southeast Pennsylvania would not prove to be financially successful. They would, however, come to constitute a network that despite the tin-pot nature of much of its equipment would serve to further connect the growing communities of southeastern Pennsylvania. Norristown was a major hub of this network, and downtown a major recipient of traffic. The combination of the two main railroad lines and the spread of light rail delivered people to Norristown from their outlying residences, making the borough a prominent destination in Southeastern Pennsylvania for both work and shopping.

Thus did Norristown, once a small and quite compact town, begin to extend its reach into every direction via rail and waterway. Faster, easier, more comfortable means of transportation among and connections with other cities and towns meant greater growth. Norristown grew only slowly when it depended solely on local roads and the Schuylkill River, but the establishment of reliable railroad service brought the explosive growth that made it the industrial boomtown it became once advances in transportation built the town—and the downtown.

3

Growth & Expansion

L ess than half a century after its creation by charter, the town became a borough. On March 14, 1812, the Pennsylvania State Legislature received a petition asking for the Town of Norris to be incorporated as the Borough of Norristown, a change that would give the new entity a separate government from that of the surrounding township of Norriton.[69] The petition received expedited treatment: it was passed by both houses by March 31, the last day of the session. The bill was signed into law by Governor Simon Snyder that very evening. The first borough election took place on May 1, though no records mention a contest for any position. Borough government began to function on June 2, 1812, at the first meeting of the Borough Council.[70] The Town of Norris was now Norristown.

When it was established as a borough, Norristown encompassed 520 acres, taken from Norriton Township. The new borough stretched west from Stony Creek to Plymouth Township. To the south, its border was now the Schuylkill River; its northern boundary had been moved northward to the flat land past Courthouse Hill. The new municipal entity comprised about 500 people in about 100 dwellings. Taverns and stores each had increased to five.[71] As a borough, the government of Norristown was initially divided between an elected burgess and an elected borough council of seven members. Burgess and council members were not paid, but could be fined if they refused to serve.[72]

As a self-governing entity, Norristown began to pay stricter attention to its growth than it had when it was part of Norriton Township. Although the town had been surveyed and laid out according to an ordered plan, lack of administrative oversight had allowed several buildings to encroach on what had been designated as streets. In December 1812, the borough council passed an ordinance designed to clear up the resulting disputes, authorizing street commissioners to conduct a survey to determine the correct lines of streets and alleys. It further directed that once the correct lines were established, the commissioners were to remove all obstructions and open up the streets to the proper width. From that point on, anyone intending to erect a building in Norristown was required to obtain the correct lot lines from the street commissioners.[73]

The original Town of Norris comprised 28 acres; when established as a borough in 1812, Norristown comprised 520 acres. The 1853 Act of Expansion grew the borough's boundaries to encompass 2,265.01 acres—the only expansion of the borough in its existence.[74] Retaining the Schuylkill River as its southern boundary, the Act extended the borough northward and westward at the expense of Norriton Township. Norristown acquired the gently rolling land north of Airy Street, broken on both the eastern and western extremities by the watercourses that form Saw Mill Run and Stony Creek. It also acquired additional land to the east of Saw Mill Run to the new borough line with Plymouth Township. Most significantly, it acquired the hill to the west of Stony Creek, thus making Norristown, as one local writer would put it, "The Town on Three Hills."[75] The new areas to the north, east and west would, over time, absorb the residential needs of the expanding population, as all who could afford it left the lower industrial area and the increasingly commercial downtown area. The land acquired greatly increased the size of the borough, and provided ample land for housing the expanding population.

Population Growth to 1912

And Norristown's population *was* expanding—and changing dramatically as it grew. When it was incorporated as a borough in 1812, its population was estimated at 500.[76] The 1830 census noted that the population had barely doubled in the ensuing two decades to 1,089. With the establishment of regular railroad service to and from Norristown, however, the population began to grow much faster. By 1840, Norristown's population had more than doubled its 1830 figure, reaching 2,937. The population doubled again in the next decade, to 6,024. Impressive increases continued. From an 1860 population of 8,848, Norristown's population grew by more than 2,000 persons per decade, reaching 22,265 in 1900. By the borough's centennial in 1912, Norristown estimated its population at just under 30,000. Its population would continue to grow, albeit at a slower rate, until 1930.

The waves of immigrants who arrived to work in the industries in Norristown during this period of explosive growth represented quite a change from those peoples who had originally settled the area. The population of Norristown, as with the rest of Montgomery County, had from the beginning drawn a somewhat diverse smattering of peoples (a legacy of William Penn), but nevertheless its mixture had drawn overwhelmingly from the British Isles and Northern Europe. As a result, Protestantism prevailed overwhelmingly, but even that faith itself was split by a considerable number of subdivisions. By mid-century the Irish had begun to arrive in large numbers to labor in the local industries, increasing the Catholic presence as well, though they remained in the minority in Montgomery County. From the 1880s to the First World War, Norristown was transformed by the same great immigration boom that brought people of every color, creed, faith, and culture to America's shores, including small numbers of Amish, Mennonites, and Jews. Overwhelmingly, however, the immigrants who settled in Norristown around the turn of the century were Catholics from Italy.

The Italians' arrival in the Norristown in large numbers was a classic example of what is known as "chain migration": immigrants from one area sponsored others from the same location, taking them in and connecting them up with earlier arrivals for aid, support and gradual acclimatization. Individuals and families from a specific region of

Italy would, upon arrival in America, settle in not just with other Italians but with specifically with other Italians from the same region of the home country. Of those who settled within Norristown proper, an enormous proportion—perhaps as much as 95 percent—came from in or around the small village of Sciacca, on the southern coast of Sicily. Italians from the central areas of Italy grouped together in a neighborhood just outside the borough line; that area came to be known as "Mogeetown," and is today part of Plymouth Township.

Virtually all the Italian immigrants to Norristown, regardless of where they had come from in Italy, were "directed" to the east end of the borough. That portion of Norristown had lagged behind in the population growth experienced by other parts of Norristown, so the land was valued at far less than in other neighborhoods and thus more affordable for newcomers. As this section of the borough became the home for the new Italian immigrants, it came to be called the East End, one of the most densely populated areas of Norristown.

The Italian Catholics encountered prejudice, and not just from local Protestants. The resident Norristown Catholics, largely from Ireland, did not mix with the newly arrived Italian Catholics—nor welcome them to the only Catholic parish in town, St. Patrick's. The ethnic antipathy appears to have been mutual, to the extent that many Italian Catholics preferred attending no church at all to belonging to one that was predominantly Irish. By 1903, the newcomers had begun efforts to organize a separate parish: Holy Savior parish. Unlike St. Patrick's, or the later-established St. Francis of Assisi, which divided Norristown between them, "Holy Savior include[d] the territory of both the other parishes, and more besides, but was exclusively for Italians."[77]

The steady influx of residents led to the gradual rationalization of the borough's terrain into an urban grid. The former town of Norris became the core of Norristown, and its original plan of rectangular lots and intersecting streets was extended beyond the original boundaries. As Norristown's population grew, so did the urban nature of life within the borough itself. The 1830 census, which counted 1,089 residents in Norristown, found 1,139 residents in Norriton Township, from which Norristown had been carved.[78] This ratio began to change in the following decades. By 1860, when the borough of Norristown's population had risen to 8,848, that of Norriton Township had increased to only 1,406.[79] This growth from near parity to a six-fold majority over its immediate surroundings testifies to the physical shape Norristown was assuming, in contrast to its rural surroundings: the urban grid.

Government Growth

Montgomery County's population also increased during this period, although not nearly as fast as Norristown's. As the population of the county grew, the original buildings on Courthouse Hill became increasingly inadequate to the county's needs. The various proposals to replace them with larger structures each faced opposition, largely for their expected cost, until two grand juries forced the issue in 1849 by declaring both the courthouse and prison unsafe. A new prison was built, not on the original county property, but adjacent to it on Airy Street. The new prison was (and still is) an imposing structure, reminiscent of a Norman castle; its sandstone crenellations and battlements still seem to glower over Airy Street.

The county commissioners then turned their attention to the courthouse. Building began in 1851 and was completed in 1855. While built largely of brick, the new courthouse's walls were faced with marble from King of Prussia, earning it the nickname "the Marble Palace." Located at the very top of the original University-granted lot, the new courthouse and its grand dome dominated the skyline of the Schuylkill valley. After the Marble Palace replaced the original county building, the county purchased a small group of office buildings adjoining the public square; these served as offices for county officials and staff. Even this expansion did not eliminate complaints about lack of space, an issue that resurfaced again within a few decades.

The borough did not provide for its officers and staff nearly as well as the county. From its inception as a borough in 1812, the Borough Council had met in privately owned dwellings or in various hotels. In 1850, the new Odd Fellows Hall on DeKalb below Main became the regular meeting place until a new Borough Hall was built in 1885 on Penn Street. On February 2, 1885, the Borough Council met at the Odd Fellows Building, then marched as a group to the new building to begin their official occupancy.[80] Within less than a decade, however, planning began for a new, larger home for borough government. This would be another brand new building, on Airy Street at DeKalb Street, which the council moved into in 1896. Despite Norristown's being a borough, this building has always been called City Hall. It accommodated government offices and meeting rooms on the second floor, while the first floor was a collection of market stalls, becoming the "borough market."

During this period of rapid growth, especially after the 1853 expansion, the borough's core area—the old Town of Norris—underwent a professionalization, in which its mix of residential and commercial interests changed. As Egypt Road evolved into Main Street, an increasing number of wholesale and retail merchants set up shop there, seeking sites as close to the Public Square as they could afford. During this period, Norristown established its position as the center of retail and wholesale trade for most of the surrounding region, as well as its link to Philadelphia and markets beyond.[81]

Early on, Egypt Road was both Norristown's commercial center and its residential center. Many industry leaders built their homes there. In 1840, for example, ironmaster James Hooven built a residence at 108 West Main Street that was grandiose by the standards of the time. In a pattern repeated in similar towns and cities across the nation, however, later generations of wealthy citizens began moving away from downtown—first to higher ground along Airy Street, then farther west and north, particularly after new neighborhoods opened up in the wake of the 1853 expansion. As regional commerce came to be centered along this street at the borough's core, a "downtown" Norristown east and west of the public square began to take shape. The core of that downtown was the six blocks of Main Street between Stony Creek and Saw Mill Run, and that core was critical to the stability of the town: during the second half of the 19th century, commerce joined with industry to finance Norristown's great period of growth.

Downtown's Business Boom

While the center of Norristown remained the Public Square at the intersection of Main and Swede streets, the gradual shift toward DeKalb Street as the borough's primary north-south route effectively created the commercial center of downtown one block to the east, at the intersection of Main and DeKalb streets. As a consequence, the first block of East Main Street, between the Public Square and DeKalb Street, became the area most sought after by savvy business owners, particularly merchants. The last private residence on the south side of Main Street between Swede and DeKalb streets was converted to business use in 1850.[82] The last private residence on the north side was not sold for commercial use until 1951, and was much remarked upon when it happened. The process of commercialization would, in truth, always remain incomplete, and people would always continue to live on this block of Main Street, although eventually only on the upper floors.

Not all buildings originally constructed as residences were easily convertible for retail use. The house at the northeast corner of Main and Cherry, built between 1802 and 1813 and featuring massive stone walls and small windows, was instead modified to house professional offices. John J. Corson, a member of a locally prominent family, operated his real estate office from the building during the latter part of the 19th century, and occupied a newer residence next door. The building thus became known as the Corson Building.[83]

In 1860, local advertisers organized and funded the first known area directory. The *Directory of the Boroughs of Norristown and Bridgeport, Montgomery County, Pa., for the years 1860–1861*, published by William Whitehead, was printed in West Chester by E.F. James, "Steam Power Book and Job Printer." This directory, as well as subsequent editions, provides a valuable view of the town's commercial health, and an important record of the downtown. The 1860 directory contained a historical sketch, followed by advertisements, and a list of individuals and businesses in Norristown and Bridgeport, and provided ample evidence that Egypt Road/Main Street was the heart of the downtown: of the 89 advertisers listed, 50 were located on that street in the stretch between Stony Creek on the west (Markley Street had not yet come into existence) and Arch Street on the east. Another 36 were nearby, with most within a block of Main Street—usually on DeKalb. Only three were in Bridgeport; six were in Philadelphia, and one was in Wilmington, Delaware.

New financial institutions—and the steadily bigger, more ostentatious buildings they commissioned—sprang up, visible evidence of Norristown's rise to commercial prominence. Chartered in 1812, Norristown's first and for many years only financial institution, the Bank of Montgomery County, celebrated its first four successful decades by relocating to a grand new building at 110 West Main Street in 1854, rendered in a faux-Grecian style complete with columns. Its exterior along Main Street was also sheathed in a local variety of marble.[84] The new bank's building touched off what was at first a modest and unacknowledged competition among such institutions. One was the Albertson Bank, on the northwest corner of Egypt and Swede streets across from the Public Square. Founded by J. Morton Albertson in 1857, a time when lax state regulation of banks inspired some investors to bank with known individuals in "private banks," the Albertson Bank became the Albertson Trust Company in 1889.[85] Another such institution was the newly organized Norristown Trust Company, which bought the lot on the northwest corner of Main and DeKalb in 1888, demolished the house there, and built an imposing new structure.[86]

The three local newspapers in Norristown before 1920 were highly competitive, vying not just for readership and advertising but also for architectural accolades; they each seemed determined to present impressive façades, and each occupied a substantial building in the downtown core area. The oldest and most conservative, the *Norristown Herald,* traced its origins to 1799, and had begun a daily edition in 1869. A staunch supporter of the Republican Party, the *Herald* occupied a large three-story building at 73–75 East Main Street. Its chief rival, the *Norristown Register,* was its opposite both politically and geographically, as the paper supported the Democratic Party, and occupied 7–9 West Main Street. It began its daily edition in 1880. In the 1890s, both were then challenged by the upstart newspaper, *The Times,* which occupied the most ornate building of the three, a dome-capped structure at 2 West Main Street. [87]

Other signs of steady growth—and wealth—in Norristown's downtown included the support services that cropped up, including the Humane Fire Company. Located on Airy Street since 1854, the fire company dedicated a new station at 129 East Main (at Green Street) on May 12, 1888, in a ceremony marred by a pelting rain. Curiously, the stone laid into its front wall at the corner says Egypt, even though by that time the street was universally known as Main Street.

There were other signs of growth. Since Norristown was the county seat, people were often obliged to travel there on legal matters, sometimes for extended periods. This led to the establishment of several hotels in the downtown area, though the names changed over the decades. One such establishment had stood on West Main Street at Stony Creek since at least 1801. Originally called the Half Moon Tavern, it was later renamed the Pennsylvania Farmer, Hartranft House, Hotel Norristown, and then, in the 1950s, Milner Hotel.[88] Nearby, on the site what had been the first house in the area (owned by John Bull), was another hostelry at 215 West Main Street. By the late 1700s, the site (not the house, whose fate is uncertain) had become the Farmer's Hotel. renamed the Lincoln Hotel after the Civil War; it would also survive until the 1950s.[89]

While new financial institutions and a fire company were proud additions to downtown, the proliferating commercial enterprises, large and small, represented the true business growth of Norristown. Many stores and service establishments appeared. Some failed, while others grew and prospered, but although national financial conditions were reflected in local "hard times," the aggregate movement was always upward from the 1830s through the 1920s. Many of the businesses left behind little record of their existence, but there during the period from the Civil War to the borough's centennial in 1912, the establishment of commercial enterprises in the six core blocks of Main Street was steady and indisputable.

Early Commercial Successes

A few businesses established during that boom period managed to prosper and remain long enough to contribute their stories to downtown's collapse in the second half of the 20th century. All were initially modest endeavors. A few expanded to become "anchors" of the downtown shopping district, while others remained relatively small yet persisted across generations. One of the earliest and most successful of the long-lasting enterprises saw clearly the advantages of the intersection of Main and DeKalb streets. In April 1862, Colonel Daniel Miller Yost and Irwin H. Brendlinger founded a partnership to sell dry goods at 102 East Main, the southeast corner of the intersection. Brendlinger and Yost's thrived, and in 1870 Brendlinger sold his interest to a Yost brother. The store was then known formally as D. M. Yost and Brother. Yost's became a fixture at the commercial core of downtown Norristown. By 1880, it was believed to be the largest store in the county, and would remain so for nearly 50 more years.[90] In time, the locals came to call this Yost's Corner.

There were other successful stores named for their owners. In 1884, an 18-year-old Jewish immigrant from Germany, Berthold Block, traveled from France to America with $2.50 in U.S. coins in his pocket—and not much else beyond his few years' experience in the dry goods business. Nevertheless, he managed to build up a successful shop by spending little and investing wisely. Block, who changed his first name to Benjamin when he became a U.S. citizen, rented a room at the corner of Main and Swede streets; not only did he live there, but he also used it to store his goods. A widely repeated local legend has it that his first horse, the only one he could afford, was blind. Soon four of Block's brothers joined his enterprise. Although one soon returned to his homeland, the remaining brothers established their first retail location at Swede Street in 1888. A year later, they added a similar store upriver in Pottstown, and soon after that another one in Phoenixville. In 1903, the family firm, now B. E. Block and Brothers, purchased the building at 11 West Main Street, added a new front, and converted it into a department store.[91]

In 1890, a young Russian immigrant named Samuel Chatlin was eking out a living as an itinerant peddler, and boarding in Norristown with another immigrant Jewish family, themselves just getting by. Young Chatlin fell in love with one of his hosts' daughters, Ida, who reciprocated his love but refused to marry him unless he put down roots. Chatlin promised to do so, and they began to save for their future life together. He acquired a horse and wagon; Ida, to prove her commitment to their planned marriage, went to work in a Bridgeport mill, despite her parents' disapproval. Each week she set aside part of the $4 she earned for her 64-hour workweek. Samuel and Ida married, and with their meager savings opened a store at the corner of Main and Mill in 1892. They labored side by side, slowly building their business enterprise. Their story is very much representative of other local firms: many took the family name of the husband, but the operations were very much partnerships.

In 1893, Gus Egolf opened a new business on East Main Street, an impressive four-story structure with bay windows and very distinctive architectural ornamentation that immediately became a Norristown landmark. Egolf, "short and stout, with a wen on the back of his neck nearly as large as his head [was] a keen dealer in old furniture and old books."[92] Antiques were a major component of his stock from the beginning; Pennsylvania governor Samuel Pennypacker, an avid collector of books and antiques, was a frequent customer.[93]

The story was repeated yet again around the turn of the century when a young Jewish man in Poland rebelled against his family's farming background and their plans to apprentice him to a blacksmith. He emigrated to the United States, and Anglicized his name to Samuel Friedman. Friedman, attracted by the retail business, began with a job as a buyer for a store in Gary, Indiana. After he had gained some experience, he and his new wife began to search for a location to set up shop, eventually choosing Pennsylvania. They first opened a store in Coatesville, northwest of Norristown, but quickly concluded Coatesville was a one-industry town—that industry was steel—with an uncertain future. Believing that Norristown's industrial diversity lessened the chances of a catastrophic collapse, in 1918 Samuel and his wife opened a store at 24 West Main Street and began the slow process of building their business, "on a reputation for quality goods and honest service."[94]

Among the numerous immigrants to Norristown from Italy, and from the village of Sciacca, was 5-year-old Joseph J. Zummo, whose family came to the United States through Ellis Island in 1888. Within a few years, young Joseph went to work at a mill as a carpenter's assistant, gradually rising to become a master carpenter. Despite his inability to learn much English, he began to do construction work for others in the Norristown area, as the quality of his work overcame his difficulties in communication. In 1908, he wed Vincenza Maggio, whose family had also emigrated from Sciacca, in an "arranged" marriage. Through his trade, he became a customer and then friend of Fred Gilbert, who owned a hardware store at 259 East Main Street. When age and infirmity moved Gilbert to sell his store, Zummo bought the business. Like many of the first-generation downtown stores, the business initially operated out of the front of the building, while the rear of the building remained a residence for years. Zummo's four sons and two daughters all participated in the family business in varying ways, according to the traditional Italian family gender roles of the time.[95] While invariably last in the alphabetical directories of the period, in the end Zummo's Hardware would be one of the very few to survive when other businesses about them were collapsing.

The problems faced by ambitious young men desiring to become merchants, even those as well respected as Joseph Zummo, meant that such businesses started out small. They were limited by what they could afford to invest, and few could buy out entire buildings or businesses when they were just starting out. In 1908, a local builder and entrepreneur introduced a novel and effective concept in downtown Norristown, the arcade—an early precursor to the mall. J. Frank Boyer constructed an unusual building at 27 East Main Street (Lot 2 in the original plan of the Town of Norris). The Boyer Arcade was a two-story structure with a central hallway from front to rear, and rooms off this concourse were rented to small businesses. While only two of these businesses actually possessed storefronts at the ground level of Main Street, all the others were easily accessible. The success of the Boyer Arcade led to the construction of a similar building a short distance away at 51 East Main Street, the Curren Arcade, named after its builder, who was a frequent business partner of J. Frank Boyer.[96]

While many of the downtown enterprises and new construction projects were the result of individual initiative, some came from early business "networking" groups. During this period in American history, fraternal lodges ranging from the ancient and widespread Masonic Order to several that derived from the Civil War, were widely popular. The old Odd Fellows building on DeKalb Street had hosted many meetings of Borough Council. After it was sold, the Odd Fellows moved in 1904 to 228 West Main Street. In 1897, a Masonic Lodge purchased the old Hooven Mansion at 108 West Main Street. Extensively remodeled, it too would become the meeting site for numerous organizations and societies.[97]

Culture

Civic pride in the borough itself began to play an increasingly prominent part as Norristown grew in size, population, and complexity after the Civil War. A town so prosperous, its leaders reasoned, should demonstrate its status through culture. One result of this feeling was the formation of the Norristown Hall Association, whose goal was "to provide a first-class auditorium for Norristown."[98] In 1874, the Association accomplished that goal by building a large Music Hall at 61 East Main Street. The Music Hall was a three-story building, reaching back 140 feet from the street and with 50 feet of frontage on Main Street, making it a quite substantial structure by Norristown standards. An auditorium occupied most of the first floor, and the second and third floors were designed for use by local organizations and lodges. Fortuitously located near the center of Norristown's prime block and a short distance from the Public Square, the Music Hall quickly became a component of regional circuits for traveling performance groups.

In 1889, two local merchants obtained a controlling interest in the Music Hall Association and renamed it the Grand Opera House. Late in the evening of December 28, 1900, a fire destroyed the interior of the building, but it was rebuilt, this time with a balcony added. The new Grand Opera House reopened on May 16, 1901.[99] The Grand Opera House hosted many ceremonial events, banquets, and lectures, each in its way a demonstration of the growing pride of the prosperous borough of Norristown. What it never hosted, however, was anything with a claim to being grand opera. The only opera on record was performed in the spring of 1888, when the building was still the Music Hall.[100] Still, it was a testament to Norristown's sense of civic pride and commitment to culture.

In 1907, an early version of a new technology called the nickelodeon premiered at the opening of the Bijou at 2 West Main Street. This modest venture marked the commercial beginnings in Norristown for a remarkable family, the descendants of Simon Sablosky, a native of Russia who had come to the United States in 1884. Simon's son Lewis opened the Bijou in Norristown, then another Bijou in Wilmington, Delaware. He and his brothers then purchased the Garrick Theatre at 216 West Main and transformed it into what was called one of the most beautiful vaudeville theatres in the East.

Next came the Empire Theatre, at 100 West Main Street. The Sabloskys incorporated as Norris Entertainment Company, Inc., in 1910. In that same year, the new corporation purchased the Grand Opera House, which until then had not been profitable. After modernization, the fortunes of the Grand Opera House improved greatly.

Over time, the Sabloskys opened additional theaters in Reading and in Philadelphia, and for the next half-century the name Sablosky would be synonymous with entertainment in Norristown and its surrounds. While some Sablosky venues offered live performances, the core of their efforts were the new "motion pictures." As this technology evolved, the Sabloskys would offer to Norristown the latest variation, from the nickelodeon to the drive-in.

Norristown's Centennial: 1912

As Norristown's centennial drew near, the borough was on the cusp of a revolution in transportation. The era of the internal combustion engine was just under way, but still in the throes of basic technological development, much as the railroad had been in the early years of its era. But where the steel tracks did not run, the horse and buggy still held sway. The automobile and the truck would play their parts in the centennial parades and other events, but the majority of the hauling was performed as it always had been, by horses.

Norristown celebrated its 100th birthday in 1912. By then it was well along in its period of expansion and growth. Prosperity and success had been the norm for so long, in fact, that its residents had come to consider this condition inevitable. There was good reason for this optimism. During its first 100 years, the borough of Norristown had seen its population grow from about 500 people scraping by in wooden cabins to 27,875 housed for the most part in sturdy buildings of brick or stone. Egypt Road had been transformed from a worn path into Main Street, paved with brick along its full length in the borough and flanked on either side with broad sidewalks. Downtown glowed at night under arc lamps, which shone down on Norristown's many paved or macadamized streets, beneath which snaked miles of storm and sanitary sewers, along with pipes carrying water, gas, and steam heat.[101] Life in Norristown was good, and there was no ominous cloud of portent hovering overhead to suggest that it might ever be otherwise.

Businesses ranged from mills and other heavy industry to professional and financial services. The 1912 City Directory listed 69 lawyers' offices in Norristown, mostly near the courthouse and dominating Airy Street from Cherry to DeKalb Street, and Swede Street above Main Street. They represented the as-yet gradual and small growth of county government. Governance had been the reason for the creation of the Town of Norris, and a constant at the core of Norristown's existence. While not yet so measurable a component in Norristown's prosperity as that of industry or commerce—the growth of government lay in the future—the guarantee that being the county seat represented certainly underpinned it.

Other businesses were thriving as well. Lower down Courthouse Hill, east and west of the Public Square along Main Street lay the commercial district. This district stretched from Stony Creek to Saw Mill Run, and was focused overwhelmingly on Main Street itself. Clusters of enterprises existed along downtown streets that intersected Main Street, including Cherry and Barbadoes, and Swede below Main Street. Their numbers declined as their distance from Main Street increased. DeKalb Street was the exception; as the primary north-south route, the stretch above Lafayette, across Main to Airy Street, became part of the commercial district.

A survey of the 1912 City Directory clearly demonstrates this geographic grouping. Within the six blocks of Main Street between Saw Mill Run (Arch Street) and Stony Creek (Markley Street had not yet come into existence) were 7 of the 13 "dry and fancy goods" stores, 5 of the 12 furniture stores, and 7 of the 11 "notions" stores (including F. W. Woolworth, which had opened at 62 East Main Street, and competitors D. M. Yost and Chatlin's). Norristown boasted five theaters, of which only the Colonial, at 301 East Main Street (the corner with Arch Street) was *not* owned by the Sabloskys, by now operating as Norris Entertainment, Inc. The Grand Opera House still presided over the center of the block at 67 East Main Street. As downtown's largest theater, it hosted the Historical Day meeting on Friday morning, May 10, before the afternoon's Centennial Parade.

The Centennial Parades wound through downtown, highlighting what seemed incontrovertible physical evidence of Norristown's shining future. The intersection of Main and DeKalb clearly constituted the commercial heart of the Borough. Trolley tracks occupied both streets, and thus intersected at this central location. The substantial bulk of the Norristown Trust Company at the block's eastern end, the northwest corner of Main and DeKalb, physically dominated the intersection. Yost's still occupied the site diagonally opposite, at the southeast corner. In the 1912 City Directory, D. M. Yost has advertisement on the title page. It also has the center stripe advertisement on every following page, including those for Pottstown, where it also had a store. The directory noted that "500 Trolley Cars stop at Yost's Corner for passengers and exchange with all communicating lines."

While March 31, 1812, was technically the day of the borough's creation, Norristown chose to hold its centennial celebration in May. This wasn't inappropriate: the original borough government had begun to function in May 1812. But more importantly, the weather in Southeastern Pennsylvania in March is very risky for any outdoor event, particularly one involving parades and floats.

Norristown devoted a full seven days to its Centennial Celebration. On Sunday, May 5, all the churches delivered special services marking the occasion. The town offered a mass meeting in the Grand Opera House in the afternoon. Monday was Municipal and Educational Day; guests of honor Pennsylvania Governor Tener and Norristown Burgess Blankenburg were among those who viewed a pageant of thousands of children in costumes. Tuesday was Civic Day, Wednesday was Industrial Day, Thursday was Fireman's Day, Friday was History Day, and Saturday was Military Day. Each day's events varied, but parades were the common denominator.

The Industrial Day parade featured floats from both local industries and commercial firms. B. E. Block and Brothers paraded a three-car float constructed to resemble a train engine and tender with two railroad cars behind, labeled as the "B.E.B. & B.R.R." to boast that Block's received "carload lots" of items for sale. Both of the Adam Scheidt Brewery trucks, electric powered and with hard tires, participated in the Industrial Day parade. One was photographed transporting what appears to be a small band and the other was piled high with cases of the company's products.

Two floats in succession from the Industrial Day parade offered a graphic demonstration of the pride that Norristown felt in its century of progress. The first float, identified only as "1812," was a mockup of a log house with the side walls cut completely away, allowing spectators to see the furniture and figures inside, all typical of the era of Norristown's founding. Immediately behind it was a second float, identified as "1912," also a mockup with both sides cut away. This one simulated a brick house, and held currently dressed figures on current furniture inside. The symbolism of "progress" could not have been more obvious.

The largest parade in sheer size was the firemen's parade on Thursday. Volunteer companies had been a tradition in Norristown, and had for some time been integral to the social structure of the Borough. Parading was a tradition among the firemen, and a very competitive one. The weather, however, had not been cooperative. It had rained or threatened to rain all week, and disrupted some of the parades, but saved its full wrath for the firemen. Thursday morning, as the *Times Herald* would much later recount, a "miniature hurricane completed the wreckage of the decorations that had survived previous rains." The heavy rain, accompanied by thunder and lightning, did clear up by early afternoon, and the volunteer firefighters, accustomed to dropping everything to risk their own lives and safety for the benefit of others, would hardly be put off by a little water. The firemen's parade went on as scheduled. A total of 81 fire companies paraded, some from as far as Delaware. "As nearly every company had a band, there was plenty of melody in Norristown that day."[102]

The week's grandest events took place on Friday, May 10, celebrating History Day. The History Day parade was smaller than the previous day's spectacle but far more colorful. The theme of progress was clearly embodied in this, the climactic event of the weeklong celebration. The pageant was built around 32 floats, each bearing costumed re-enactors portraying an event in Norristown history, from William Penn to the modern day.[103] The pageant director, the Rev. Dr. Theodore Heysham, a Baptist minister, knew nearly everybody in town, and talked almost all of the borough's prominent citizens and civic organizations into participating, in costume and either marching, sitting on a pageant float, or astride a horse.[104]

While the Historical Pageant was the climax of the celebration, it was not the last activity, nor the last parade. Saturday's Military Day offering included the entire Sixth Regiment of the Pennsylvania National Guard, survivors of the Civil War (who rode in automobiles) and four Norristown troops of Boy Scouts.

Anyone attending the Centennial festivities could be excused for believing that the town would continue to grow and prosper forevermore. How could it fail? Every parade of the weeklong celebration marched down Main Street, through the borough's commercial core and past the array of stores in its jammed downtown. The buildings that served as each parade's backdrop were almost all of two or three stories. While overwhelmingly of brick, some had plaster finishes. A number of the larger buildings boasted elaborate facades along their rooflines and some sported wooden canopies built out over the sidewalk. A few elaborate cupolas, such as that atop the Grand Theatre, dominated the skyline.

Virtually every building on Main Street—as well as the P&W Bridge—was bedecked with red, white and blue bunting. U.S. flags flew everywhere. Above the bunting was strung a virtual spider's web of electric lines. The poles along Main Street carried from four to six horizontal members, with a plethora of wires strung along each and crossing Main Street from side to side. All this testified to the commercial success that characterized the borough in 1912. The large crowds that lined the decorated streets waved flags and cheered as the parades proceeded past. While people may have cheered hardest for their particular favorites, what they all cheered was the message delivered by the passing parade of floats: Norristown's residents should be proud of being where they were, when they were. Each resident was a part of a growing, prosperous borough that could boast of both its industrial and its commercial success. They celebrated their past because they enjoyed their present and believed that their future would bring more of the same.

The formal report of the Centennial festivities, sponsored by the Historical Society of Montgomery County, was written by the Rev. Theodore Heysham, the event committee's chairman and pageant director. Heysham's slim volume, modestly entitled *Norristown: 1912*, was more than just an account of the Centennial festivities. The book included a brief history, but its text, photographs, and maps focused on the overall state of the borough in 1912 with great pride. At Heysham's behest, there were many photographs taken of the festivities, and these were delivered separately to the Historical Society. This montage of images provides a glimpse of a Norristown that was prosperous, secure, pleased with the past and confident of the future—the Norristown that had successively benefited from its connection to each new mode of transportation as it had appeared: the Schuylkill Navigation, the local roads, then the railroad and light rail. Norristown was still on the rise.

The Centennial celebration would have left any citizen feeling proud and filled with hope and optimism for the future. The centennial celebration was every bit as successful as Norristown itself, except in one regard. The *Herald* offered great praise for the event, proclaiming, "It was a spectacle that will linger long in the memory of every man, woman and child who witnessed it. It was instructive; it was dignified; it was historically accurate in every detail—what more could be asked, what more could be expected?"[105] The lone negative result was financial. The participant groups defrayed their own expenses, but an appeal went out to the general populace in early spring to cover the larger amount needed for everything else. Donations did not meet expectations, and the Borough Council was forced to add a half a million dollars to that year's tax levy.[106] It was not a good omen.

4

Enter the Automobile

At the time of the centennial, trains were still critical to Norristown. By 1912, the latest, best-built and most long-lasting of the region's light rail lines drastically altered the very core of downtown. The Public Square offered virtually the only open space remaining in downtown, and that little open area itself was about to be compromised—in a major way. For the previous five years, the Philadelphia and Western Railway (P&W) had been constructing a trolley line from West Philadelphia northward from its 69th Street terminal. Unlike most of the previous trolleys, the P&W used its own dedicated track bed, which was an enormous improvement over the undulating local roads with dubious foundations upon which trolleys usually traveled. P&W also invested in heavier materials and better construction.

As the centennial approached, the company had nearly completed an extension of its line from present-day Villanova to Norristown, where it was to connect with a 10-year-old line of what was by then the Lehigh Valley Transit Company that led north to Lansdale. The P&W built a high bridge across the Schuylkill with an elevated extension that carried the tracks over both the Reading and Pennsylvania lines to a bridge over Main Street that terminated at Penn Street, about halfway up Courthouse Hill. There it joined the existing tracks up Swede Street then east on Airy Street to DeKalb Street, whose right of way it occupied as it exited the borough to the north. While the P&W Bridge over Main Street added to the borough's transportation network, its construction effectively divided Main Street into two parts, blocking the view of one from the other. The effects went beyond cosmetic changes, as will be seen later.

Although the Borough Council welcomed the arrival of another major route for people to reach Norristown, it turned down the P&W's request for a terminal in the Public Square. The P&W instead made arrangements with the owner of the Rambo House, a hotel on the corner of Swede and Airy streets and directly opposite the County Courthouse, to accommodate P&W's ticket counter and waiting room. The first trolley made its run to Norristown in August, although the line at that time was open only to Centre Square. Full service between Norristown and Allentown began in December of 1912.[107] Norristown now stood at the crossroads of three rail lines: two (the Reading and the Pennsylvania) connected it to Philadelphia to the east and to western Pennsylvania to the west, and the third (the P&W and Lehigh Valley lines) connected the borough north and south from Philadelphia to Allentown.

Given that its prime midway location among a great number of locations in Southeastern Pennsylvania and beyond made it an important hub, it's not surprising that Norristown's era of growth continued for some time after the 1912 centennial. Norristown had been built upon the railroads, but by that time more upgrades were done on the local bridges and roads than on the almost fully built-out railroads. The *Norristown Study*, the name given to the collection of scholarly articles and book that tracked Norristown's development from 1900 to 1950, ultimately concluded that Norristown's period of growth lasted into the late 1920s, followed by a period of "stability" from 1930 to 1950.

Some aspects of life were more stable than others, of course. By the period just after the centennial, borough residents were bifurcated along a broad ethnic and religious divide. On one side were the Italians; on the other side was everyone else. The principal expression of this division was the continued confinement of Italians to the East End. DeKalb Street came to be recognized as the informal boundary line between the East End and the rest of Norristown in the downtown area, allowing a few Italian businesses access to the borough's prime shopping area.

The descendants of the county and the borough's original founders, almost exclusively of northern European ancestry and Protestant religion, had in the beginning dominated the borough's business, financial, legal and political affairs. They had also defined the borough's prime residential ground by occupying what became known as the North End, essentially the flat ground above Courthouse Hill. The white Anglo-Saxon Protestant (WASP) elite built their mansions along northern DeKalb Street. The less well-off families occupied the streets to the east and west of this artery, often in neat, well-ordered townhouses or twins.

The less upscale portion of Norristown west of Stony Creek experienced a pattern of independent, smaller-scale development made possible by its relative isolation due to the creek. It by now had acquired not only its own fire company but its own shopping cluster along West Marshall Street, and had become Norristown's West End. The West End boasted mansions along Main Street that, though fewer in number, rivaled those on DeKalb Street for opulence. The vast majority of the housing there, however, was lower quality brick row housing. Both the West End and the North End shunned Italians and people of color. The melting pot was a myth. This was instead a carefully sewn quilt, with the sections neatly fitted to the gridlines of the old colonial plan.

Driving Change

Nevertheless, Norristown grew. People drawn by the favorable location, industrial diversity, and the guidance of chain migration settled into the maturing borough, and the downtown flourished. From a small grid filled with the clatter of carriages on cobblestone and hoof beats on gravel and macadamized paths, Norristown swelled to a bustling town with shops and services housed in imposing multilevel brick and stone structures. Train and trolley tracks carried people and products in and out of the town, and the future of Norristown seemed secure and predictable.

And then came the automobile.

In addition to the heavy and light rail that allowed people, products, and materials to move in and out of Norristown, there were also still the two main roads that had served the area for almost two hundred years. Both Ridge Pike and the State Road were well established, if not well maintained. Both spent portions of their 19th-century life as private roads called "turnpikes." Ridge Pike had become a turnpike in 1812; a turnpike for the State Road south of Norristown had been authorized in 1848, while the stretch north of Norristown had been chartered in 1868. Neither was a financial success, as was the case with so many of their predecessors.

The turnpike north of Norristown was freed by legal process in 1890, with the company receiving $11,000 in recompense. Five years later, DeKalb Pike south of Norristown was freed, with its company receiving an identical sum.[108] Ridge Pike became a free road in 1888 when the turnpike company defaulted on its bonded debt to Philadelphia.[109] This period saw the freeing of bridges as well as turnpikes. The bridge over the Schuylkill at DeKalb Street, which dated from 1828, was rebuilt in 1861, still as a toll bridge. The bridge was freed in 1885 with the payment of $111,322 to the company in compensation, and became owned by the county. The Ford Street Bridge, however, remained in private hands, and charged a toll to cross.

Tolls were highly unpopular, and never seemed adequate to properly maintain the roads. There was a more fundamental reason for the failure of the turnpikes, however. To many people, the ideas of private ownership of roads and being charged for their use seemed antithetical for a free country. While this feeling had existed from the start, in the second half of the 19th century, public attitudes turned decisively against private roads. This marked the end of the "First Turnpike Era."

While turnpikes were the subject of frequent complaints over the state of their maintenance, they were in much better shape than other roads in Montgomery County. The turnpike companies each made at least some provision (albeit usually inadequate) for maintenance. For the "public roads," funding was considerably less certain. Up until the middle of the 19th century, each township was responsible for all highways within its territory, meaning that little work of lasting quality on the public roads was done.[110] In the mid-1890s, support began to coalesce for what were termed "good roads." By that time the township-level work gangs to pay off the road tax had largely been abandoned. Farmers' organizations had long agitated for better roads, and by the end of the old century they were joined by another group agitating for better roads, the Wheelmen—those people caught up in the latest transportation craze, the bicycle.[111]

Without question, the greatest impetus for road improvements was the growing popularity of the automobile. Automobiles had begun to appear on the roads of Montgomery County just before the turn of the century, with the first sighting in 1896.[112] An 1899 *Herald* editorial, pontificated that "the progress of the human race is illustrated by the advance in methods of transportation," and observed that, "a comparatively new invention, the automobike [sic], promises to make further inroads upon the horse as a means of transportation, if not also upon railway lines."[113]

Norristown's first automobile owners typified the first such generation elsewhere: professional men, particularly doctors who employed the vehicles to make individual visits to patients, or members of the local business elite demonstrating their status. The area's first automobile was purchased by Dr. Charles H. Mann, of Bridgeport, in 1904. Dr. Mann visited his patients in a vehicle of unspecified make that featured a one-cylinder engine and tiller steering. Peter V. Hoy, proprietor of the Montgomery Hotel on the south side of East Main, also bought his first car in 1904. Harry Stahler, owner of the Stahler Drug Company at 2 East Main Street, bought a White Steamer in the same year.[114] The first industrial firm in the area to join the automotive age appears to have been the Adam Scheidt Brewery on lower Stony Creek, which in 1905 purchased two electric-powered vehicles, with an aggregate capacity of five tons, to make local deliveries. The beer, transported in trucks with no suspension and solid rubber wheels over the bricked streets of Norristown, must have arrived in a rather more agitated condition than when it set out.

Gradually, as the number of vehicles on the roads increased, the state began to respond to the demand for better roads. Unfortunately, the increase in the number of vehicles outstripped the rate of support. In 1911, there were 43,000 automobiles were registered in Pennsylvania, which inspired then-Governor John K. Tener to sign an act of the General Assembly that placed 8,835 miles of roads connecting county seats and other population centers under the State Department of Highways. While this legislation undoubtedly helped, the popularity of the automobile burgeoned far more quickly than the government's plans to accommodate its manufacture and use. By 1918, the total of vehicle registrations in the state had jumped to 395,000.[115]

Within about a decade the automobile was no longer just a curiosity but a firmly established mode of transportation and industry. The automobile had not only come to Norristown, it had come to downtown. The 1912 City Directory listed six establishments for the sale and service of automobiles. By the 1920, the town directory listed 61 firms that sold either sold automobiles or their frequently replaced components, or serviced them. These last were the most prevalent: 26 of the 61 were garages. And most of those service stations were downtown, with 36 of them located along Main Street within the borough limits, and 21 of them located within the six-block core of downtown. The borough even had its own vehicle manufacturer, the J. Leitenberger Company, which built bodies for motor trucks.

Change was gathering strength. A fundamental change in the dominant mode of transportation was taking place across America, though its progress slowed somewhat during the Depression and war years. The automobile was becoming the favored means by which people traveled to downtown America, including Norristown, to shop. And now the borough was faced with two looming problems that had no simple, overnight solutions: how to get the increasing stream of automobiles into the downtown area, and what to do with the automobiles while their occupants went about their business of shopping, dining, and purchasing goods and services.

Changes in Transportation

Thanks to the state's rich coal deposits, the railroads serving Norristown continued to prosper during this period. Things were different for light rail, however. During the

1920s, the trolley system in southeastern Pennsylvania began to suffer; by the latter part of the decade, the bus had clearly displaced the trolley. In 1927, the *Norristown Register*, commenting on the ending of trolley service to the northwest, observed that "Discontinuance of the trolley service between Pottstown and Boyertown by the Reading Transit Company marks one of the first abandonments of trolley lines in this section due to the use of the automobile and the introduction of busses [*sic*] for transportation of passengers."[116]

Another conspicuous component of Norristown's transportation infrastructure was in obvious distress. Norristown's wooden bridges across the Schuylkill were relics of an earlier era. The covered bridge over the Schuylkill at DeKalb Street was by this time public—and thus free—but the bridge that crossed at Ford Street was still owned (indirectly) by the Reading Railroad and by now accommodated automobile traffic as well, for a toll. Its maintenance needs had not been adequately met for some time, and by the 1920s the bridge had become quite rickety.[117] The year 1924 was a bad one for Norristown's bridges: fire destroyed the DeKalb Street Bridge on April 14, and another fire destroyed the Ford Street Bridge on July 10. The county commissioners quickly had a temporary bridge erected to span the river at DeKalb Street, and sought bids for a concrete replacement. The bid accepted for $500,000, and its plan was approved despite controversy over the fact that the plan did not address the longstanding problem of the railroad crossings at the foot of the bridge. The cost to resolve these crossings was deemed excessive and the bridge was built without any provision for the problem. The new DeKalb Street Bridge opened to traffic on November 11, 1925.[118] Despite the considerable shortcoming of the grade crossing at its northern end, the new bridge was a major improvement over its predecessor. Its concrete construction eliminated the danger of fire, and made it far more resistant to the periodic rampages of the Schuylkill. While traffic crossing the DeKalb Street Bridge benefited from the new structure, the problem of congestion at the grade crossings remained. So did the desire in Norristown to eliminate this longstanding problem.

The Shape of Things to Come: Suburban Square

Not just in Norristown but throughout the Philadelphia region, traditional downtowns were beginning to encounter new problems brought on by what might have been a desirable combination: population growth, increasing disposable income, business success, and a new mode of transport. Acceptance of the internal combustion engine, while slow at first, was becoming commonplace. This fascination with personal transportation by automobile, however, meant that urban centers were discovering the need for something with which they had little previous experience: parking spaces—lots of them. Increasingly, people were coming into the downtown areas by way of the automobile, and finding fewer available places to park.

Architect Fred W. Dreher, Sr., studied these problems, and realized the hopelessness of reconciling many downtowns' compact urban grids with need to accommodate large numbers of cars. His solution was one of the country's first "modern" shopping centers. Dreher designed a cluster of retail spaces on an open tract of land in the Philadelphia suburb of Ardmore, a short distance from both rail and road transportation. Christened Suburban Square, the project presaged much of what was to come after WWII. Suburban Square was built in accordance with a comprehensive design, with coordinated materials and colors, ample parking by the standards of the time, and even provision for future expansion. Major stores opened at this location, including a Strawbridge & Clothier, the first branch of a major urban department store to be opened in a suburban location.[119] The Strawbridge & Clothier store prospered, as did Suburban Square itself. Depression and then war would seriously delay future applications of this innovative concept, but the lessons learned would be retained.

The Golden Years

Norristown's commerce thrived during this period. The 1920s were golden years for downtown. Local business owners were investing and re-investing, the value of Main Street frontage was growing, and the banking industry continued its construction of substantial buildings. The older, established firms, as well as many new ones, prospered. New, more ornate buildings replaced older ones, and downtown property values rose steadily. Yost's still dominated the intersection of East Main and DeKalb streets, the commercial core of downtown. Yost's advertisements are ubiquitous in the directories of the 1920s: each edition shows a full-page on the inside cover, and at least one smaller one per page thereafter. For the first half of the 1920s, Yost's inside cover advertisement referred to itself as a dry goods and carpet store that also offered such related items as awnings, window shades, linoleum, and custom upholstery work. By the publication of the 1927–1929 directory, Yost's more closely resembled today's department store, with the focus having shifted to include a broad array of clothing-related items.

Norristown's formal core remained the Public Square at the intersection of Swede and Main streets. This small patch of ground had long been quite literally overshadowed by the substantial buildings to both the east and west. Since 1912 the Square had been further marginalized by the black steel P&W Bridge that blocked the afternoon sun and deposited passengers at its northwest corner. To the east, old Lot 1 of the Town of Norris, now 23–25 East Main Street, had become the site of the Montgomery Trust Company. The Public Square's neighbor at 1 West Main Street was, after 1925, the magnificent multistory Norristown–Penn Trust Company building, a grandiose new bank opened to the public on December 15, 1925.

Business appeared to be booming downtown. In 1925, the Montgomery Trust Company purchased the neighboring Boyer Arcade Building, at 27 East Main Street. The business disavowed any plans to change the arcade layout, saying it was "fully teneted," [sic].[120] The newly named Montgomery Trust Arcade prospered, as did the similar Curren Arcade Building, at 51 East Main Street. In 1923 Samuel Friedman, who had been operating his piece goods store at 24 West Main, moved to 16 East Main Street, and christened his new enterprise the New York Store. His firm prospered at this central location, targeting the more upscale women's apparel market.[121] Further east, the unique structure of Egolf's Furniture Store at 113 East Main continued to feature, as it always had, expensive antiques.

In 1926, Samuel and Ida Chatlin, who by now had begun to expand by acquiring the adjacent buildings, retired and turned control of the business over to their son Morris. He would, in turn, expand the business even more, and make Chatlin's into downtown Norristown's eastern anchor.[122] The building at 67 East Main, where first the Music Hall and then the Grand Opera House had stood, burned again on December 18, 1922. The Sablosky brothers built yet another theater, which they named the Grand Theater. The new building was dedicated in August 1924, amid much oratory and praise.[123]

While the residential areas continued their self-imposed segregation, the downtown businesses were more cosmopolitan, or perhaps just more pragmatic. Italian-owned businesses cropped up on Main Street east of DeKalb Street, and rather than freezing them out, some older establishments, most significantly Chatlin's, accepted the ongoing change as progress and welcomed the Italians—first as customers, and then as employees. It was probably during this time that the informal tradition began in which the Italians among the Chatlin's sales staff adopted "American" names (that is, WASP names) and referred to each other using them while in the presence of non-Italian customers, a practice still common in 1950.[124]

West Main Street had always existed somewhat in the shadow of East Main, but the expansion of old businesses or the opening of new ones provided this stretch with some of downtown's most iconic structures. B. E. Block & Brothers Department Store, which had occupied 11 West Main Street since 1903 and had also expanded next door, decided in 1927 to raze the separate buildings and construct one large store extending back to Penn Street. The new three-story Block & Brothers Department Store—which featured an elevator—opened in 1928.[125]

Downtown Norristown acquired a large new building on its western boundary during the 1920s. The new business managed to be a continuation, an expansion, and an exception, all at the same time. The Stritzinger family bakery, which had occupied the corner of Main Street and the valley of Stony Creek since 1908, was purchased by the Continental Baking Corp. That company in turn built a much larger building, and thus continued to fill the air with delicious smell of baking bread every morning of the next several decades.[126] As an addition to Main Street, however, it was clearly an exception. The new, much larger building was a factory—the only one in downtown Norristown at the time, and the only one of any significant size, ever.

Local newspaper competition in Norristown largely ceased by the end of the 1920s. The grand buildings that had graced the first block of East Main Street over the previous decades reflected that change. The *Norristown Register* had gone out of business soon after the end of WWI, reflecting the fortunes of the Democratic Party in Montgomery County. Its building became McDivitt's Pharmacy. Not long after that, in November 1921, Ralph Beaver Strassburger, a wealthy businessman and graduate of the Naval Academy who resided on a grand estate in Blue Bell, Montgomery County, purchased the oldest of the Norristown newspapers, the *Herald*. Strassburger built a new printing plant at Markley Street near Airy, and began printing at the new location in

June 1922. He then purchased the *Times*, and in 1923 he consolidated the two as the *Times Herald*.[127] The former *Times* building also became a conventional retail establishment, and in the process lost its dome. In 1924, a new *Norristown Register* reappeared, attempting to compete with the *Times Herald* at a slightly cheaper price. It struggled for seven years before going bankrupt in June 1931.[128]

The Valley Forge Hotel

Downtown's general prosperity did not seem to benefit one important component of Norristown's business structure, its hotels. Ironically, the frequent and reliable rail transportation that helped Norristown grow had at the same time dramatically reduced the number of people who had to stay overnight to conduct county or other business. Now few overnight travelers stayed in Norristown as a part of a longer journey. By the 1920s it seemed that the steadily more popular leisure activity, "tourism," promised to more than make up for the decline. Some members of the business community considered how this new pastime, tourism, might benefit the town. Sadly, they saw at once that Norristown was poorly positioned to take advantage of the growing number of visitors to nearby Valley Forge because of the state of its hotels, which dated back to a time not long after that of Valley Forge itself.

The Montgomery Hotel, in the core of downtown at 22 East Main, still possessed stables at the rear of the property, which dated back to 1804. The Hotel Penn, at 16 West Main Street, was equally worn out, and in 1928 it was converted to a dry goods store. At the corner of West Main and Barbadoes streets sat the historic Lincoln Hotel. Though its name dated only to just after the Civil War, its purpose as a hotel itself dated back to the late 1700s, and it was more than showing its age. Behind the streetfront hotel was the site of John Bull's house during the Revolutionary War. Finally, at the very west end of downtown sat a building that had housed a hotel since 1801. At that time it was called the Milner Hotel, but it had begun life as the Half Moon Tavern.[129] In short, the borough could offer only a handful of old, shabby, ill-maintained, and seriously out of date places to stay—"an embarrassment to Norristown."[130]

By the mid-1920s, the perception among Norristown business owners was that the borough needed a "first class hotel." This, they believed, would result in an example of civic pride, one that would become emblematic of Norristown itself. A political, industrial and commercial center of Norristown's stature, they reasoned, needed a hotel worthy of its surroundings. This conclusion dramatically influenced the events that would follow. While the substantial prosperity of the times underlay the endeavor's financial projections, the fundamental motive for building the an new hotel was civic pride. The business community was so caught up in the imagined prestige of having such a hotel that they seemed not to have burdened themselves with any sober look at the potential profit or loss. The hotel project was not the singular work of an entrepreneur or a corporation, but an effort by the residents of Norristown itself. The borough's commercial, social, and political elite provided the leadership for the effort, which included the sale of the common stock to the local community, a marketing effort clearly built on community pride.

The financial plan, as it emerged for public scrutiny, was built on an agreement with the American Hotels Corporation wherein 50% of the new company's stock was given to the corporation in exchange for construction supervision to ensure the new hotel would be built to the proper specifications, and a 30-year agreement to manage the hotel. The remainder of the stock would be sold by local subscription.[131]

Two decisions were made early in the planning: where to locate the new hotel, and what to call it. The site chosen was 22 East Main Street, on the south side of the first block of East Main Street. This placed the new hotel at the historic center of the borough's downtown business district. Other, cheaper sites were considered, but the allure of Main Street, in the middle of downtown, won out.[132] After much deliberation, the choice of what to call the new hotel came down to two names. One faction favored the General Hancock Hotel, after Winfield Scott Hancock, Norristown's "favorite son," a hero of the battle of Gettysburg and Democratic candidate for president in 1880. However, another faction preferred the more general appeal of Valley Forge, the "crucible of American Freedom," whose cachet ran high in the United States in that exuberant, patriotic era. Valley Forge won.[133]

The new corporation formally purchased the site July 1, 1924, for $225,000.[134] This relatively low price for downtown frontage was largely due to the poor condition of the existing structure, the Montgomery Hotel, by then a shabby and aging relic housing just a few long-term, low-rent tenants. A multifaceted marketing campaign saturated the local area with publicity from several sources, including a cooperative *Times Herald*. The benefits of a new first-class hotel for Norristown were widely proclaimed in publications by the new company. A booklet from 1924 intended as a sales tool for the stock purchase campaign spelled out the case for the new hotel. "The Beginning of a Greater Norristown" proclaimed the hotel's potential contributions to the local business climate, both as a prestigious revenue producer and as a community center for social, fraternal and political gatherings.[135] The latter predictions, at least, came true.

The local stock subscription campaign climaxed between July 21–28, when over 200 volunteers, themselves purchasers of stock, fanned out to collect pledges and deposits from the local citizenry. By all local accounts, the campaign was successful. It is believed that about one thousand persons subscribed during this week.[136] With sufficient funding in place, the Valley Forge Hotel Company engaged an architect to plan the new structure.[137] Like the vast majority of downtown Norristown's buildings, the new hotel would be of brick, but at six stories high it would rise above all but a few, and dominate the center of town by the sheer bulk of its façade. The lot dropped off at the back, allowing for a basement and a rear entrance; a small parking lot was squeezed behind the building. The design featured two storefronts flanking the Main Street entrance, to be sublet to firms willing to pay top dollar for a prime location. The dining room, coffee shop, and barbershop occupied the first floor, a mezzanine led to meeting rooms, and the hotel rooms occupied the upper floors.

Work on the new building began in November 1924. Construction proceeded apace, and was complete enough by November 1925 for the formal opening ceremonies to be announced for a four-day period beginning December 9. Several front-page articles in the *Times Herald* celebrated the opening of the new hotel. The planned events went off to the approval of all, if published reports are to be accepted at face value. The size, accommodations, and fittings of the new structure received effusive praise. The *Times Herald* thanked the citizens who had sold stock in July of 1924 by naming them. The 30-year agreement with the American Hotels Company to operate the hotel was repeatedly stressed as testimony to the quality the new hotel's patrons could expect to encounter.

It being a community project, the Valley Forge Hotel printed a brief summary of its annual financial report in the *Times Herald*, beginning with those for 1926–1927. Thus, the entire community soon became aware that the rosy predictions for the Valley Forge Hotel were not being met. The hotel's first full year of operation, 1926, was a severe disappointment, with a net loss of $10,152.44. While a portion of this loss was due to expense inefficiencies typical of fledgling establishments, the fundamental reason was seen clearly: low occupancy of the hotel rooms. The year 1927 saw rigorous cost-cutting and a resultant smaller loss of $1,122.48, but as the annual report for that year made clear, room occupancy continued to be the problem. Management admitted that, "the revenue from bedrooms has again been disappointing. The daily average percent of rooms occupied for 1927 was 39.8%, an increase of only 9% over 1926, thus making the daily average of vacant rooms for the year over 60%." The prediction for the future was equally clear: "Until the room patronage materially increases, there will be little or no opportunity for any substantial profits." For its part, the American Hotels management was equally clear as to the solution: "It is in the hands of the people of Norristown and the traveling public to make your hotel, now rendering excellent service to the community, a profitable investment."[138] Norristown had its mission: get travelers to the hotel.

On December 1, 1928, the American Hotels Corporation terminated its agreement with the Valley Forge Hotel Company, some 27 years short of its 30-year lifespan. The termination's official reason was "inasmuch as the American Hotels Corporation was unable to earn any dividend on the preferred stock of your company." The annual report for 1928 listed a net loss for the year of $3,270.41, and restated the official net loss from the 1927 report from $1,122.48 to $3,923.23. While acknowledging these numbers, Valley Forge Company President J. Frank Boyer delivered a pointed address aimed at those who did not see that a greater good, something beyond financial profits, was supposedly accruing. Criticizing those small stockholders who did nothing but complain about the enterprise and its management, Boyer declared that the Valley Forge hotel existed "not as an enterprise for gain but as a civic necessity and for community advancement."[139] This was true, but not exactly what had been pitched to the Norristown community.

The Board of Directors' assumption of absolute control over (and thus responsibility for) the operations of the Valley Forge Hotel in late 1928 proved to be unfortunate timing. Whatever the chances might have been for early profits, the Depression in 1929 postponed them. The early years of the Valley Forge Hotel clearly established three fundamental points about the venture: first, profits would be rare; second, it would never be profitable as a hotel; and third, it would nonetheless become the very emblem of Norristown itself. The pattern established at the very beginning, of revenue from food and beverage exceeding that from room rental by a substantial margin, would continue for the entire life of the enterprise. The refrain about lack of room rentals would also be continuous.

Since the fundamental reason for building the Valley Forge Hotel had been civic pride, not profits, it could be said that the goal of its founders was more than achieved. The Valley Forge Hotel was much more than just another business to the Borough of Norristown from its very beginning and for its entire existence. The Valley Forge Hotel would come to be viewed as a symbol of the borough itself. While few locals ever stayed overnight there, many generations of Norristownians would remember major events of their lives together with the Valley Forge Hotel, as thousands of confirmations, weddings, graduations and a plethora of other events took place within the confines of this downtown landmark.

Divisions and Diversity

As the *Norristown Study* suggested, Norristown "had by the late 1920s reached a plateau of development beyond which it did not significantly advance in the next 30 years [but] such stability does not indicate complete dormancy." There was substantial turnover in both the population and businesses. The "stability" was statistical, and occurred despite the Depression, which gutted many other towns and small cities. Norristown did not suffer from any extreme of the Depression. While individual situations varied, and the area's major employers cut back, jobs remained available.

While the population of Norristown remained stable after 1930, events began to demonstrate the effects of the significant migration of Italian Catholics that had taken place prior to WWI. The 1930s saw this rising ethnic group break the long-held grip on government of the descendants of the original Protestant founders. Italians would increasingly become the "movers and shakers" of the Norristown business community. While it certainly did not seem that way to those Italians who pioneered in government, they were to a degree stepping into a void—a small one at first, but one that grew larger until the middle of the century.

Thanks at least in part to the automobile, and to the lack of available space in the tonier parts of the downtown grid, the period 1930 to 1950 saw a population movement out of Norristown that was not represented in the statistics: the resident upper class, the descendants of the borough's founders and long-time movers, left for the suburbs. The 1930 Census recorded 35,853 residents in Norristown, and in 1940, the number had barely changed, dropping slightly to 35,181. The *Norristown Study* recognized that this statistical stability masked a significant rate of in-and-out migration among the population during different decades of this time period: "Even for the two decades between 1930 and 1950 there was a turnover of at least one-third of the community's population despite the fact that the net change resulting from migration approached zero." Further examination of the statistics revealed a fundamental change: the borough's traditional commercial and political elite, the Protestant descendants of those who had arrived earliest, were heavily represented in the exodus. They were being replaced—in sheer numbers—by peoples whose culture and religion differed from that of the county's founders. The traditional financial and governmental elite steadily exited the grand mansions along upper DeKalb Street and western Main Street, and Norristown itself, bound for the countryside, or the Main Line west of Philadelphia.[140]

During the Depression Norristown continued virtually unchanged the by-now traditional ethnic-religious division of its population. While Italian immigration into Norristown had been largely curtailed by recent revised immigration statutes, the younger generation of native-born Italians in Norristown began to exert influence as a group, as many rose from the laborer class into the local professional business and commercial hierarchy.[141] With professional and commercial ascendancy came political influence. Italians began to appear on the political scene, initially representing the by-now overwhelmingly Italian East End. The November 1931 general election saw the first two Italian-Americans added to the Borough Council, with Michael Ciccarone representing the Ninth Ward and Paul Santangelo representing the Fifth Ward. Both would prove to be skilled politicians, and be regularly re-elected.

Both Ciccarone and Santangelo were elected in what was a transitional election for the makeup of Borough Council, as Norristown surrendered its special charter and came under the General Code of Pennsylvania Governing Boroughs. Before the change, Norristown possessed 12 wards, each electing three council representatives, which packed the Borough Council with an unmanageable 36 members. The downsizing took four years to complete, but ended with one council representative per ward. This greatly benefited both Ciccarone and Santangelo, who each represented wards with a high percentage of Italian-American voters.

Statistics and formal accounts exist to describe post-WWII period of Norristown's history. But personal recollections from those who lived it provide a richness that can't be gleaned from numbers and bald facts. Many Norristown residents, past and present, contributed stories to this book, and their tales share a common thread: the remembrance of this time as pleasant, filled with the happy routines of daily life. No doubt these happy memories have been burnished to a fine glow by the passage of time, and the sharper edges dulled by the years—these people who lived through the Depression, WWII, and the post-war era were children and teens then, and they are senior citizens now. While people never truly forget some parts of their youth, they often forget that they viewed life then through children's eyes, and that this often imparts a rosy glow that can obscure the harsher reality. One woman who shared her story, Mary Early, summed it up this way: "If we were poor, we didn't know it, because nobody else had anything more than we did."

One man who shared his insights was Joseph Verunni, the son of an immigrant Italian laborer from the East End. He was 10 years old in 1929 when the stock market crashed, his father lost his job at a local fabricator, and hard times fell on the Verunni family. Verunni's father, having heard that there were openings, sought a job at Alan Wood Steel in Conshohocken; each day he packed a meager lunch, walked the almost five miles to the company headquarters, and sat in the front office all day—nine hours—waiting for word. He would then walk the five miles home again. After three months of this, he got a job at the plant. Joseph was still in school. There he discovered that students had to pay 15¢ for the wood they were going to use in shop class—money his family could not spare. The WASP students, whose parents were generally better off, were able to buy their wood, and Joseph was left to beg them for the scraps that fell from their workbenches.[142]

Kenneth Randall was born a decade later, the year of the market crash itself, into a working-class family in the West End. The Depression hit his family hard. Though his father eventually found work with the Works Progress Administration (WPA), but money was always tight. One of Randall's earliest memories was being given two dollars by his parents right before Christmas—one was to spend on a present for his mother and one on a present for his father.[143]

Florence Johnson, a year older than Ken Randall, was born and raised in the North End. Hers was a decidedly middle class family, by no means wealthy, but extraordinarily conscious of their relative status in the community. She and the remaining cultural survivors of the upper-class exit consciously aped the manners and beliefs of the people who had founded Norristown and seen it grow. Florence was aware of limitations during the Depression, but suffered nothing like the indignities of Ken Randall, let alone Joe Verunni.[144]

Horace Davenport shared a neighborhood with Joe Verunni—the East End—but he was different in two ways. One, he was black. And two, his family was better off. He was descended from the blacks who had lived in the Norristown area since the era of the Civil War. A paperboy in the 1930s, Davenport distinctly remembered the dispersal of black families among the Italians in the East End. His route might include two or three black families among 10 or 12 Italian families.[145]

Downtown and the Depression

As it was with population, so it was with industry, which produced only minimal net growth in the next two decades, and whose small fluctuations "more closely paralleled the pattern of Norristown's population growth than the fluctuations of the business cycle." [146] Yet fundamental changes in Norristown's industrial base did occur. Borough-based industry, although shaken by the economic downturn, survived the Depression relatively well. During the Depression, business turnover continued, for the usual combination of reasons typical of any retail center, but the commercial core of downtown Norristown, sustained by the relatively high employment level of the area's population, remained the unchallenged retail shopping center for the region. In fact, the dark days of the early Depression saw the construction of Norristown's two most architecturally prominent buildings of the twentieth century, the Norris Theatre and the Philadelphia and Western (P&W) Terminal.

Commerce remained the economic backbone of Norristown. No broad threat to downtown Norristown emerged during this period of the Depression and the war. Retail and service businesses opened and closed for individual reasons, or broader changes in taste, but during the period downtown Norristown consolidated its role as the regional center for retail trade and services.[147]

Main Street's big night continued to be Friday, and on Friday nights, the place to be was the corner of Main and DeKalb. Depression or not, the sidewalks continued to be crowded with people, shopping, and just being seen. On those Friday evenings that her father—a borough policeman—was assigned to work, Mary Early remembers a family tradition. He would drive the family car downtown, and park it as close as possible to the corner of Main and DeKalb before reporting for work. His wife and children would later walk to Main Street to do their shopping. They would then go sit in their car until her father got off from work, watching the parade of people going past. "My mother used to always say 'I'd love to live at Main and DeKalb; everything happens at Main and DeKalb.' "[148]

August 1933 brought the welcome news that Sears, Roebuck and Company had leased the property at 227–231 West Main, the old Norristown Hotel. The building was extensively remodeled "in conformity with the scheme of Sears store design and layout."[149] The Sears store boasted a 40-foot frontage on Main Street and extended back to Penn Street, where the frontage expanded to 127 feet. The new floor plan offered customers 10,000 square feet of retail goods off Main Street, and another 2,480 square feet along Penn Street of automobile service and parts department.[150]

On a cold January night in 1935, a fire began at 14 East Main Street. It quickly spread first to Samuel Friedman's New York Store at 16 East Main Street, and then to the clothing store at 18 East Main Street.[151] Despite massive losses, Friedman saw an opportunity to rise up from the ashes by expanding, and to establish a unique presence in downtown's core as well. He purchased the 14 East Main Street lot—and what was left of the building, which was basically the bare bones—and combined the two stores. He had builders install roof trusses that spanned the two original buildings and added new exterior walls. His reopened New York Store could thus boast a 40-foot span between the side walls with no interior supporting columns, which gave the store a unique feeling of spaciousness.[152] Visitors came, sometimes from as far as Philadelphia, to view this curiosity. The sturdy walls required to support the trusses also made it possible to convert the structure to a three-story building, which added to Friedman's prominence downtown. He demonstrated his marketing savvy by employing only local contractors for the remodeling work, and was rewarded for this loyalty over and over again when the former workers brought their families to the New York Store to shop and to show off the work they had done.[153]

Chatlin's survived the Depression, and even managed to expand. Morris Chatlin steadily increased the store's size and offerings. He added first one adjoining store and then another to the east of Mill Street. For access, he connected them internally with doorways and ramps (to accommodate different floor levels), but retained the individual building exteriors.[154]

Across the street, the Joseph J. Zummo Hardware Company, with a much smaller retail base, saw diversification as a survival strategy. The second generation was beginning to take over. While Joseph Zummo continued to be active, more and more of the responsibility was passing to Anthony, the oldest of his four sons, while the younger brothers, Charlie, Vincent and Paul provided more of the labor. Anthony, obsessed from the start about not just survival but long-term expansion, began to add new lines of hardware. More significantly, he had the store bid on the hardware contract for large projects. This revenue stream would help get the Main Street store through hard times, from the Depression of the 1930s and beyond.[155]

As might be expected, the Valley Forge Hotel had a hard time in the 1930s. The 1930 Annual Report revealed a drop in overall business of approximately 15% from the 1929 numbers, producing the corporation's worst loss yet, $15,657.50. The Board of Directors was clear in attributing the blame to the times rather than the business itself. "The management was very efficient but the business just was not available."[156] The losses continued to mount in 1931, and revenues to decline in 1932, and only with rigorous cost-cutting could the annual loss be pared to $14,990.81. A glimmer of hope was found in the repeal of Prohibition, as the hotel continued to earn more from the sale of beverages and food than from room rentals, which lagged badly.[157] Delivering the annual report for 1933, new Board President A. T. Eastwick managed to be both blunt and hopeful. Acknowledging the obvious, he declared, "It is needless to discuss these figures. They show that last year was the low ebb in the volume of business done by the hotel since its opening in 1925." Revenue for 1933 was only $79,659.71, a decrease of almost 60% from its high point of $183,791.21 in 1929. The net loss was pegged at $24,503.32.[158]

It is uncertain how 1934 turned out; the *Times Herald* carried on its tradition of printing a report of the annual meeting of the board and stockholders in January 1935, but included no figures whatsoever.[159] For 1935, the *Times Herald* again broke the tradition, printing no report at all. The tradition resumed in January of 1937, and reflected the improving times. A front-page article reported that current Board Chairman William A. March cited total revenue of $149,226.05 and claimed an "operating profit," before depreciation.[160] In 1937, drastic cost-cutting actually produced a profit after depreciation of $15,322.18, the first in the history of the hotel.[161] The combination of circumstances that had produced 1937's profit would not be repeated. The annual meeting of the Board of Directors and stockholders for 1938 reported a net loss of $1,854.73.[162] Income dropped again for 1939, and the result was a loss of $564.72.[163]

Nevertheless, while the Valley Forge Hotel continued to struggle, by 1940, evidence that business was picking up in Norristown overall was palpable. The downtown had survived, and even the Valley Forge Hotel made a profit in 1940. At $1,280.43, that profit was a modest one, but it was still interpreted as a sign that happier times were ahead.[164] People seemed to emerge from this period with the same convictions as those who had witnessed the centennial celebrations of 1912: Norristown had weathered the Depression and post-War years, so surely things would only get better...right?

Many of those optimistic people grew up to be the very ones who shared their stories for this book. Most were never so overcome with nostalgia as when they spoke of how the Depression years were brightened by "the movies." The 1930s were, after all, the beginning of the so-called Golden Age of Hollywood, too. Norristown's theaters had participated in the transition from stage to screen, and by 1930 all had seen better days. The Garrick on West Main Street had adopted survival strategies that included jitterbug contests between the two halves of a double feature, as well as amateur night on Fridays. The Grand on East Main was reduced to similar circumstances.[165]

That changed in 1930. The Sabloskys, Norristown's first family of entertainment since the turn of the century, opened the decade with what would be their greatest achievement: the Norris Theater, the largest and grandest theater Norristown would ever see. Formal groundbreaking for the new theater took place on May 8, 1930, in a ceremony that saw State Senator James S. Boyd praising the Sablosky brothers, and proclaiming that "This new theater will be erected by Norristown labor, supervised by Norristown contractors, and, when completed, will be the latest type of playhouse, rivaling in appearance and appointments the metropolitan amusement buildings in the East."[166] The dedication of the new theater took place on December 22, 1930. More than 2,000 people packed the auditorium for the ceremony. The *Times Herald* dedicated almost its entire December 22 issue to the new building, with pages of praise from locals and from contractors and materials suppliers.[167]

The Norris Theatre was a colorful and imposing Art Deco building. Its Main Street frontage was three stories high, with an entrance marquee done in gold and polychrome terra cotta, surrounded by additional terra cotta in cream and orange. White flood lights and neon lighting in green, red, orange and blue beckoned gaudily, and the entrance ceiling of polished aluminum reflected light onto the sidewalk below. The lobby was another riot of color, from silver and pastels to red and brown, the whole lit by indirect ceiling lighting. The foyer was considered perhaps the most attractive room of all. Its color scheme was comparatively muted, the better to show off the two murals, each 50 feet long and 8 feet high along the side walls. Each end wall featured two large oval mirrors, their perimeters carved in floral designs and supported on black and gold marble bases. The lounge on one side of the foyer featured walls of an imported wood, its grain forming an overall diamond pattern, and windows of leaded glass depicting the arts. The auditorium itself was done in a color scheme of Tuscan red, silver and gold, with intricate lighting fixtures located in alcoves and the ceiling. The screen was located at the rear of a stage, as live shows were to be featured along with motion pictures. Frances Zummo, daughter of Anthony Zummo, remembers the effect of all this decoration. When you were among the paintings, wall hangings, and curtains, she said, "You felt like you were in a really important, beautiful place."[168]

While the modern technology and sophisticated décor hinted at a new and better world, in some ways it was just window dressing. The Norris Theater may have been new, but in at least one way it remained mired in the unenlightened past: it segregated its patrons, as all Norristown theaters always had. The Grand and the Garrick Theaters seated all non-white patrons in the balcony area. The West Mar, a component of the West Marshall Street shopping area, and representative of the overwhelmingly white West End, did not admit people of color at all. The Norris restricted them to the balcony only. There were, of course, no signs announcing this discriminatory policy. Any non-white patrons who approached the box office were simply given balcony tickets by the people issuing tickets; ironically, these counter operators were often black. Bill DeAngelis, a white boy who grew up near black families in the East End, preferred the balcony. To be seated there, he had to wait until after the opening newsreel to enter the Norris Theater. Only then, with no one as witness, would the black ticket taker allow him to go up into the balcony and watch the movie.[169]

Another Significant Birthday

Depression or not, 1937 marked the 125th anniversary of its establishment as a Borough, and Norristown was determined to celebrate. Unlike the 1912 Centennial Celebration, which was held in May, Norristown elected to observe this anniversary in the fall. In May, Burgess Anson B. Evans appointed funeral director D. Rae Boyd, commander of the local American Legion post and already active in civic affairs, to chair the celebration committee.[170] By August, planning was in full swing for the week of festivities, which began September 12 with church services on Sunday morning, and a community service in Elmwood Park in the afternoon.[171] On Monday, an evening event at City Hall honored "Old Norristown" with displays of artifacts and pictures, followed by a speech by local historian S. Cameron Corson. Parades began with the Industrial and Civic parade on Tuesday, with floats by industrial, civic and patriotic organizations. Thursday saw a large parade of high school students and the laying of the cornerstone of the new high school. The Merchants Bureau sponsored a Mardi Gras celebration on Thursday evening, and offered the "Special Anniversary Sales Day," a "gigantic" sale in borough stores. Saturday was the big parade, with a combination of veterans' groups, military units, and fire companies participating. While the vast majority of participants were local, some came from a distance, the longest probably being the drum and bugle corps of the Harvey W. Seeds Post of the American Legion, who traveled all the way from Miami, Florida.[172]

The committee commissioned the production of a moving picture to mark the event, titled *It Happened in Norristown*. The venture was funded by several local businesses, and the technical aspect of actually making a movie was arranged through the Sablosky brothers. The original 16 mm footage has since been transferred to videotape and DVD disc. The scenes were shot with local actors, and the dialogue was dubbed in later. The plot, such as it was, involved two friends who have just graduated from nearby Ursinus College, and travel to the hometown of one of the friends—this, of course, is Norristown. The local proudly squires his friend around town, and they tour firms who contributed to the production. The visitor falls in love with the sister of his Norristown friend, and they plan their wedding, which naturally requires visiting more shops that obviously paid for their inclusion. It ends with the three young people attending the big 125th Anniversary parade. Amateurish production values aside, the movie does paint the picture of a borough surviving the Depression in good order.

The P&W Terminal

After the Norris Theatre brightened the Depression Christmas of 1930 for the Norristown, the New Year brought an announcement that would bring to the borough its other signature building. The P&W trolley company had purchased the property at 2 East Main Street, the southeast corner of Main and Swede streets.[173] The company tore down the old brick structure there to build a striking new terminal in the very core of Norristown. The Art Deco exterior of the new three-story building was more low-key and muted than the flashy, colorful Norris Theatre. The exterior was monochrome, but the wall above the first floor displayed a sculpted finish that evoked columns. The windows were trimmed with aluminum, faux curtains, and decorative plaster, and the terminal's façade was dominated by tall windows that extended from the second to the third floor.

The new terminal was formally dedicated on November 14, 1931. The P&W invited several hundred guests to board one of its new "streamline" electric cars at the 69th Street Terminal in Philadelphia and travel to Norristown for the ceremony. Upon arrival, the travelers were greeted by a downtown Norristown bedecked for the occasion. Norristown merchants sponsored the celebration, termed "Norristown Day," strewing bunting along Main Street and offering sales on merchandise. One of the new P&W electric cars was placed on display in the Public Square (on temporary tracks placed on the sidewalk), and open to the public. Burgess Walter A. Wilson, in an acceptance address printed in its entirety in the *Times Herald*, used the construction of the new terminal as a rallying cry against the negativism inspired by the deepening economic Depression:

> This magnificent, palatial station reflects [the P&W Railway's] confidence in this community. This confidence permeates the atmosphere of this entire borough and all its environs. They are leading the way to renewed prosperity. Let us be imbued with the Philadelphia and Western spirit on the occasion of the dedication of this handsome new terminal. Let us follow this example of true American confidence. If every man and woman within the sound of my voice will do his and her part Norristown will be a leader in the restoration of a finer faith and courage, and will be among the first communities to enjoy tomorrow's sunshine of prosperity.[174]

After the dedication ceremonies, the new station was thrown open to the public, which toured the building in large numbers. The festivities ended with a band concert in the Public Square that evening.

The southern approach tracks continued to be elevated, and passengers embarked and disembarked via the waiting room on the building's second floor, which could be reached using stairs or an elevator. The P&W placed its offices on the third floor, while the first floor housed small concessions. This new terminal replaced the old waiting room and ticket counter at the Rambo House on Swede Street across from the courthouse. As the line included the northern service to Allentown, the bridge across Main Street at Swede Street was retained. In fact, to accommodate a slightly changed track layout, several square feet of the Public Square were covered over by the foundation for the tracks to allow room for a pedestrian walkway across the bridge over Main Street.[175]

Trolley Trouble

When the protagonists of *It Happened in Norristown* arrived on the P&W trolley, they were traveling on a remnant of a bygone era. By 1937, most of the local trolleys had been replaced by buses. Southeastern Pennsylvania, Norristown included, appears to have witnessed the local effectiveness of the nationwide conspiracy, financed largely by General Motors, which bought up many of the nation's trolley lines to replace the trolleys with buses. This effort, outlined in Stephen Goddard's *Getting There*, was locally effective in Montgomery County.[176]

Trolley service between Norristown and Chestnut Hill in Philadelphia, in continuous operation (under successive corporate names) since 1894, ended in December 1931 due to "steadily diminishing patronage." Buses replaced the trolleys in the county's eastern area, but unfortunately, the lines did not offer service to Norristown.[177] In November 1932, the Schuylkill Valley Traction Company went out of business, ending trolley service from Collegeville through Norristown to Conshohocken, and from Norristown through Bridgeport to Swedeland.

While the remaining trolleys passed over Main Street on the P&W steel truss bridge, the still-very-frequent trains continued to cross lower DeKalb Street at grade. This had been a problem ever since the trains began to stop at stations adjacent to DeKalb Street. Road traffic was frequently blocked by passing or idling trains, and accidents were an ever-present danger. In early 1930, the matter was brought before the State Public Service Commission. In May, an agreement was reached among the railroad companies, the streetcar service, the borough of Norristown, and the county government. After that, the tracks of both train lines were raised by about seven feet at DeKalb Street, and DeKalb Street below the tracks was lowered by about 11 feet. Both the Reading and the Pennsylvania stations were relocated, and several residential properties along Lafayette Street were ordered to be vacated. The new Reading Railroad station was opened to the public on December 18, 1932; the Pennsylvania Railroad station opened on July 30, 1934.[178] A 1934 agreement between the Reading and the Pennsylvania allowed patrons of each to use the other's line by transferring between the two new stations at DeKalb Street via a tunnel without changing or purchasing new tickets. This led to the location being referred to as Norristown's Union Station, where passengers could catch one of 138 trains each day bound for Philadelphia, or 128 trains from Philadelphia headed for points west.[179]

The railroad's need for a slow grade increase from that of its original tracks to the new height for the stations forced the closing of several streets south of Lafayette Street. A steadily rising wall blocked everything farther south. Mill Street, which had earned its name as the path to a mill at the riverbank and had prospered during the first railroad construction era, was cut off from the river, becoming merely a block-long street between Main and Lafayette.[180]

The Ford Street Bridge was a private entity owned by the Federal Bridge Company, a subsidiary of the Reading. The company had maintained the bridge, inadequately, until 1939 when it was deemed dilapidated and unsafe, and demolished. Local attempts to have the borough or county take title to the bridge were to no avail. While little mourned at the time, the loss of the Ford Street Bridge meant that from that point on Norristown could only be entered from the south at one point, the DeKalb Street Bridge. The coming of WWII postponed any further consideration of a second bridge—until problems forced the issue again.

The Traffic Ordinance

While access by road into Norristown had greatly improved with the elimination of the DeKalb Street grade crossing, travel within the borough was becoming increasingly congested. The reason was simple: despite the grim economic climate, people were still coming to Norristown from the surrounding areas to shop, as they always had. By now, however, they were increasingly coming via private automobiles and, from still-agricultural Montgomery County, light trucks. As late as 1918, at the conclusion of WWI, there had been 395,000 such vehicles registered in Pennsylvania. By 1940, there would be 2,268,000.[181] While the numbers are small compared with what would follow, they represent the sea change flooding across the country: Americans fell in love with cars. In the second half of the century, this love affair would prove tempestuous, providing high drama in Norristown, and across the nation.

In 1934, the Borough Council decided to design and implement an overall plan for its streets, governing direction of travel, curbside parking areas, signage and the plethora of related issues involved with automobiles. The result was this:

> An Ordinance regulating traffic conditions in regard to the use and operation of vehicles on the streets and alleys of the Borough of Norristown, restricting parking on certain streets, prohibiting double parking, providing for angular parking, providing for one-way streets, providing for designation from time to time of spaces to be reserved for public convenience and imposing penalties for the violation thereof, approved the third day of April 1934.[182]

This would become known as the Traffic Ordinance, and all subsequent changes in the coming decades would technically be amendments to this original ordinance. Its parking component required diagonal parking, which had the effect of prioritizing parking over traffic flow since diagonally parked cars protrude farther into the roadway do those parked parallel to the curb. Additionally, leaving a diagonal parking space requires drivers to back into the main roadway against the flow of traffic, then stop before proceeding forward. This formalized the nascent struggle between traffic and parking. This struggle would divide Norristown internally, and be a recurring irritant to a borough government and population that increasingly had to struggle to survive in a fundamentally changing world.

While the issues of traffic and parking and their many ramifications would often become lost in their own complexity, they at all times operated within a physical reality that was hard, simple and unchangeable. Downtown Norristown between Arch and Markley streets was just under six-tenths of a mile long, a little more than 3,100 feet. Five cross streets (plus Strawberry Alley and Green Alley on the south side of East

Main Street), clearance for bus stops and fire hydrants, and myriad other circumstances placed physical limits on curbside parking. Main Street's ability to accommodate anything that was both new and substantial in terms of traffic was almost nonexistent. The intersecting side streets offered some nearby parking spaces, and downtown's on-street parking thus extended both north and south along these streets, effectively between Lafayette and Airy streets.

Individual downtown merchants made many attempts to improve their specific parking issues. Here the historic lack of development along Lafayette Street, the result of the railroad's stifling presence, benefited the businesses on the south side of Main Street. Several open lots lay along this stretch, some of them conveniently at the back doors of enterprises located on the south side of Main Street. Chatlin's was particularly fortunate in this regard, and others sought to take advantage of open spaces as parking lots. Many of these lots, however, were owned by the railroad companies, who used them for storage or for employee parking. This occasionally led to conflict with the borough government.

Parking Meters

The 1934 Traffic Ordinance offered governed many aspects of on-street parking, but failed to address one important factor—namely, the length of time a space could be occupied. Downtown merchants had recognized early on that if number of parking spaces was largely fixed, turnover was critical. Merchants certainly didn't want people who were done shopping or transacting their business to occupy the limited number of spaces and prevent others from being able to park and conduct *their* business.

This was not a problem unique to Norristown, of course, and the solution was one borrowed from other municipalities: the parking meter. The primary purpose of the parking meter was, and still is, to promote turnover. Its perceived secondary financial benefit derived not only from the initial charge to occupy the space, but also from the considerably more expensive penalty paid for overstaying allotted time. Parking meters promised more efficient use of available spaces—people would park, pay, shop, and then leave—so others could find places to park. The initial charge to occupy the space, plus fines, provided revenue to the municipality. This revenue would prove to be more important than was initially thought.

The first parking meters appeared on downtown Norristown streets in 1940. The initial resolution offered on January 2 contracted for 525 meters from the Dual Parking Meter Company of Oklahoma City, Oklahoma. The meter manufacturer would receive 75% of the revenue from the meters (the remainder went into the borough's coffers) until the meters were paid for in full. From that point on, *all* revenue would go directly to the borough. The resolution passed its first and second readings, and was laid over for final decision at the next regular meeting.[183]

Reaction to the proposal was mixed, to say the least. Borough Council's method was questioned as much as its goal. Questions arose as to why no other bids had been solicited, let alone offered in a public meeting, before the contract was signed, and why no total price for the contract was announced. Main Street merchants held even deeper suspicions. While they admitted that in theory parking meters would aid the con-

51

gested parking situation by increasing the turnover rate of the metered spaces, many suspected that the Borough Council's true motive was not so much to aid Main Street as to garner additional revenue.[184]

At its regular February meeting, the Borough Council accepted some amendments to the proposed ordinance, including one that prohibited people from adding extra money to a meter at the end of its original time. The proposal passed on its third reading.[185] The questions raised about the cost of the contract had some effect: at this second meeting the members revealed that the 525 meters were being purchased at a cost of $58 each (they stressed, of course, that no initial cash outlay was required). Councilman Ciccarone, who had headed the parking meter study effort, attempted to rebut criticism about the Borough Council's motives by insisting that there were not installing meters for revenue but with a view to solving Main Street's perplexing parking problem. Borough Council approved the ordinance.[186]

The first of the meters went into formal use along Main and DeKalb streets between Lafayette and Airy on May 1, 1940. They were extended to both sides of Main Street from Markley Street to Green Alley and on streets intersecting Main Street in the downtown area, including DeKalb, Swede, and Lafayette. For the first time in Norristown history, people had to pay to park on Main Street. The rates were 1¢ for 12 minutes, and 5¢ for one hour. There was also a 10-minute "extension period" after the end of the one-hour paid period until the meter's red tag fully showed. After that point, continued occupation of the parking space would bring a $1 fine. There was no charge for Sundays and holidays.

Public reaction to the new meters was again mixed. There was confusion on the part of some drivers as to whether to put the coin in the meter in front of or to the rear of their automobile. The *Times Herald* wrote of the complaint of a clergyman, who now had to pay to park his car in front of his rectory. The same article, however, told of a merchant who sold a refrigerator to a customer who was now able to park right in front of the store. In early June, local baker John Entenmann added a touch of whimsy to the situation (and provided the *Times Herald* with a an excellent photo opportunity) when he drove his horse and wagon into downtown, parked them both at a metered spot, put in a coin and then walked to the Peoples National Bank to conduct business. Whatever the extent of initial confusion, the meters quickly proved their ability to generate revenue, generating $1,534.18 in their first fifteen days of operation.[187]

Downtown merchants would later insist, in print (and in Leonard Friedman's case, to the author personally), as would the *Times Herald* in editorials, that the original reason for the installation of parking meters was traffic control, not revenue. Their fundamental purpose was to put an end to any individual's extended occupation of a parking space. They would also claim in the coming decades, and the *Times Herald* would concur, that their reluctant acquiescence to the initial installation of the meters had been based on the unfortunately unwritten promise that once the initial cost of the meters had been paid to their manufacturer, all future proceeds would be used for the improvement of downtown. Anecdotal evidence supported that claim, but the Borough Council immediately saw the meters' potential as revenue generators and began to apply that revenue to its general fund. Parking meters brought in revenue of $35,853.36 in the first year of operation. By the end of 1945, revenue from parking meters had totaled $216,446.95. This was estimated to constitute 10% of the borough's total revenue during that period.[188] Although the issue of designating parking meter revenues for specific parking improvements would reappear more than once over the succeeding decades, whenever the subject would arise, the Borough Council made their revenue the overriding consideration.

Downtown During the War Years

As war replaced the Depression as the national focus, Norristown's businesses were faced with a dilemma. In the downtown world of retail and service, the war meant two contradictory things. The first was a local population with steadily increasing purchasing power, as unemployment yielded to the demands of wartime production. All the merchants welcomed this. The second result, however, which would be even more quickly felt, was that constraints on business from lack of demand would be replaced by constraints from lack of supply. The military would have first priority on essential materials, with the production of civilian goods shunted aside. Downtowns across the United States were in a similar bind, one that they could not patriotically escape. They could not promote spending to meet private desires; they could, however, appreciate at long last the steadily more apparent fact that their customers had money to spend, and look forward to the day when they could again profit from meeting that demand.

Rationing began to affect Norristown and Montgomery County in 1941, with automobiles and tires being first on the list. Sales of gasoline were restricted by a curfew from 7 p.m. to 7 a.m. beginning in August. December saw the last special lighting downtown for the Christmas season until 1945. Automobile production ceased in 1942, and by 1943, the Office of Price Administration (OPA) had even issued a directive largely banning pleasure driving. Norristown merchants were quick to react to the resulting belief that shopping constituted "pleasure driving." The *Times Herald* printed one such clarification, stating that people may use their automobiles for shopping "when no other transportation is available, or where the goods are too bulky to be carried, as well as for going to work, or meeting an emergency.... But civilians may not use their cars for social calls; for touring or vacationing; to attend places of amusement, entertainment or recreation; or to dine out where home cooking facilities are available." A few days later the local representative of the Office of Defense Transportation requested that the ban on recreational travel should be extended to include travel by bus, and specifically called on local bus companies to *not* increase service, as was being requested.[189]

As gasoline rationing and tire shortages combined to greatly restrict travel by private automobile, the parking problem was temporarily solved, but the simple act of getting downtown became for a chore for many people. Bus service helped to meet this challenge, but the then-customary habit of walking, recently reinforced by the Depression, continued to serve for most people. As Mary Early said, "Of course gas was rationed, but we were used to walking everyplace, you know."[190]

Main Street stores, particularly the larger ones, did not just await customers who had to make an increasingly difficult trip into town. Some sought ways to keep in touch with their rural customers. Block's Department Store hired drivers who would go out into the countryside, pick up rural families as previously scheduled, then drive them into Norristown, stopping, naturally, right in front of Block's.[191]

Of course, getting downtown was only part of the problem. Once people arrived on Main Street, they still had to figure out where to find persistently scarce items. Many of those interviewed for this book recalled standing in line with a large number of people, all patiently waiting for an item that had been previously unavailable and would be again soon. Mary Early's mother, trying to cope with shortages and irregular deliveries of basic items, became very responsive to this. "When my mother saw a line, [even if] she didn't know what they were selling she figured it must have been something we might need, so she joined it." One day, as she got closer to the head of the line, she realized the only item being sold was cigarettes. She was not a smoker, but her husband was, so she stayed. When it was her turn, she asked for a pack of Pall Malls, her husband's brand. Sorry, came the reply, only Viceroys. She thanked them and left without buying a pack. At dinner that night she mentioned that she had stood in line "forever" only to discover that they were selling cigarettes. When her husband's eyes lit up, she added, "I know you smoke Pall Malls, not Viceroys, so I didn't buy any." Mary recalled, "My father was not a violent man. If he had been, he would have killed her." Other interviewees offered similar stories. Judging solely by the lines generated, rationing's most significant shortage on Main Street was cigarettes.

A common dilemma for downtown stores was the relative absence of young people. Three of Joseph J. Zummo's four sons—Charles, Vincent, and Paul—entered the service. Anthony, the oldest, had a wife, children, and flat feet, and so was not called up. This unintentionally served the founder's purpose since Anthony had always been destined to take over the business. He worked at the store beginning in childhood, while he was in college, and after he got married. His parents planned his wedding ceremony around when he could be spared from the store. As the war—and the demand for manpower—continued, at one point it appeared as if Anthony, flat feet and all, might be called into service. Had that happened, it would have been the end for Zummo's Hardware: founder Joseph had aged, and would not have been able to handle the full responsibility again. Anthony's younger brothers had all labored at the store from an early age, too. Paul, the youngest, was the one who most longed to do something else, somewhere else. He was, for example, a swimmer of considerable prowess. His army career took him to places and into missions that he could not disclose in letters home (nor did he speak of them in later years). Once the Zummos received a call from the army suggesting that they attend the Norris Theater during the run of a specific "Movietone News" segment that accompanied the feature. They did, and on the screen they briefly viewed Paul with other members of his (unspecified) outfit, not only swimming but diving from high platforms.[192]

Each business concern faced specific problems, and not all overcame them. Yost's, one of downtown pioneers, had been on the decline during the Depression and clearly

began to suffer during the war. The store's once-plentiful ads in the Norristown directories dwindled. The war only hastened the decline. In the 1944 edition, Yost's displayed just a single half-page ad—a considerable comedown from its glory days
through the 1920s.

The Valley Forge Hotel, never profitable to begin with, weathered the war years
largely as it had weathered the Depression. It remained unprofitable overall, but continued on as a Norristown tradition. And by the end of the war, the hotel corporation
could point to *some* achievements. In the annual statement for 1942, Board Chairman
Leon Kohl observed that the hotel had survived Prohibition, the Depression, and wartime rationing. The hotel did have the advantage of being a community institution. For
one thing, this meant that local banks held the mortgages, and when things were tight
the banks required that interest payments be made, but made no demands for amorti-
zation of the outstanding principal.[193] A gradually improving financial picture allowed
management to pay off portions of the mortgage, reducing it from $125,000 in 1939 to
$50,000 by the end of 1945.[194]

5

Transportation Crisis

I n early September 1945, with Japan's surrender barely a month old and the troops just beginning to come home, the *Times Herald* was ready to launch what it considered a long-overdue campaign to improve Norristown's transportation infrastructure. The newspaper called on the Borough Council to take the lead in seeking state and federal funding for such improvements. The editorial, "Build for the Future," focused on the need for new bridges across the Schuylkill. Citing Norristown's growing population, it called for two such bridges, one in the east and one in the west.[195] In the coming years, the *Times Herald* would publish a number of editorials on various infrastructure needs, all springing from the same source: the desire to see Norristown, and the downtown in particular, not only retain its traditional prominence but expand it. The newspaper argued that the key to this goal was access to transportation, and the means of access to Norristown were insufficient, old and in disrepair.

The Borough Council and the downtown businesses shared the *Times Herald*'s concerns. During the post-war period, many people were concerned about transportation infrastructure. Each group saw the issues differently, but all shared a common realization that the means of access to, from, and within Norristown needed both major repairs and fundamental upgrades. As elsewhere in the nation, the war years had forced Norristown to postpone much-needed maintenance and improvement on its rails, roads, and bridges. The *Times Herald*'s editorials over the next few years lost no opportunity to remind readers of the importance of retail business to Norristown, adhering to its opinion that "One of the most effective proofs of a town's progress is the success of its retail stores."[196]

Deferred maintenance would soon encounter pent-up demand, as industrial production returned to peacetime output. Among the great many things that followed was a steadily quickening increase in the number of automobiles traveling on roads and bridges that had shown their inadequacies even before the war. The result was a transportation crisis for Norristown and its surrounding area, years before the Pennsylvania Turnpike became anything more than a vaguely understood highway somewhere to the west in Pennsylvania. For Norristown, that crisis had three components. Two of them, traffic congestion and parking, were closely interrelated and by the end of the war had already taken prominent positions. The third—and very different—crisis involved the railroads.

The railroad and Norristown had grown up together, and by now were experiencing fundamentally similar problems. Both possessed an aging infrastructure, overused and under-maintained, with all but the most necessary renovations long delayed. The local lines of the Reading and the Pennsylvania Railroads had been heavily used during the war, with only critical maintenance and replacements being done. In the first years after the war, Norristown continued to be well served by both railroads, which offered frequent service to Philadelphia as well as points west, but even those major lines were beginning to feel the decline in patronage and revenue as people became ever more enamored of their automobiles. The coming crisis of the railroads would play itself out on a national stage, with the competing lines along the Schuylkill decidedly minor, but typical participants.

Things were even worse for the remnants of Norristown area's light rail network. The only remaining lines in town were the P&W and the Lehigh Valley Transit Company. The latter had been having trouble maintaining its tracks, end experience had made the Borough Council members suspicious that the company was planning to abandon the trolley and switch to buses, leaving the borough to pay for the overdue roadwork.[197] This suspicion would prove to be well founded.

The most prominent components of Norristown's post-war transportation crisis were not just interrelated, they were two sides of the same coin: traffic congestion and automobile parking. Traffic congestion was a multifaceted issue, whose source components—automobiles, trucks and buses—each imposed differing physical requirements for their safe and expeditious entrance into, passage through, and exit out of downtown. These requirements would prove to be extraordinarily difficult to accommodate within the context of Norristown's old colonial Pennsylvania Town Model. Making things even more difficult was the competing need for parking spaces on the very same streets carrying the new traffic. Parking problems and traffic congestion were always discussed together, as one led to the other, and vice versa.

The principal area of traffic congestion downtown was at the intersection of DeKalb and Main streets. The problem itself was exacerbated by the elimination of grade crossings at the foot of the DeKalb Street Bridge. This action in the 1930s had eased congestion on the bridge itself and in Bridgeport, but only by shifting the location of the problem north. During the 1930s and 1940s, traffic congestion spread from the intersection of Main and DeKalb streets first to adjoining intersections, then to whole blocks, and finally to nearly every part of the downtown area.

The first major effort to address the problems had been the parking meters, installed in 1940. Whatever their contribution toward parking-space turnover, the meters had clearly not solved the parking or congestion problems. The problems had continued to worsen. The meters had, however, demonstrated their worth as revenue producers, especially after the wartime restrictions on private vehicles. In 1946 they enriched the borough coffers by $44,500.91, an increase of more than 20% over their 1945 total, and the highest ever since their installation.[198] This financial reality would underlay much of the maneuvering over these meters in the coming decades, shaping the debate and restricting the options.

Norristown's two primary access roads now carried the U.S. highway shield logos, but they were still the same two roads that had evolved with the borough itself. Ridge Pike, now U.S. Route 422, was still the main route from Philadelphia to its northwest. DeKalb Street was by now U.S. Route 202, a component of the primary road from Southeastern Pennsylvania to New York City. Complicating the issue further was the fact that the state was tasked with the actual responsibility for the maintenance and improvement of these roads, despite their U.S. designation. Thus, the state claimed authority in decisions involving the roads' traffic flow. The Norristown area authorities soon discovered that their plans for Main and DeKalb streets were at odds with the wishes of the state of Pennsylvania. It became increasingly clear to Norristown officials that the state's priority was traffic flow, at the expense of on-street parking.

The borough was thus caught between the state's desire to expedite traffic, which borough officials shared, and the concern of downtown merchants over the loss of badly needed parking spaces. With local prosperity at stake, borough authorities responded to state proposals with efforts to substitute conditions more favorable to local merchants. Between 1946 and 1950, the borough and the state engaged in a contentious back-and-forth over how to expedite traffic flow on DeKalb Street. The dispute centered on the removal of parking spaces to expedite traffic, but included a proposal by the state to make DeKalb Street one way northbound. After much back-and-forth, the state at least tacitly backed off of its proposals, and even allowed Norristown to reinstall most of the meters it had made the borough remove. This would not be the end of the problem, however.

By late 1948, the steadily worsening traffic congestion was reaching a crisis point. In November the implications for downtown merchants were spelled out by Francis A. Pitkin, executive director of the State Planning Board of the Department of Commerce. His message was that traffic congestion and lack of parking spaces were hurting downtown merchants in many municipalities in Pennsylvania and beyond. He cited a survey that revealed during the rush hour in many such municipalities, perhaps 27% of all vehicles on a street were simply circling the vicinity, looking for a place to park, or just trying to pick up or discharge passengers. Downtowns were already paying a price for this frustration. "The trouble is when people pass through an area with a situation of this kind now existent in many cities and towns, they are not likely to stop in that area but somewhere beyond where they can find a place to park." He noted that the number of "branch stores" now opening in suburban locations was evidence that people wished to keep out of heavily traveled areas.[199]

The spring of 1949 saw a fundamental change in the relationship between traffic flow and parking along Main Street, which demonstrated where the state's focus lay: traffic flow. Downtown parking had been diagonal when the meters were installed, but in September 1948 the state formally proposed changing to parallel parking to expedite traffic flow. By early 1949 borough council had agreed, and made the decision to switch to parallel parking.[200] Not only did this require that each meter be relocated, but the additional curb length required for each parking space meant a net loss of 40 parking spaces, and thus their meters. A *Times Herald* article starkly portrayed what had by now become the adversary relationship between traffic flow and on-street parking: "Although the change from angular parking is expected to help move traffic through the business district, it also provides more trouble for motorists seeking to park during shopping hours. The decrease of 40 spaces in the already-crowded Main Street area is expected to force drivers to park at greater distances than ever from stores."[201] The decision to implement parallel parking resulted in the almost-simultaneous authorization for additional parking meters on Main Street east and west of the original downtown area, and on Lafayette Street (which had also reverted to parallel parking). This action of the Borough Council in immediately authorizing new meters to compensate for the revenue to be lost speaks to what had become their priority.

The Tempting Chimera: A Bypass

One of the main points of discussion among those who dealt with transportation issues was the importance of handling both through traffic and local traffic. For the most part, given its already-unwieldy traffic problems, Norristown wanted to divert through traffic, and entice local traffic. Many other urban centers across the nation had done this by constructing a bypass section of the major highways that passed though the cities, and this was also Norristown's desired solution. The idea was that diverting through traffic on U.S. Route 202 around Norristown would lighten the load on downtown streets, freeing up some of the congestion and making it easier for local traffic. The concept wasn't new; it had been introduced in the late 1920s, and would remain a favored tactic nationwide to adapt the nation's system of old, local roads to the automobile era.[202] Norristown Borough officials, downtown merchants and the *Times Herald* embraced the idea eagerly. A bypass seemed the solution to the chronic traffic congestion, and perhaps even to its parking problems since it would render moot the incessant struggles among downtown merchants and state and borough officials over traffic flow versus parking on downtown streets.

WWII, however, postponed everything but dreams for Norristown, as it did for many other communities. With the war's end the publicity and political effort began again; the *Times Herald*'s September 1945 editorial was couched in terms of a bypass, and the newspaper would return to the subject again and again, whether the subject was traffic congestion, downtown parking or downtown prosperity. Readers would have their hopes for a bypass raised, then tempered, then squashed, only to have them raised yet once more as the cycle begin anew. The issue would never actually die, but Norristown never did get its highway bypass.

Downtown Norristown reflected very broadly the national experience of the immediate post-war period. Hopes soared quickly, but such wartime remnants as rationing and shortages would persist in the short term. As the economy adjusted to peacetime production, first the rationing and then the shortages would each decline and then vanish. Downtown merchants discovered that pent-up demand was real, and rejoiced as supplies of products increased. A sense of returned prosperity was palpable in downtown by the late 1940s. Even the Valley Forge Hotel would share—somewhat— in the return to prosperity.

By the end of WWII in August 1945, downtown Norristown was already planning for the long-delayed return of good times. In October came the glad tidings that downtown Norristown, Main Street from Markley to Arch, would be lit for the Christmas holidays for the first time since December 1941. By December, local merchants claimed to have found the evidence they sought that shoppers were indeed indulging in shopping sprees "denied them during the war years."[203]

There had been virtually no construction in downtown Norristown during the war years. Nevertheless, one of the earliest examples of post-war construction did take place downtown. Before 1945 had ended, the corner of Main and Barbadoes streets, on the site of the former U.S. Post Office (almost the only available lot of any size downtown), appeared a brand new automobile service station.[204] Significantly, its construction prompted a *Times Herald* editorial to sound yet another alarm over the need for off-street parking by pointing out that the new station's construction was costing Norristown "one of its largest downtown parking lots."[205]

Two of downtown's two most prominent residents, Sears and W. T. Grant, upgraded their stores immediately after the war, demonstrating that even the faraway corporate management of both firms felt confident about the economic future of Norristown. Both remodeled Main Street locations opened in June 1946. Word spread in advance that W. T. Grant would feature a stock of such hard-to-get items as nylons and menswear, strongly desired by the rationing-deprived population. The result was close to a mob scene: eight police were needed to handle the crowd, which threatened to block Main Street. Sears reopened its improved store less than a week later with less fanfare—and less chaos. Still, the investment in Norristown by a firm with the tradition and reputation of Sears was duly noted by the *Times Herald*, which opined, "A store of this type is a credit to the business district of Norristown, and an asset to the entire community. It not only attracts its own larger patronage, but it brings new customers for other merchants."[206]

Together with returning prosperity came the inevitable lesson that nothing lasts forever. Yost's had dominated the southeast corner of Main and DeKalb since 1862. Daniel F. Yost, son of founder Daniel M. Yost, who had administered the firm since his father's death in 1912, announced in April 1946 (the firm's 84th anniversary) that he had sold the company. The new owner was quick to assure everyone that not only would the store remain, but so would its personnel. Later that year came the news that another venerable downtown institution was undergoing fundamental change. B. E. Block and Brothers, at 11 West Main Street, was sold to an outside investor. The firm continued to do business as B. E. Block and Brothers, but as with Yost's, old-timers felt that something had been lost.

Some economists say "a rising tide floats all boats," which might even apply to one as heavily laden and underpowered as the Valley Forge Hotel. In January 1946, the hotel's stockholders reviewed what Board Chairman (and Norristown Burgess) William A. March termed "one of [the hotel's] best and most prosperous years," then accepted management's initiative and voted a $2 liquidating dividend, the third in as many years. The focus on strict cost control and paying off the mortgage had caused shares of preferred stock in the hotel, which carried a par value of $100 and had been selling (if at all) for $5 during the Depression years, to be valued at about $18. While this policy had substantially reduced the amount of the mortgage, it had meant that stockholders had received no regular dividends. By the end of 1946, the mortgage had been pared down to $30,000. The expectation was that once the final mortgage amount had been paid off, the company would be in a position to start paying regular dividends. By 1948, the Valley Forge Hotel had paid off this remainder, making the hotel debt free for the first time in its history. Hopes were high for a dividend payment in 1949.[207]

In 1949, the corporation enjoyed two positive events: the promised dividend, and a buyout offer. Philadelphia businessman Frank A. Libbon made an offer in early summer to buy the company's preferred stock for $46 per share. Rebuffed, in October he increased his offer price to $60. This failed to impress the management; in what the *Times Herald* termed an "unofficial meeting," the company's stockholders declined the offer. Chairman March was of the opinion that the turnpike's new terminus at King of Prussia was an opportunity for the hotel to increase its transient traffic, and had been the reason for the offer the company had received.[208] Two weeks later, the board of directors declared the first regular dividend, $2 per share (on preferred stock only) since the hotel opened in 1926.

Surveying the Situation

By the late 1940s, a consensus among local merchants had been established that traffic congestion in the downtown shopping area was hurting business. This was particularly true from on Friday nights and all through Saturdays, traditionally the heaviest shopping times of the week. Traffic jams and lack of parking were driving shoppers away from downtown, and business was suffering.[209] The frustration that resulted led to pressure for a formal survey to quantify what everyone was experiencing. Such a survey was the necessary first step for the borough in seeking financial support for its proposed projects; the statistical results from this survey would provide the basis for any claimed priority on state and federal funding. Downtown retailers were the primary movers. When the Montgomery County Commissioners voted in early 1949 to fund an Origin and Destination Traffic Survey for the major routes into and out of Norristown, borough merchants were greatly heartened. Equally heartening was that the amount voted by the County Commissioners included Norristown's share of the cost. The good news was somewhat tempered by the reality that much time would elapse before any results were made available, especially since the survey would not be undertaken before the spring, to ensure a more realistic estimation of traffic flow. The survey would then take at least three months to compile. Tabulation and analysis of the data obtained would take an additional six months at minimum. Still, the announcement was well received.[210]

By May, the work had added a second survey on parking. While the Origin and Destination Traffic Survey analyzed an area that extended out the main routes past Norristown itself, the Parking Survey focused on the central business district. Work on the Origin and Destination survey began in June. Easily the most conspicuous aspect of the process was the need to interview between 50–66% of motorists traveling over the relevant roads. In a significant aside to an early August article monitoring survey progress, the *Times Herald* noted that "heavier-than-anticipated traffic has caused many more interviews to be conducted."[211] The Origin and Destination Survey was complete by August 12, and the Parking Survey began on August 19, so the initial part of the schedule was essentially kept. Unfortunately, the second part—tabulation and analysis of the data—was not. The final survey report was not released until September 1950, almost 13 months after the compilation work had been completed. The actual numbers were outdated, but the trends appeared to hold true. One conclusion deserves note: over 75% of travelers used private automobiles, trucks or taxis, and only 22.5% rode the bus.[212]

The schedule for the Parking Survey fared even worse. The formal results of the survey were not released until July 1951. The Parking Survey did, at least, provide hard numbers to substantiate the common knowledge, reporting 2,395 spaces in the central business district available to accommodate customer vehicles. Of these, 1,086 were curb spaces (on Main Street and connecting streets between Arch and Markley), while various public lots offered 1,216 spaces. Only 148 cars could be accommodated in garages. During the course of this statistical 10-hour day, the 1,086 curb spaces accommodated 8,375 vehicles, while the 1,216 spaces on private lots were utilized by 2,247 cars.[213] That each curb space was occupied by just over seven vehicles in a statistical 10-hour day indicated that parking meters were having a positive effect by forcing vehicle turnover. By contrast, the turnover rate of fewer than two cars per 10-hour day in the public lots and the statistically zero turnover rate in the garages indicated that these spaces were most likely being used by those employed in or near the central business district. This meant that shoppers had little chance of finding a space in a parking lot and zero chance of finding one in a garage. As there was also no chance of increasing the number of curb spaces in the central business district, the conclusion was obvious: "It is evident that all additional parking spaces provided must be off-street facilities."[214]

Perhaps it was only fitting that 1949, a year in which the borough focused on parking meters and their effect on business, should have closed with an embarrassing reminder that Norristown, for all its pretensions, was a small municipality governed by part-time politicians and subservient administrators. In a December 22 front-page article, the *Times Herald* revealed that the same borough officials who had been complaining about the lack of downtown parking spaces had arranged for a private business to sell Christmas trees on the Public Square, and had reserved one adjacent metered parking space for the vendor of the trees. The article revealed also that two metered spaces at Main and Cherry streets were being rented to vendors selling merchandise from the spaces themselves—and these two were nephews of a current councilman. Merchants were predictably angry, charging that the borough was now renting Main Street itself for individuals' business purposes. The next day the council president released a statement saying that he was "outraged" by the rentals, and that they were merely the result of a "misunderstanding."

As 1950 dawned, downtown Norristown retained its long-time dominance as the area's retail and service center. By then, however, its deficiencies had also become glaringly obvious to all. Its physical plant was built out and aging. Norristown's six-block downtown was unable to offer adequate space for either the smooth travel of vehicles through the area or their parking within the area. To this problem was soon to be added that of traffic from the Eastern Extension of the Pennsylvania Turnpike. The number of such vehicles, and the form that they would take—automobiles, trucks and buses—became a subject of major concern. Yet it is clear that regardless of the number of vehicles the turnpike might bring, they would add to a traffic situation in the Borough of Norristown that had already reached the crisis point.

The Coming of the Superhighways

The original Pennsylvania Turnpike, which opened on October 1, 1940, was an immediate success. Even before its opening, the first steps were undertaken to extend the original road to both the eastern and western borders. The once-questionable idea of building a limited-access highway across Pennsylvania quickly proved its worth, though actual construction of the extensions had to wait out the duration of the war. Soon afterward, however, planning began again.

The route that would become the Schuylkill Expressway first appeared on a map in 1932, when the Regional Planning Federation proposed a parkway system into and out of Philadelphia along the lines of those built by Robert Moses in New York. Initially termed the Valley Forge Parkway, the four-lane, limited-access roadway was to connect Fairmont Park in Philadelphia with Valley Forge State Park. As with the New York parkways, this road would be built strictly for automobiles (low stone bridges would keep out trucks and buses) and laid out with an eye toward both aesthetics and efficiency of travel. The project remained a dream: actual highway planning focused on arterial routes to relieve congestion on long-existing arteries.[215] It was not until the Pennsylvania Turnpike's Eastern Extension from Carlisle was becoming a reality that the necessary components fell into place. Traffic congestion on local roads, regional political support, and state funding combined to forge the "engineering mentality" identified by historian Bruce Seely as necessary to overcome the many obstacles that would be encountered.[216]

In 1947 the line on a map connecting Philadelphia and Valley Forge reemerged, but with fundamental changes in concept. The new highway would intersect the Pennsylvania Turnpike at its new eastern terminus, an area of farmland in Upper Merion Township, just east of Valley Forge itself. The "parkway" approach had been discarded for an "expressway," a four-lane limited-access highway that could accommodate not just cars but also the large trucks and buses that traveled the turnpike. This conceptual change was driven by the highway's new purpose: to lure as much traffic as possible away from U.S. Route 202, which led north to New York City, and toward Philadelphia instead. An expressway connection to the turnpike would also minimize the amount of traffic being dumped onto the local roads.[217]

While the turnpike's extension eastward encountered little substantial opposition, the Schuylkill Expressway most certainly did. As a result, the completion times of the two superhighways did not align. Official groundbreaking on the Expressway did not take place until April 26, 1950, several months later than the original prediction. Then the delays really began.

King of Prussia

The area of Upper Merion Township that would host this intersection of modern highways had always been farmland. Close to the planned intersection for the super-highways was the nexus of DeKalb Pike (U.S. Route 202) and Gulph Road (Pennsylvania Route 23). DeKalb Pike was the primary north-south road in the area west of Philadelphia, passing through Bridgeport and then Norristown on its way to New York. Gulph Road proceeded in a generally east-west, although quite meandering, direction. The road crossed county lines, and its financing was supported by the state. Considerably less traveled than DeKalb Pike, Gulph Road had over the decades remained a minor roadway and was much less substantial in layout and construction.

An imposing stone building stood at the intersection of these two roads. This was the King of Prussia Inn, built in 1769 by Daniel Thompson, a Quaker and veteran of the Revolutionary War. Thompson named the inn after the monarch known in the United States as Frederick the Great, who was King of Prussia from 1740 until his death in 1786. The King of Prussia Inn had already acquired iconic status by the time the superhighways appeared literally at its doorstep. Deep connections with American history—and several legends—had arisen from its proximity to Valley Forge and its connection to the bedraggled Continental Army's winter encampment there. One such legend asserts that the inn was the site chosen by George Washington to induct the Marquis de Lafayette into the Masonic Order. A later legend dates from 1793, when Jefferson, Madison, and Monroe were said to have taken refuge there to escape the yellow fever epidemic then raging in Philadelphia. None of the stories has been substantiated sufficiently to please professional historians.

By 1948, the coming Pennsylvania Turnpike began to take on real importance to the few residents of King of Prussia and to local governments in southeastern Pennsylvania. The *Times Herald*, in a parade of articles, kept its readers informed over the summer on the progress of construction and its expected completion date. An August article made public the effects of construction on the local residents. Approximately 125 acres of Upper Merion Township would be taken by the turnpike's road and new terminus; 11 property owners would lose portions of their land.

A review of the coverage in the *Times Herald* on the arrival of the Pennsylvania Turnpike in King of Prussia produces the inescapable conclusion that almost everyone involved saw the event as being a net loss to Upper Merion Township. During this entire period, the focus of the local press and pundits was on what would be physically lost and how what remained would be adversely affected by the coming of the super-highways. Homeowners who would lose property to the roads were listed, and careful records made of what they would lose. Ample voice was given to those who predicted

64

traffic chaos. What was glaringly missing from local accounts at the time was much consideration of what *positive* changes the superhighways might bring. A comment from an Upper Merion Township official in August 1949, while little more than a footnote amid the proceedings, serves as ironic testimony to this rampant negativism. Noting that between them the Turnpike Extension, the Expressway, and the Schuylkill River de-silting project (already well under way, and unrelated) had removed some 400 acres from the Upper Merion tax rolls, "most of which has a high assessment value," this less-than-prescient official viewed the construction as costing the township tax revenue, thus damaging its financial status.[218]

Not everyone, of course, saw what was coming in terms solely of loss. A handful of visionaries and entrepreneurs was active, if quietly so. By 1949, some landowners began receiving inquiries from gasoline companies interested in purchasing property for service stations, and from unidentified people interested in local land for "tourist cabins, lunchrooms and way stations."[219] March 1950 saw the first governmental response to such inquiries. Upper Merion Township received a request from the Gulf Oil Company to construct a service station close to the terminus, and on ground still zoned residential. The request was denied, but the company, "foreseeing a prospective business future at the turnpike site," decided to go before the Township Board of Adjustment to ask for a variance. Joseph K. Shoemaker, president of the Upper Merion Township Supervisors, revealed that Gulf had "several months ago" approached him, as the owner of a piece of property they felt would be suitable for a service station. Shoemaker turned down the offer.[220] Where there are roads, however, there must be services, and eventually some of the offers were accepted.

In the coming decade, many businesses did indeed appear in the King of Prussia area, including service stations, motels, and restaurants for travelers. But there were those who saw in this busy intersection the perfect place for their then-unique vision of a new way of living, working, and shopping to take form. These were the people who ensured that the name King of Prussia would become known nationwide, as its pioneering project proved successful and was copied again and again and again across the local and national landscape, altering the countryside beyond all recognition. These were the dreamers who would eventually create the King of Prussia Mall.

6

Mid-Century Norristown

Though in 1950 "stability" still dominated in Norristown, forces of change were stirring, with some already under way and some still just beginning. In the coming decades, Norristown's traditions would be tested by broader social forces on a level never before encountered. Norristown lay in their path, as with so many other American communities. Yet change was not going to depend solely on anonymous social forces, it was already under way, spurred by local individuals dissatisfied with "the way things had always been."

The U.S. Census Bureau reported that there were 35,126 Norristown residents in 1950—evidence of the second straight decade of population decline, however slight. The 1940 Census had reported 35,181 residents, a decline from the 35,853 listed in 1930. The 1950 figure represented slightly more than 10% of Montgomery County's 353,068 residents, up from 289,247 in 1940. By this time, the considerable majority of Norristown's population was native-born, as the descendants of the pre-WWI immigrants were now native-born Americans. Most of Norristown's foreign-born residents continued to be Italian.[221] Despite the passage of time, however, and the changing status of the borough's Italian population, Norristown's stability in population was matched by stagnation in the relationship among the ethnic groups that comprised it, along the traditional ethnic/religious divide. As a consequence, residents of the three residential "Ends" of Norristown still grew up and lived largely in isolation from one another. In 1950, in Norristown, the melting pot had barely heated up.

The West End—In 1950, with very few exceptions, the people of the West End had three things in common: they were white, they were not rich, and they were not of Italian descent. Norristown's ethnic/racial divide had directed all but a few Italians and African-Americans to the East End; the West End had been the last settled, and the descendants of the borough's founders that came to comprise the elite had long since settled in the North End. The West End had made a game attempt to be recognized as a status neighborhood—at least along West Main Street—but by that time, visitors arriving from the west along Main Street would see that the old and once-spectacular mansions had seen better days. The original families that had built and occupied these elaborate homes had left the West End, as had the original owners of those on North DeKalb Street, as part of the flight of the "resident upper class" referred to in the *Norristown Study.*

The West End's geographic isolation had conditioned both its physical development and the attitude of its residents. The volunteer spirit kept the local fire companies staffed, and the merchants of Marshall Street had organized for their common interests. These separate institutions at the same time had channeled and focused that spirit locally; the result was competition with the other sections and institutions of Norristown rather than cooperation. In all fairness, that sense of "difference" was returned in full measure by both individuals and institutions of the other two "ends."

The North End—The North End of Norristown had been the preferred area of settlement for Norristown's giants of business and commerce. As the borough had expanded, the residences of its elite steadily grew in size and moved farther northward. What was distinctive about the North End in 1950 was the makeup and attitudes of its residents. Wealth was no longer a major factor; the wealthy had exited for the suburbs. Despite this, the North End's residents were evidence that the declaration of the *Norristown Study* that "Norristown proper lacks a resident upper class" was rather overstated, if "upper class" also refers to a collective mental outlook.[222] The wealth may have departed, but the attitudes of superiority and entitlement remained entrenched in North End residents. The North End's residents, while economically a shadow of their former status, nonetheless remained the descendants of the founding elite, in ways more significant than family connections or level of income. While they could not afford the lifestyle of those who had previously dominated Norristown, these residents continued to hold onto the beliefs, outlooks and traditions of their ancestors—the majority of whom had also been something less than rich. Those traditions included service to local institutions, to the borough, and to the county. Among the North End's residents were those who occupied posts of responsibility, in law and government, including county judges.

The assumption of superiority that underlay the tradition of service was a combination of the longstanding Protestant domination of Montgomery County and of the status of residence—particularly long-time residence—in the North End. In a reflection of "old Norristown," the North End remained not only overwhelmingly white, but also overwhelmingly Protestant. Congregational membership both determined the alleged "differences" among them, and differentiated between them and the Catholics. Divided as they were among Episcopal, Methodist, Lutheran, and Baptist, as well as a number of smaller sects, they were still proudly aware that while a few were Catholic, fewer still were Italian. With the 20th century half over, the old barrier still held: Italians were still unwelcome north of Fornance Street. Prospective homebuyers of Italian descent found nothing available: "They just wouldn't show you the house."[223] The few exceptions were those Italians who had accumulated sufficient prestige, as well as income, and who purchased substantial homes above the never-exact boundary between North End and East End, particularly if their family name was ambiguous, as with the Constable family.[224]

These people strove to perpetuate and preserve the world they had grown up in, largely retaining their upper-class Protestant value system, only slightly altered by their lack of individual wealth. While religion was central, what really mattered was one's behavior, not one's income. Behavior was the means on which others were largely judged, beginning with church attendance and involvement, but extending across a wide scope. Florence Johnson, who as a young woman had begun working in Philadelphia during the late 1940s, often found herself walking home from the DeKalb Street Station to her home in the North End. Her father cautioned her about this, and advised that if she was returning late at night, she should use Powell Street rather than DeKalb Street to walk north, even though it added time to her journey. Her father's reasoning was that if she had a problem, the poor people of Powell would open their doors and help her, while the "rich people" of DeKalb would not.[225] Florence Johnson married Robert Young, and together they carried on the traditions and attitudes of the old North End, minus the wealth. Robert served on several borough voluntary committees, and Florence "Johnny" Young became a pillar of the Historical Society of Montgomery County.

In 1950, these were the people who still dominated Norristown religiously, socially, and politically. The brief overview above, focused as it is on the huge and obvious ethnic/religious divide in Norristown, glosses over the actual complexity of groupings and relationships among the Protestants in the North End, and in Norristown itself. These groupings and relationships had deep roots, and one of the social attitudes carried on by those who clearly identified with their ancestors had been to perpetuate these "differences."

The East End—Norristown's East End had expanded along with the immigrant population, and in 1950, its unofficial (but well understood) western boundary was DeKalb Street, just one block to the east of the borough's historic core. Likewise, its northern boundary stretched north to Fornance Street, well above the ridgeline of Courthouse Hill. A rough and irregular "dividing line" between North and East Ends was the rugged ravines of Saw Mill Run; some of the poorest residences of the East End lay near here, always under the threat of quick and damaging flooding.

The borough's residents may have mixed at work, across the ethnicities and even across racelines, but in 1950 the geographic divisions within Norristown were as strong as ever. When a cross-ethnic acquaintance led to an actual visit from a West or North End family to the East End, as at a wedding, the experience was akin to visiting "a whole different world."[226] The food was strange, as were the customs surrounding the event itself. The East End in 1950 was overwhelmingly Italian, and close to a self-contained community, due to the long exclusion of Italians from the Protestant-dominated social structures in Norristown. East Main Street was its backbone. Main Street east of DeKalb contained several Italian-owned shops, some quite Italian-oriented in their offerings. Everyone's religious center, Holy Savior Church, sat at East Main and Walnut, and several of the Italian clubs, such as the L.A.M (Sons of Italy) could be found along Main Street east of Arch.

In 1950, Norristown's Italians were grouped together and separated from others even in death. The only Catholic cemetery, on DeKalb Pike in East Norriton north of the borough, was (and still is) called St. Patrick's, after the traditionally Irish Catholic parish that owned it. All Italians who inquired about burying a relative there would be taken past the front rows, replete with mausoleums and elaborate gravestones on ample sites to the very rear of the cemetery. There they would see only a large number of simple stones, closely crowded together, and be told that this was where all Italians were buried. Take it or leave it.[227]

Agents of Change

Horace Davenport—African-Americans had been a presence, albeit a small one, in Norristown for generations. One notable local man, Horace Davenport, had as a youngster delivered papers to both Italian and African-American families on his route. After graduating from Norristown High School and then completing his service in the military, he studied at the University of Pennsylvania. In 1950, he was awarded both a law degree and a master's degree. In 1951, upon being admitted to the Montgomery County Bar, he returned to Norristown and opened his own office. It was small, just one story and only two rooms, but it was located on Swede Street— Norristown's "lawyers' row."

An African-American attorney was a rarity there at that time, but as Davenport recalled, "I had no racial problems at all. I was accepted in the legal community as just another lawyer from the very beginning." He recounted his experience shopping for furniture for his new office, noting that he had inquired at D. M. Feldman's Office Supplies on West Main Street about second-hand items. David Feldman, the owner, demurred, saying it was a bad idea and would give the wrong image. He instead offered to sell Davenport the necessary new furniture, allowing him to pay when he was able. Struck by the merchant's kindness, Davenport accepted the offer. He repaid Feldman's within a short time.[228]

When Davenport returned to Norristown to begin his legal practice, he brought his new wife, Alice. Like her husband, Alice had come from the upper strata of the African-American population in her hometown—but her hometown was Washington, DC. Good-looking, educated, poised, and articulate, the young Alice Davenport immediately impressed everyone she met. She had been a teacher in Washington, and once in Norristown she applied for a teaching job in the Norristown public school system. She was accepted, and became the first African-American public school teacher in Montgomery County. She was assigned to an elementary school on East Marshall Street, where most of the African-American and poorer Italian children attended.

Alice Davenport provided an interesting "outsider's" view of Norristown in the 1950s. "I missed Washington when I first came here because I didn't have anyone here that I had anything in common with," said Alice. The African-Americans she encountered in Norristown mostly worked at the state hospital, or as domestics; she was used to "something better." Going downtown comforted her because, as she put it, "People knew me, and wanted my business." She spoke fondly of downtown Norristown in the 1950s. "I remember downtown Norristown as a hustling, bustling center of shopping on Friday evenings."[229]

Samuel Friedman—If African-Americans can be said to have existed below Norristown's social structure, then the even smaller Jewish community can be said to have existed outside it. Jews had been prominent in downtown Norristown for some time, and many had attained personal and professional success. In 1950, they were significant players within the merchant community, but were still largely excluded from the social structure and the groups of influence in that venue. The experience of Samuel Friedman, longtime proprietor of the New York Store, was typical. His attempts to purchase a house in the better sections of Norristown or in the adjoining West Norriton Township were rebuffed; when he purchased a house on West Main Street in the far West End, his neighbors immediately put up a For Sale sign (they later relented, and stayed). Friedman's son Leonard recalled hearing the epithet "dirty Jew," and getting into more than one childhood fight over the slur.

Friedman desired to be admitted to the Masonic Order, which in Norristown as in many places in 1950 signaled perhaps the ultimate acceptance by the "insiders." Like other Jews previously, he was initially the kept out by the "blackball" system. Unlike the others, Friedman had a connection: a friend was a past master of the Lodge, who supported his reapplication. The second time he was admitted. In the years that would follow, his son Leonard's experiences showed that change, while slow in coming, was at least taking place. Leonard joined the Kiwanis Club, then, largely to please his father, applied for admittance to the Masons. He was accepted without problem, and eventually rose to become Lodge Master.[230]

Harry Butera—Another familiar Norristownian is Harry Butera, who by 1950 was already a legendary figure among Norristown's Italian community, having becoming a major player in real estate. Ignazio Butera ("Harry" was the contribution of a childhood employer) was an immigrant, having arrived with his family in 1906, at the age of 7.[231] His family's arrival was a typical example of "chain migration," with the way having been paved by Harry's older brother Tom who, upon completing his compulsory service in the Italian army, had returned home and announced his intention to go to America. He did so in 1904.

Like many local families, the Buteras came from Sciacca, Sicily. Patriarch Charles "Big Charlie" Butera initially found work in the borough's woolen mills. He and his wife—heeding the advice of their sponsors, who understood the critical importance of education, including learning English—initially placed young Harry in a local public school. Due to his sensitive nature and inability to speak "proper" English, he met with both abuse and ostracism. He transferred to St. Patrick's, a Catholic school. There, as Butera related in his memoirs, "I really learned the real depth of what was spontaneous prejudice versus Italian boys who, in those days, were considered as intruding foreigners and showered with epithets not permitted in print." Butera's memoirs recounted beatings suffered at the hands of American-born Italians who joined in the abuse heaped on the immigrants despite their common ethnicity.

Butera's parents, when they first registered him for school, had added three years to his actual age—a typical ruse at the time to make it possible for kids to obtain working papers early; in the 1900s, the minimum age for working papers was 14. Thus it was that Harry, at age 11½, left school and took a menial job at the James Lees Woolen Mill across the Schuylkill River in Bridgeport. Along with about 150 boys, girls, and women on the fifth floor of the mill, he worked initially as a "doffer," removing spindles wound full of yarn and replacing them with empty ones. His hours were typical of the times: 6:45 a.m. to 5:45 p.m. on weekdays, and 6:45 a.m. to noon on Saturdays. For this he received $3.50 per week. After four months, he secured a job at the Rambo and Regar Hosiery Company, located along East Main Street in Norristown. The new job freed him from having to cross the Schuylkill twice a day; the rickety old Ford Street Bridge charged a penny for each one-way pedestrian crossing.

Butera held various jobs and learned several skills (including barbering) during his youth, but his one consistency during this period was studying: he labored assiduously in what little free time he had to overcome the handicap of a fourth-grade education. He was accepted at the Schlissler Business College at 208 DeKalb Street, perhaps because the school was in serious financial straits and needed his $16-per-month tuition too much to check the fourth-grade graduate's credentials. Butera's intelligence and diligence impressed his teacher so much that she agreed to become his tutor. He studied hard and did well, but just before graduation the Schlissler Business College was abruptly shut down by its creditors.

Butera's mastery of both English and Italian, with an emphasis on the proper grammar and pronunciation of each, had always greatly impressed his family and their acquaintances, many of whom spoke little English and only the Sicilian dialect of Italian. His ability to read Italian led to Butera being proposed for membership at age 16 (officially 19) in one of the many local Italian self-help societies then active; he was accepted, and was elected recording secretary. He was soon helping other members, providing translations and interpreting legal documents. This was the beginning of Butera's stellar reputation within the Italian community.

In the fall of 1922, an elderly real estate broker named D. L. MacDonald, a daily customer at the barbershop run by Harry's brother Frank, confided that he was not in good health and was looking for a young salesman to help represent his agency. Frank recommended Harry. Butera interviewed, and got the job, at straight commission. Although MacDonald's agency had focused on rural properties, Butera saw an opportunity in Norristown, particularly among his fellow Italians. Those that had managed to accumulate savings were reluctant to deal with existing realtors, and with good reason. In addition to the common one of blatant discrimination against Italians, the real estate profession during this time was virtually unregulated. Butera, through his assistance of fellow Italians, already knew that in local real estate, "Competition among brokers was fierce and on a 'dog-eat-dog' basis, usually devoid of normal business ethics."[232]

Butera's reputation for knowledge and honesty in the Italian community brought him quick success. MacDonald made him an equal partner after only three weeks, and began to plan for his own retirement, upon which Butera opened his own little office (9 feet by 20 feet) on Swede Street on May 1, 1923. His clientele and his reputation grew steadily. Banks at first treated him shabbily, not wanting to advance mortgage money to Italians, but that reluctance changed as Butera's business grew.

His expertise in property values led by the 1930s to a series of appointments as an appraiser, first by the Borough of Norristown for condemnation work, later by the state of Pennsylvania, and then by the U.S. government itself in its efforts to counter the growing Depression. Throughout the Depression, Butera was a low-key but well known benefactor of the needy among the Italian community, often administering—at no charge—the small savings of acquaintances who were forced to work elsewhere. He even covered the mortgage payments of people who were about to lose their houses.[233]

In real estate Butera not only found a successful career but his life's cause: combating the discrimination that virtually all Italians in the area had encountered in every aspect of their lives. A fundamental component of that discrimination had been the "ghettoization" of Italians in the East End. Harry Butera dedicated his real estate efforts to breaking that barrier. He later described the general process in his memoirs, phrased in the polite and proper tone that characterized his writing:

> Anglo-Saxon folks strongly resisted my suggestions that they sell their homes, located in Anglo-Saxon neighborhoods, to my Italian clients, despite my personal assurance that their fears of neighborhood deterioration and depreciation of home values would most certainly not be the result. After assiduous efforts, I succeeded in effectuating home sales between Anglo-Saxon and Italian clients to a gradually increasing degree.[234]

Many who observed his work had another name for it, of course: Block Busting. The pattern was simple and repetitive: Butera would sell a house on a previously restricted street to an Italian. The neighbors would get upset, imagine a future of lowered property values, and decide to sell their homes. Harry's son Robert, whose legal and political career would familiarize him with the process, was open and honest about the result: "So who would they go to to sell their house? They would go to him. This not only hastened the acceptance of Italian-Americans and helped to Americanize them by not forcing them to live in one ghetto, but for him it meant increased business." This was not a strategy, Robert Butera insisted, but simply what happened. "[My father] wanted to show that Italians could live like everybody else, be industrious, earn good wages, acquire businesses."[235]

Three people interviewed for this book used the exact same phrase about Harry Butera: "[He] wanted to put an Italian family on every street in Norristown." These three friends of Harry's included an Italian, a Jew and an African-American, which says a great deal about Harry Butera's humanity. To those still striving to retain the Old Norristown, however, Butera and his efforts would receive an entirely different verdict: As "Johnny" Young succinctly put it, "Harry Butera was the man who destroyed Norristown." In 1950, Butera's efforts were under way, but just barely. The final verdict would come more than two decades later, when it would be the Italians fleeing the borough for the suburbs.

A Fractious Borough Government

Unsurprisingly for a municipality thus riven, the government of the borough of Norristown was itself divided. Rather than setting aside minor complaints and petty arguments and cooperate to solve the town's issues, the Borough Council expended most of its energy on controversy and internal disagreement. Its resulting inaction would lead to the accusation, still repeated today, that the death of the downtown came at the hands of its own government. The failure of Norristown's government to deal decisively with the steadily widening crisis is a matter of record. This inaction was the result of a combination of a divided population and a governmental structure whose system of local representation reinforced and multiplied that division.

In 1950, Norristown was governed as a Borough under the General Code of Pennsylvania Governing Bureaus, as it had been since 1930 when it surrendered its original charter. The borough structure concentrated power in the Borough Council, which had 12 members, one elected from each of the borough's 12 wards. Executive power, such as there was, was vested in a burgess, who was elected. The burgess had the power to veto legislation, although that veto could be overridden by the Borough Council as long as there was a two-thirds majority (8 members) present and voting. The burgess possessed, at least nominally, control over the police department. By 1950, however, the Borough Council, through its committees and control of the budget, had all but usurped the burgess's few powers. Thus, the Norristown Borough Council largely controlled both the legislative and executive functions of government. Its ordinances became law upon the signature of the burgess, or after overriding the burgess's veto. The council then supervised the execution of these ordinances by the very committees that had drafted them, meaning that there was no effective oversight or separation of powers; government was exercised by a committee of elected amateurs. Norristown possessed no office with executive authority even comparable to that of a borough manager, although citizen pressure for a more professional government had already begun, and would continue for decades.

In the Borough Council, legislative and executive policies were divided among standing committees (seven of them, in 1950). Proposed ordinances were generated by those committees, then either accepted or denied by the full council. Any ordinance that passed was implemented and enforced by its authoring committee—which is how it happened that directors of the various borough executive departments, including the police, found their budgets and salaries were controlled by a committee that scrutinized how, why, and where every penny was spent.

Such a structure gave considerable power to the chair of each committee, limited to a large degree only by the personality, agenda, energy, and commitment of the individual chair. The system did not, however, degenerate into entirely independent fiefdoms, but only because each of the standing committees of the Borough Council could be, at least in theory, composed of all 12 members of the council. The reality had evolved into something different, with the standing committees possessing from 8 to 11 members, and each committee chair being carefully watched by the members of the committee. This supposedly acted as a check on any attempts at "empire building." It also promoted the making, and subsequent breaking, of alliances among factions of the council, which contributed to the many false starts, U-turns, reversals, and abandonments of the most basic policy measures.

Any study of Norristown borough government, even a peripheral and limited one such as this, quickly reveals the critical, central factor in borough government, and therefore borough politics: the election of each and every council member from an individual, different ward. The burgess was the only borough official with lawmaking responsibilities who was chosen in a borough-wide election. This simple structural fact is of enormous significance in describing and analyzing Borough Council's performance during the crises facing the downtown. The effect of election by individual ward on local politics is obvious: a member of the Borough Council ultimately needed only to profess concern for what was good for his individual ward rather than the borough as a whole. While this led to each member of the Borough Council being in close touch with the residents of the ward, and certainly led to good constituent service, it promoted self-preservation over civic cohesiveness, and worked against any attempt to think on a larger scale. It took a special personality to occasionally rise above the parochial viewpoint necessary for political survival as a council member, and the voters of Norristown found that few people possessed that ability to weigh what was best for both ward and borough.

The politicians produced by Norristown's deeply divided electorate would remain divided among themselves and, on the whole, never rise above a fundamentally neighborhood-centric view. In the coming years of crisis, the individuals produced by Norristown's ward system, and retained in office by their constituents, would almost universally prove to be "very small thinkers," extraordinarily provincial in their outlooks, to whom "you could not appeal to…on an intellectual, conceptual level."[236] In the face of the admittedly overwhelming challenges to the nation's downtowns that in 1950 were only beginning to stir, the Norristown Borough Council would debate, decide, debate again, and usually postpone (and thereby abandon) virtually all proposed responses.

The issue was not party politics. Norristown, divided though it was, suffered very little inter-party strife. Every member of the Borough Council was Republican; that party had dominated Norristown and Montgomery County since the Civil War. This allegiance had only been shaken during the Depression and by the allure of Franklin D. Roosevelt, but during the prosperous post-WWII years Republicans slipped back into control. Eventually even that would change, as population migration in the coming decades rendered Norristown a Democratic-leaning municipality in a Republican-remaining county, but in 1950 that was years away from happening.

Between 1950 and 1975, the effect of this political sea change on the day-to-day governance of the Norristown was virtually nil. On the municipal level, for dealing with such issues as whether to purchase a truck for the highway department, ideological differences were wholly irrelevant. By the time Democrats achieved sufficient council seats for such differences to arrive, the cash-strapped condition of Norristown's government rendered ideological differences even less relevant. Players in the political arena aligned themselves with either the Republican or the Democratic camps, and contested each election along this divide to determine who would sit on the Borough Council, but once they took office, party membership largely disappeared as a consideration. In the 1950s, council Republicans would split into factions; later, Democrats who joined the Council would simply join in the game of constantly rearranging factions of willful individuals. These factions would cross party lines, with little regard for the political consequences, because there were virtually none. With no significant inter-party considerations, all politics was personal. The Borough Council was composed of 12 separate personalities, and the interactions among them were as might be expected: complex and constantly changing, with constantly shifting temporary alliances being built then destroyed, as 12 individuals with no structural reason to act otherwise sought to advance their individual and neighborhood agendas.

The ward system in a one-party municipality is a recipe for such divisions, but in Norristown the theoretical isolation of a ward system had decades ago been caught up in the larger isolation along the traditional ethnic/religious divide. By 1950 this had produced a curious mutation of the social relationship among the borough's ethnic and racial components. The African-American community, dispersed in small components among the majority white population, possessed no political power at all. By contrast, the Italian-American community possessed influence out of proportion to its numbers, or even its representation on Borough Council.[237] Such a claim, given the previous discussion of the isolation and subjugation of Italians in Norristown, requires an explanation, which has two components: the impersonal impact of numbers, and the very personal impact of one individual.

Norristown's long history of internal division had shunted the arriving Italian immigrants to the eastern part of the borough. Crowded in the East End, their very numbers ensured the election of an Italian in East End wards once the acculturation process had proceeded far enough. Any Italian council member who remained in close touch with constituents and represented the neighborhood interests would be re-elected, time and time again. This is exactly what happened. The first two Italians to be elected to Borough Council, in 1931, Michael Ciccarone from the Ninth Ward and Paul Santangelo from the Fifth Ward, were re-elected every four years thereafter for decades. Thus, every Borough Council had to contend with those two individuals and others like them who, once they demonstrated their staying power, could not be ignored or gone around. They had to be accommodated, and thus they achieved influence in Borough affairs. This applied, of course, to both the Italian and non-Italian members of council, according to each person's personality.

Control over a large and reliable voter turnout not only ensures re-election, it offers a voice in larger political councils. In this the Italians excelled. Their ability to deliver votes to the candidate favored by their council members gave those members influence in county and state elections. While Italian names will predominate in the coming narrative, it should be kept in mind that the extraordinary parochialism demonstrated by the specific individuals discussed was hardly a genetic, ethnic characteristic. Many other individuals of Italian descent, including some blood relations, exhibited extraordinary vision, openness to new ideas, and ready acceptance of reasoned debate. This includes but is hardly limited to the Genuardis, Tornettas, and Gambones, many of whom would lead the development of residential communities and shopping malls in the countryside surrounding Norristown. But this is not their story. This is the story of control of the Norristown government by a stubbornly single-minded few—to the detriment of many.

Paul Santangelo was unquestionably the most stubborn-minded of the few. He was Norristown born, to immigrant parents Saverio and Ignazia Santangelo on October 13, 1900, on Moore Street in the East End. The Santangelos, like so many of their neighbors in the East End, had come from Sciacca, Sicily. Except for an 8-month period beginning in 1908 when his family temporarily returned to Sciacca, Santangelo spent his entire life in Norristown. When he died in 1995, he still lived in the East End.

Little is known about Paul Santangelo's life before his election to the Borough Council, or about his private life afterward. Rumors and innuendo abound, but evidence is lacking. While he would be in office for 62 years, his very public presence in the borough was balanced by a very private life, which he protected fiercely to the very end. His *Times Herald* death notice on January 10, 1995, stated simply that he had been married and produced four children (two of whom pre-deceased him), and that from 1931 to 1960 he had been employed "in the maintenance and shipping departments" of the Conte Luna pasta factory on East Main Street that had been founded by his father-in-law, Vincenzo Arena. There is a brief, polite reference to a later alliance with a woman, but nothing else about his private life; the rest of the article is filled with recollections of his extraordinarily long political career.[238] This is clearly as he wished it. Santangelo's life was an essentially simple one, driven by one all-encompassing passion: ward-level politics. He would live out his obsession for more than six decades, and never retire. When he was finally defeated in his ward, in the general election in November 1991, he was 91 years old.

Santangelo had ample time to focus on his obsession with local politics. The bare bones in his death notice about his relationship to the Conte Luna pasta factory hinted at the story behind how he earned a living. He was the beneficiary of a fortunate marriage and the even more fortunate timing of two deaths. Vincenzo Arena, founder of the Conte Luna plant, fathered two sons and a daughter. By the time Santangelo had courted and married the daughter, Vincenzo's sons were operating the business. They did not like him, and originally put him on the loading dock. Then fate intervened. Vincenzo Arena died, leaving two healthy sons but a terminally ill daughter, Santangelo's wife, who did not long survive her father. According to the most reliable version of the story, both brothers had come to despise Santangelo so much that had their sister died before their father, they would have fired him. But she survived her father, albeit briefly. She was heir—again, very briefly—to one-third of the business, which upon her death passed to Santangelo. Some negotiations followed.[239] As his obituary later stated, he would remain technically an employee of the Conte Luna Company until management passed from family hands, which it did in 1960 when it was sold to a large corporation still making pasta at the plant today.

Judging from the amount of time that Santangelo would subsequently spend on politics, it appears that his job placed few restrictions on his time. After his arrangement with Conte Luna ended, Santangelo quickly secured other employment; he served as Montgomery County Inspector of Roads and Bridges from 1961 until he reached mandatory retirement age in 1970, and this job seems to have been as undemanding of his time as his first, for his political activity was not curtailed. His income arrangement gave Santangelo an enormous advantage. In typical American governmental tradition, service on municipal councils was largely unpaid. Thus Borough Council members had been almost invariably been successful businessmen. Time spent governing Norristown was time taken away from businesses, and many a retirement would be spurred by the eventual realization of the financial cost that being elected to local public office could entail. Santangelo, however, could afford to be a constant presence at City Hall, and he took advantage of it. No one ever accused Paul Santangelo of lacking in energy.

The residents of his ward were the focus of that energy—particularly the newer, poorer immigrants. Santangelo was their guide, their interpreter and their defender; he knew his constituents because he had visited many, if not most, of them in their homes. He was always available to help fellow Italians navigate any of the small obstacles of municipal life. He was notorious for having parking tickets "exonerated." This was a privilege afforded to each member of the council, but Santangelo used it more than the others combined. As one Norristown police officer explained it, "You didn't ticket Italians in those days [late 1950s], because he would fix them all. He would come into City Hall with a pack that big and have them exonerated."[240]

Santangelo did not just campaign door to door. He would go to a home, sit down and listen to the complaints of "his people," visiting home after home after home until late at night, in any sort of weather. He would listen, and often he would help. Santangelo also carefully instructed each of his constituents in the intricacies of the voting process. Robert Butera told of how Santangelo, pleased to aid a fellow Italian, campaigned heavily for Butera in his first race for state representative. They went door to door together, and Santangelo, by then in his 60s, would never be the first one to quit—never. "He was tireless," said Butera. Santangelo had a model voting machine built for him, complete with levers that moved—a small but exact replica of the machines at the polls, including a space for name tags for each lever. These Santangelo would insert (or ignore, depending on his opinion of the individual). The replica was made of steel, and quite heavy, but Santangelo lugged it everywhere, and refused all Butera's offers to help him carry it.[241]

Paul Santangelo delivered for his constituents, and they in turn voted as he instructed. This loyalty was something he expected in return for his efforts on his ward's behlaf, and he remembered anyone who did not seem sufficiently supportive. He was obsessive about every vote. In Robert Butera's first primary in 1962, he won Santangelo's ward by a margin of 422 to 19. Reporting the ward vote that evening, Santangelo wondered aloud, "Who were those 19 people?"

Santangelo had a passionate hatred of being photographed—an unusual attitude for a man in public life, but one befitting his personal, often confrontational political style. In 1972, he and three other present and former Borough Council members were summoned by the State Crime Commission to a meeting. As Santangelo emerged from the building, a photographer attempted to take his picture. Enraged, he tore two cameras from the man's chest and threw them away, destroying both cameras and slightly injuring the cameraman. "Santangelo's aversion to having his picture taken is well known by his colleagues, as well as others," said one article. "In a similar incident at a meeting in borough hall, he was restrained by a police officer when he chased a photographer in an attempt to grab his camera."[242] Santangelo was 71 years old at the time.

Santangelo's intense focus recognized no distinction between the personal and the political, and he did not hesitate to ask for political favors from those he felt were indebted to him. Bill Giambrone, whose immigrant father had been befriended by Santangelo, knew many Italian people, as he had quickly learned English and would assist new immigrants with translation and cultural problems. One day Santangelo asked him to perform some unspecified "under the table" task. Giambrone's father never revealed what Santangelo had asked him to do, but he was so offended that he never spoke to Santangelo again.[243]

A "no" response to Santangelo, however, was rare. He was famous statewide for his ability to turn out a large number of voters (often several times the turnout in other wards), all of whom voted as he instructed. This made him valuable to politicians involved in county and statewide races.[244] Santangelo knew how his constituents would vote, but he still took no chances. One of his regular tactics involved his wife, a woman about which little is otherwise known. Before a primary election—even if he were running unopposed, as he usually was—he would have his wife file for the ward seat as a Democrat. She would often win the nomination, and then always drop out before the general election, leaving her husband unopposed.[245]

But it was on election day itself that Santangelo demonstrated his true power. His disdain for the rules governing election procedures was virtually complete. Every election saw him at his polling place (an Italian-American club) all day, buttonholing incoming voters, often inside the polling place itself, which was and remains a violation of the rules. He routinely assisted voters in the booth itself, another fundamental violation of election rules. As Bill DeAngelis, an activist in the Democratic Party and thus a frequent opponent of Santangelo, put it, "You could go down to the polling place and see two sets of legs behind the curtain." One pair, of course, belonged to Santangelo. He would routinely arrange for residents of his ward who were not citizens to vote, entering the booth with each and helping each to vote.[246] Outside the polling place, supporters of other candidates physically feared him. Complaints of verbal and even physical intimidation were common. He often removed the posters of the opposition, tearing them up.

While the voters that day each received careful attention, and the result was really never in doubt, Santangelo always carried a trump card in his coat pocket, and never hesitated to use it: a large number of absentee ballots, all filled out, that he would deposit and have counted. Santangelo's playing this trump card in the 1984 general election earned his ward the title "The Miraculous Fourth Ward" (electoral ward boundaries had changed by this time). It also demonstrated that while Santangelo was a rock-ribbed Republican, he was an Italian first. Paul cast 88 absentee ballots that day. Each absentee ballot cast reliably Republican votes for every slot but that of president/vice president. All 88 votes were cast for Mondale/Ferraro, as the presence of an Italian on the national ticket outweighed his Republican allegiance. Santangelo continued this practice to the very end; in his final, losing campaign in 1991, he submitted 81 absentee votes, all for himself.

Santangelo would almost certainly be in the news after each general election, when reports of his behavior would be printed in the *Times Herald*. People would threaten to sue, and then later quietly decide that the effort just wasn't worth it, as people willing to actually testify were hard to find. Santangelo got away with what he did because, as Bill DeAngelis said, "He controlled the polling place." Every election official, including the Judge of Elections, would owe his position (and one day's pay) to Santangelo, who had gotten them their jobs.

Consider the following events leading up to the general election of November 1965. The basic sequence had occurred before. The amount of attention Santangelo received by that time was due largely to the by-then significant Democratic Party in Norristown. The result was the same. Santangelo was in the middle of his term, and not even on the ballot. In late October, Montgomery County Democratic Chairman J. Phil Doud delivered a speech at a Norristown Democratic Party dinner during which he said that Democrats would be carefully watching the Fifth Ward, as in the last election 115 people voted there who did not live there. This was followed by the filing of a petition asking the court to appoint overseers for the upcoming election. The petition claimed that approximately one-tenth of the voters registered in the Fifth Ward didn't live there. The court appointed two overseers, but their presence did not appear to faze Santangelo. He was present at the polling place all day, where he apparently engaged in his usual actions. After the election, another petition was filed, asking the court to invalidate the result in the Fifth Ward based on 41 people having received illegal assistance and on 12 who voted despite not being ward residents. The petition also claimed, "The said election was also illegal because the Councilman, Paul Santangelo, intimidated the voters."[247] On December 23, a county judge dismissed the petition.

One reason Santangelo got away with so much was his personality. On this subject, opinion is unanimous: he was loud, rude, crude, and did not observe even the basic boundaries or proprieties in his dealings with others. Regardless of how a dispute might have started, Santangelo would immediately go on the attack, and that attack would always be *ad hominem*. Any opponent, anyone who offered a proposal he did not like, or simply anyone who voiced a contrary opinion could expect to be personally attacked. His ability to single-handedly disrupt public meetings of the Borough Council was by 1950 already the stuff of legend, and he would continue to add to it for decades. When the Council would retreat to private chambers to resolve one of its more-or-less-continuous internal disputes, Santangelo's bellowing voice could still be heard. Much of this was bluster, a tactic. Its message was clear: *you cannot go around me, and I will always be here, so you must give in to me on this point.* Often, the council would do just that; or, more in keeping with its actual proclivities, it would simply delay the issue Santangelo opposed.

Bluster there certainly was, but it was no bluff; it did not pay to be Santangelo's enemy. Here he also held a trump card, and held it for 40 years: membership on the Borough Civil Service Commission, usually as the chairman. The Civil Service Commission had jurisdiction over hiring, promotion, and firing of borough personnel, including those of the police department. Santangelo clung to this seat with his usual tenacity, rebuffing several attempts to remove him from the Commission. Here, within the (unrecorded) meetings of the Commission, Santangelo manipulated the true levers of power and authority in Norristown.

While opinion is unanimous that Santangelo had no political ethics whatsoever, opinions as to his honesty differ. Most give him high marks for financial honesty; the exceptions focus more on his activities in the Civil Service Commission than in the Borough Council. While this was an opportunity for financial gain, it was also an opportunity for personal political gain. For Santangelo, whatever the extent of his financial gain, personal political gain was always the most valuable currency.

When it came to power—both in obtaining and exercising it—Santangelo observed as few rules after his elections as he did during them. By 1950, he was already a senior figure in borough government. Many of those in borough staff positions had been put there by him, or had at least earned his approval. Seniority, a doggedness that even his opponents admired, and the cumulative effect of his loud, vituperative personality had combined to make Paul Santangelo the large, immovable rock in the channel of Norristown Borough Government.

Unfortunately, Santangelo was a man of limited vision—limited in fact to the boundaries of his ward. This is the unanimous opinion of those interviewed who were in any way involved with borough affairs, and an examination of the historical record supports this judgment. Some would go so far as to view Paul Santangelo as, in Horace Davenport's words, "one of the major factors that kept Norristown from progressing." While a series of Borough Councils during the period that follows would offer up a great many of what Bob Butera termed "small thinkers," Santangelo would stand out for his dogged, unrelenting opposition to any project that might either raise taxes or increase higher governmental oversight of how he and the borough government in general were carrying on their business.

Santangelo was not the only "small thinker," of course, and he was not the only rock in the channel. His fellow Council members were themselves products of the individual ward system, and while none ever possessed the combination of characteristics that Paul did—certainly not his frequent beastliness—few would simply lie down before him. Santangelo was a great maker of "backroom" deals, but his peers on the Norristown Borough Council were well known for the same activity. Santangelo was a member of the Borough Council committees that each other member chaired, and thus kept a close eye on each of them. However, they all belonged to the committee that he chaired, and returned the favor with vigor. The result would be a succession of alliances, all publicly unacknowledged, accompanied by feuds that were also all too public. At no time in the future should Norristown Borough Council and Paul Santangelo be thought of as congruent; overlapping yes, but his doggedness often led him to maintain a minority opinion, despite all attempts at "back-room" deals. More than one ego and temper—even one as monumental as Paul Santangelo possessed—was required to produce the sad, quarrelsome and indecisive performance of Norristown Borough Council during the next 25 years.

County Government

There was another government presence in Norristown—aloof, but always there, very close to downtown. This was the government of Montgomery County, the reason for which Norristown had come into existence, and a neighbor ever since. In the 138 years since Norristown's incorporation as a borough, county government had expanded in response to Montgomery County's growing population, although far from proportionately, in conformity with the political tenor of the day. The original courthouse and jail were long gone, with a 19th-century courthouse of excessive grandeur on its original site, and an imposing—and glowering—gothic jail on Airy Street. Additional office space had been a periodic need, and the country grounds had slowly expanded, mostly along Airy Street east from Swede Street.

The relationship between the borough of Norristown and Montgomery County had changed considerably from the early days when Norristown largely *was* Montgomery County. Between 1812 and 1950, the county's population remained largely rural and overwhelmingly Protestant. The early 19th-century Irish immigration to Norristown had begun to differentiate Norristown from its surroundings. The much larger Italian immigration that followed, not to mention the less substantial but even more obvious increase in the African-American population, completed the process of establishing Norristown as "different." That difference played out in the political arena. The trip into Norristown for county business largely precluded the county office workers from living too far from the borough. Most county employees, therefore, were borough residents. However, few Norristown residents ever gained (elected) positions of authority in the country government, at the row officer level, or as County Commissioner. Norristown's "differentness" in population made it suspect with county politicians. In addition, there was the feeling that with so many county employees resident in Norristown, "Norristown already had its jobs."[248]

In 1950, Montgomery County was in the early stages of the most spectacular population increase in its history. The post-war years saw the townships immediately surrounding Norristown, previously quite rural, begin to give way to suburban development. Also expanding was people's perception of government—at all levels—and its responsibility. These two forces were already in collision in 1950, and their combined result would be a considerable expansion of personnel employed by the county government. This time that expansion would aim at Main Street. The government of Montgomery County would, in fact, exert the most direct negative influence on Main Street for the entire 1950s and early 1960s.

This book may occasionally give the impression that the Montgomery County government was unified outside force, a powerful individual rather than a collection of varied offices and efforts. That is certainly an oversimplification, but a necessary one here in the context of how county agendas and decisions affected Norristown's downtown. The processes by which the county commissioners reached their decisions and determined their courses of action were likely as complex, multifaceted, and fraught with internal debate as those in the borough. To further complicate an understanding of the county's role, there is also the fact that the county judicial branch was also involved in many of the decisions involving expansion, and the commissioners and the courts were often at odds with each other over which policy to pursue. Exploring the positions and thought processes of all the county officials and departments would probably triple the size of this book and is beyond the scope of this work. Therefore, with apologies to the many people who actually played a role in the decision-making, the Montgomery County government is treated here as though it could and did speak with a single voice.

7

Main Street by the Numbers

What follows here is not merely a nostalgia-driven meandering through pica-yune minutiae. The next pages describe downtown Norristown in the early 1950s in very specific detail: who occupied the buildings, what they did there, down to the sights and smells. This is an attempt by the author to recreate a mi-lieu now almost forgotten: the multi-textured experience of shopping along Main Street in a classic American downtown. A steadily decreasing few remember their lo-cal version of this ritual, but it is foreign territory to the young. It is included because to truly understand what happened to the downtown, it is important to know what was there that drew people to that six-block core at the heart of Norristown. To understand how downtown could fail, you have to know first what made it succeed.

Who, What, Where, and Why

The borough of Norristown was and always had been the center of legal and adminis-trative affairs for Montgomery County, Pennsylvania. But in 1950, the county's resi-dents saw its more important role as the area's leading provider of retail products and services. The *Norristown Study* offered a succinct and balanced summary of Nor-ristown commercial centrality at mid-20th century:

> Reflecting Norristown's important role as an economic center is the relatively large number of service and trade establishments located in the borough. By 1950, Norristown employed almost 6,000 persons in trade or service. Its banks, department stores, specialty shops and automobile agencies attracted buyers from a broad farm and small industrial area north of the Schuylkill. To the south, the trade area was restricted by the fact that Philadelphia suburbanites along the southern borders of Upper Merion Township shopped at the more fashionable stores of Wayne, Bryn Mawr, and Ardmore, or bought directly from New York or Philadelphia. Nonetheless, in 1950, Norristown was the trading and service center of an area that encompassed some 220 square miles and embraced some 160,000 persons.[249]

The *Times Herald* was in complete agreement. An August 1950 article, citing a na-tional business survey, put it this way: "Norristown stands out as a rich market, with income and spending at a level above that of most cities in the United States." Furthermore, the trend was up: Norristown's retail business had increased over the previous year, despite an economic climate that saw retail business declining nationally by 1¼ percent. In 1950, prosperity was the byword for downtown.

The most significant of those "service and trade establishments" were located along Main Street, tightly concentrated in the six central blocks between Markley and Arch Streets. From whatever point of the compass you had arrived, once you reached downtown Norristown, you found yourself within a densely grouped, interdependent business community. The six-block stretch of Main Street between Arch and Markley streets boasted an integrated grouping of retail stores, trades and service offerings. In 1950, Norristown's Main Street was a community dedicated to servicing the needs of not just the residents of Norristown, but those of the surrounding area, as it had been doing for over a century. At the time, there were 312 "for profit" businesses packed into that six-block core of Main Street. Of these, 217 possessed first-floor storefronts on Main Street beckoned shoppers with wares displayed behind large glass windows. Above the considerable variety of their advertising signs, hung the smaller, less demonstrative signs of the 100 other businesses that occupied the second or third floors of the tightly packed buildings.

Norristown's adherence to the Philadelphia Town Model had dictated its original core layout, and had continued as downtown developed. Compactness and tightness was the consistent theme. The six-block core of Main Street was overwhelmingly constructed of brick buildings of two or three stories, with infrequent exceptions adding variety to the skyline. The buildings along both sides, regardless of their specific design and adornment, were built all the way out to the sidewalk, which in turn abutted Main Street.

As with the original plan of the Town of Norris, streets intersected at right angles, and some alleys continued to divide blocks. However, while the original plan had featured lots of a consistent shape—a rectangle—with consistent dimensions, nearly a century and a half of successive businesses and real estate deals, with sub-divisions, consolidations and other accommodations had created a welter of different (and occasionally contradictory) sizes and dimensions in the downtown lots. This was occasionally revealed along Main Street by the existence of odd-sized buildings, or by such addresses as 80.5 East Main Street, as from Main Street back to both Penn and Lafayette streets, the platting picture had become much more crazy-quilt.

The Public Square marked the very core of Norristown, as always. In 1950, the Public Square was visually something of a void, a small space overshadowed by the imposing banks on either side, and elbowed out of a portion of its western boundary by the P&W Bridge over Main Street, which had its northern anchor firmly in the upper end of the square itself. The Montgomery Trust Company immediately east of the square had a marble frontage featuring Roman columns, while immediately across Swede Street to the west was the Norristown-Penn Trust Bank (its then-current name), which was both wider and taller, with even more marble.

The first block of East Main Street retained its long-held position as downtown's core block, with 126 businesses listing the block as their address. This number includes the Montgomery Trust Arcade at 29 East Main Street, which had 31 occupants (22 of them businesses), and the Curren Arcade at 51 East Main Street, 20 of whose 29 tenants were also businesses. The two Arcades housed five specialty retailers, and a self-described department store (Kerson's, which also had a ladies wear store at 42 East Main Street), and a Sears catalog service. Offices, whether of (largely medical) professionals or of companies, comprised the most frequent tenants. Medical offices included those of a dentist, optometrists, opticians, and physicians. W. T. Grant and the Southern Railway Company had district offices in the Montgomery Arcade. Seven offices sold insurance, some together with real estate.

The more substantial reason for the first block of East Main Street's commercial dominance lay more in the long-time presence of several large firms, both locally owned businesses and representatives of national chain stores. The towering presence of the Valley Forge Hotel and the Grand Theater contributed to the image, if not the reality, of solid, successful businesses. Squeezed in among this array of retail stores and service businesses on this core block were two buildings that were not occupied by retail businesses. One was 80 East Main, which housed a local headquarters of the Bell Telephone Company of Pennsylvania. The other was 35 East Main, home of the Mitchell brothers, Morris G. and Herbert D., who had been proprietors of the venerable Mitchell Brothers Clothing Store (by then David Mitchell Clothiers) at 18 East Main. This was the only building in the entire six blocks of downtown Main Street that was used solely as a family residence. The building had housed the Mitchell family for over 60 years.[250]

The second and third blocks of East Main Street continued the compactness and tightness of the first block, but with fewer nationally or even regionally recognized business names. Brick exteriors continued to dominate, but there were exceptions. The striking four-story Egolf Building, with its large bay windows and elaborate plaster scrollwork, dominated the second block of East Main Street. Much less striking (and in fact, rather tattered) was the antique wooden awning that extended out from the building over the sidewalk to the curb. Such overhangs had once been common on Main Street, but few were left by 1950. Further east was another atypical building, whose tall first floor with roll-up doors housed the Humane Fire Company No. 1 at the corner of Main and Green streets.

West Main Street, the three blocks between Swede and Markley streets, was somewhat more varied in its structures than East Main, but was still overwhelmingly of brick buildings two or three stories in height. A striking, anachronistic exception to the brick and glass fronts of most downtown buildings was the ancient stone structure at 33 West Main Street. The building, constructed between 1802 and 1813, had been built of thick stone walls with small windows, which made it unsuitable for conversion to retail use. Since the late 19th century, it had been called the Corson Building for attorney John J. Corson, who had used the building for his office. Though that John J. Corson was long dead, the name had stuck, but with good reason: among the five professional office listings at 33 West Main Street were C. Russell Corson (lawyer) and very much alive John J. Corson (real estate). By 1950, the building's distinctive stone had been plastered over with a uniform whitewash.

In 1950, the most unique building on West Main Street was still the Art Deco gem, the Norris Theater. The theater continued to be, as it had since its opening in 1930, Norristown's premier movie theater, and was still owned by the Sabloskys, who also owned the Grand and the Garrick theaters. Other exceptional structures included the Masonic Temple at 108 West Main Street, which once been the mansion of local iron-master James Hooven, and the Montgomery National Bank next door at 110 Main Street, also adorned with marble and columns. While the site had housed the original Bank of Montgomery County, the borough's first bank, since 1812, the current structure had been built in 1854.

There were many reasons to be on Main Street in 1950, and many people came there to shop, to eat, to be entertained, or some combination of all three. Ken Randall remembered, "Everything you wanted was located on those few blocks on Main Street. This was where you did your Christmas shopping, or your everyday shopping."[251] Friday night was prime time; the phrase "you could hardly walk the streets" came from the lips of several interviewees, who well remembered the hustle and bustle of crowds. The intersection of Main and DeKalb streets was the center of it all, as it had been for decades.

A trip along the six blocks of downtown Main Street might give the impression of an overall sense of prosperity and well being, but that sense did not emanate from every building. Downtown had 10 empty storefronts in 1950: six on East and four on West. But empty did not necessarily mean abandoned: six were in transition and would shortly be listed in subsequent directories with new businesses. Two of these 10 storefronts, however, would never again be occupied. They were torn down to become parking lots.

1950s Main Street

The Norristown City Directory for 1951 contained a total of 524 entries in the six-block downtown of Main Street. Curiously, for a stretch of downtown so devoted to business, the largest single category was that of Residence at 174. That number would decline but Residences would still top the category for each succeeding Directory. The distribution demonstrates, however, that residences were subsidiary to business establishments, with the 174 residence entries distributed over 69 addresses. There were often apartments above street-level retail stores. The Blackfan Apartments at 28 West Main Street listed 17 tenants, the largest number of any address within the survey area. Rothman's Apartments at 200 East Main Street was the next largest, listing 12 tenants. Five locations listed four tenants each. A majority of residence entries however, listed between one and three tenants per address. It is clear that residences were of only secondary importance in downtown Norristown.

Businesses

Downtown Norristown was all about business. The total number of "for profit" businesses on downtown Main Street in the 1951 business directory was 323. These encompassed an enormous range of both physical size and business volume, from the major department stores to a shoeshine shop. They also included Main Street's three schools, as all were privately owned and offered training by professionals in dance, voice and cosmetology. While for statistical purposes each of these entries counted equally, this was not true with respect to their presence on Main Street itself. Such obvious differences as size, showroom stock and sales volume were measures of relative value within the business community, but other, less quantifiable distinctions also existed. These related to reputation, tradition, ethnicity, length of time on Main Street, and, most important, local ownership. This last was a major advertising point in 1950, when some of the older businesses were selling to so-called outsiders.

In a discussion of downtown Norristown, the important distinction among the businesses of Main Street for the purposes of this book was whether or not they occupied a "storefront." Those that did were usually the ones whose success was most affected by borough government decisions, which is why they are more frequently mentioned here. Only those enterprises that occupied the first floor of an address for general business purposes were considered "storefronts," a distinction that eliminates businesses that operated from an upper floor, regardless of their nature. It also disregards such situations as an address that was merely a doorway providing direct access to the upper floors, or those few instances, such as the ancient stone building at 33 West Main Street, where the very structure of a building had resisted attempts to make it over for public access. It does include all Main Street locations (whether "business" or not) that had some form of physical presence at street level, whether they employed that presence to lure shoppers inside, or simply to signify their offerings, such as gasoline stations. The focus of the public and government discussions, and of this narrative, largely concerns those business establishments that shoppers saw as they walked down Main Street glancing at the window displays at street level.

Consider the special case of the Montgomery Arcade Trust Arcade and the Curren Arcade, both products of downtown's golden years, built by and named after prominent local businessmen specifically for the small business or profession. The 1951 directory listed 31 tenants at the Montgomery Arcade and 28 tenants at the Curren Arcade. The Montgomery Arcade had been constructed so that only two of those tenants could display their wares through glass windows on Main Street; the Curren Arcade had only one such storefront.[252] With both arcades, shoppers had to enter the central area to access any of the stores, including the storefronts, but these three businesses— and only these three at these two addresses—were classified as storefronts. The survey area listed 209 such "storefronts." Ten of these were listed as Vacant or No Return in the 1951 City Directory. Thus Main Street within the six block length of its core area featured 199 storefronts "open for business."

The majority were of a similar pattern, if different variations; a central door flanked by, and set back from, glass windows on both sides. The exceptions that did exist along Main Street were, of course, those most noted and pointed out to visitors. These ranged from the classical-style banks, sheathed in marble, through the Art Deco Norris Theater and P&W Buildings and included the design-specific Block's Department Store or Valley Forge Hotel and the one-of-a-kind Egolf Building. By contrast, Chatlin's was not a unity, but the cumulative smaller conventional type of stores, modified externally only by the raised roofline of the end building along its Mill Street side. The business of Main Street was, overwhelmingly, retail. Wholesale businesses were scattered around the borough, but only one such listing in the 1951 Directory was located within the survey area: the A. L. Banham Company at 275 East Main Street in the extreme east end, which wholesaled tobacco products.

Department Stores

The directory listed 15 self-described "department stores." These included prominent national names like Sears Roebuck, W. T. Grant, W. W. Woolworth, and S. S. Kresge. The Grant, Kresge, and Woolworth stores sat squarely in downtown's core, the first block of East Main Street. All three were located on the south side of this block, and all three were at that time still representatives of the "five and dime" store, offering lower-end merchandise as the name implied. Woolworth's was the largest of the three, but its primary attraction was its soda fountain/lunch counter. Most of those interviewed recalled that counter with great pleasure.[253] In addition to generations of shoppers, Woolworth's soda fountain had refreshed generations of local business owners, who often had coffee there early in the morning.[254] Sears sat at 227 West Main Street, adjacent to the Continental Baking Company factory at the corner of Markley Street. Though it was downtown, it already included goods that met the physical needs of suburban and rural customers, offering tools, hoses, mowers and the like, in a building that stretched back to Penn Street.

These firms may have had the big, prominent names, but in the 1950s department stores of local origin still dominated downtown Norristown, including Yost's, which had occupied the southeast corner of Main and DeKalb streets since 1862. No longer family owned nor considered Norristown's most prominent store, Yost's had failed to change with the times; it was still a "dry goods" store, selling cloth, needles, thread, as if the farmer's wives were still coming into town for such goods to make clothes.[255] Its pneumatic tube system of sending customer payments to the office upstairs was, like Yost's itself, a visible symbol of the past.

B. E. Block & Brothers, the venerable downtown institution at 11 West Main Street, often laid claim to being Norristown's signature retail store, although the city directory listed furniture as the store's only offering. There was furniture for sale, but Block's advertisements in the *Times Herald* justify its categorization as a department store, and a prominent one. It was four stories tall, and featured an elevator, a rarity in Norristown in 1950. Block's had for decades been the sponsor and prime focus of Norristown's Thanksgiving Day celebration; the arrival of Santa Claus officially opened the area's Christmas shopping season. Santa arrived by train, stopping at the old station at West Main and Markley streets, then climbed aboard a fire truck. He was given a police escort to Block's, where a reception area for the area children was always constructed. The crowds at this event at times were so big that Block's had to board up its large glass windows at street level, fearing the press of the crowds.[256]

Despite claims by B. E. Block, Chatlin's was arguably the most prominent individual retail business on Main Street in the early 1950s. The post-WWII years had seen Chatlin's, under the guidance of returned veteran, owner, and founder's son Morris Chatlin, steadily increase in size, offerings, and customers. No other store was so typically Norristown as Chatlin's. While Block's was older, its local family connections had ceased. Unlike Block's, which had expanded by tearing down the old and building a new building, Chatlin's had expanded by takeover, and retained the structure of the previously existing buildings. It had no consistent roofline or frontage. Inside was an array of departments and displays connected by openings cut in the masonry walls between the individual buildings. The different buildings had had slightly different floor heights, so short staircases or ramps were everywhere. The floors were wide-planked wood, and squeaked constantly. Virtually everyone interviewed who shopped at Chatlin's remembered the squeaky wooden floors, and the need to pass through portals and go up or down ramps to move between the interconnected buildings that housed the store. There was nothing fancy about the interior: wooden tables held the merchandise, and bare light bulbs in the ceiling provided the lighting.[257] The sales staff itself was quite large; the store's division into separate little rooms and floors required this, along with additional workers hired—usually over the holidays—to watch over the security of the items squirreled away in so many different locations.[258] Chatlin's had also managed to secure one of the very few parking lots for an individual store, by its rear entrance on Lafayette Street.

Chatlin's sold primarily clothing, along with carpet, shoes, and other household items. The store catered to the lower-end customer, and was famous for its bargains. Mary Early spoke for many when she remembered this: "They would give you wonderful bargains.... We had a lot of places to dress your children—Fliegelman's, Bellak's Kiddie Korner—but Chatlin's gave you the best deal."[259]

A great many transactions at Chatlin's did not involve money at all. A regular, well-known customer would be given a coin with a number on it, which was used rather like a store credit card: if you had no cash with you at the time, you showed the coin at the register, and your transaction was recorded. Chatlin's management was confident that such payments would be made. Chatlin's also provided a layaway service, with no credit charge; you simply paid installments on your item until it was paid for. With so many of Chatlin's customers in the lower income bracket, this service was utilized particularly between Thanksgiving and Christmas.[260]

Amidst these community giants (as tiny as each would seem to us today), a few small, self-declared "department stores" strove to exist. These included the Quaker City Store (120 East Main Street), Shuman's Variety Store (200 East Main Street), Martin's Department Store (262 East Main Street), the Economy Cut Rate Store (29 West Main Street), and Kramer's Cut Rate Store (160 West Main Street). These smaller stores offered competition to the larger firms in specific, carefully selected lines of products, generally in the lower range of prices. Martin's Department Store attempted to compete with Chatlin's, but its much smaller size and a particularly unfortunate location, almost next door to Chatlin's, prevented the business from ever becoming a major retailer. It must be recorded, however, that Martin's Department Store remained in business after Chatlin's Department Store had closed.

Specialty Retailers

While the large department stores and the imposing banks drew the most attention, Main Street's backbone was the wide variety of specialty retailers. These numbered 114 in the 1951 City Directory, not including restaurants or grocery stores/markets. Specialty Retail, the second-largest category after Residence, encompassed a very diverse group. There were clothing stores, shoe stores, jewelry stores, and furniture stores, but the array of the offerings available along Main Street was wide indeed.

Clothing stores (a combined number, for men, women and children) constituted the largest subgroup of specialty retailers. They numbered 37. Four specialized in hats; this *was* the 1950s, after all. Four stores advertised as general "clothiers," including the vaguely named Schnably's Union Store at 121 East Main Street. A solid majority of these were locally owned, although some were representatives of regional firms, such as Adams Clothes at 2 West Main Street. Among those that had occupied Main Street for a considerable time was the venerable David Mitchell Clothiers, at 18 East Main Street, a conservative, upscale shop. By now a Norristown institution, this last store was a lingering remnant of a bygone era, with the all-male staff seeming as old as the building they inhabited.[261] It is not hard to imagine their customers being the same men who patronized Main Street's four hat stores.

Novell's may have been the most "upscale" women's shop, with the most fashionable clothing, but Friedman's New York Store, a Norristown institution since 1918, had become the most well-known.[262] Founder Samuel Friedman's son Leonard continued the family tradition of "honest service." Piece goods had always been their primary offering, from cheesecloth to silk. As tastes switched to ready-made dresses, Friedman's began to purchase these from manufacturers in Philadelphia, and they were able to obtain new stock in an afternoon thanks to the frequent railroad connections between Norristown and Philadelphia. The store carried many forms of underclothes for women. After the war, nylon stockings became a big draw. The only men's items Friedman's sold were gloves and socks. The smaller stores had each generally aimed at a price range to fit in a "niche" on Main Street. Main Street shoppers could find not only upscale firms such as the aforementioned David Mitchell Clothiers, or Ralph T. Steinbright at 117 West Main Street but an array of others, down to the self-explanatory Norristown Bargain House, at 124 East Main Street.

Furniture had been sold in downtown Norristown since the days when farm families came to Norristown in horse-drawn wagons. No fewer than 11 stores specialized in furniture (not including Block's), with five on the south side of the 100 block of West Main Street. Each carried their specific lines of furniture, although the degree of overlap cannot be ascertained. Gus Egolf Furniture at 113 East Main was the exception, as it sold only rare, collectible, and antique furniture. "Antique," in fact pretty well summed up everything about Egolf's: the building had never been renovated, and even retained its original antique wiring, switches, and electrical fixtures. The term could also be applied to Gus Egolf himself, the son of the firm's founder, a frugal man from a frugal family. He was notorious for refusing to tip anyone, even the shoeshine boys who regularly spiffed up his brogans. In 1950, he could still be found sitting outside his store, but few patrons entered and fewer still purchased anything. The days when his father counted the governor of Pennsylvania among the store's frequent patrons were long past.[263]

Shoe stores had been a longtime staple on Main Street, and in 1950 there were 10 retailers (this does not include shoe repairs or shoe shiners). As with furniture stores, the stores were no longer manufacturers; the sold shoes made elsewhere, of varying in quality and price. While most were locally owned, others were regionally or even nationally owned, such as Dial and Hanover Shoes.

Downtown boasted seven jewelry stores. Some of them offered higher-end items, particularly those on the first block of East Main Street, such as Snyder Jewelry (12 East Main Street), Jennings Jewelers (57 East Main Street), Dales Jewelers (75 East Main Street), Rogers Jewelers (83 East Main Street), and Morris Jewelers (88 East Main Street). Lantz Jewelry's presence in the Boyer Arcade, although on this core block, indicated a lower focus, as did that of Sid Richmond at 123 West Main Street, the only jewelry store on West Main. Shoulberg's, at 106 East Main Street listed jewelry among its offerings, but was actually a pawn shop.

Main Street had seven stores offering a wide array of automobile-related items; these were exceptions to the generality that specialty stores were largely locally owned. Well-known franchise names predominated in this category, such as Pep Boys (105 West Main Street), Penn-Jersey (147 West Main Street), Goodyear (200 West Main Street), and Dunlop (212 West Main Street). These offered stiff competition to local competitors such as Harry Lutz (161 East Main Street), Colonial Auto Supply (139 West Main Street), and Lincoln Battery and Tire Company (215 West Main Street). In the opinion of one police officer who walked Main Street on a daily basis during this period, Pep Boys was "the busiest store in town."[264]

Retail stores selling automotive parts and accessories were prospering, but those who sold and serviced automobiles were already being crowded out by the lack of space downtown. Service stations in particular suffered in this regard, losing their curbside gasoline sales while simultaneously coming up short in space to accommodate the increasing number of automobiles that needed service. Downtown had four auto service stations, within three of them clustered in the 200 block of East Main Street, including Gambone's Atlantic Service at 201 and the Rawn Garage at 209. Their buildings were old, as both had evolved from the days of street side pumps and the (Pennsylvania) prohibition against advertising the price of gasoline. They serviced most makes, and, as a sideline, sold the occasional used car.[265]

The last surviving auto dealer downtown was Walter Wood Autos at 222 East Main Street. Automobile dealers had faced the fundamental incompatibility between downtown Norristown and the automobile first, in the most fundamental way. The inherent size of the product they were selling caused difficulty from the start: only a few autos could be squeezed into a showroom in any downtown location. The only solution had been to go up, and it had been tried, but the difficulty of lifting the autos from floor to floor had caused attrition among downtown auto dealers in the preceding decades. Only Walter Wood, opposite Mill Street from Chatlin's, had been able to hang on, and by 1950 it was basically a car lot with just a small office.

It had been more than half a century since Norristown had experienced the bicycle craze, and only one shop on Main Street still existed to sell and service them. Bill Glass, at 202 West Main Street, typified the type of small businessman, retail or service, who made a living on Main Street in 1950. He not only sold bicycles, he loved them, and his love reflected itself in his demeanor. He "always had work clothes on, always had a bicycle in his hand…. He was just in love with them bicycles; it was something about him; when you went in there you knew that you were talking to somebody who wanted to help you."[266]

There were other specialty retailers. Main Street had only two hardware stores, but both were institutions in the community. Lloyd H. Daub, at 106 West Main Street, featured an extensive array of nails, screws, and fasteners in large metal bins, from which you scooped what you needed in bulk and weighed it, paying by the pound. Daub also operated a similar store in Bridgeport. Joseph J. Zummo Hardware, at 259 East Main Street, was still the place to go to find the odds and ends you couldn't find anywhere else. The family's connections with builders and long-accumulated collection of odd bits of builders' hardware made it the store for those seeking more than a common nail. "You could get anything you wanted in there."[267]

A very diverse array of individual retail stores filled out the ranks of those that cannot be easily grouped. Tobacco and cigars, sold separately and together, remained strong sellers in 1950: A.D. Schulte sold cigars and tobacco on the first floor of the P&W Railroad Terminal at 2 East Main Street; Albert L. Banham sold just cigars at 131 West Main Street, and the Philadelphia Tobacco Store at 104 East Main Street offered a wide array of tobacco products. Frank Jones Sporting Goods at 228 West Main Street (the first floor of the Odd Fellows Building) was a pioneer in a field that would grow in the future; he not only sold generic products at his store, but he supplied the local sports teams, which were usually sponsored by local businesses, with custom, name-imprinted T-shirts. Also on Main Street you could find stores that sold generic "gifts" and such things as candy, flowers, and books. For homeowners there were stores specializing in such offerings as paints, wallpaper, electrical appliances, and vacuum cleaners. Local businesses and two levels of government were steady customers for the local stationery and office supplies stores, Ziegler's at 59 East Main Street and D. M. Feldman at 10 West Main Street. Other stores sold records, newspapers and magazines, eyeglasses, hearing aids, and arch supports. While out-of-state visitors would have found it curious that they could buy retail liquor (i.e., by the bottle) at only one location, Pennsylvanians were already long familiar with Pennsylvania's state monopoly on the product. Downtown's sole manifestation of this monopoly was the Pennsylvania Liquor Control Board Store at 217 West Main Street.

Grocery Stores/Markets

In this analysis, grocery stores were those establishments that largely sold food for preparation at home; meat markets were grouped with grocery stores, as they overlapped considerably in their products. Restaurants (a category that includes independently located luncheonettes), sold prepared food. In the early 1950s, downtown had seven grocery stores, ranging from small meat markets (two of them kosher) to local representatives of two large chains: Food Fair, which had a store in the first floor of the Tone Building at 105 East Main Street, and Acme, which had built a new store at 210 East Main Street. The Acme store was typical 1950s, though not so typical for Norristown, with its sloping, quarter-round style roof. Also unique was Acme's parking lot at 218 East Main Street. The Family Food Center and James Castenova Grocery were both smaller versions of the standard market; Taglieber's Market at 28 West Main Street offered general groceries along with a substantial meat counter, competing with the Norristown Poultry Market at 256 East Main Street, Vitabile Meats at 273 East Main Street, and Zarcone's Meat Market at 247 Main Street. The Norristown Poultry Market sold live chickens: customers selected a chicken, and the clerk would weigh the bird, put it upside down on a special jig above a funnel, then slit the bird's throat and let the blood drain into the funnel. This was followed by quick dip in hot water, then the carcass was held up before a large wheel with rubber flappers that would spin and knock off the bird's feathers, rendering it ready for the trip home.[268] Both Vitabile's and Zarcone's had profitable sidelines supplying meat for the many festivals that the Italian organizations would sponsor during the year. Zarcone's owner was also a hunter, so his market would feature venison in the fall season.[269]

Main Street had only one bakery, perhaps because there were so many bakeries elsewhere in the borough. Perfection Bakery at 34 West Main Street was just one of the firm's retail outlets, while its actual bakery was off Haws Avenue in the West End. The Continental Baking Company at the very western end of Main Street was a substantial presence that anchored the western end of downtown Norristown. The company also operated a retail store that sold day-old items at reduced cost, but this store was never mentioned in the City Directories.

Restaurants/Snack Shops

In 1950, downtown shoppers or residents in need of refreshment could find 19 establishments that served prepared food, including a delicatessen, all locally owned. These were mostly luncheonettes and sandwich shops; six had "lunch" or "luncheonette" in their titles, while the sandwich shops demonstrated the influence of Philadelphia tradition (itself Italian) with "steak" or "zep" shops. The "steak" in this instance meant "cheesesteak," and the "zep" is the Philadelphia-area variation of an Italian sandwich usually referred to as a "hoagie," but without the lettuce.

While the Philadelphia influence dominated sandwich shop menus, downtown Norristown's most popular eating establishment claimed an American regional origin from far away, however dubiously. This was a small shop, the Montgomery Lunch, at 145 West Main Street, where the specialty of the house was the Texas Hot Weiner, cooked on a grill in front of the main window, with the resulting steam usually obscuring the window itself. Ned Offner, a street patrolman during this period, clearly recalls a steady parade of customers, with lines often into the street itself.[270] John Ashton, a floor layer for Frank Batdorf Floor Wall and Window Coverings at 204 DeKalb

Street, recalls being called in every few years to replace the linoleum worn down by the feet of so many customers in search of this particular delight.[271]

Downtown's eating places with the best claim to restaurant status were the Grill in the Valley Forge Hotel and the modestly named Roma Café. None of Norristown's downtown restaurants even approached gourmet status, a fact that is more reflective of the size of the community and the nature of American cuisine in this period than anything specific to Norristown. Even those placed that advertised themselves as restaurants, such as the Keystone Restaurant at 127 East Main Street, or the Blue Jay and Arthur Brooks Restaurants at 22 and 239 West Main Street respectively, tended to have a counter at the front and booths at the rear, in the conventional luncheonette layout. The Blue Jay served "All-American" food such as roast beef, mashed potatoes, and string beans. The Arthur Brooks, by contrast, was better known as the "Double D" (for Dine and Dance), as it featured booths up front, a more limited menu, and a juke box in the rear. The Keystone Restaurant had no source of music, but it did have a bar, and more pub-style food offerings such as fried oysters and oyster stew. Its Greek owner and proprietor, Theodore Katsias, also offered furnished rooms on the second floor of the building.[272] The Keystone's location on East Main meant that it drew a mainly Italian clientele, and many late nights at the bar saw both the owner and his customers, all substantially lubricated, revive and rehash ancient Greek/Italian quarrels. Despite the volume and intensity of these exchanges, all was forgiven in the next morning's light, and those same customers would return.[273]

Service Businesses

The term "service business" is suitably ambiguous. The point of differentiation is that a business so classified provides a service as its primary market offering. This allows such businesses to be differentiated from the many primarily retail businesses who service what they sell. Discussed here are Professional Services and Trade Services, distinctions with clear class ramifications. A self-employed photographer is a "professional," whereas a barber practices a "trade." These often have nothing to do with differences in income: the most frequent "professional service" on Main Street was that of Notary Public, a part-time side business offered only on an occasional, as-needed basis, and paying not much at all.

In 1950, downtown Norristown had a total of 40 service businesses; 14 "professional service" listings and 26 "trade services." Nine were notaries, all located in banks or other offices. The Professional subcategory included an interior decorator, two photographers, a commercial artist, and a producer of commercial blueprints. The 26 trade listings featured an even division—seven each—between beauty parlors and barbers, plus three each of tailors and clothes cleaners. Two businesses repaired shoes while one shined them; one repaired watches and one stitched hems. Businesses whose specialized service was providing financial arrangements were given a separate category, Financial Services. In 1950, Main Street had 15 of them, most located on a floor above the retail store below with which they were affiliated.

There were 50 professional service businesses downtown in 1950, drawn there no doubt by the prime location that put them within easy access not only of local residents, but employees of surrounding businesses (including the county government offices) and shoppers from outlying areas. Most of the individual proprietors were in the medical profession, with 8 dentists, 4 general physicians, 3 chiropodists, 1 practical nurse, 9 vision specialists, 8 optometrists, and 1 optician. There were also 7 self-employed attorneys, 10 insurance firms (of which 6 also sold real estate), an employment agency, a CPA, and a structural engineer.

The classifications used here are those assigned by the city directories of the time. It must be remembered, however, that the reality of Main Street was more complex than can be determined solely from the such listings. Consider the cases of Bill Glass at 202 West Main Street and Butwin's at 242 West Main Street. Glass listed himself as a retail store, for bicycles and hobbies. He also repaired bicycles, whether he had sold them or not; in fact, bicycle repair was the most likely activity he would be engaged in at any one time. Butwin's, by contrast, listed itself strictly as offering a service, "washing machine repairs," but also sold the machines.[274]

Another example of the blurry difference between retail and service can be found in the category of automobile service. There were four businesses that were listed as servicing automobiles—two connected to national brands (Atlantic Oil at 201 East Main Street and Gulf Oil at 165 West Main Street) and two locally owned shops that focused on service (Rawn Garage at 209 East Main Street and the Harry Fosbrenner Garage at 220 West Main Street). All four sold gasoline; all four also serviced automobiles; and almost certainly all four sold the occasional car, suggesting that the distinction between retail sales and service is of little actual importance.

Company Offices

The 17 company offices located along Main Street testified to Norristown's significance as a regional center. These varied widely. Three were the regional headquarters of national firms (Southern Railway, W. T. Grant, and the Reuben H. Donnelley Corporation). Among regional firms, the Bell Telephone Company of Pennsylvania occupied a building at 80 East Main Street, while Schuylkill Valley Bus Lines operated a small office in the Curren Arcade. Local firms included Norristown Broadcasting (call sign WNAR), Norris Amusements (the Sablosky brothers), and a building contractor. Downtown also had three business who offered classes and were thus classified as Schools, although they were all for-profit businesses: the Norristown Beauty Academy (115 West Main Street); the Doris School of Dancing (an upper floor of the P&W Building at 2 East Main Street); and Julie W. Kane, who offered vocal lessons at the Odd Fellows Building at 228 West Main Street—which had Frank Jones Sporting Goods in its storefront.

Theaters

Downtown's three theaters were all owned by Norris Entertainment—the Sablosky brothers—who had long ago established niches for each. The Norris Theater at 125 West Main Street offered first-run films, while the Grand at 67 East Main Street and the Garrick at 214 West Main Street offered B-movies, serials, and the like. Only the Norris had been built originally to accommodate both movies and stage performances.

The Grand and the Garrick were from an earlier era. In 1950, the Garrick Theater was clearly the weakest of the three, tawdry and ill maintained.[275] None of the three had dedicated parking, and they were thus significantly affected by the rise in automobile usage. The Sabloskys were well aware of the changes the automobile was bringing to the downtown, and had opened two drive-in theaters in New Jersey as early as 1945. In 1950, they opened a drive-in theater on Ridge Pike, just east of the borough line in Plymouth Township. However, in 1950, motion picture theaters everywhere—not just on Main Street, Norristown, but on Main Streets throughout the United States—were beginning to face a new technological challenger: television. The devastating effect of the rising popularity of this new technology would dramatically cut into the business enjoyed by Norristown's motion picture theaters as they would for similar motion picture theaters across the country.

Hotels

Even a single trip down Main Street would have likely revealed to the observer that three of downtown's four Main Street hotels had sadly deteriorated. The best of the lot was the Valley Forge Hotel at 22 East Main Street, but downtown's three other hotels, all on West Main Street, were old and decrepit. All had ceased to seek the tourist trade and had become renters to Single Room Occupancy (SRO) tenants.[276] Arena's Hotel, the westernmost at 252 West Main Street, was essentially a bar that rented a few rooms upstairs. The other two hotels were relics of the 19th century, with elements of even earlier times. The Milner Hotel at 231 West Main Street dated back to 1801, and had operated under several owners. By 1950, the hotel had become so rundown that one police officer interviewed for this work referred to it as a "flophouse."[277] The other officer was more charitable, admitting that "we had some problems there," and describing the Milner as "a little bit more sophisticated than the YMCA."[278] The Lincoln Hotel at 201 West Main Street was even older, with portions dating back to the late 1700s when it had operated as the Farmers Hotel. The street-level building fronts of both hotels had been subdivided into small storefronts, with the hotel rooms upstairs.

These three somewhat seedy establishments served a necessary function for a few residents, but they were not the type of hotel the Chamber of Commerce would point to with pride. That role had always been filled by the Valley Forge Hotel, planted squarely in the core of downtown at 22 East Main Street. It was an imposing brick building, six stories tall, just west of Strawberry Alley, which in 1950 led down to the hotel's small parking lot; there was a side entrance to access the building's lower level. The main entrance to the hotel was centered between the large display windows of two retail stores that were part of the building proper, and could only be entered through the hotel, though each possessed a separate street address. In 1951 these were occupied by two long-standing tenants, Hanover Shoe Store at 20 East Main Street and Bud White Haberdashery at 26 East Main Street.

By 1950, it would have been clear to anyone who examined the Valley Forge Hotel's financial records that the hotel portion of the business—the temporary housing of transient guests—had never lived up to expectations. And now, more than 20 years after its opening, the Valley Forge Hotel itself was a relic of past tastes. Its small rooms had initially lacked air-conditioning, although a retrofit project was under way. Several rooms on a floor shared a common bath, which was customary in the 1920s but increasingly unpopular since the advent of the bedroom-bathroom combinations offered by motels catering to automobile travelers. This brings us to what was perhaps the Valley Forge Hotel's most telling weakness: its parking lot had always been capable of accommodating only a handful of cars. By 1950, it had already been insufficient for years. This boded ill for the only hotel in Norristown still serving transient guests.

The Valley Forge Hotel may have played an insignificant role in Southeastern Pennsylvania, but its importance to Norristown went much deeper than that of any other business. It was the heart and soul of Norristown; its existence touched the core of Norristown's image of itself. The Valley Forge Hotel was identified with Norristown because its owners were the residents of Norristown. The hotel had been conceived and built as a physical testimony to the commercial success of Norristown, built because a "first class town" like Norristown needed "a first class hotel." Its stock had been purchased by Norristown residents as a testimony to their love of and faith in Norristown, not for the potential profit. The Hotel's Board of Directors always had been composed of the business elite of the community, serving without pay and lending their business expertise to manage the hotel, leading the valiant efforts to sustain the business for its image, not its profitability. If it had been just another downtown business, the Valley Forge would have disappeared well before 1950. The Valley Forge Hotel was, however, Norristown's mirror on itself; it was not allowed to fail.

The building's location just down the hill from the county courthouse and offices made its grill and bar a favorite of county employees, from county judges to office clerks. Civic associations such as the Rotary regularly met there; the banquet room could accommodate perhaps 200 guests, and was host to wedding receptions, dances, luncheons, dinner meetings, and all the social/business events of a thriving community.[279] Each year the graduating class of Norristown High School had traditionally held a dance and a dinner there.

In 1950, the Valley Forge Hotel was entering what would be its best financial years. The steadily improving financial picture of the late 1940s made 1950 the most profitable year ever. Although 1950 got off to a bad start—a strike by kitchen employees crippled efforts for the first three months of the year—revenue was reported to have rebounded sharply for the remainder of the year. The new hotel manager's report attributed much of this increase to the opening of the eastern extension of the turnpike. The hotel's unprecedented profitability even produced an offer from a private investor to purchase ownership of the hotel, the second in as many years. A February offer from attorneys representing "unnamed principals" offered $400,000 for the company and all its assets. At that point, the balance sheet of the Valley Forge Hotel showed an excess of current assets over current liabilities of $14,217.58. The offer specified an initial payment of $40,000 upon stockholder approval, with the balance paid within three months. The offer contained promise that the buyers would continue to operate the site as a hotel for at least 10 years.

The proposal would have netted a holder of preferred stock about $70.00 per share, which was a $10 per share increase over the previous year's offer. Still, the opposition was vocal, loudly reminding others of the hotel's history and intimate connection with the borough. They argued that historical difficulties had caused past losses, and that the opening of the turnpike extension heralded a new era of profitability. A special meeting of the hotel's stockholders in March formally rejected the offer by a slim margin: 2,710 shares in favor outvoted by 3,310 shares opposed (of the total of 9,123 shares of preferred and common stock outstanding).

In 1950, William "Bill" Giambrone, a veteran whose war experience had included being shot down on a bombing raid and sent to a German prison camp, was working as a barber at a shop in Bryn Mawr. He heard that the Valley Forge Hotel's barber was going to retire. He applied, and became the hotel barber in December 1950. His shop was on the first floor, past the entrances to the two shops, and had an entrance off Strawberry Alley, with the traditional barber pole above it. Giambrone would remain the hotel's barber until the very end, in 1974, making him a first-hand witness to the downtown's collapse. He made a good living, and always felt "tuned in" to the community, as his clientele included several local merchants, doctors and bankers, a large number of attorneys, and even a County Commissioner.[280]

Nonprofit Residents of Main Street

Main Street's nonprofit organizations will receive short shrift here, mostly for lack of reliable statistical data. While each of the business directories contained listings for such organizations as unions, fraternal organizations and industry organizations, the enormous increase in such groups in the 1960 directory suggested that they had been seriously underrepresented in most of the editions before and after. There was also the question of the nature of the presence on Main Street of most of the nonprofit organizations. Both the Masonic Hall at 108 West Main Street and the Odd Fellows Hall at 228 West Main Street housed such organizations, although actual reporting of which ones varied from year to year in the directories, so the actual extent of their presence is conjectural. The Valley Forge Hotel regularly listed such organizations as the American Business Club (AMBUCS) and the Traffic Club of Norristown, who utilized the hotel's larger rooms for their periodic meetings/luncheons/banquets.

Two other frequent addresses for nonprofit organizations were the Montgomery Trust Arcade and the Curren Arcade. Some of these "organizations" were actual offices, and others something closer to a mail drop. No fewer than four unions—the United Steelworkers of America, the Federation of Telephone Workers of Pennsylvania, the Montgomery County Industrial Union Council (a component of the Congress of Industrial Organizations, the CIO), and the Electricians Hall of the International Brotherhood of Electrical Workers (IBEW)—had locations in one or other of the buildings. The Chamber of Commerce had its office in the Curren Arcade, as did the Norristown Community Chest. The Fraternal Order of Orioles, in an exception from the many fraternal organizations listed at either the Masonic Hall or the Odd Fellows Building on West Main Street), had its own listing at the Montgomery Trust Arcade. The Girl Scouts of America were listed at the Curren Arcade.

Survival Strategies: Competition & Cooperation

The previous pages outlined the 524 entries for downtown Main Street in the 1951 City Directory. As mentioned, the categories were somewhat arbitrary, and are useful here primarily just for organizational purposes. It has already been mentioned that the separation, for example, between "retail" and "service," masked a deeper and more complex reality, but the point requires further elaboration. Main Street Norristown in 1950 was an organism, and like all such entities, its components were interdependent. Competition was its lifeblood, and the stakes were high; yet that competition was carefully calculated, and the entire mix was leavened with cooperation, even friendship.

A review of the businesses on Main Street in the 1951 directory gives evidence of the changes under way in American consumer goods. Reflective of the United States itself, the time was one of transition from home-made to store-bought, especially in the broad category of clothing. The mix of offerings on Main Street demonstrates the nature of this change. Rudolph's Dry Goods at 108 East Main Street by its very name recalled the former era, as did Yost's, with its continued focus on "yard goods"—which had nothing to do with landscaping. Ready-made clothing was by 1950 a staple offering of most department stores and specialty retailers. Main Street's specialty clothing retailers sold almost entirely ready-made clothes, from the inexpensive to the almost-fashionable, but there were also two businesses that sold only sewing machines, Chinchilli's Sewing Machines (251 East Main Street) and Singer Sewing Machine (109 West Main Street). For those well enough off to have others do their sewing, Main Street could still claim three millinery shops, two of which—Smarte Shoppe at 61 East Main Street and Emily Shainline at 63 East Main Street—occupied their own buildings on downtown's core block. Chatlin's was large enough to effectively split the difference. It offered both yard goods and clothing, although most of its clothing offerings were in the lower price ranges, due to its location and clientele

Business survival strategies in Norristown included many specific examples of what is today termed "niche marketing." Among local retailers this led to close attention to what, with whom, and at what level competition would take place. Those stores who were components of national or regional chains of course had their general strategies, as well as their product lines, determined by their corporate management. Locally owned stores had more flexibility in their policies, both as to sources of products and marketing strategies. Careful marketing permitted specialty retail stores to compete on a partial—and carefully selected—basis with the department stores, even Chatlin's, and be successful. Friedman's New York Store, physically the largest of the specialty retailers with its "double wide" store, offered both lines of clothing and "yard goods," plus the accessories for making clothes. This put them in competition not only with other clothing stores, but also the department stores, primarily Yost's and Chatlin's. Anthony Zummo's wife, despite the success of the family business, still made all her children's clothes. She preferred Chatlin's for the fabrics, but the New York Store for threads and accessories.[281]

Downtown's department stores competed with each other, but also with specific specialty retailers on specific lines of products. These department stores competed amongst themselves in patterns that were the result of long familiarity with equally long-established competition. The stores were quite familiar with the offerings of each of their neighbors/competitors. Depending on the individual's store's focus, this would result in avoidance of competition in some products/lines and quite direct competition in others. Block's was an all-around department store, with a reputation for furniture. Sears at this time sold mostly household maintenance items, and did not compete with Main Street stores in the clothing market. Thus, Chatlin's, Block's and Sears were less directly competitive than their common designation of "department store" would suggest.

Block's focus on furniture eased its competition with the other department stores, but placed it in direct competition with the 11 downtown specialty retailers of furniture, which offered a wide range of product lines and price spectrums. With such competition, Block's could not depend on its "upper class" image to sell furniture. It offered its own form of credit: someone who bought a piece of furniture would pay a deposit of $5 or $10, and have the furniture delivered. The customer then paid off the balance in small weekly installments. Block's had a man who worked the neighborhoods of Norristown collecting these payments.[282] Cumulatively, these offerings had the curious effect of separating the furniture shoppers themselves into niches, whose specific combination of style and price might be accommodated in one particular store, but not another. The specialty furniture stores had long since come to an unofficial and unspoken agreement that should a particular store not have something in the line a customer was seeking, the proprietor would freely recommend another store in the downtown area that *did* carry that line. The assumption, of course, was that the reciprocal would be true. Such a policy did have its limits; indications are that the same courtesy was not often extended to Block's.[283]

The result of such careful marketing strategies was a complex web of competition among local retailers. If, for example, Friedman's had advertised and sold an item also sold by Chatlin's, it would often find last week's price for that item undercut—often by as little as a penny—in Chatlin's advertising for the next week. Small price wars would result, but only on carefully selected items, and never at a level broad enough to jeopardize the survival of one or the other enterprise—just enough to keep things interesting, and to keep the customers flowing in.[284]

Downtown Norristown always operated under a distant but powerful restraint on its commercial aspirations: the city of Philadelphia. The 20 miles between the two downtowns had been connected by rail since 1835, and competition between the Reading and the Pennsylvania Railroads ensured that rail service was both frequent and reliable. In 1950, the fact that Philadelphia was only a short train-ride away played a significant role in the business plans of Norristown retail merchants. That role cut both ways. It both served the interests of many Main Street retail firms and acted as a ceiling on their aspirations. Philadelphia housed numerous wholesalers of a great many products. Several Main Street retail firms utilized them as warehouses, where they might themselves obtain a specific product asked for by a customer in their store that was not in stock. A customer who ordered a particular product on Main Street one morning would be told to stop by the next day to pick it up. When he did so, he would find the product there, and pay for it, not realizing that the previous day a store employee had quite possibly phoned around among his network of wholesalers until he found the desired product, then traveled by train to Philadelphia, picked it up and returned to Norristown. Main Street's purveyors of upper-level products, such as Friedman's New York Store, often employed this device.[285]

Philadelphia's proximity thus promoted the business interests of several firms. Yet each retail firm in downtown Norristown understood fully that the very same proximity and frequency that allowed their employees to utilize Philadelphia also allowed their customers to do the same thing. Many of Norristown's middle-to-upper-income families shopped in Philadelphia on a regular basis already, reflecting not only their incomes and/or devotion to fashion, but as a method of demonstrating their status, both to others and to themselves. Harry Butera's wife, the genteel native-born Italian-American who had bet her future on an immigrant from Sicily, was one such frequent shopper.[286] Other shoppers, the vast majority of them with less family income than the Buteras, would use the train to go shopping in Philadelphia on a more select basis, but would usually go on a Saturday. Philadelphia possessed draws like Wanamaker's and Strawbridge & Clothier, who not only offered the latest styles, but offered a prestige that no firm in Norristown could match. With such retail giants a short train ride away, Main Street's larger retail merchants were always reminded that their status in Norristown was tiny by comparison. With such giant shadows looming not too far away, Main Street Norristown's merchants kept their marketing sights on a regional audience, focused around Norristown itself.

Some retailers had either wholesale or service contracts to provide additional sources of income. Feldman's Office Supplies at 10 West Main Street also had a contract with the borough and county to provide office supplies, including furniture, which would prove to be the store's salvation.[287] Norristown Furniture at 223 West Main Street was aided in its efforts among so many furniture stores by being a supplier to local builders. Zummo's had for some time established a design service for local builders, which was certainly useful in the years ahead.[288] Albert L. Banham supplied his store at 131 West Main Street with cigars from his wholesale business at 175 East Main Street. Some of these arrangements would last, and provide the difference between success and failure. Others were less fortunate. Weiss Brothers, at 130 East Main Street, were wholesalers of paper goods such as paper bags to other retailers, and they had previously supplied local shoe repair shops with bulk leather, rubber for soles and specialty nails. This profitable sideline would dry up as the local retail stores that had long been their customers themselves declined and failed.

Gilbert J. Farrington straddled two unusual categories. In addition to his real estate business at 236 West Main Street, Farrington was a "magistrate"—a local judicial official now referred to as a district justice—holding court at the same location. Cecil C. King went him one better, selling real estate and insurance and serving as justice of the peace, all out of his office in the Curren Arcade.

Norristown's Main Street was clearly less divided by ethnicity or religion than was the borough itself. The lessened importance of ethnicity was due to two fundamental realities: first, businesses on Main Street for over a century had been owned by a wider representation of ethnicities and religions than existed in the population of Norristown as a whole, and second, Main Street's compactness—the Philadelphia Plan—placed religion and ethnicity alongside one another, close enough to make clear their common interest in the larger concept of "downtown." From the interaction of these factors had evolved a community that was internally competitive, yet cooperative, even within those subgroups of specialty retailers in direct competition with one another. The religion and ethnicity divisions that still divided Norristown had less effect on Main Street. There is also substantial evidence among the business owners of mutually beneficial relationships that crossed ethnic, racial, and religious lines. The downtown business community clearly (and early on) recognized the fundamental nature of the challenge that was about to confront them and strove to overcome the many internal obstacles to a united response that their diversity presented.

While the role of the Norristown people of Italian descent has been discussed here, there are two other groups whose collective role on Main Street exceeded their proportionate presence in the general population. These were the Jewish and Greek communities. Jews had been part of Main Street's merchant community from early on, and this continued to be true in 1950, when Jewish-owned firms were sprinkled among the retail and service businesses alike. These businesses had long since ceased to conform to any pattern, and could be found at all levels of Main Street commerce. Some, like Chatlin's and Friedman's—both moving into their second generation of family ownership—were clearly among the premier businesses on Main Street. Jewish names appeared frequently among the several professional listings of lawyers, doctors, dentists, and opticians scattered along Main Street. For Norristown's Jewish merchants, however, one thing had not changed. Friday night services at Synagogue still began at 9:00 p. m., the closing time for stores on the week's busiest night. Leonard Friedman, by 1950 an integral part of the family store, thus joined the generations of Jewish merchants, his father among them, who consistently showed up late for services.[289]

Individuals of Greek extraction possessed a presence on Main Street out of proportion to their percentage of the borough's population. Greek-owned businesses in the general downtown area varied, but sale of food in various forms dominated. In 1950, LaModerne (26 West Main Street) was, despite its name, Greek-owned, as were the Family Food Center (168 West Main Street), Perseo's Lunch (154 West Main Street), the Keystone Restaurant on East Main, the Blue Jay Restaurant on West Main, and several other establishments. The Coney Island Luncheonette was Greek-owned, and its unfortunate location a few doors down from the enormously popular Montgomery Lunch—also Greek owned—demonstrated that cultural affinity need not get in the way of business competition.[290]

By 1950, however, it was the Italians that most conspicuously challenged the traditional Anglo-Saxon Protestant domination of Norristown business, and even established a substantial presence. Most Italian-owned businesses on Main Street were located to the east of DeKalb Street, the western boundary of the East End. They had, however, preceded their general population by jumping over the unspoken boundary, and establishing themselves on West Main Street. Arena's Hotel and Bar was downtown Main Street's westernmost business, bordering on Markley Street.

Still, in 1950, it was on Main Street east of DeKalb that the Italian presence predominated. This was true not just of the business names, despite their greatly increased numbers, but of the individuals who could be seen on Main Street itself, collecting outside certain businesses, sharing news and gossip. The most obvious examples of "Old Italy" behavior were the barbershops, like the Bono Barber Shop at 205 East Main Street, and in particular the DeStefano barbershop at 272 East Main Street. Both had become daytime hangouts for the older men, usually sitting on the steps, talking of the old country and the old times. Small groups of them could be seen virtually any daylight hour at both locations, discussing local affairs. These discussions centered on the activities of the Italian social clubs, their upcoming feasts and frequent activities. This time-honored social pastime was not without its critics, however: the owner of the building next door to the DeStefano Shop grew so tired of men gathering in front of his shop that he had a contractor enclose the steps and place a door at their base to keep the men from his premises.[291]

Deep in the East End sat the Italian housewives' favorite place to shop: Chatlin's. Chatlin's policies toward its clientele and its staff reflected the nature of its second-generation owner, Morris Chatlin. They provide in microcosm a lesson in ethnic and business relations in a community as ethnically divided as Norristown. Chatlin's always sought patrons from the still largely Protestant West and North Ends of Norristown, as well as from the entire surrounding region. The store's no-frills approach and subsequent low prices made Chatlin's the store of choice for all families on a tight budget, regardless of their ethnicity. Still, its location deep in the East End had led to considerable Italian patronage. Chatlin's welcomed all, regardless of ethnicity, and was patronized by a considerable array of customers.

Chatlin's rabbit-warren layout required a substantial sales staff. The store's focus on clothing and other items traditionally of particular interest to women had early on led to Chatlin's employing young women as salesclerks. By 1950, Chatlin's location in the East End had ensured that a considerable majority of its sales staff was Italian. This had brought into existence a custom among its sales and floor personnel that speaks volumes about the ethnic divisions in Norristown. Each of the Italian salesgirls adopted a WASP first name, to be used when tending to non-Italian customers. When waiting on Italian customers, or conversing among themselves, they reverted to their Italian names.[292]

Chatlin's and Zummo's had existed across from one another on East Main Street for close to half a century. Both had established reputations that extended beyond the East End, and even Norristown itself. Zummo's drew considerable customers from the East End, but it had long since gained a regional base that was oblivious to its ethnic heritage. These two very disparate businesses are linked in the memories of those interviewed as the two most well known stores on East Main Street. As Joseph Verunni put it, speaking of an earlier period, "My dad was always at Zummo's looking for hardware, and my mother was always at Chatlin's."[293] In the process, Anthony Zummo and Morris Chatlin established a close friendship. This friendship would serve Anthony Zummo well as he raised his three oldest daughters: when each was old enough, she began to work at Zummo's itself, but always in the basement, "counting cans of paint."[294] No female Zummo waited on customers. As the girls reached their middle teens, Anthony "strongly directed" her to Chatlin's for work. As the oldest daughter, Fran, remembered it, "Their employees liked working for them. It was a little bit like home…. You were with people you were comfortable with, people you liked, and you were meeting up with people you saw all the time, went to school with, and their parents, all the time."[295] Fran and two of her three sisters each worked in turn at Chatlin's. By the time Rory, the youngest girl, had come of age, however, Chatlin's was gone.

By 1950, the long-existing ethnic-religious boundaries had been crossed by the younger generation, with Italians marrying Irish—Fran Zummo became Fran Doyle— and even WASPs and Jews. Charlie Shoulberg, the Jewish owner of a pawn shop at 106 East Main Street, married an Irish Catholic woman. They had two children: the son became a priest and the daughter a nun.[296]

Organizing Downtown

The merchants of downtown Norristown had a long, if inconsistent, record of attempts at organization. Downtown merchants, despite their inherently competitive position, had as early as the second half of the 19th century shown the ability to organize, especially to address specific issues. By 1950, downtown's merchants had organized within the Norristown Chamber of Commerce, forming an active Merchants Division (this structure changed substantially in the coming decades). Organization and membership in the Chamber of Commerce had by 1950 allowed Main Street's merchants to establish a degree of uniformity within their community. The coming decades would first test their tenuous relationship among one another, and then destroy it entirely, along with many of the individual businesses themselves. Efforts by Main Street's merchants to counter this onslaught would founder, for a variety of reasons. Chief among them, however, were the internal divisions among these businessmen, divisions that had little or nothing to do with religion or ethnicity.

In 1950, the primary division among Main Street's retailers was not that of religion or ethnicity, but a decidedly more fundamental one: the nature and location of their business ownership. The majority of Main Street's businesses were locally owned, but several of the substantial ones—Sears, Grant's, Kresge, and Woolworth most prominently—answered to management in distant locations, with different perspectives. Other, newer chain stores that were gaining a national reputation, particularly in the automotive field, were represented in Norristown, such as Pep Boys, Goodyear, and Dunlop. There were also representatives of regional chains, such as Adams Clothes or Sun Ray Drug Company.

In response to the trials to come, downtown's merchants would find their common efforts consistently hamstrung by this division. There would be a more or less constant uncertainty as to who would join in a particular effort and who would not. Those businesses that were a component of a larger chain were the most questionable. The locally owned stores provided not only the more active membership, they provided the leaders for the merchants' organizations, such as Morton "Bubby" Weiss, the owner of Gilbert's Clothes at 132 West Main Street, and Morris Chatlin, both of whom would play a major part in organizing downtown in the coming years.

The lower-cost efforts to promote Main Street, such as joint advertising for an announced sales event, would generally receive ample support, perhaps even from the chain-store branches. However, in the face of the larger issues the spirit of cooperation would be sorely tried, particularly when financial contributions were called for. In the coming decades the downtown merchants would offer up an array of ideas and display a general willingness to implement these ideas. This must not be overstated, as obtaining a consensus from such a disparate blend of inherently independent and competitive individuals was almost by definition impossible, and dispute and disagreement within the business community would always manifest itself.

While Main Street's merchants could largely overcome the ethnic and religious divisions of the community in which they did business, and avoid the paralyzing disputes typical of Borough Council, they did share the crippling parochial attitude of their fellow residents and elected representatives. While organizing to protect downtown, they could not overcome an innate bias toward their geographic portion of downtown. The subject of parking lots and then parking garages would consume much thought, planning and funding in the coming decades. Each proposal would discover this truth in its turn, as the matter of location within six blocks would to a large extent drive and determine its fate.

A geographic bias sufficient to doom proposals within (or on the edge) of a six-block stretch also rendered impossible any substantive attempt by Main Street's merchants to think outside their six-block core world—and kept them from recognizing their common cause with Marshall Street merchants. In the coming age, as "thinking big" in retail took on larger and larger dimensions, Main Street's merchants continued to think within the traditional physical parameters. They did not so much "think small" as simply fail to recognize that the world's ideas had expanded up around them, thanks to the automobile.

A Feeling of Security

Norristown's Main Street merchants, though diverse and competitive, shared one enormous asset: a close relationship with the Norristown Police Department and in particular the officers who patrolled Main Street itself. This close, often personal relationship was emblematic of urban America of this time, and symbolized by the cop walking the beat. Such a police officer learns about the people and the buildings over the course of many such walks; what was normal, and what should be looked at further. The officers got to know the people who lived or worked on their beats, and played a major part in the making of a local "community."

During this period, a young man named Frank Ciaccio joined the Norristown Police Department. Ciaccio was the son of an immigrant who had lived in Norristown, but had moved to Brooklyn, New York, when Frank was born in 1923. When the family returned to Norristown, the father plied his trade as a shoemaker, owning shops at different locations, including one at 88 East Main Street. Frank Ciaccio was one of the young shoeshine boys who mentioned never having been able to coax even a penny tip from Gus Egolf.

Young Ciaccio's hardscrabble upbringing was rather typical of lower-income Italians of the period. His formal study ended after the eighth grade; he would later earn a G.E.D. After service in the military, Ciaccio and one of his brothers tried professional boxing. While it was common for fighters to be known by a nickname, it was an absolute *necessity* for a young fighter whose last name rhymed with "Sissy-O." Thus, Frank Ciaccio became "Hank Cisco," first as Frank's professional name, then as the name he preferred to be known by. Thus it remains to this day. "Hank" started as a foot patrolman, graduated to the motorcycle division, and remained with the Norristown Police Department until his appointment as a county detective in 1976. Outgoing, voluble, always ready with a smile and a handshake, and possessing a singular talent for self-promotion, "Hank Cisco" became the public face of the Norristown Police Department. He initiated a bike inspection and licensing program, and spoke frequently to groups at the local schools. When the borough established a group of "meter maids," it was Hank who equipped and trained them. He was involved in a legal dispute over promotion with Paul Santangelo, and won, but he never did realize his ambition of becoming Norristown Chief of Police.

Hank Cisco's appointment as a police officer was typical of the day: he was recommended by a friend of a friend who knew somebody. There were no job requirements, and no previous experience was necessary. For Ned Offner, who became a police officer in 1954, it was the same. Norristown born and bred, Offner was recommended by a member of the Borough Council. Neither he nor Hank Cisco had previous experience, except in the military, but both were put on the beat immediately to learn on the job while paired with a veteran officer.

Downtown in 1950 was divided into two police districts. Together they encompassed the area between Arch and Markley streets on the east and west, and Penn and Lafayette streets on the north and south. Swede Street was the dividing line between District 1 to the east and District 2 to the west. The two districts thus encompassed virtually all of downtown, and the core of each was Main Street. The police officers worked eight-hour shifts. In Districts 1 and 2 that meant walking along half of downtown Main, Lafayette, and Penn streets, plus the shorter blocks of the connecting streets; DeKalb, Green, Mill, and Arch to the east and Swede, Cherry, Barbadoes and Markley to the west.

The police presence symbolized by the cop on the beat was especially obvious on Friday and Saturday evenings, when additional officers were placed at Main Street's intersections with Swede and DeKalb streets, at each end of the business community's core block. Their job was to just stand there, keeping an eye on things, but more significantly acting as a comforting symbol of safety for the individuals that made up the throng. As Ned Offner recalled it:

> We came on, on a Friday [or Saturday] night; it was so busy that if [I] were on 4 to 12 [p.m.] I would go down to Main and Swede Street, or Main and DeKalb, wherever they sent me, and stay there from 4 to 6. At 6 [p.m.] you went and got dinner, and then you had to be back on the corner at 6:30 to 9:00. You weren't supposed to leave that corner.[297]

Main Street merchants appreciated the steady police presence during the day, as well as the extra police presence during the heavy evening shopping hours, but they knew that their real security lay with the police presence after their stores had closed. The beat officers on the 4 p.m. to midnight shift were required to check the stores on Main Street, including the locks of the doors, front and rear. The midnight to 8 a.m. "graveyard" shift repeated the process, and woe betide the officer who neglected to check a store that was later discovered to have been burglarized, as happened to Block's Department Store in 1957.[298] Such a routine resulted in the officer's gaining an intimate knowledge of downtown. As Ned Offner, who walked a downtown beat for 14 years, put it, "I got to know everybody on that beat. If I was on midnight to 8 a.m., and you as a stranger would be coming down there at 3:00 in the morning, if I had never seen you before, I would watch you."

While the graveyard shift was lonely, with suspicion thus falling on almost anyone moving about at that time, the beat cops found that the final hours of their shift brought not only light but people, people who belonged there, people who worked there, as people before them had done for over a century. It was a reassuring symbol of the daily reawakening of a prosperous community. As Hank Cisco remembered, "It was great to watch the town come alive." After hours of darkness and stillness, the light brought the signs of life. The first people to appear on Main Street in the morning would be the window washers and street cleaners, between 5 and 6 a.m. Then the drivers making deliveries to the stores began arriving. Some of those deliveries were of freshly baked bread products from the Continental Baking Company; a delicious smell hung in the valley of Stony Creek and greeted anyone crossing it from the west. The store proprietors by this time would have begun to prepare for the day. Steps and sidewalks were washed, a practice that was generally practiced, but not universal. Neon lights blinked on. Store workers joined the people about, and Main Street, Norristown, Pennsylvania, woke up.

Activity on Main Street during the day largely followed the patterns allowed by the weather. While southeastern Pennsylvania can experience most of what winter brings, the region's summers bring a combination of heat and humidity that contrasts sorely with the weather of but a few months earlier (or later). In 1950, virtually no retail building on Main Street possessed air conditioning, and the need for first-floor security meant none of the display windows could be opened, at least none of significant size. This brought many of the proprietors of Main Street businesses out of their buildings and onto the sidewalk where, even in the hottest weather, it was likely to be more comfortable. An additional motive, and one that promoted standing outside one's store even in cooler weather, was to attract passersby into the store. Thus Main Street had a fairly steady population of "street people," those who could be found on the sidewalk in the same location day after day. Unlike those associated with the term today, these were individually and collectively the pillars of the business community. Not only were they storeowners, many were involved with the community as a whole:

> All these business people along here had a different personality, they all had a character, something about them, and a story to tell when they would meet. You would get to know them; they would talk about their wives, what kind of food they would make. Whether they were German or Italian, Jewish...they would always wind up talking about food, or about the good old days, often back in their country, wherever they came from."[299]

The range of personalities was considerable. The proprietor of the Norristown Maytag shop at 253 West Main Street, known to all as Joe Maytag, used to sit outside his store all day long, singing, making jokes, with something to say to everyone who passed by. Gus Egolf, by contrast, sat in front of his store on East Main Street, spoke much more sparingly, and seemed to rarely have shoppers actually enter his store.

Main Street's merchants knew they were being watched over, and some would show their appreciation to the police force in tangible ways, such as temporary shelter from the cold, or a cup of coffee. The merchants were also reliable customers for local fund solicitations. The police department lacked a pension fund at the time, and thus had to solicit funds from the local community. This put them into personal contact with local merchants. Specific merchants did even more. The proprietor of DiRocco's Tavern at 235 East Main Street liked to go crabbing at the Jersey shore. He would bring back his catch, make up a large batch of crab sauce and spaghetti, and invite the local patrolmen into the back of his restaurant for a free meal. He would also send some sauce and a bowl of spaghetti up to the police headquarters for the desk sergeant.

Not all the merchants were as generous. The proprietor of Wilks' Mens' Furnishings at 20 West Main Street in 1951 was a vocal supporter of the police department. A few years later he gave a gift certificate for a new suit to each police officer, redeemable after Christmas. Two days after Christmas, the first officers went to collect their promised suits and found the store cleared out, and the proprietor vanished.[300]

The blanket of security that enveloped and protected the merchants was also extended to others who did, on occasion, violate the law. Much of this was the informal, take-care-of-the-guy aid to a lost drunk, who might be directed to one of the rooms available for those who could not get home. Of course, if that drunk was a local official (say, a Borough Councilman), who had imbibed too much at the Norristown Club at 61.5 East Main Street (a stairway, not a storefront address), he would likely be given a ride home in a police car.[301]

Christmas 1950

The prosperous year of 1950 culminated with the Christmas season, traditionally the retailers' busiest period. Growing production during the year had allowed manufacturers, wholesalers, and retailers to build up substantial inventories, and they were thus able to avoid any shortages that might result from the recent increase in defense orders generated by the outbreak of the Korean War. One solid financial indicator was a note accompanying the December 14 issue of the *Times Herald*: "Today's *Times Herald* contains the greatest volume of advertising it has ever published in a 48-page paper. Due to restricted newsprint supply, all the advertising scheduled for today could not be published for lack of room. Those important gift messages will be in Friday's paper." The pages were packed with advertisements. Merchants in downtown Main Street predominated in the issue's early pages, offering sales on everything from food to furniture. Sears splashed ads over several pages, featuring housewares and appliances. All the downtown clothing stores had ads, as did the jewelry stores. Even Zummo's Hardware offered seasonal home-oriented gift items.

Main Street's core blocks were again lit up for the season. The borough provided the lights and installed them, but each merchant was assessed a fee according to the building's Main Street frontage.[302] These seasonal lights, strung from Main Street's existing light poles, and combined with the lights on the various stores, made central Main Street seem like a classic urban American winter wonderland as shoppers thronged Main Street throughout the holiday season. As before, the season opened with Santa Claus arriving by train at Main and Markley. He threw candy and gifts to some of the hundreds of children that thronged around him as he paraded to Block's in a fire engine, under police escort. The throng was especially large around Block's, whose owners once again had boarded up the display windows to protect the glass from the crush of spectators and prevent a tragedy.

When the Christmas shopping season was over, downtown merchants were quick to proclaim it "one of the largest, if not the largest, in the history of the borough of Norristown. Some individual merchants enjoyed the largest amount of business in the history of their stores." The Merchants Division of the Norristown Chamber of Commerce reported that shopping was consistently heavy, right up to Saturday's deadline of 6:00 p.m. It was a prosperous end to a prosperous year.

Such boosterism is not to be taken as hard evidence. Yet whatever the specific numbers may have been, in the aggregate they spelled prosperity. War clouds hung over the period, but the mood on Main was positive and upbeat. The future looked bright. Once again the people of Norristown were convinced that their downtown was happy, healthy, and successful, and that it would remain so long into the foreseeable future. Once again, they can be forgiven for not seeing the other dark clouds on the horizon.

MAIN STREET IN 1950

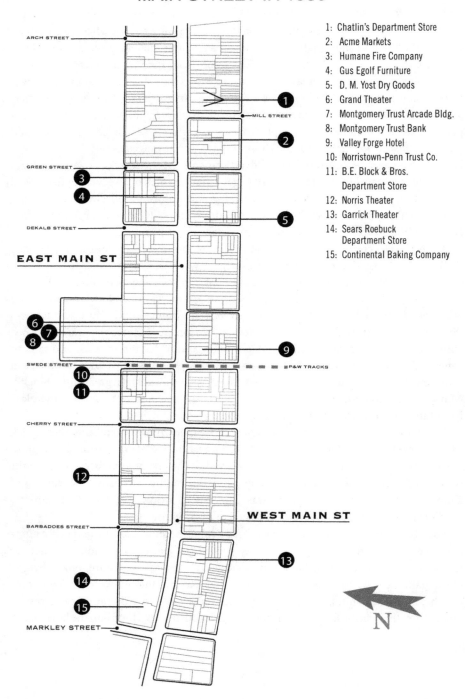

ARCH STREET

MILL STREET

GREEN STREET

DEKALB STREET

EAST MAIN ST

SWEDE STREET

P&W TRACKS

CHERRY STREET

BARBADOES STREET

WEST MAIN ST

MARKLEY STREET

N

1: Chatlin's Department Store
2: Acme Markets
3: Humane Fire Company
4: Gus Egolf Furniture
5: D. M. Yost Dry Goods
6: Grand Theater
7: Montgomery Trust Arcade Bldg.
8: Montgomery Trust Bank
9: Valley Forge Hotel
10: Norristown-Penn Trust Co.
11: B.E. Block & Bros.
    Department Store
12: Norris Theater
13: Garrick Theater
14: Sears Roebuck
    Department Store
15: Continental Baking Company

The P&W building and bridge over Main Street at Swede Street. The Valley Forge Hotel is visible at the left. The Public Square is across the street. People used to say "meet me under the clock." (Photo: Coll's Custom Framing)

Next to the Public Square: the Montgomery Trust Bank and the Arcade Building.
(Photo: Coll's Custom Framing)

The Valley Forge Hotel, in good times. (Photo: Historical Society of Montgomery County)

The Norris Theater, early 1940s. (Photo: Coll's Custom Framing)

Chatlin's staff, assembled before the Christmas season, 1949. (Photo: Coll's Custom Framing)

Paul Santangelo holding forth. (Photo: The Municipality of Norristown)

The "Pigeon-Hole" Garage. (Photo: Coll's Custom Framing)

Demolishing buildings for a parking lot for the bank across the street. The Norris Theater (at left) was quite run-down by that time. (Photo: Coll's Custom Framing)

MAIN STREET IN 1975

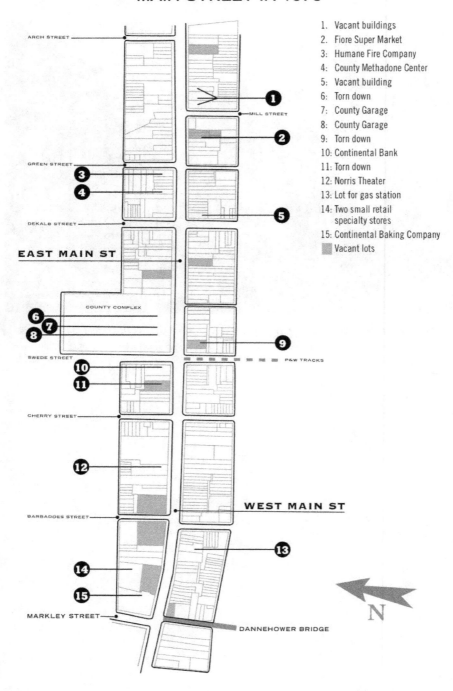

1. Vacant buildings
2. Fiore Super Market
3. Humane Fire Company
4: County Methadone Center
5: Vacant building
6: Torn down
7: County Garage
8: County Garage
9: Torn down
10: Continental Bank
11: Torn down
12: Norris Theater
13: Lot for gas station
14: Two small retail specialty stores
15: Continental Baking Company
Vacant lots

Part II

The Beginning of the End

8

The Automobile Age

Downtown Norristown's prosperity by 1950 already demonstrated the double-edged nature of the emerging automobile age. People who shared their recollections spoke of a bustling, busy city. Shoppers could find anything they needed downtown, from buttons to brassieres to brogans. Young people could share a soda at the fountain counter to the strains of Frankie Laine, Patti Page, and the Mills Brothers playing on the jukebox. The streets were alive with laughter and music, punctuated by the occasional car horn or train whistle. Moms and pops would glide by in their gleaming Buick Roadmasters, Studebaker Commanders, and Plymouth Suburbans to pick up or drop off their teens, leaving the sidewalks awash in a rainbow of short-sleeved sweaters, poodle and pencil skirts, and Bermuda shorts. Good times.

But while the sidewalks were crowded with shoppers and people enjoying all that Main Street and downtown had to offer, the streets themselves were choked with traffic. Often the moms and pops weren't just cruising around the block to show off their beautiful new chrome-glinting automobiles, they were trying desperately to get through the jammed streets, and to find someplace—anyplace!—to park. Officer Ned Offner, often on foot patrol on the corner of Main and DeKalb, remembered those times. The parking spaces were almost always full, he said, and "people would be just waiting for a space to open up; people would cruise around looking for a space."[303]

The years after WWII had quickly acquainted Norristown with the twin problems of traffic and parking. By 1950, these interrelated problems were all too familiar to shoppers, Main Street merchants and the Borough Council. The month before the *Times Herald* had proudly proclaimed Norristown to be a "rich market," it had published an article that added balance to the overall view, admitting that all was not well downtown: "As benefits a contented community, Norristown has few major complaints about its immediate surroundings. It would like to have U.S. Route 202, which now embarrasses DeKalb Street with its burden of through traffic, bypass the town. Too, like other communities with a sizable shopping and business district, it has a parking problem."[304]

These two issues—traffic congestion and parking—would dominate discussions about and actions on behalf of downtown for the next two decades and beyond. They were the opposite sides of the same coin. One focused on expediting the entry of people by automobile into, about, and out of Norristown as quickly as possible; the other focused on what to do with the automobiles of those who arrived in Norristown to do business. This twin-faceted problem already appeared to be intractable; anything done to improve the situation for those traveling by automobile within Norristown only worsened the situation of those attempting to park there, and vice versa.

There were two parts to the parking portion of this two-faceted problem. The first was that there were nowhere near enough curbside parking spaces to accommodate shoppers. "People really resented that that every [space] was filled and there was no place to park."[305] Those who drove around seeking a space added to the congestion problem regardless of whether the search was successful. The second was that once you found a parking space, you had to pay to use it. This had been a fundamental reason for objections to the first parking meters a decade before, and it still rankled. The amount had not changed; it was still a penny for 12 minutes. If you let the meter expire, however, the fine was one dollar. People could not understand why they had to pay a dollar just for not inserting a penny in time. It is little wonder that residents often sought out their Borough Councilman to seek exoneration of their ticket.[306]

While people driving about downtown seeking a parking space were no doubt contributing to the traffic problem, all were aware that there were several other contributors. The desire to identify and put specific numbers to these contributors had been behind the aforementioned Traffic Origin and Destination survey of 1949. The long-awaited report based on the survey was finally released to the public in September 1950, more than a year after the time of its data collection, and largely just put numbers to what everybody knew: there were frequent, heavy traffic jams on both DeKalb Street (Route 202) and Main Street (Route 422). The report concluded that 38% of the traffic into and out of downtown either originated in the downtown area or had a downtown destination. The remaining 62% were just passing through downtown to another destination. This would have perhaps been a useful quantification in 1949. In September 1950, however, the report was overshadowed by the pending arrival of the Pennsylvania Turnpike, which promised to render the survey's numbers obsolete, if they were not already.

A *Times Herald* December editorial's answer to the problem of traffic congestion was to again call for a bypass for U.S. 202. This long-discussed project would re-route U.S. 202 away from DeKalb Street—and potentially Norristown itself, depending on where the crossing was anticipated—thus removing the north-south through traffic that clogged downtown Norristown streets on a daily basis without contributing business or parking revenue. The *Times Herald* had been a frequent promoter of the project in concept (although it had waffled on both location and cost), and its news coverage at least gave the impression that most of Norristown's "movers and shakers" supported the idea.

That was rather an exaggeration, however. There was opposition, and the leader of that opposition was none other than Harry Butera. Butera, in January 1950, wrote a letter to *Times Herald* vice president William Shelton, outlining what he termed a "master plan" for Norristown's traffic woes, which the *Times Herald* published. As the area's foremost real estate expert, Butera was certainly in a position to examine what was proposed from a knowledgeable viewpoint. Yet he did much more than that. Examined more than a half-century later, Butera's letter to Shelton stands as the lone vision of what was happening to Norristown.

Although the Eastern Extension had not yet reached King of Prussia, he had already grasped the broad outlines of the process that would engulf Norristown—lines sketched by the new superhighways that would meet just across the river in King of Prussia. Butera realized that the connection of the Pennsylvania Turnpike and the Schuylkill Expressway would create a superhighway that would draw away considerable east-west traffic from Norristown. This understanding lay at the core of his opposition to the U.S. Route 202 Bypass. While the bypass would be less of a superhighway than the turnpike/expressway, it would still pull north-south bound traffic away from Norristown. Since the through traffic would already be diminished by the superhighways, Butera believed that a bypass would isolate Norristown and sound the first tones of its death knell. "By one grand stroke, it seems to me, Norristown will be reduced to a community located along secondary highways to be seen only, practically speaking, by 'local people,' " he wrote.[307]

And as it turns out, he was right.

Viewed through the lens of more than half a century, that statement sums up what did in fact happen to Norristown. Butera was not magically blessed with second sight. He was merely attuned to the grand scheme of things, of what was happening outside the borough as well as within its confines. The central component of his "master plan" was to move U.S. 202 away from DeKalb Street, but not Norristown itself. This did happen eventually, but by then it would not matter. The bypassing of Norristown took place on a scale larger than Butera—or anyone else at that time—could have imagined, and U.S. 202 had very little to do with it.

Enter the usual suspect in the death of the downtown: the shopping mall. It is a sign of Butera's grasp of current events that in addition to warning of the dangers the new superhighways posed, he was at the very same time involved in planning Norristown's first such mall. It is also one of the little ironies of history that while Butera was warning of dangers ahead for downtown's commercial supremacy, he was developing the new shopping model that would destroy that very supremacy. To be fair, he did not envisage anything like what would one day become the King of Prussia Mall. He did not heartlessly set out to replace downtown with a one-stop-shopping mini-city far from Main Street. But he was taking the first step in abandoning downtown, the first move to the periphery in Norristown's commercial history.

To the Periphery: Logan Square

That first step was Logan Square. The project itself was not Harry Butera's idea but the brainchild of his nephew, Joseph, son of his older brother, James. After returning from military service, Joseph Butera had gone to work for his Uncle Harry, but in the words of Harry's son, Robert, they proved to be "like oil and water." Harry Butera was a social progressive, but he was at the same time a businessman, and a conservative one at that. Joseph, by contrast, dreamed grandiose ideas. When Joseph proposed that they jointly build Logan Square, Harry demurred. Though the initial planning, was done jointly, he limited his participation to that of exclusive leasing agent for the planned center; Joseph was the owner. Harry's expertise in land values and his unexcelled connections across the Norristown community were necessary to the success of what, at the time, seemed an audacious and risky venture.[308]

The Logan Square project *was* both audacious and risky, but it was not actually new. The basic concept, and indeed the basic design itself, was patterned after the Suburban Square project in Ardmore, one of America's early planned shopping centers. Joseph Butera set his sights on a portion of very northernmost Norristown, where the by-now combined Swede/Markley streets met the ill-named Johnson Highway, just a two-lane asphalt road whose intersections lacked traffic lights. The tract of land being eyed for this project was largely undeveloped, but residences dotted the area, thus requiring rezoning—and hence a decision by the Borough Council.

Joseph Butera, representing Logan Square Inc., took the proposal to the Borough Council in January 1950. There were two parts to the land being proposed for rezoning. Tract 1, bounded by Markley Street, Johnson Highway, and Logan Street, was to be rezoned for commercial us, with eight stores and a theater, and provision for the off-street parking of 195 automobiles. Tract 2 would be rezoned for residential use, for apartments on the land adjoining Tract 1. The plan was given a first reading, and referred to the Borough Zoning Commission for examination and recommendation.[309] The Zoning Commission favored the proposal. The Council Building and Zoning Committee then considered the matter. On March 7, the committee recommended accepting the rezoning request for Tract 2, allowing apartments, but also recommended rejecting the commercial request for Tract 1.[310] Despite the fig leaf of approval for Tract 2, this was tantamount to a flat rejection of the Logan Square proposal. The Borough Council agreed, and the ordinance to enact the *partial* rezoning passed its first and second readings unanimously.[311]

Curiously, the one specific objection voiced by an unnamed council member concerned not the stores, but the theater, and he allowed that other (also unnamed) council members shared this concern. His (and implicitly, their) opposition was based on the fact that Norristown already had enough theater seats, information he admittedly obtained from David Sablosky—and no one was better positioned than a Sablosky to know the number of existing theater seats. Substantial discussion ensued. While no one ever specifically identified the downtown merchants objecting to the rezoning, the subject of "special interest influence" was repeatedly mentioned. It seems obvious that the addition of another theater would be viewed by Sablosky as competition, not civic improvement. The weight of the opinion, including an editorial by the *Times Herald*, was that the Borough Council had rejected a proposal that would benefit the borough. Undeterred, the Borough Council passed the resolution approving only Tract 2, again unanimously, on April 4.[312]

Five months of negotiations followed. After Logan Square Inc. notified the council that the theater component of the plan would be dropped, the Borough Council again took up the plan at its August meeting, and gave the first two readings to an ordinance that set up a new business district classification to accommodate the Butera proposal. At this third council meeting on September 5, the ordinance passed, and included a long list of permitted and non-permitted businesses. Immediately after the ordinance had become law, the real estate firm of Harry Butera, Inc., announced that it would immediately open negotiations with the number of business and professional firms reported to be interested in the project.

The conception, planning, and approval of the Logan Square project would prove to be a seminal event in the history of Norristown in the 20th century. It was the first planned commercial development in the Norristown area of the type of commercial enterprise later to be termed a "shopping center." Unlike other commercial parts of Norristown, Logan Square could not be reached by train or trolley. Most people could not walk to it from their homes or place of work. Roads provided the only access to Logan Square, but by 1950s standards the shopping center would offer extensive parking—with no meters. The site was large, but commercially undeveloped. All the structures would be built specifically for their tenants, unlike on Main Street, which had long ago been built, modified, and modified again.

Logan Square was thus, from the beginning, a full-frontal challenge to Main Street. The elimination of a theater was inconsequential to the plans; the site appeared to have considerable commercial potential. Here Harry Butera played a key role; as Norristown's undisputed king of local real estate, his reputation as a careful businessman undoubtedly lent considerable credence to the Logan Square project. In just a short while, Logan Square would establish one the basic principles of a successful shopping center: land a major tenant, and build a large custom structure to create an "anchor store." Another note in the death knell sounded, for Logan Square's anchor store would be a long-time tenant of Main Street.

The decision by Sears to leave Main Street and become the cornerstone of Logan Square made Joe Butera's shopping area into an indisputable success story. The new Sears store had triple the amount of square footage of its old Main Street store. Its name and reputation provided the nationally known draw that pulled shoppers into the shopping area, where they could then shop not only at Sears but at any of the 16 smaller stores and a food market. Most significantly, the stores were set amidst seven acres of land, much of it paved to accommodate 500 automobiles, with not a parking meter in sight. *Free, ample parking.* Those three words sent shudders down the spine of the downtown merchants.

Logan Square's official groundbreaking ceremony took place on July 9, 1953, and its official opening (and that of the Sears store itself) on August 12, 1954. The Sears representative was effusive in stressing the firm's traditional connection with Norristown, proclaiming, "This new store will make Norristown a still greater trading center. Sears will continue its community interest and help Norristown grow to greater heights in the future."[313] While this may have been true for Norristown as a borough, Logan Square at its inception clearly presented a major challenge to Main Street, particularly for the patronage of the rapidly increasing number of residents in the nearby suburbs. Within two months of the center's opening, Logan Square Inc. was back before Zoning Board of Adjustment. Joe Butera proclaimed that the success of the new center was "so overwhelming" that additional parking was needed.[314] In November, the Norristown Zoning Board of Adjustment turned down the request for additional parking. Logan Square Inc. quickly appealed the denial to county court, contending that the additional parking was necessary. In August, the court granted Logan Square Inc.'s appeal to expand its parking area, giving the shopping center permission to expand its *free, ample parking* from 500 to 1,000 spaces. For the downtown merchants, this was the stuff of nightmares.

Logan Square continued to add tenants. In November 1956, it hosted its first car show, arranged by the Norristown Automobile Dealers Association to show off the new models. The Dealers Association had sponsored indoor events of very limited size since its inception in 1938. In July 1955, downtown Main Street had been closed to traffic and Norristown's first outdoor automobile show was held along its center stretch. The show attracted considerable interest, but the event on Main Street was the first and the last. The reasons should by now be obvious: it disrupted traffic, and there was nowhere for people to park, so it disrupted rather than enhanced business for the downtown stores. The outdoor show relocated to Logan Square in November 1956, timed to feature the new models from Detroit, with 11 dealers participating. The show was held again at Logan Square in November 1957. (A November event held outdoors, however, was at risk given southeastern Pennsylvania's unpredictable weather, so the event was rescheduled for April after 1958.)

Logan Square instituted another, quite symbolic, challenge to downtown, where each year Santa Claus had traditionally arrived at Main Street by train. At Logan Square, he arrived by helicopter.[315]

By September, Joe Butera was back before the Council's Building and Zoning Committee again, this time to request the rezoning of 26 acres at the rear of the location to accommodate yet another expansion, the largest yet. An additional location for "a complete major department store," together with approximately 20 smaller shop locations—and, at this stage, possibly an office building—would more than double the overall size of Logan Square. The council delayed for over six months before finally voting 8:4 to reject the request.[316] A sense of the behind-the-scenes negotiations comes from a quote by Paul Santangelo. "I gather a lot of merchants from Main Street are very much interested in this not being approved. They want other things in their favor, and don't like it if we don't go along with them."[317] Santangelo supported and voted for the rezoning request.

Shopping Centers in East and West Norriton

Logan Square was just a stepping stone from downtown toward the periphery. It was quickly followed by other new commercial centers, which began to appear at the intersections many of the area's roads. For the people moving into the area's new housing developments, these centers offered an increasing number of stores, more choices and inventory, and were often closer than downtown Norristown. And, of course, there were those three magic words: *free, ample parking*.

DeKalb Pike and Swede Road had long been the existing roads to the north. Not far from the borough they intersected the equally ancient Germantown Pike. This area had previously been served by the P&W trolley, whose route roughly paralleled Swede Road through East Norriton Township. There had long been businesses at the intersections of Swede Road and DeKalb Pike with Germantown Pike, beginning with inns to host colonial-era travelers. As the 1950s progressed, these ancient intersections spawned collections of stores that grew with the area's population. Some were small, of the type now known generically as "strip shopping centers," or "strip malls," consisting of one small row of businesses set behind a combination driveway and parking area, closely parallel to the highway. They rarely had formal names, or if they did, the names changed often, seemed tacked on as afterthoughts, or were easily forgotten. Penn Square, a typical small strip center on Germantown Pike west of Swede Street, was an exception; its name survives to this day.

In very little time, the intersection of Swede Street and Germantown Pike began to see even larger projects. One was the Swede Square Shopping Center, which featured a Genuardi's supermarket (another local Norristown Italian business success story), 20 additional stores, and, of course, free, ample parking. By late 1961, plans were being offered for a shopping center a short distance down Germantown Pike at its intersection with DeKalb Pike, also in East Norriton. (Representing the developer, DeKalb Square, Inc., was attorney H. Kenneth Butera, a son of Harry Butera.) Already, in 1955, Food Fair Properties Inc. of Philadelphia had purchased a 26-acre tract of land at the intersection of DeKalb Pike and Germantown Pike. The development was to include a Food Fair market, a department store, one or two "five and dime" stores and up to 20 smaller retail locations. Construction began in the fall of 1956, by which time the list of tenants included Grant's and Kresge's.

The area to Norristown's west, along Ridge Pike, was not far behind in the population and construction boom. In 1956, work began on another shopping center at Trooper Road, the connection to the first bridge across the Schuylkill west of Norristown, at the village of Port Kennedy adjacent to Valley Forge. This plan, which called for 18 stores and parking for 150 cars, was the inspiration of Lawrence Tornetta, another of the area's rising new generation of Italian-American entrepreneurs—Tornetta, Gambone, Genuardi—the "broad thinkers" who looked beyond their front steps toward regional locations for larger markets. Although they largely seized on business opportunities outside the borough and thus are absent from this narrative, their contributions should be kept in mind. They saw what was happening to the Norristown area and across the country, and found a way to make it work.

Today we look at such small-to-medium-size shopping centers and shrug off their relative importance. But in the 1950s, it only took a handful of these to have a major, collective effect on Main Street. Added together, their explosive impact reached critical mass and caused Main Street to begin its irreversible implosion even before the more visible effects of the King of Prussia Mall that was yet to come. The incremental effects of these smaller shopping centers have been largely overlooked, overshadowed as they have been by the giant malls. Collectively, these smaller shopping centers popping up everywhere constituted a serious threat to Main Street, and were the primary reason for the slow decline of Main Street during the late 1950s. Regardless of their size, whether they were individual enterprises, or tenants of centers that may have possessed names or not, they sprung up in an arc north of Norristown from west to east. Collectively, they not only absorbed the shopping income of the new residents, but also began to alter the shopping habits of Norristown's residents themselves; the slow decline in the number of businesses on Main Street during this period testifies to this.

So do the memories of this book's interviewees. Joseph Verunni, who had returned to live in Norristown after WWII service in the Pacific but had found a job and a career in Wayne repairing watches and clocks, moved to Plymouth Township in 1952. Possession of an automobile had given him alternatives, and he decided to pursue the American dream of owning a house with some land around it and some space from his neighbors. He was one of the first of the long-time residents of his street in the East End to leave, and one of the first to sell to African-Americans. In time, his neighbors followed suit, in both respects. "We all eventually sold to black people." Once he moved out, he returned to Norristown only to attend his church, Holy Savior, for which he served as choir director for 72 years. "As we got into the cars, and businesses were starting to open up on the outskirts of town, we didn't go downtown anymore."[318]

Mary Early remembers a large store called Atlantic Thrift. It was not in a shopping center, but it was on the outskirts, on DeKalb Pike just short of Germantown Pike. "What we would consider Wal-Mart and K-Mart, that's what Atlantic Thrift was like.... I lived there every Wednesday, which was sale day." By the early 1960s, "I was torn between Atlantic Thrift and Chatlin's."[319]

In all of this, the unfortunate fact for Main Street, Norristown was that more and more of the new residents were essentially asking themselves the same question: if a shopping center is easier to get to and provides plenty of free parking right near the stores I want, why bother with Main Street, or for that matter, with Norristown itself? By 1962, the local shopping centers that had been and were still coming into being around Norristown had changed people's shopping decisions and destinations, to the detriment of Main Street. The number of local shopping centers, and their impact on the downtown, would only increase in the years ahead. Just then, however, the big challenge, one that would dwarf the others in both size and scope, was looming almost literally on the horizon, across the river in Upper Merion Township, adjacent to the Turnpike interchange at King of Prussia.

Meanwhile, Across the River

In April 1950, the Pennsylvania Highway Planning Commission, an 11-member panel appointed by Governor Duff to "develop a long range highway program for the Commonwealth under the provision of Act No. 537 of 1949," held a public hearing in the main Council Chamber of the Philadelphia City Hall. The Norristown Chamber of Commerce sent a representative to present a statement about what was quickly becoming a major concern in Southeastern Pennsylvania: traffic congestion expected at the new King of Prussia terminus, extending into nearby municipalities. The Chamber's statement is revealing for its belief about the relationship between the turnpike and the expressway:

> We estimate that the traffic on Route 202 will be increased nearly 200% because approximately 85% of the Turnpike traffic will be through traffic taking advantage of the superhighway and traffic headed for New York and the New England states will certainly use Route 202 through Norristown.... We are informed that the Turnpike will be opened for the traveling public sometime during the latter part of 1950. At that time there will be no outlet for the motor vehicles from the turnpike other than the present existing roads, which were not designed to accommodate this type of traffic. It is true that the Valley Forge Expressway has been planned to take traffic from the turnpike to the city of Philadelphia, but as near as we can learn only two short sections of this expressway has been let out to contractors and it probably will be at least two or three years before this expressway will be completed as far as City Line, Philadelphia.[320]

Norristown was by no means alone in its concern. Local governments and other interested business and civic groups beginning with Upper Merion Township, where the Philadelphia Extension would terminate, shared a common attitude toward the turnpike's pending arrival: dread. The equally shared reason for this was fear of traffic congestion. The unavailability of the Schuylkill Expressway for what promised to be at least a year substantially increased this concern.

Officially, the State Department of Highways disputed the idea that any such congestion would occur. Its figures claimed that fewer cars would enter the completed expressway from the turnpike than from Route 202; in other words, local and already-existing traffic exceeded what the turnpike would bring. State officials also disputed the "common local belief" that the extension would generate a large volume of traffic on Route 202 headed north. State figures showed that only 728 cars per day would exit the turnpike at King of Prussia and proceed north through Norristown.

The Turnpike Commission also did what it could to allay local fears about traffic the extension would deliver. The Commission predicted that once the expressway was completed, traffic eastbound for the Delaware River basin would exit the extension at the Pennsylvania Route 100 interchange in Chester County. From there, it said, traffic would proceed to U.S. Route 30 at Exton, and then travel Route 30 to Philadelphia. In anticipation of this additional traffic, the Pennsylvania Department of Highways was upgrading Pennsylvania Route 100 between the new interchange and the intersection with U.S. Route 30. As for eastbound traffic bound elsewhere, the department did not foresee any great increase of traffic on state or township roads during the period before the opening of the Schuylkill Expressway. In fact, it predicted that the only major road congestion would occur on U.S. Route 202 after the completion of the expressway, and would be due not to the extension, but to local traffic to and from Philadelphia. Nevertheless, the State Department of Highways by that time had decided to reverse its previous decision on using directional signs to guide traffic exiting the extension. Although originally they had decided to not designate any formal routes to Philadelphia in the King of Prussia area, they eventually sided with local officials and posted "To Philadelphia" signs on all local roads affected by the King of Prussia terminus of the extension.

The Turnpike Arrives

October 23, 1950, dawned rainy and cool, and continued that way, the type of raw fall day so familiar to residents of southeastern Pennsylvania. By mid-morning, close to 500 of those residents, according to local press reports, had gathered despite the weather to celebrate the official dedication of the King of Prussia Terminus of the Pennsylvania Turnpike's eastern extension. The area all around was farmland, but the spot on which they now gathered possessed all the rawness of an unfinished construction site, made even muddier by the recent rain. Two ribbons of concrete began (or ended) there, and stretched just over 100 miles to Carlisle, where another not-quite-finished construction site was connecting them to the two ribbons that a decade earlier had initiated a revolution in transportation in the United States.

Local dignitaries, together with a delegation from the Commonwealth led by Governor Duff, gathered around a ceremonial ribbon stretched across the roadway at the terminal gates. After cutting the ribbon, Governor Duff gave a short speech extolling the benefits of the turnpike, both those it had already brought to the central portion of the state and those it would now bring to the Philadelphia area. The speech emphasized the long-range vision that had brought about the turnpike. "This is a wonderful day for Pennsylvania," Duff opined. "Now the industrial ports of Philadelphia and Pittsburgh are connected." This was of course, not strictly true; there still remained the not-inconsiderable matters of the distance between the western terminus of the turnpike at Irwin and Pittsburgh, and between its new eastern terminus and Philadelphia. Everyone present, however, expected those final connections would be made. At the ceremony's end, the dignitaries of the state delegation bade farewell to the local officials and boarded a multicar caravan, departing westward down the right-hand ribbon, quickly drawing out of sight.

As ceremonies go, this one had been nothing much. A good part of the reason was that it would have to be repeated—including the short speech by Governor Duff, slightly altered as required by the changes in location—again and again, at each of the interchanges along the new extension to Carlisle, the turnpike's previous eastern terminus. Another was that the population in the general area around King of Prussia knew that this dedication would not open the extension to traffic; work remained to be done on guardrails, traffic signs and road shoulders.

That evening, in the state capital of Harrisburg, a banquet concluded the day's ceremonies. Governor Duff gave yet another speech, one that emphasized the significant yet transitional nature of this extension of an already-long successful roadway. In his speech, Duff announced that the Turnpike Commission, the quasi-state agency responsible for the turnpike, had proposed the construction of a further extension, this one from its new terminus at King of Prussia to the Delaware River, Pennsylvania's boundary with New Jersey. This new proposal, combined with the extension of the turnpike westward from its original terminus at Irwin to the Ohio State line, would bring into being a limited-access highway the entire length of Pennsylvania.

Closing the gap between King of Prussia and Philadelphia was imminent, as area residents well knew. While attention that day focused on the concrete ribbons heading west, in the ceremony's background were two more such ribbons whose pavement began a short distance from the new terminus and then proceeded southeast for a few miles. It was a road that on this day connected nothing and led nowhere. But that would change, as construction on additional sections of what was officially known as the Schuylkill Expressway was already in the works.

While the Philadelphia Extension was formally dedicated in repeated ceremonies along its route on October 23, it actually opened to the public on November 11 without fanfare. For anyone desiring to travel the length of the new extension between King of Prussia and Carlisle by automobile, the toll was $1.20. The full trip, to the new western terminus at Irwin cost $2.50. The actual opening of the eastern extension, and the first traffic passing through Norristown, provided the *Times Herald* with an opportunity to fulminate yet again on the problem of traffic congestion.

An editorial in December 1950 reviewed the "Traffic Problem," and issued yet another call for both the state and the borough to take "immediate action" to solve the issue of downtown congestion. The editorial named the newly opened eastern extension of the Pennsylvania Turnpike as a new contributor to the problem, but tried to have it both ways, claiming that that the opening of the eastern extension was "largely responsible for the position in which Norristown finds itself," while simultaneously admitting that "Norristown had a traffic problem—one made up of local traffic—long before the State started building the extension." The fundamental problem, it continued, was that Norristown possessed "business area highways designed for horse and buggy days." The editorial did observe that Norristown was hardly alone in this and claimed that similar towns had solved *their* problem. No names were mentioned.

While the amount, nature, and destination of additional traffic due to the eastern extension may have been open to debate, Norristown at the end of 1950 certainly viewed the future of local traffic with dread. The December release by the American Automobile Association of information to motorists on how to reach the new turnpike entrance at King of Prussia from New York, Philadelphia, the eastern shore of New Jersey, and points south brought home a chilling message: while in the future, truck traffic would probably follow the most developed roads, access to the turnpike was open to virtually all vehicle traffic in the Delaware Valley. As the AAA directions would show, Norristown lay squarely in the way of this access. Local officials continued to worry, as the AAA's preferred, suggested route between New York and King of Prussia was via U.S. Route 202—squarely through downtown Norristown.

Reliable data on the effect of the Pennsylvania Turnpike on the areas adjacent to its termini and interchanges prior to 1950 is sparse. The most relevant seems to be Henry K. Shearer's PhD dissertation in economics submitted to the University of Pennsylvania. Shearer, writing in *The Economic Effects of the Original Section of the Pennsylvania Turnpike on Adjacent Areas*, had this to say in 1955:

> The area as a whole through which the original section of the Pennsylvania Turnpike passes has not experienced more or less favorable overall economic trends since its opening in 1940.... Thus there would seem to be no evidence that the original section of the Turnpike has had any marked overall economic effect on the area it might have been expected to affect.[321]

This pattern would not be repeated at King of Prussia. The first development proposals to reach the Upper Merion Board of Commissioners were for small business designed to accommodate travelers, such as service stations, restaurants, and motels. This was largely in keeping with the experience of interchanges of the original turnpike. The largest of these early-phase developments was the General Lafayette Motel, along DeKalb Pike adjacent to the turnpike interchange. This project was another one belonging to Lawrence F. Tornetta who, along with a handful of investors, had purchased a tract of land for $50,00 and built the motel, originally 53 rooms. They subsequently expanded its size, and by the time it was sold to a national syndicate in 1956, the General Lafayette boasted 105 rooms. Other large motel projects followed, each seeking to locate as close as possible to the King of Prussia Interchange. In 1956, the Howard Johnson company sought and received a zoning change to locate its planned 100-unit Motor Lodge at the intersection of Route 202 and the ramp from the Schuylkill Expressway.

A second phase—largely residential developments—followed. The bulk of construction in the King of Prussia area would be residential through mid-decade. In 1954, construction in Upper Merion Township totaled $1,836,821.00; in 1955, the total skyrocketed to $5,438,595.00, a 300% increase. The 1955 total represented permits issued for 410 single-family homes and five industries. A shift in these totals was evident in 1956: the total value of construction increased again, to $6,098,066.50, but this time the number of single-family homes was just 270, while industrial projects had increased to 18. The shift toward industry and offices had begun in earnest.

This third phase would soon reach previously undreamed-of proportions. A proposal announced in April 1955 to erect a $4 million office building (then termed the Graphic Arts Co-Operative Center) was an early project offering what would become a familiar refrain: access to major highways. In early 1956, General Electric Company announced that it would build a "multimillion" R&D center on a 110-acre site virtually overlooking the turnpike itself. The company proudly proclaimed that the new facility would employ at least 2,000 people, with a payroll of at least $10 million. As the international "space race" heated up, this project would quickly grow into the General Electric Valley Forge Space and Technology Center. By the end of the year, Automated Temperature Control Company had purchased a 12-acre site adjacent to the Schuylkill Expressway just south of the turnpike interchange to house its new plant, which had 70,000 square feet of floor area. In 1958, the American Baptist Convention, at its meeting in Cincinnati, voted to consolidate its New York and Philadelphia headquarters into one location—at Valley Forge. The Convention was clear as to the reason for its decision: "It [the Valley Forge location] is near the convergence of three great super-highways, one from the West, another from the South, and still another from New England and New York."[322] The new headquarters featured a striking circular shape that led to its nickname, "The Holy Donut."[323]

One result of this great interest in relocating to King of Prussia was that several of those local landowners who had been worried about the arrival of the eastern exten-sion became wealthy. In March, 1953, a group of investors purchased the 90-acre "An-derson Farm Tract" in King of Prussia between U.S. Route 202 and Allendale Road, for a price reported to be in excess of $450,000. The purchase was speculative, for future development. In 1957 Cabot, Cabot and Forbes Inc. purchased the land of Alexander D. and Aimee Irwin, about 800 acres, for what was quoted to be "considerably more than a million dollars." There would be several more such purchases.

The Upper Merion Township Board of Supervisors was generally receptive to the plans, due largely to the financial bonanza that was coming its way. In April 1958, the Board approved the creation of a new "suburban-metropolitan" zone on what had been the Irwin land. When Cabot, Cabot and Forbes issued its initial plans for a "modern industrial center" (one- and two-story buildings "of attractive design" and no "smoke stack" industries included), it pegged the cost of the project at between $50 and $60 million dollars. Daniel G. Wheeler, vice president of Cabot, Cabot and Forbes, proudly pointed out that Upper Merion Township would realize at least $1 million per year in taxes from this site alone. Furthermore, this new industrial center would have an assessed valuation almost equal to that of Upper Merion Township's entire residential housing stock. Thus all the township's residents were going to benefit, and for a considerable time.

As the 1960s began, virtually all those involved in or observing the process of ex-pansion in Upper Merion believed that the decade-long transition from rural farmland to industrial, commercial, and residential developments would not only continue but accelerate. A *Times Herald* editorial in early January 1961 caught the prevailing mood: "Where a few short years ago there were pastures and farm lots and tangled woodland, today stand supermarkets, retail stores and the foundations for massive apartment buildings, huge industrial parks and hundreds of new, well-built homes." The edito-rial was entitled "Just the Beginning."[324]

And it was. Housing developments and local industries meant commercial busi-nesses to service the new homeowners and workers. A November 1956 article in a Montgomery newspaper informed its readers of a new, substantial shopping center being planned for Upper Merion. It also cast the center as a challenge to downtown:

> One of the greatest needs has been the types of conveniences normally associ-ated with "downtown." Historically, Upper Merion residents have depended upon Norristown and Wayne for these conveniences but, with rapid popula-tion growth, closer facilities became both desirable and economically feasi-ble. In 1953 a group of local residents began a study to determine what these facilities should be and where they should be located.[325]

The result of this study was the rezoning of a tract of 36 acres on the northwest corner of Henderson Road and DeKalb Pike (Route 202) to "shopping center," and the construction of the Valley Forge Shopping Center. Construction began in the spring of 1955. The center opened in November 1956, prospered, and in 1960 an expansion plan was announced that would not only add to the center's total of stores, but also include a 32-lane bowling alley and a new King of Prussia Post Office—all adjacent to 8,000 square feet of office space, 5,000 square feet of medical space, and 142 "garden apartments." And, of course, *free, ample parking*.

The Valley Forge Shopping Center was a substantial commercial challenge, and one clearly aimed at downtown Norristown. However, despite this quite substantial increase in size and scope, the Valley Forge Center itself was about to be relegated to secondary status.

Early Plans for King of Prussia

In the summer of 1954, residents of Norristown first became aware of the shopping center that would forever define their future. The July 24 edition of the *Times Herald* proclaimed in its lead article "Big Shop-Center for King of Prussia." The reason for its conception was clear from the article's lead sentence:

> Plans are well advanced for the development of the suburban commercial district to be built on a 93-acre tract in King of Prussia, where the Pennsylvania Turnpike, the Schuylkill Expressway and Route 202 and 23 join to create the principal traffic center of the Greater Main Line–Norristown Region, with a population of a million within 30 minutes.

In its initial appearance, the center was to be developed by the American Stores Company, and the 10 or 12 stores would be built around an Acme Supermarket. The same article quoted LeRoy Little, director of the Montgomery County Planning Commission, as he predicted that "King of Prussia will become as well-known as 42nd and Broadway.... All Roads will lead here."[326]

Little was not far off. But first the concept of a "shopping center" at King of Prussia would have to go through some striking changes. In 1956, the Centers Corporation took over the site and the project from American Stores Company, along with six other sites in the Philadelphia/Wilmington area. Planning and construction continued, but the big change was still to come. What would become the King of Prussia Mall was truly born in 1959, when the M. A. Kravitz Company (later Kravco) took over planning for and management of the shopping center. The result would be, developed in stages, a shopping center on a greater scale than had ever before been contemplated in the area—what would become the prototypical "shopping mall" before the end of the 20th century. The limited-access highways made possible this retail bonanza of multiple "anchor" stores together with many smaller stores, all easily accessible to shoppers from every direction, supplemented, of course, with free, ample parking.

By 1961, the basic plan we now associate with malls had begun to emerge: a massive structure that combined both enclosed and open shopping areas. The new plan added a J. C. Penny Store to the original Korvette's, with a third large store promised in the near future. All this required more land, which meant purchasing another estate from a local property owner, and another request to rezone that land for shopping center use. By now, however, some 20 local organizations, all alarmed by what was happening, had banded together as the Upper Merion Civic Council, and attempted to fight the center's expansion. Their protests went nowhere. All legal obstacles to this massive project were duly overcome. The result, even in its initial form, was to effectively double the size of the shopping center. That expansion made the King of Prussia Plaza more than *twice* the size of the newly expanded Valley Forge Center, less than a mile north on DeKalb Pike.

All that was to come in King of Prussia rested on two physical factors. The first was abundant undeveloped land. The farm fields surrounding the King of Prussia Inn provided that, and more, for the several other industries and businesses locating huge new plants in the area. The second and by far the most important factor, however, was ease of access, even from considerable distances. The intersection of the Pennsylvania Turnpike and the Schuylkill Expressway allowed people from a vast area to drive rapidly, and with little difficulty, to the new shopping center. A retail store, even a modest one, in the evolving King of Prussia Plaza thus had a huge potential marketing area, beyond anything before conceivable except for the very few dominant Philadelphia department stores in a day of less available transportation. That enormous marketing area was also rapidly accumulating new residents, steadily increasing the number of potential customers. Virtually all of these customers would arrive via the roads: the King of Prussia Mall never possessed a rail link. It would be included on local bus routes, but the overwhelming majority of customers would arrive by automobile.

It was in 1961, as this new mode of shopping made possible by superhighways was taking shape, that the University of Pennsylvania published its collection of research papers about Norristown between 1900 and 1950. The book was called *The Norristown Study: An Experiment in Interdisciplinary Research Training*. It included introductory and summary comments from the project's faculty supervisor and the work's editor, Sidney Goldstein. He noted the arrival of the superhighways between 1950 and the work's 1961 publication, and viewed this as a promising event for the borough, predicting that "the stability which had come to characterize Norristown proper by mid-century may very well give way to a new era of growth."[327]

Rarely has a prediction been proven so wrong so quickly.

9

Downshifting Downtown, 1951–1961

The decline of downtown Norristown between 1950 and 1975 can be divided into two periods: the 12 years prior to the opening of the King of Prussia Plaza, and the 12 years afterward, with 1962 as the transition year. An examination of the *Polk City Directories* reveals that Main Street's decline began in the middle 1950s. By the time the King of Prussia Plaza opened in 1963, Main Street had been in a steady—and accelerating—decline for years. Years before the King of Prussia Plaza opened, Norristown's commercial supremacy had been challenged by both external and internal competitors, and their combined effects would leave Main Street weakened and vulnerable. The King of Prussia Plaza was simply an exponentially greater threat, as was the additional challenger soon to appear, the Plymouth Meeting Mall.

What makes this story a tragedy is that during the period leading up to the coming of the malls, both the borough of Norristown and the merchants of its downtown were well aware of the danger. They knew that they were being attacked by the twin nemeses of traffic congestion and parking problems. For slightly more than a decade, downtown Norristown would invest a great amount of thought, time, effort, money, and prestige to fend off these problems, and would fail spectacularly. The consequences of that failure would cripple them, and leave downtown all but helpless when faced by the twin giants of competition, the King of Prussia Plaza and the Plymouth Meeting Mall.

Railroads

In the background of events prior to the coming of the malls is the regional and national decline of America's railroads. Locally, the decline of two of the nation's great railroad systems, the Reading and the Pennsylvania, delivered successive blows to Norristown's rail communications to the east and west. The decade would see both cutbacks in the number of trains connecting Norristown to Philadelphia and points west, and periodic fare increases to ride the trains that remained.

The trains between Norristown and the communities to the west were the first to go. The Reading continued to run trains, but on a greatly reduced schedule, and the Pennsylvania had already ended some services west of Norristown. Though ridership to the east (linking Norristown with Philadelphia) had always been higher, even those routes had become unprofitable for both lines. When the Pennsylvania petitioned the Public Utility Commission (PUC) in August of 1952 to end its service between

Philadelphia and Norristown, E. W. Smith, vice-president of the line's Eastern region, very clearly stated the reasons:

> [T]here is no longer enough business for two railroads paralleling the Schuylkill with so many people there using the family automobile, bus, and trolley.... Patronage of Pennsylvania trains beyond Manayunk has dropped more than one-third since World War II, although the area has grown substantially in population in these five years.[328]

The PUC rejected the request to cut service entirely, but permitted cutbacks first on weekdays, then on weekends. By late 1953, it had allowed cutbacks on weekday service and the elimination of weekend and holiday trains. By 1960, the Pennsylvania's second petition to end all service between the Borough and Philadelphia was quickly approved. The last train between Norristown and Philadelphia over the Pennsylvania Railroad's Schuylkill Branch ran on Saturday, October 29, marking the end of 76 years of service by the Pennsylvania between Norristown and Philadelphia.

While the Reading Railroad (at least its Schuylkill Valley branch) fared better than the Pennsylvania Railroad during this period, the same fundamental problem of declining ridership on its regional trains plagued it as well. A major schedule reorganization in the fall of 1954 discontinued 49 area trains and consolidated others. The company cited a major operating loss on its commuter lines the previous year as its motivation. The Reading joined with the Pennsylvania in requests for fare increases in 1951, 1955 and 1957, citing declining ridership as the reason.

Despite these persistent efforts, events would demonstrate that both the service cutbacks and rate increases were inadequate responses to a fundamentally changing national as well as local landscape. Those Norristown residents who continued to ride the train to Philadelphia during this period suffered on two levels. First, the steadily decreasing number of the trains themselves and second, the repetitive increases in the cost of making the trip on those trains. Together, they combined to further reduce the numbers still riding the trains, continuing the vicious circle.

From Trolleys to Buses

While the nation's railroads were engaged in a desperate struggle, with local evidence in Norristown, the borough's remaining "light rail" connections were suffering from a condition even more acute than their heavy rail cousins. The last trolley ran north from Norristown in early September 1951, replaced by bus service. Thus ended the upper half of a trolley service between 69th Street Station in Philadelphia and Allentown that had begun in 1912. The Borough Council members' fears in the mid-1940s of being abandoned by the trolley companies and being left to pay for overdue roadwork turned out to be well founded. The Borough Council undertook negotiations with the Pennsylvania State Public Utility Commission over the course of several years following the trolley abandonment, seeking funds for the tracks' removal. The PUC declined. An agreement was finally reached in late July 1958 between the two entities when the state agreed to fund a portion of the cost.

The retirement of Harry S. Bergey in July 1956 provided a personal insight into both the era that was ending and the one taking its place. Bergey had begun work as a trolley motorman with the Reading Transit Company in 1917, making the night run from Chestnut Hill in Philadelphia to Boyertown, west of Norristown. When the Reading Transit Company trolleys were replaced by buses, Bergey became a bus driver after 16 years as a trolley motorman. He observed that being a motorman was easy, although cows could be a frequent nuisance. As a bus driver, things started easy but grew more difficult. "In the early days of the bus, it wasn't too much of a problem. There weren't too many cars on the road and the traffic problem was simple. But as the years went by, the cars and traffic increased, and so did the problems."[329]

The End of the P&W Bridge

With the trolleys gone, there was no more need for the P&W Bridge. Discussions began in 1951, and finally in the spring of 1953, the P&W offered a proposal: retain the old bridge, but abandon the station at Main and Swede streets and replace it with a small ticket office and waiting room at the north end of the bridge at Penn and Swede streets. The Borough Council denied the request, amid much bitterness over the run-down condition of the station and bridge. In February 1954, the P&W released preliminary plans for terminating the tracks on the south side of Main Street, and reinforcing the old P&W building structurally to allow the tracks to terminate there without the support of the bridge. In January 1955, the P&W formally petitioned for permission to demolish the bridge. The PUC agreed, and the big event took place September 28–29, 1955. On September 30, the *Times Herald* announced that the bridge was down, with only cleanup work on both ends remaining. With obvious pride, the paper reported, "An obstructed view on Main Street in Norristown's business district was possible, today, for the first time since 1912."[330] The large clock that had served as a focal point for the community ("meet me under the clock") was saved and installed on the Borough Hall.

Limited-Access Highways

While the railroad network that had nourished Norristown for over a century was deteriorating and all but disappearing, the network of limited-access highways that would replace it was taking shape in the Delaware Valley Region. In the first half of the 1950s, the Pennsylvania Turnpike pushed eastward to the Delaware River and over a bridge to connect to the New Jersey Turnpike, one of several such limited-access highways inspired by the original Pennsylvania Turnpike. Simultaneously, plans were announced for the Pennsylvania Turnpike's "Northeast Extension" connecting to the turnpike west of Norristown and up (eventually) to Scranton.

The bridge over the Delaware River that connected the Pennsylvania and New Jersey Turnpikes opened on May 25, 1956. The *Times Herald* article announcing the bridge's opening observed that by that time, progress on other state turnpikes had reached the point where it was possible to drive from New York City almost to Chicago on limited-access toll highways. Work on the Northeast Extension continued, and would for some time (a tunnel was needed in the Lehigh Gap section, and there was no pre-existing railroad tunnel to widen), but by 1956 the basic network of limited-access highways in Southeastern Pennsylvania seemed complete. It wasn't, but that construction took place after the period covered by this book.

As the regional network of limited-access highways began to develop, a quick glance at a map seemed to put Norristown at the region's core as the nexus of an increasingly wide-ranging highway network. A closer look would have revealed even then, however, something very different, and disturbing: Norristown's centrality was a myth. The highways did pass near the borough...but they did not actually connect with it. This was a fundamental difference from the spread of the railroads in the previous century; Norristown was directly connected with railroads, and they served to nourish its growth. The borough would never possess a truly direct connection with this new network of highways. The areas immediately adjacent to the local interchanges of these highways would find themselves connected, and the results of these connections would propel them into the new world of the automobile. It would be the exact opposite for Norristown.

The Pennsylvania Turnpike and the Schuylkill Expressway were the highways that would largely dictate Norristown's future. Their early impact—and their significance—are largely obscured by what was to follow shortly: the Interstate Highway System. The Interstate System would absorb the existing turnpikes and extend their reach beyond all original imagining. Yet it was these early limited-access highways, born of state inspiration (and federal funding) that would bring national recognition to the local term "King of Prussia," and bring ruin to Main Street, Norristown.

A Missed Opportunity?

Norristown showed an immediate, intense interest when the Pennsylvania Turnpike Commission proposed in March 1952 to extend the route from King of Prussia to the Delaware River, skirting Norristown proper and crossing the Schuylkill just east of the borough; an interchange with Ridge Pike would be located less than one-half mile from the borough's eastern boundary. Objections were raised in Upper Merion, Plymouth, and Whitemarsh Townships about the route as it passed through each, but in Norristown the objection was to the interchange.

The Borough Council met on April 17 to consider the issue. It unanimously passed Resolution 1011 opposing the interchange. The full text of the resolution is printed here (complete with typographic error):

> WHEREAS, the Pennsylvania Turnpike Commission has announced the route of the Delaware River Extension from King of Prussia to join the New Jersey Super Highway, and WHEREAS, the present plans call for the location of an interchange on Ridge Pike at a point about 0.7 of a mile southeast of Norristown, and WHEREAS, it is the feeling of the Norristown Borough Council that increased traffic congestion will result on Main Street, Norristown, because of the interchange being located on ridge Pike, east of Norristown, to the detriment of Norristown merchants and

business, Therefore be it RESOLVED, that the Norristown Borough Council go on record as favoring the location of an interchange onto the Delaware River Extension of the Pennsylvania Turnpike in the Germantown Pike area, Plymout [sic] Township and not at Ridge Pike, southeast of Norristown.[331]

The sole reason given for this opposition was increased traffic congestion, though there were clearly broader, if unspoken, reasons. Former mayor and longtime political activist William DeAngelis adamantly described Paul Santangelo's vociferous opposition to the proposal, saying that the interchange had not been built "because [Santangelo] didn't want it."[332] Santangelo was among the most vocal opponents to the interchange, and DeAngelis's assessment of the situation rings true: Santangelo *always* opposed *any* proposal that might have weakened his political control over his electoral ward. The proposed interchange would have placed his Fifth Ward clearly in the crosshairs of powerful real estate developers. Whatever the result might be, the Fifth Ward as he had known it would be irrevocably changed, and most likely not to his benefit. Santangelo was hardly alone in his objections, however. The Borough Council's unanimous passage of the resolution testifies that. Even Harry Butera opposed the interchange, a curious stand given his earlier analysis of Norristown's pending isolation, and testimony to the virtually unanimous local feelings.[333]

Norristown's arguments won quick and firm support from the Montgomery County Planning Commission, which adopted a resolution calling for the intersection to be located instead at Germantown Pike, north of Ridge Pike. David D. Longmaid, the commission's executive director, used the 1949 Traffic Survey to make his case. He pointed out that in 1949 through traffic already constituted 45% of traffic on already-overloaded Main Street, which would be unable to handle the additional traffic: an interchange at Ridge Pike, in his estimation, "would render Norristown's Main Street worthless as a shopping area."[334]

The Turnpike Commission turned conciliatory, and the proposed interchange quietly disappeared from the plan for the Delaware Extension and was relocated at Germantown Pike as had been suggested by both the borough and the County Planning Commission. Though the interchange would be formally designated the Norristown Interchange, it did not actually connect to Norristown, nor to any main road entering Norristown. For the next several decades, drivers new to the area who exited at the Norristown Interchange and failed to see the small signs at several Germantown Pike intersections could easily miss Norristown entirely.

The question of what might have happened had the Pennsylvania Turnpike built its Norristown Interchange adjacent to Norristown lies only in the realm of speculation. The general decline might have continued unchanged. An interchange at the East End of Norristown might also have accelerated the decline of Main Street. But it is also possible that the East End of Norristown would have grown dramatically, as King of Prussia and Plymouth Meeting did in the decades to come. If anything like the appreciation in land values and uses that occurred at both those locations had also happened just east of Norristown, the borough as a whole would have benefited, and perhaps some of that new wealth and energy might have jump-started the dying batteries of downtown. But it was not to be.

Decline: By the Numbers

The 12 years between the 1951 and 1963 editions of the *Polk City Directory*, the basic reference source drawn upon by this book for indicators of the life and health of Norristown's downtown, provide ample raw data to isolate, quantify and analyze the changing status of Main Street before the opening of the King of Prussia Plaza. The data from those seven directories revealed that Main Street was already in the throes of a broad and alarming decline long before the appearance of the malls. The 1955 directory revealed few differences from the 1951 edition: total entries dropped from 524 to 496, while the number of storefronts had actually risen, from 209 to 215. Given the statistical imprecision of the directories, this amounts to no change. Thus, it can be argued the "Period of Stability" identified by the *Norristown Study* extended from 1950 to at least 1954. The following summary of the 23 categories through the 1963 Directory (there were no Auto Sales entries after 1951, nor Government-State entries after 1957) illustrates the widespread nature of Main Street's decline prior to any competition from the malls:

Directory Year	1951	1963	Net Change	% Change
Total Entries	524	460	-64	(12%)
Storefronts	209	193	-16	(8%)
Category				
Auto Service	4	2	-2	(50%)
Bank	4	5	+1	25%
Company Office	17	12	-5	(29%)
Financial Service	15	16	+1	7%
Food Service	19	15	-4	(21%)
Government, County	2	1	-1	(50%)
Government, Federal	2	2	-	—
Grocery Store/Market	9	3	-6	(67%)
Hotel	4	2	-2	(50%)
Manufacturing	2	2	-	—
Other/Unknown	4	2	-2	(50%)
Parking Lot	1	1	-	—
Professional Office	50	37	-13	(26%)
Retail-Department Store	15	7	-8	(53%)
Retail-Specialty	114	102	-12	(11%)
School	3	1	-2	(67%)
Service-Professional	14	2	-12	(86%)
Service-Trades	26	20	-6	(23%)
Tavern	4	7	+3	75%
Theater	3	1	-2	(67%)

(continued)				
Directory Year	**1951**	**1963**	**Net Change**	**% Change**
Transportation	3	1	-2	(67%)
Wholesale	1	1	-	—
No Return/Vacant*	14	36	+22	157%

Adjusted number, accounts for addresses disappearing temporarily from Directory

The most significant number among those above is the rise of the number of No Return/Vacant entries. This combined category contains both Storefront and non-Storefront entries (a single-room residence might be listed as "Vacant" for example), so certain distinctions need to be drawn. They will be. First, it should be pointed out that this category of No Return/Vacant is the only category that was adjusted across the 12-year period covered by the directories to account for the Main Street addresses that disappeared intermittently from the directories. The No Return/Vacant category thus reflects more closely the actual reality of Main Street. The 1951 Directory listed 14 No Return/Vacant entries; 9 were storefronts. By 1963, these entries would increase to 36, 21 of which were storefronts. The raw number of No Return/Vacant entries would thus increase by 157%; the number of storefronts listed as No Return/Vacant would increase by 133%.

Sadly, the category of Parking Lot was never accurately reported in the directories. Acme Market's lot is the only consistent entry. The reality on Main Street was different, however, and that difference increased over time, as buildings began to come down and not be replaced. Small and very unofficial parking lots would thus appear, although not be listed in any Directory. The actual number of such lots cannot be determined with any accuracy.

Another sad and closely related subject not revealed by the city directories adds to the already-depressing picture: the number of buildings razed and not replaced. These addresses simply disappeared from the directory. Their numbers must be inferred from a combination of tracking the fate of each address and reference to news stories. Most of the interviewees recalled that many more buildings were torn down in the 1970s and 1980s, but the process had already begun in the late 1950s.

A Good Beginning

Despite the losses of a few downtown businesses here and there, the early 1950s were overall rather prosperous years. Each year in that period the *Times Herald* published annual summaries prepared by *Sales Management* magazine that compared Norristown's economic situation with that of the rest of the nation. These reports were invariably bullish, ranking Norristown high in volume of retail sales, even in a national context. The optimistic report that opened the decade in 1951 again ranked the borough high as a consumer market, indicating the overall prosperity of its residents. By 1953, the annual report indicated that not only had retail sales increased over the previous year, but sales figures indicated that "Norristown families generally earn more than their counterparts throughout the country."

140

The 1954 Federal Census of Business confirmed the picture of increasing prosperity, revealing that retail sales in Norristown increased 49.2% during the six-year period from 1948 to 1954. This exceeded the overall figure for Montgomery County of 46.7%. Within Pennsylvania during the same period, Montgomery County was second only to Delaware County in retail sales, and Norristown Borough was second only to York.[335] Thus, statistically speaking, downtown showed stability. Changes in the overall data and the individual categories were attributable to the coming and going of individual businesses, and there were no major alterations in the numbers of any significant category. Two department stores disappeared: the Quaker City store at 120 East Main Street and the Kresge location at 4 East Main Street. The former was but one of the smaller, lower-priced stores to come and go on Main Street. S.S. Kresge was a well-known national concern, but the Kresge store at 4 East Main Street had become redundant since the store at 64 East Main Street had opened. Downtown also lost its last auto dealer, with Walter Wood closing up shop, making him Main Street's last-ever entry in the Auto Sales category.

In late 1951, downtown witnessed one last memory of an older time, and yet another intrusion of the new. In November came the news that the Mitchell brothers, Morris G. and Herbert D., had sold their residence at 35 East Main Street to two Norristown businessmen, who planned to convert it into stores. The building had housed the Mitchell family for over 60 years, but the house had been an anachronism for much longer than that, as the only solely residential building on the first block of Main Street. The last such house on the south side of the block had been converted into a business back in 1850. Somewhat earlier, the new had intruded with the application by the Montgomery National Bank to construct Main Street's first "drive in" banking window at its 110 West Main Street. In September, the Borough Council approved the request, allowing the construction of a driveway on the west side of the building from Main to Lafayette streets. The work was completed and the new drive-in window opened in March of 1952.

Downtown's statistical stability during this period is deceiving, of course. The stores there were not all of equal importance to downtown. In late 1952, rumors that had long been circulating turned out to be true: the Sears store at 227 West Main Street was closing. This was a major blow to downtown, for two reasons. First, it removed a major retail presence from downtown. Sears was the best-known of the national "chain stores"; Sears had first opened its Norristown store in late 1933, in the depths of the Depression. Now, with an unprecedented period of national prosperity getting under way, downtown had to face the fact that one of its biggest presences was leaving. By the numbers, Sears represented only one storefront (the Sears catalog order shop in the Curren Arcade at 51 East Main Street remained open until 1956), but it was a big store. An important store. The departure of Sears was a major blow to Main Street; Sears had been a bulwark of Main Street's western end, traditionally less prestigious than its core, and less patronized than its eastern end, and thus even more important.

The second blow was its choice for its new Norristown location, already touched on earlier: Sears was moving to Logan Square. The decision by Sears to stay in Norristown but to leave Main Street was perhaps the loudest, most visible warning that the downtown was in trouble. The November announcement to the public was starkly clear as to the reasons for the move:

> Sears, Roebuck and Co. will move its Norristown store to the Logan Square shopping center where their customers will be afforded free and ample parking facilities and three times more floor space than its present store.[336]

Sears needed two things in Norristown: room to expand their floor space, and adjacent free parking for patrons who were arriving at its store in private automobiles. *Free and ample parking.* Main Street could provide neither. Sears would not be the last to come to this conclusion.

Less than a year after Sears announced its departure from West Main Street, another West End institution closed, though this one did not reopen elsewhere. The Garrick Theater and the three storefronts between 212 and 224 West Main Street were sold by their owners, Norris Amusement Company (the Sablosky brothers). Included in the deal was another Norris-owned and -operated theater, the WestMar, and its two shops at 704 West Marshall Street, as well as a garage and a parking lot at Lafayette and Barbadoes streets. The entire package was sold to the "unnamed client" of a local attorney, with the provision that neither movies nor live theater were to be offered in either theater location by the new owners.

The loss of this aging component of downtown cannot be blamed entirely on either traffic or parking problems. The movie-theater experience had come under assault from the new medium of television, and moviegoers had a far grander place to view what movies they did see at the Norris Theater on West Main Street. Still, the departure of these storefronts would open a sore on West Main Street that would never really heal. The Garrick and its storefronts were torn down in 1954, and the site converted into an automobile service station with adjoining parking. Edward Hocker began his sad obituary for a Norristown institution this way: "Space for automobiles is needed more and more these days, so the Garrick Theater, Main Street below Markley, has been demolished and the site is to be a parking lot."[337] This razing and conversion of the site meant the net loss of three businesses along West Main Street, a loss that was permanent.

The County Comes to Main Street

Main Street faced two challenges in the period leading up the sesquicentennial, one external and one internal. The external threat came from the individual stores, strip malls, and shopping centers that were increasingly beginning to appear in the borough's immediate environs. That external threat was diverse and diffuse, and its true impact cannot be accurately measured. It would continue to gather strength and eat away at downtown's commercial position.

The internal threat was very different. It was unitary, and its effect on Main Street can be measured quite precisely, at least in terms of businesses lost. The source of this internal threat was the government of Montgomery County, although a simple comparison of the numbers in the Government-County category in the 1951 directory to those in the 1963 directory completely obscures its impact on Main Street. The actions of the government of Montgomery County constituted a severe and lasting body blow to the commercial health of Main Street. That blow would arrive in two stages, several years apart, but it was one blow nevertheless.

It began in 1954. Planning for a much-needed county courthouse expansion had been "in the works" for several years. County officials looking for room to expand in the immediate area of the courthouse had debated two obvious alternatives: to the east, along East Airy Street east of the existing annex, or to the west across Swede Street to the site mostly occupied by the Rambo House, a decidedly run-down hotel. Expansion to the east would follow in the familiar pattern; the country had built the previous courthouse extension on land along the south side of Airy Street, some of which it had purchased as early as 1871. It already purchased a portion of the land needed should the expansion be eastward, the former site of the Montgomery Hose Company, when the firehouse moved in 1938.

As the decade dawned, courthouse expansion planning centered on this eastern alternative. The perceived space requirements steadily increased under pressure from county officials, however, and by the end of 1953, the project's scope had already increased several times. County commissioners Fred C. Peters, Foster C. Hillegas, and Raymond K. Mensch formally announced in January 1954 that they had abandoned plans for the eastward extension along Airy Street, saying, "We are now considering other plans." While the commissioners did not elaborate, the *Times Herald* did, indicating that the negotiations were not exactly secret. "Court House observers believe the County authorities are 'eying' the acquisition of the property which housed the former Montgomery Trust Company, which extends from Main Street to Penn Street, and the Historical Society of Montgomery County building, adjacent to the bank building on Penn Street."[338]

This made some sense. The Historical Society was already planning to move to a property on DeKalb Street in the North End. The Montgomery Trust Co. had recently merged with the Norristown-Penn Trust Co. and was now, as the Montgomery Norristown Bank and Trust Co., in the process of transferring most of its banking activities to the large building at Swede and Main. This made it amenable for an offer not only for the bank building itself, but for the Arcade next door, which it owned.

Indicators seemed to confirm this was the county's plan. In February the HSMC sold its building on Penn Street to the Montgomery-Norristown Bank and Trust Co., with the provision that the bank would sell the property to the county at no increase in price. The Society's Board of Directors had approached the county commissioners directly, and had found them "genuinely interested in buying the property, but not ready to enter into any transaction."[339] The bank obviously believed the same thing.

The county's extension southward onto Main Street, claimed a *Times Herald* article in January, would save the taxpayers upwards of $12 million, as "it would be considerably cheaper for the County to modify those buildings for use than to buy the church property, raze the former fire house, and erect a new building."[340] This was an attractive point in favor of expansion onto Main Street. The county government naturally wished to keep taxes low. And by mid-summer, an agreement was in place. The county announced that it was purchasing the Montgomery Trust Bank and the Montgomery Trust Arcade on Main Street, and the HSMC building on Penn Street, for $665,000. The county commissioners were proud to point out that they had in one stroke both relieved the overcrowding problem *and* saved the taxpayers at least two and a half million dollars by purchasing rather than building.

In their announcement, the commissioners went even further, however, claiming that in addition to alleviating the existing overcrowded conditions, " [the purchase] will give us plenty of office space to expand in the future."[341] There is reason to question the sincerity of this claim for a long-term solution. It is difficult, in fact, to see this decision in retrospect as anything more than a decision to postpone making a decision. The bank and the arcade would certainly serve to ease the pressure for a period of time, but the addition of three buildings, each showing their age, cannot realistically have been considered a long-term solution. The HSMC building, after all, was the original Borough Hall, and dated back to 1884.

In addition, it was by now clear that despite the claims for the future of the Main Street buildings, further planning on a greater scale was already under way. The same press conference in which the commissioners had claimed that the three buildings would provide "plenty" of office space for future expansion also produced an interesting—not to mention contrary—admission. Speaking specifically of the Montgomery Trust Arcade (which dated back to 1908), the Commissioners conceded, "However, eventually it may be torn down, and until the county needs the area for building space, it may be used as a parking lot."[342] It is reasonable to infer from this that while the physical nature of the county's intrusion onto Main Street was yet uncertain, its presence would likely be permanent.

Settlement occurred in mid-December when the county formally took title to all three buildings. Renovations would begin on the HSMC building immediately, on the Arcade once the last of the existing tenants' leases had run out, and on the Montgomery Trust Company building in July 1956. In the meantime, the county tried to address its need for employee parking by razing the former Montgomery Hose Company building on East Penn Street. Even with that new parking lot, it was not long before pressure began to build for still more parking spaces.

It was not until 1961 that a coherent plan was presented to county residents. The formal announcement came in October. As long had been expected, the plan called for the razing of both 25 and 29 East Main Street—the bank and the Montgomery Trust Arcade building. By now however, the scope of the project had again expanded at the expense of Main Street. The county announced that it would purchase the two properties to the east of the Arcade. These were 35 East Main Street, the long-time Mitchell residence now occupied by the Paris Linen Shop (with offices above), and 37 East Main Street, occupied by Schnably's Men's Store (also with offices above). The new administration building would extend across these four properties back to Penn Street. Construction was set to begin in the spring of 1962, and completion before the end of

1963. This was ambitious, particularly since responsibility for these country government expenditures was shared between the county executive and county judiciary, with
a county court needing to approve both construction plans and payment of costs.

The county commissioners directly addressed the concern over the project's effect
on downtown, proclaiming, "The new administration building and proposed governmental center will add to the health and well-being of Norristown. Its construction
will enhance and increase property value on Main Street, the community's major artery."[343] Exactly how this would happen was not discussed. The county commissioners
merely repeated the alternative if downtown expansion was rejected, and added a vague
assurance about replacing the lost storefronts. They drew attention to the fact that they
had decided to remain in Norristown itself, rather than avail themselves of an alternate
location elsewhere (a county-owned farm that straddled East and West Norriton had
been mentioned). The press release featured this theme, proclaiming with much fanfare
that the expansion downtown was in fact "a debt of gratitude to Norristown, the
County seat, historically, traditionally and geographically."[344] It also attempted to address, vaguely, concerns over the loss of storefronts to Main Street and tax revenue to
the borough. The developing plans were reported to include shops on the ground floor
of the new building's five-story Main Street frontage, to be rented to businesses. This
would ostensibly restore both the borough's revenue and downtown's appearance.

Regardless of how the matter was phrased and whatever future considerations were
promised, the razing of four buildings at downtown's core was a severe blow. The net
loss was 22 businesses, 5 of them storefronts, and all in the middle of downtown. Replacing them with storefronts in the new building would have mitigated the blow—if
that new building had ever been built. But it was not to be.

The Damage to Main Street

The county's takeover of two Main Street locations significantly, and negatively, affected the very core of downtown Norristown. The 1953 Directory had three entries
for 25 East Main Street, the Montgomery Trust Company building: the bank, an attorney, and a notary. The directory listed 28 entries at the Montgomery Trust Arcade at
29 East Main Street, of which two were vacant.

By the time the 1955 directory was being compiled, there had been a 100% turnover in building tenants in the Montgomery Trust Arcade. The 1955 directory had 13
entries for the Arcade, one of them No Return. The Federal Government had two offices, both occupied this time by military service recruiters. The remaining 10 were
bureaus of the county government. The bank continued a bare existence at 25 East
Main Street, but would disappear by the time the 1957 directory was being compiled.
The bank's ancillary services had ceased in 1953, thus removing both the listings for
an attorney and a notary.

The taxpayers' money may well have been saved, but the county's action was a blow
to downtown commerce. The purchase of the properties and removal of the commercial and professional tenants cost downtown a total of 20 businesses and the offices of
two unions and one fraternal organization, all in the very core of downtown itself. The

county continued to occupy the buildings at 25 and 29 East Main Street for the remainder of the decade. As the planning process continued on its tortuous and slow path, the county fell behind in maintenance of its buildings. Three vacant storefronts at downtown's core gradually began to be three increasingly shabby and run-down buildings falling to ruin—a major embarrassment in the heart of Norristown's commercial district.

The Interval: 1954–1960

The county's intrusion onto Main Street was mainly reflected in the changes in the two affected addresses, but it had broader results. The 1955 City Directory reported that total entries continued to decline, from 512 to 496. This decline would prove to be continuous for decades, but no one at the time seemed aware of the attrition. Despite the county's elimination of three storefronts, the directory recorded a net gain of one, reaching 215. This would prove to be highest number in any of the directories consulted for the 12-year period between 1951 and 1963. After 1955, Storefronts joined Total Entries in declining.

Yet the band played on. The *Times Herald* continued to speak with confidence about Norristown's economic future, trumpeting *Sales Management* magazine's annual issue for 1955 on its front page. The magazine reported that the total volume of Norristown's retail sales in 1955 exceeded that of 1954 by just under $4 million. Of course, that figure applied to the borough as a whole: there was no breakdown of the figures between the downtown area and the rest of Norristown, which by that time included not only the western shopping area on Marshall Street but also Logan Square as hubs of retail activity.

The Chamber of Commerce did its part to promote optimism, sponsoring the annual joint sales event in July that had become a fixture of downtown. The 1955 event's theme was "Downtown Norristown Progress Sales Days," and was held on Friday and Saturday, July 22–23. The event promised both "Sensational Savings" and a contest to win a free trip to Nassau, the Bahamas. The *Times Herald* promotional article on July 19 said that 103 stores would be participating in the event. One significant change, and a nod to the pressing problems, was that the 1955 event included free bus transportation to the downtown shopping district. In promoting this feature, the article walked a fine line along the parking problem, and tried to have it both ways. It advocated using the bus, "thus avoiding the problem of finding a parking space for the family car, although there's plenty of parking space on lots at the rear of many stores."[345]

The period after the 1955 could not be as easily whitewashed, however. The numbers before 1955 had been more down than up, but not so dramatically that they were obvious signs to the average Norristown resident. The statistical changes between the 1955 and 1957 directories, however, begin to paint precisely this picture of slow decline. Total entries dropped from 496 to 475; more significantly, Storefronts demonstrated their first decline since 1951, dropping from 215 to 211. Retail Specialty Stores also dropped, from 118 to 112; Grocery Store/Markets declined from 8 to 5. The categories of Company Office, Financial Service, and Service-Trades all recorded small losses of one or two. Main Street gained an additional bank, but this "gain" was illusory, as Philadelphia National Bank added simply added its Penn Centre Branch listing to the Montgomery Office already listed at 110 West Main Street. The consolidated category of Food Service rose by one but once again, this number showed only the net gain and did not reflect the many "sub" and "zep" shops that come and gone during the year.

A significant reason to date the beginning of slow decline with the 1957 directory is found in the (adjusted) category of No Return/Vacant. This significant, and very noticeable, category recorded its first real rise, increasing from 16 to 20—19 of them Storefronts. The reason could be found on West Main Street, where several businesses had encountered hard times in the wake of Sears' departure. The previous year had seen the quick decline of the properties between Continental Baking Company at 257 West Main Street and the former Sears store at 227 West Main Street. Five storefronts clustered around the old Milner Hotel at 231 West Main Street closed down, including a small restaurant, a second-hand furniture store, and the hotel itself. The properties were supposed to be auctioned off in December, but the auction was postponed due to lack of bidders. No one wanted the dilapidated old buildings. Not too surprisingly, in 1958, the buildings at 231 through 237 West Main Street were torn down and converted into parking, another lot never acknowledged in the directories. Only Gus's Steak Shop, at 239 West Main Street, survived that particular architectural massacre. The net physical loss to downtown was four storefronts. The loss was permanent.

In 1956, the Central Montgomery County Chamber of Commerce formed a Downtown Norristown Merchants Division (DNMD). Elected to head up the new subdivision was Morton "Bubby" Weiss, owner of a Main Street clothing shop. Weiss would prove to be another major personal asset to downtown in the years ahead, and not just in his role as president of the DNMD. And downtown received *some* positive news in 1956. In September, 150 West Main Street, which for the last 40 years had housed the Boston Store, was sold to James V. Bondi, owner of a furniture store at Arch and Chestnut streets. Bondi, a Norristown veteran who had opened his Arch Street store in 1927, demonstrated his confidence in downtown Norristown by moving his store to the new location. The building had a rear alley to Lafayette Street, essential in Bondi's case as it allowed him to move his furniture stock in and out through the rear. While statistically this was a wash, in reality it constituted a step up. Bondi, who moved his store to the Main Street location "because it was the place where everyone shopped," would prove to be a lasting and active component of downtown through the hard times ahead.[346]

Most of the news was not good, though. In December 1956 yet another downtown institution failed. The prominent and architecturally unique Gus Egolf Furniture Store at 113 East Main Street, a fixture downtown since 1893, closed after the death of its owner. The surviving owners sold the building and the stock inside.

The Lincoln Hotel followed the Milner into extinction in early 1957, when the property extending from 201 to 215 West Main Street was leased to an out-of-towner, Frederick S. Veterlein of Baltimore. Unlike the Milner, whose dilapidated buildings still tarnished the downtown for another year, the Lincoln Hotel and adjacent stores were torn down quickly. The razing of the Lincoln Hotel removed the last vestiges of John Bull's original Mansion House. Five storefronts, including the hotel, were torn down and replaced by—naturally—more parking, plus a gas station and, in place of what had been the Lincoln Tire Store, a Firestone Tire Store. This was physical net loss of four storefronts. While the razing proceeded quickly, the remodeling at 215 West Main Street took some time. The finished Veterlein Firestone Tire Store did not open until May 1958. By 1960, both the Milner and the Lincoln hotels had disappeared. The two remaining Main Street hotels now represented the extremes: the Valley Forge Hotel and Arena's Hotel.

Between 1955 and 1957, four more storefronts disappeared from the 200 block of West Main Street. Two addresses on either side of the service station at 220 West Main Street were torn down and converted into…yes, parking lots. Again, the parking lots failed to be accounted for in subsequent directories, and thus the addresses simply disappeared from the listings. Again, the loss was permanent.

By this time, Main Street's merchants had a clear understanding of the problems facing them, despite the optimistic phrasing of most of their public quotations. So did the broader economic and political groups within Norristown, and many of the residents. The *Times Herald*, which had tried to balance boosterism about the present with every scrap of hope for the future that could be reported, announced in March 1957 that there would be a meeting of a brand new organization calling itself The Committee for Civic Progress. This new group, advertising itself as a non-political, non-partisan group of people interested in the future of Norristown, met at the Valley Forge Hotel. They quickly identified and ranked the three major goals: (1) "Solution of the Downtown Parking Problem"; (2) "Elimination of Traffic Congestion and Bottlenecks"; and (3) "An Additional Bridge over the Schuylkill." The *Times Herald* article reported that the group was sketching out a 12-point program to attack these problems.[347] Whatever that program was, it never saw print in the *Times Herald*; in fact, the group was never heard from again. The problems facing Norristown in the mid-1950s were clear; the solutions were not.

The year 1958 was, at least according to the *Times Herald*, a good year for Norristown's business community, particularly in contrast to the national economic slowdown. In May, the paper again featured an article from *Sales Management* magazine in which it declared the Norristown area (with no definition of exactly what that comprised) as a "retail sales market area that will go against the national recessional trend for this month." The magazine's complex formula for ranking retail sales areas rated Norristown as one of the 59 "high spot" cities in the country.[348] Presumably the calculation covered an area greater than Main Street and downtown.

In July 1958, the Montgomery County Bank and Trust Company announced plans to open another "drive-in" bank, this time at the corner of East Main and Mill streets, the former site of Walter Wood automobile sales. A lane for traffic was constructed between Main and Lafayette streets so that when the new bank opened in June 1959, patrons could do their banking without leaving their cars. Automobiles had truly taken over Norristown.

In 1958, Joseph J. Zummo, founder of the hardware store that had for so long been a Norristown institution, lost his long battle with cancer at age 74.[349] The store was prospering, and the family had just purchased Harry Lutz's tire store next door, at 261 East Main Street, to use for storage. While this lowered Main Street's number of storefronts and Specialty Retailers by one, it was still a gain for the downtown, as it helped another commercial enterprise dig in, survive, and prosper. Zummo's sons Anthony, Vincent, Charles, and Paul were already running the hardware business by then, and Anthony already nursed dreams of even further expansion.[350]

Zummo's death was followed not long by the loss of another familiar downtown figure. In September, less than two weeks before the 66th anniversary of Chatlin's Department Store, Ida Chatlin, widow of Samuel Chatlin, died. After opening their first store in 1892, the Chatlins had slowly built their business on East Main Street. Ida had retired along with Samuel in 1926 when their son Morris took over the business. Then in February 1959, news broke that *Times Herald* owner and publisher Ralph Beaver Strassburger had died in Paris. His 1921 purchase and merger of the other Norristown newspapers had resulted in a local newspaper monopoly, but one that had reflected a viewpoint that was consistently local, if not always consistent.

Perhaps it was the shock of so many deaths in a short period, but something shook up the downtown merchants. In 1959, after edging toward the concept for years with their annual sales events, they formally adopted an inclusive and year-round promotional program that would employ consistent advertising, emphasizing the periodic special sales events. In announcing the new approach, stationer Maurice A. Ziegler, then Chairman of the downtown merchants division of the Chamber of Commerce, minced no words: "One of your prime duties is to revitalize downtown Norristown, to return the glamour to Main Street."[351] As it turned out, Ziegler himself would not be lending his own hand to those efforts: four days later, just after closing his store for the day, Ziegler collapsed and died.

The *Times Herald* addressed the issue of revitalizing downtown in an editorial in September, but only with the underlying purpose of promoting advertising in the *Times Herald*. The editorial quoted an article in the *Windsor Missouri Review* that said, "The chief competitors of the small city retailer are not other local merchants. His most serious competition comes from nearby metropolitan centers." Then came the disturbing question: if prices are generally the same everywhere, and if low overhead sometimes gives the small city merchant an advantage, "Why, then, do so many shoppers travel 50 or a 100 miles to buy the same items they could obtain at home for the same price?" Unfortunately, the *Review*'s answer to its self-posed question was limited to "inadequate advertising." This allowed the *Times Herald* to make its point that "the local newspaper is the outstanding medium for the retailer."[352] The larger issues—ease of access and parking—may have been avoided in both articles, but it was certainly on the minds of Norristown's Main Street retailers.

Although the editorial cast events in a positive light, 1959 provided substantial if indirect evidence of the difficulty Main Street merchants faced with respect to getting financial help from the borough government. The May 1959 primary election reminded the elected officials of that government—in no uncertain terms—that they represented a conservative constituency almost reflexively opposed to increased borough expenditures. With a number of long-postponed improvements becoming necessary, the Borough Council had unanimously approved an $800,000 bond issue and submitted it to the voters for approval at the May 19 primary election. The bond issue was to fund several projects, including a new Borough Hall on East Airy Street.

Despite the unanimous vote of the Borough Council and the support of many local organizations, the voters decisively rejected the measure. It was not even close, and it was consistent: *all* of Norristown's voting districts rejected the proposal. Although no one seems to have made the connection at the time, at least in print, the subtext seemed to be that a council that could not even raise enough support among its constituents to replace its own decrepit meeting structure was not likely to commit tax revenue toward aiding a "special interest" such as the Main Street merchants.

By the publication of the 1960 directory, the No Return/Vacant category had risen by seven from the 1957 directory to 27; 24 of these were storefronts or, in some cases, newly vacant lots. In fact, by 1960 the number of vacant or not responding storefronts listed had almost tripled from the directory from 1951, and risen 10 just since 1957. The 24 vacant or non-responding storefronts in the 1960 directory were almost evenly divided between east and west, with 13 on East Main and 11 on West Main. The East Main Street entries present the occasional location spread out along the three blocks, with the only contiguous sites the Montgomery Trust Bank and the Montgomery Arcade, now merely "Vacant" entries. The Grand Theater had closed, and was now in the directory reported as Vacant.

The West Main Street entries presented a similar picture for the first two blocks. Then there was a substantial gap between the Continental Baking Company and the site of the old Sears store. Numbers 231, 235, 237, and 239 West—the old Milner Hotel and the small business near it—were all now Vacant. This was the first substantial gap in what had been for many decades a solid lineup of stores along both sides of downtown Main Street. The lack of any investors wanting to use the old buildings was by no means surprising, but for the site itself to remain undeveloped did not bode well for Main Street or for Norristown in general.

Another gap had in fact opened on Main Street, one that the ebb and flow of business would disguise in the city directories, but which was clearly visible to those passing by, even if they missed the symbolism. The old Lincoln Hotel, again with associated small businesses, had been sold and replaced by a Firestone store for auto parts and service, and a substantial area for parking cars being services. This single new business replaced five former businesses, and their street addresses simply disappeared. By the end of the 1950s, property on West Main Street could reap more value as a parking lot for a single business repairing automobiles could several businesses combined. This was just one of the many unpleasant discoveries to come.

For Main Street merchants—and the older residents of Norristown in particular—1960 was a big year for loss. Two familiar landmarks changed hands. One then crumbled under the wrecking ball and the other, though it remained standing, crumbled in its own way. The year was but a few days old when the *Times Herald* revealed the shocking news about Norristown's most storied commercial business site. The D. M. Yost Dry Goods Store building had passed out of the Yost family in 1946, and by the 1950s had ceased to be a major presence on Main Street in terms of retail sales, but it still loomed large in the collective memory of the town. Many of the older residents still thought of the southeast corner of Main and DeKalb as Yost's Corner. So there was widespread dismay when the community learned that as part of a complicated deal between local merchants Novell's and Dial Shoe Company (54 and 56 East Main Street, respectively), Yost's would not only close, but the building would be torn down. Indeed, after knocking the old building down, Dial Shoe Company opened its store in a new building. That was good news, in a way, but still very unsettling for the town: there was no longer a Yost's at Yost's corner.

Main Street had hardly had time to digest the news about the Yost building it was hit with another salvo of bad news. An even bigger—if newer—Main Street landmark was going out of business. The Norris Amusement Company announced in January that it had leased the Grand Theater at 67 East Main Street to John's Bargain Stores, Inc. Residents were shocked. They knew that the Grand Theater had fallen on hard times, but it was still a firm part of the childhood memories of local residents. It was hard to imagine it as just another five-and-dime. But it was. The new tenant leveled the floor and installed a suspended ceiling below the balcony and loge seats, transforming the hall into one large open area for retail sales. This was a sad comedown by any standard. Though the directory would show a new Department Store entry, downtown Norristown can hardly said to have gained anything. Interviewees remember John's Bargain Store as cheap, tawdry and disorganized.[353]

Between 1960 and 1961, the organization of Norristown borough merchants reached a new level of cooperation. This in itself is testimony to the decline of Main Street, as by now The Central Montgomery Chamber of Commerce featured three Norristown subgroups, representing Main Street, Marshall Street, and Logan Square. Main Street had long regarded Marshall Street as an inferior location (with considerable justification), but the rapid emergence of Logan Square was an entirely different matter. The three merchants' organizations opened the Christmas shopping season with an unprecedented demonstration of cooperation, simultaneously turning on the Christmas lights at all three centers on Thanksgiving Eve.

Cooperation extended further in 1961, as what were by now commonly referred to as "Norristown's three major shopping districts" coordinated not only their light displays, but agreed to be open identical hours during the Christmas shopping season, twelve hours, 9 a.m. to 9 p.m. For individual stores that competed against one another, and shopping areas that did the same on a broader scale, this was a remarkable display of unity. The reason of course, was obvious: whatever their locally competitive status, they shared common enemies in the similar stores by now proliferating within a few miles of the borough. The *Times Herald* joined the unified approach, publishing a late November editorial in which it again urged shoppers to buy locally and not be enticed by stores away from the area.

The Valley Forge Hotel

The fortunes of the Valley Forge Hotel between 1950 and 1962 followed much the same pattern as for downtown as a whole. The years through the middle of the decade were among the most profitable period in the hotel's history, with 1951's net profit of $33,404.94 the best ever, breaking the record set in 1950. Net profits declined slowly in 1952–1954, but in 1954 the corporation paid not one but two dividends to stockholders. Then 1955 saw the first serious decline in net profits, to $28,770.46, followed by another drop, to $27,619.12 for 1956. The hotel's reported net profits would decline through the latter half of the decade, to $20,278.96.[354] The reality behind the figures is murky. It is clear that the hotel's expenses were carefully managed. Renovations were phased in; air conditioning, for example, was spread over several years. Actual figures were missing, however, from 6 of the 11 annual reports up to 1962. The breakdown of expenses was even more incomplete, and often missing. From the data available it appears that income from room rentals continued in the tradition of underachievement it had long ago established, hovering around 35% of gross income and never exceeding 37%.

A lack of specific financial information in the annual *Times Herald* articles about the annual meeting of the Valley Forge Hotel Directors and Stockholders inhibits detailed analysis of the hotel's status during the period of the late 1950s. The figures, while incomplete, nevertheless suggest that the not much had changed: income for room rentals lagged dismally behind sales of food and beverages, and function room rentals. This had only grown worse with the promulgation of new motels appearing in King of Prussia.[355] There was one highlight in 1960: presidential candidate John F. Kennedy came to town in October and appeared at a rally at Roosevelt Field. Afterward the politicking, he spent the night in a suite in the Valley Forge Hotel.

The annual article for 1961 posted the best financial figures the hotel had seen for a long time—or would ever see again. This was achieved, as Manager Andrew Malone made clear, despite the fact that, "This hotel has a lot of competition, for both rooms and functions, with 1,050 motel units in the area."[356]

10

Power Struggles

Norristown spent the 1950s engaged in struggles on several fronts, but the chief battle involved problems stemming from a fundamental change in transportation. Americans, including those in Norristown, loved their automobiles. Yet other struggles beset Norristown at this same time, reflecting other changes in post-WWII America. Two of these, the struggle over Municipal Planning and the periodic revival of efforts to change the structure of borough government itself, will be discussed briefly in this narrative. Their history provides context for the focus on the Borough Council's efforts to deal with the issues of traffic and parking, both by outlining the Borough's fundamental conservatism, and by demonstrating that the Borough Council's method of handling its traffic and parking problem was not an exception, but rather the general practice.

Municipal Planning

Of all the proposals offered to counter Norristown's already-perceived decline, few became more controversial than the concept of Municipal Planning. Montgomery County had created a Planning Commission in 1950, but such a commission at the borough level faced determined opposition. Planning was the type of "government interference" that encountered virtually instinctive opposition among many of Norristown's political leaders. Paul Santangelo was invariably at the center of that opposition. His overriding personal issue was control of his ward, and a Planning Commission clearly threatened that control. Santangelo was elected Council President in 1954, 1955, and 1956, thus ensuring that the subject of a Planning Commission would remain dormant over this time.

In the early part of the decade, the *Times Herald* expressed a favorable view of Municipal Planning. This attitude was surprising given the consistently conservative and virulently antisocialist credo to which the *Times Herald* subscribed. Against the backdrop of the Cold War, the phrase conjured up visions of creeping socialism. Yet in a July 1954 article, the plaudits flowed almost as thick as the platitudes. The editors of that decidedly conservative newspaper seemed to be absolutely unaware of the ideological irony involved in the praise they lavished on Municipal Planning:

The value of sound planning to insure the continued growth and prosperity of a community is something that has, quite properly, been given increasing importance by our progressive public officials in recent years.... Men who are experts in the field of municipal planning know from experience that proper planning will prevent the creation of blighted areas, provide for sound commercial and industrial expansion, insure adequate recreational space and coordinate all these objectives in a way that will contribute to the general well-being of all.[357]

The idea of a Planning Commission did not gain a majority on the Borough Council until 1961. Even then, its path toward existence was both tortuous and revealing. At a meeting on August 9, 1961, the council approved the creation of a Planning Commission after the third reading of its enabling ordinance, #1535. The vote was 6:4, with Paul Santangelo in opposition.[358] Merritt W. Bosler (he began as a burgess, but had just become the mayor), however, vetoed the ordinance. His veto message made clear the broad ideological background to the specific local issue. Norristown, he contended, already had effective zoning and oversight. The real reason for establishing a Planning Commission was that such an institution would be necessary to obtain federal funding for future projects. For the mayor (as for many others) however, federal funding also meant federal oversight, and that was unacceptable.[359] The issue came to a head at the October meeting. The *Times Herald* account revealed the depth of the emotion. After much discussion and controversy, even bringing a veto motion to the floor proved difficult. Santangelo objected vociferously, as only he could, contending that the motion was illegal. When the vote was finally taken, Mayor Bosler's veto was overridden by a 6:3 vote; Santangelo did not vote, continuing to object that the motion was illegal.

The Borough Council formally appointed the five initial members of the Planning Commission at the November regular meeting. D. Rae Boyd, a mortician and a man well known for his enthusiasm about and contributions to Norristown charities and beneficial events since the 1937 celebration, was named chairman. He was given a five-year term, while the four others were given initial terms of different years to ensure a staggered order of succession. One member declined his appointment, and Main Street hardware store owner William E. Daub was appointed in his place.

The Planning Commission's controversy-laden creation would presage its equally controversial existence. This was particularly true with the commission's chairman, D. Rae Boyd—a passionate and articulate voice for Main Street and for the borough whose view of the Planning Commission's mandate nevertheless often clashed with the Borough Council's traditional way of doing business, which led to considerable difficulty. Those clashes substantially lessened any positive contribution that an effective Planning Commission might have had on the deteriorating situation.

Governmental Change

The continued inability of the Borough Council throughout the 1950s to come to grips with the problems confronting Norristown, and the ease with which resistance could force delays or postponements of any idea bold enough to actually tackle a problem, caused some individuals to think past the usual questions of personalities and alliances. They set their sights on a fundamental reform: replacing the ward system with a system that featured legislative members elected at large. Under the laws of the State of Pennsylvania at the time, such a change would require Norristown to formally change from a "borough" to a "city."

These were not the first attempts to change the Norristown ward system. There had been four previous attempts, dating back to the 19th century, when Norristown was gaining its reputation as an efficiently run municipality. An 1881 proposition to adopt a city charter failed in the November election. No actual tally of the vote was made; an unofficial newspaper-arranged vote check indicated that the proposition had failed in every ward. There was another such attempt in the general election of 1888. This time the votes were properly counted; the city charter proposal received 823 votes, while those opposing the idea registered 1,338 votes. A third attempt in 1913 came closer, being defeated by only 423 votes. The fourth attempt took place in 1957, but the petition to put the proposal on the ballot was ruled invalid as it included signatures of people who lived outside the borough.

This latest attempt to convert Norristown from a borough to a city also failed. The petition appeared on the November 1960 ballot, and was soundly defeated by 4,768 to 2,041. The more than two to one victory margin can be largely attributed to the innate conservatism of Norristown's residents. While they recognized the weaknesses of their existing leaders and bemoaned their inability to work together, the voters of Norristown were almost universally opposed to change. Paul Santangelo was the most vocal in this, but his attitude and that of his fellow council members must always be understood within the matrix of the borough. This issue would flare up again in 1970; when it did, the old issues and the old emotions would virtually replay themselves.

The "Comprehensive Plan"

Borough officials had met many times with both the county and state highway departments to discuss traffic problems. The state had recently begun pushing to make DeKalb Street into a one-way northbound route, and argued with the borough over which street to make one-way southbound. In 1951, the Borough Council announced a fundamental restructuring of the traffic flow into and out of the borough from all four points of the compass. On October 10, they passed, unanimously, "A Resolution Declaring the Intention and Policy of the Borough of Norristown With Regard to the Regulation of Through Traffic."[360] Quickly dubbed the "Comprehensive Plan," this proposed radical changes for Norristown's core. Main Street would become one-way westbound between Ford and Markley streets; Lafayette Street would become one-way eastbound between the same two streets. DeKalb Street would become one-way northbound from Lafayette Street all the way to Johnson Highway, the borough's northern border; Markley Street would become one-way southbound for the stretch.

The plan's claim to the title of "comprehensive" was quickly jeopardized. Since the State Department of Highways administered the U.S. route system, agreement by the state was required to implement one-way traffic along both DeKalb Street (U.S. Route

202) and Main Street (U.S. Route 422). In December, the Borough Council passed two resolutions formally requesting state approval for the DeKalb Street portion of the plan only.[361] Significant errors in the original ordinances were apparently discovered, because at its March 1952 meeting, the Borough Council passed two replacement ordinances for those passed in December.[362] This seems to have resolved the issues, although the actual changeover was postponed until November to allow for the resurfacing of Markley Street and the changes in traffic signals. The Borough Council formally passed the ordinance establishing the new north-south traffic pattern on November 10, 1952. The plan went into effect a week later.[363]

There was no official comment as to why the Main Street portion of the Comprehensive Plan had been abandoned, but none was needed. To convert Main Street to one-way traffic had enormous ramifications for downtown businesses, rendering the east-west portion of the 1951 Comprehensive Plan much more controversial. Nonetheless, by 1951, the future course of the long-standing traffic vs. parking controversy was clear: expediting traffic would win. DeKalb Street had been made one-way, and the Borough Council was at least on record as *considering* plans to make Main Street one-way as well. This second step had been postponed, but remained an option, a veritable sword of Damocles hanging over Main Street.

The Pursuit of Parking

Main Street's merchants, working with and through the Chamber of Commerce—and, to an extent, the Borough Council—spent the 1950s and early 1960s trying to secure desperately needed parking. Some members of the Borough Council would be sympathetic to this effort, but most seemed far more concerned with how to extract the maximum revenue from the parking meters than with actually solving the parking problem. They were also concerned about avoiding the financial commitment sought by parking advocates.

Regardless of the pros or cons of parking meters, or of any further changes in traffic patterns, the indisputable need was for substantial *additional* parking spaces. It was equally obvious that, as the *Times Herald* expressed it, "It is evident that all additional parking spaces provided must be off-street facilities."[364] Unfortunately, while the will to seek solutions existed, finding those solutions remained elusive as long as "possible" meant "affordable." Main Street's merchants were faced with the fact that any effort substantial enough to address the parking problem would entail enormous risk, and might exceed their collective ability to finance. They would turn to the Borough Council for assistance, but receive none. In the coming decade and beyond, the Borough Council would propose, debate, postpone, and endlessly argue over proposals to secure off-street parking. The struggle would reveal the internal fissures, both political and social, that survived from decades past and continued to work against any effort to deal with the parking problem.

In 1956, a report prepared by the Montgomery County Chamber of Commerce that appeared as one of a series of articles in the *Times Herald* outlining community problems effectively summarized both the reasons for Norristown's parking problem, and the fundamental problem involved in dealing with them. The article argued that the local parking situation was illustrative of what was happening across the nation. However, it contended, Norristown's situation was worse than the average, and the future less bright, for three reasons. The first was Norristown's location at "the center of the highway of the Eastern seaboard"—through traffic headed between Philadelphia and New York. The second was the rapid suburban growth occurring all around, which had been greatly accelerated by the new expressways, with local highways the only means of connecting these burgeoning areas. The third reason was the only problem specific to the borough itself, but also the major obstacle: lack of space downtown. The report concluded on a rather somber note, pointing out the threats rising all around the borough, but offering little hope: "The threat of new shopping areas in suburban sections remains a specter that downtown business is well aware [of] and local merchants see the need for early and intelligent action in making what solutions are possible."[365]

It all came back to the Philadelphia Plan. The same plan that had made the town compact, efficient, and appealing to shoppers back in colonial times was now the reason that shoppers could get to the downtown but not be able to stop there easily. There was simply no space. Norristown's horse-and-buggy era blueprint had produced the largely typical "downtown" of buildings abutting one another and built out to the sidewalk. The streets could not be widened, and there was no space between buildings. Except, of course, when bankrupt businesses left and the buildings were razed. Ironically, it seemed that as long as there were thriving businesses, there was nowhere to park, but when the businesses started to fail one by one because of that fact, more parking opened up.

The First Parking Authority

Something had to be done. The obvious answer was to purchase unused lots; several existed along Lafayette Street. Unfortunately, Pennsylvania law forbade municipalities from owning land other than that used for government operations. Provisions had been written into state law, however, to allow for the establishment of an "Authority," a subsidiary component of a borough or township, created specifically to own and manage property. Thus, the first step toward acquiring additional parking lots was to establish a Parking Authority. Naturally, establishing a new part of borough operations was itself controversial, so as usual the Borough Council wasted a great deal of precious time debating the issue before finally creating the Parking Authority at its December 1953 meeting. Proposals for and discussion on such an authority had been under way for some time, but the issue was complicated by a simultaneous controversy over establishing a Borough Planning Commission. The combination of two such radical changes, the potential expenditure each involved, and the consequent loss of a degree of control over borough affairs distorted the debate over each, and delayed both. By late 1953, an apparent "gentlemen's agreement" to delay the Planning Commission proposal and proceed with the establishment of a Parking Authority had been reached, and an ordinance to create the Authority was being written.

When the Borough Council formally created the Parking Authority in December 1953, it soon had to demonstrate the council's ability to move quickly if absolutely required: the original ordinance establishing the Authority turned out to be defective, and a replacement was prepared. The original ordinance was given its third reading and was unanimously voted down. The new ordinance was then introduced, given the three required readings, and passed, all in the same night.[366]

In its final form, the ordinance created a five-man board to manage the Parking Authority. The members were given staggered terms so that only one board membership per year would become vacant. Morris Chatlin was among those appointed to this first board. The Parking Authority was empowered to buy or lease ground for parking purposes, to obtain this property through condemnation if necessary, and to operate the lots or lease lots operated by others. The Parking Authority was given the power to issue bonds or notes, and to negotiate loans.[367] In creating the Parking Authority, however, the Borough Council also clearly indicated that it would be unwilling to commit revenues to any future projects that might result.

While embroiled in discussions over the establishment of both a Parking Authority and a Planning Commission, the Borough Council proceeded to cloud the already-complicated issue of off-street parking with one of its all-too-frequent controversial actions. The Borough Council held a special meeting in July 1953 that, according to the *Times Herald*, had been "planned and held with a high degree of secrecy." With two members absent, the Borough Council, by a 6:4 vote, authorized the purchase of a tract of land along Saw Mill Run, between Airy and Marshall streets, "for the purpose of providing facilities for off-street parking of vehicles and for general borough purposes."[368] Which of these two motivations was primary—and to a substantial degree, the proposal's merits—were quickly lost in a storm of controversy over the legality of the special meeting itself. Burgess March reacted to the controversy by returning the bill authorizing the purchase without signing it. This was the equivalent of a veto, and at next month's regular meeting, his veto was sustained.[369] There the matter remained for the time being. The borough's need for space was real, however, so the matter did not go away. Despite his persistent opposition to most spending, Santangelo actually supported this purchase, citing the need for parking. The lot's potential to clean up a rather decrepit area of the East End may have also been a consideration. There were also rumors, unsubstantiated but persisting even until today, that Santangelo had a financial stake in the property.[370]

By October 1953, the now-functioning Parking Authority submitted a request to the Borough Council for funds to conduct another parking survey. The previous one dated back to 1949, and its methodology had not been directed specifically at downtown. The new survey would be conducted by a private firm under contract, so delivery of the results could be expected much more quickly. Some Council members grumbled, but at the next month's meeting they voted to spend $7,500 to contract out the survey.[371] The Parking Authority contracted with Ramp Buildings Corp. of New York, and the survey itself began on March 1, 1955.

The company did indeed produce a faster report; it was made public in early May. The survey found that the central business district (defined essentially as Main Street, Penn Street between DeKalb and Cherry streets, and those streets intersecting Main

Street back to Penn or Lafayette streets, respectively) possessed 2,726 parking spaces, only 1,655 of which were available to the public. The others were tied up in a variety of individual arrangements by the county and by private concerns, including the railroads. On an average business day, 9,274 vehicles entered the central business district in search of a place to park in these publicly available spaces. Automobile turnover (presumably spurred by the existence of parking meters) accommodated a portion of these, but it was estimated that at least 2,735 automobiles were forced to park a "substantial" (unspecified) distance from their destination. The report identified two particularly acute problem areas within the central business district. One was bounded by Main, Swede, Penn, and Cherry streets; the other was bounded by Lafayette, DeKalb, Penn, and Strawberry Place (the small alley adjacent to the Valley Forge Hotel). Within these areas, a total of less than three square blocks, excess demand totaled more than 1,600 spaces. That is, 1,600 automobiles per day could not find a place to park.

Armed with figures from the survey, the Parking Authority set to work identifying potential sites to purchase for use as parking lots. However, the Parking Authority was five men working part time on a correspondence-heavy task—in the days before email and cell phones. Thus, despite the acknowledged abilities and organizational acumen of Parking Authority Chairman Judge Alfred L. Taxis, the group did not present its report to the Borough Council until April 30, 1956—more than a year after the survey had begun.

The report recommended the purchase of four sites deemed close enough to the critical areas. Two of the sites were owned by the Pennsylvania Railroad, and preliminary negotiations for their purchase had been completed. The Parking Authority planned to provide the purchase and administration funding through a bond issue. The Borough Council would lease the four sites from the Parking Authority, and revenue from the lots would be used to pay off the bond issue first, and after that was paid off, to contribute to the borough treasury.

The central question was whether the four lots—275 new parking spaces—would generate enough revenue to liquidate the bonds. If they could not, then the Borough Council would have to tap tax revenues to make up any difference. By the end of 1956, the Borough Council had examined the numbers within the Bond Issue, and concluded that a yearly operating deficit of $15,000 was a possibility. If this was the case, then they had to decide whether and to what extent the Borough Council should subsidize downtown parking. The question they grappled with was, "Is downtown important enough to the Borough of Norristown to justify the expenditure of tax revenues to support it? And if so, how great an expenditure?"

On this subject, the Borough Council deadlocked. However much it may have desired to follow through on the recommendations of the Parking Authority it had appointed, the prospect of tapping tax revenues found a solid majority of council members opposed. A joint meeting in mid-November of the Borough Council, members of the Parking Authority, and officials of the Norristown Chamber of Commerce saw Parking Authority Chairman Taxis strongly urge the Borough Council's approval of the $665,000 bond issue. According to Judge Taxis, the Parking Authority had performed the task it was given: "We think the time has come for action." For Judge Taxis, the main issue was not the potential financial deficit, but whether Council had faith in the downtown area and its merchants. At a later public meeting of the Council Finance Committee, Chairman W. Earl Seltzer disagreed, arguing that the issue *was* a financial one. He questioned whether tax revenues should be expended to benefit only one section of the borough, and if so, why not other projects in other sections?

By February 1957, in the face of continued deadlock in the Borough Council, the five members of the Parking Authority gave up. In the ten months since they had presented their report, nothing had been done. They formally resigned as a group, stating for the record that their job had been accomplished. This "reason" was not designed to fool anyone, nor did it. Everyone knew that the mass resignation was a protest against the Borough Council's inaction. Nevertheless, the Borough Council accepted the resignations. Council President Paul Santangelo then appointed four Council members, including himself, "to meet with the newly formed Downtown Merchants Liaison Committee in reference to the parking problem at its request."[372] The Parking Authority continued to formally exist, but with no members.

Meter Maids

Revenue to Norristown Borough from parking meters for the period prior to the coming of the malls is shown below:

1950	$48,972	1956	$59,333
1951	$49,308	1957	$59,277
1952	$54,998	1958	$57,879
1953	$57,000	1959	$62,845
1954	$59,699	1960	$63,221
1955	$57,663	1961	$59,756

Parking meters provided a revenue stream to Borough government that rose steadily through the first half of the 1950s, peaking at $59,699.00 in 1954. This revenue stream had, in fact, steadily increased from its low of $35,575 in 1944. The revenue totals jumped from 1952 to 1954 primarily due to their extension into the West End along Marshall Street in 1951.

Revenue from the meters had peaked in 1956, and after a minor decline in 1957 showed a more substantial decline in 1958. This set the Borough Council to thinking about not just how to secure more revenue, but how to do so without further taxing the regular police patrols who were writing the parking tickets. As 1959 dawned, Norristown Borough Council decided to employ some of its existing force of school crossing guards—all women—as "Meter Maids," thus freeing regular patrols from the task. The borough possessed a solid cadre of such crossing guards, under the supervision of Frank "Hank Cisco" Ciaccio, who was rapidly becoming the police department's jack of all trades (he had initiated bicycle inspections, and was the public face of the police department through his many visits to the borough's schools). Ciaccio had insisted that the crossing guards be uniformed, and had trained them as a group, trying

160

to establish an *esprit de corps*. Their training had a military air, and the crossing guards had received a considerable amount of such instruction as how to stand at attention, dress their lines, and march in step. Ciaccio extended this approach with those designated as Meter Maids, insisting that they be uniformed as closely as possible to regular police officers to demonstrate their authority and instill respect in the unhappy motorists they were bound to encounter frequently.

Borough Council gave final and unanimous approval to the Meter Maids ordinance in March.[373] Burgess Bosler, however, vetoed the ordinance, objecting to the provision that placed the force under the supervision of the Finance Department; he wanted them under the authority of the Police Department. Council overrode his veto—again unanimously—at the April meeting, and the ordinance became law.[374] The new Meter Maids were deployed and proved to be an immediate success; revenue from parking meters jumped almost 10% in 1959, and reached $63,221 in 1960.

Burgess Bosler's veto is revealing of the nature of Norristown's borough government, its essentially feudal structure, and the contradictions this produced. Council had created the Meter Maids program to increase revenue collection. This was the same Borough Council, however, that routinely exonerated every parking ticket submitted by a council member, as a matter of courtesy, thus reducing potential revenue from those meters every time Council met. When Burgess Bosler asked for the program to be placed under the considerably more professional direction of the police department, Council's unanimous response was to place this new program under a department chaired by one of its own. Had the program been placed under the police department, the actions of the Meter Maids would have been largely out of the Borough Council's control.

Professionalism (and revenue), while ostensibly the reason for the program in the first place, in the final analysis took second place to the preservation of the authority of individual council members. This was a fundamental weakness of the Borough Council, regardless of the decade, and regardless of who sat on the council at any given time. It was most likely the fatal weakness. But Main Street, not the Borough Council, would pay the price.

The "Pigeon-Hole" Garage Debacle

The proposal that would entice Main Street into the greatest debacle of this entire period first saw the light of day in August 1958. A joint committee of merchants, borough officials, and representatives of the Chamber of Commerce had been quietly formed to study a promising new technological approach to an old problem: the lack of available space downtown. Their printing of this proposal launched the effort for what would be known as The "Pigeon-Hole" Garage.

The most attractive part of the proposal was that it enabled a parking garage to be built in what seemed the ideal location: on Lafayette Street, behind the Valley Forge Hotel. That would place the garage close to the very center of Main Street; shoppers would have the shortest walk regardless of their destination, east or west. Thus, the issue of favoring either East or West Main Street was avoided. This fundamental—although unspoken—point lay at the core of subsequent approvals of the project by local merchants and banks. Unfortunately, this particular location, while excellently located and available, suffered from the same flaw as had other tracts the Parking Authority had considered previously: its lack of size. There had never been any question of its use as a parking garage; it was too small to accommodate a multi-level garage of conventional design. Any garage that included the access ramps and driving lanes required to access the parking spaces would have almost no room left over for the parking spaces themselves.

The need for a central location and the lack of an even marginally large enough lot led the Borough Council to propose a new and largely untried parking technology whose design would do away with access ramps and driving lanes altogether. Drivers would maneuver their automobiles onto a dolly, lock the doors, then exit. A lifting mechanism would then raise the auto to one of eight "floors" above and deposit it into a space just slightly larger than that required for the automobile itself—hence the adoption of the term "pigeon hole." When the shopper returned, ideally laden with purchases from the nearby Main Street stores, the auto would be extricated by the machinery and returned to first-floor level. The process of insertion or extraction was proclaimed to take no more than 30 to 40 seconds. Thus equipped, the garage was to accommodate 240 automobiles at one time.

The critical issue of whether to ask for financial support from the Borough Council elicited two financing plans. One would finance the project solely from revenues, the other would have the Parking Authority operate the garage under a lease-back arrangement with the borough. This latter option meant, of course, that the Borough Council would potentially have to back the project with tax revenues if the user revenues proved insufficient. Previous events had shown that this was a sham choice, and events quickly demonstrated which method would be accepted.

There was a second issue: the Parking Authority at that time lay in abeyance, its members having previously resigned and no active replacements appointed in their stead. A re-staffing of the Parking Authority would have to be the first step in pursuing the project. The Borough Council acted quickly, proof positive that the ground had been laid in advance, and a resolution approving the "pigeon-hole" garage concept was approved unanimously at the next regular meeting, in September. That resolution specified that the Borough Council was "in favor of the plan and of financing solely from the revenues from the project itself, and not in favor of the lease-back method of financing."[375] Five new members were appointed to the Parking Authority, again with staggered terms.

In Norristown, no matter how well the ground had been laid, complications and controversy tended to arise, and so it was in this case. Burgess Bosler refused to sign the bill, citing his objection to a provision allowing a member of the Borough Council to also sit on the Parking Authority, an issue relating to whether a member of the Parking Authority could be paid. Citing differences in the requirements contained in Pennsylvania's 1935 Municipal Authorities Act and 1947 Parking Authority Act, Burgess Bosler and the Borough Council could not come to an agreement. At its October meeting the Borough Council proceeded to override Bosler's veto—again unanimously—thus clearing the way for the project.[376]

The total cost was estimated to be $450,000. Absent any contributions from the borough, the original plan was for the Parking Authority to raise $400,000 of the total through issuing bonds. The remaining $50,000 would be raised by subscriptions from local merchants. By November, the *Times Herald* reported that the merchants had received pledges totaling almost half the amount needed.

Three downtown banks—Montgomery County Bank and Trust Company, Peoples National Bank of Norristown, and the Montgomery Office of the Philadelphia National Bank—agreed in January 1959 to provide the major share of the financing, relieving the Parking Authority from having to sell bonds. Despite this considerable vote of support, downtown merchants at this point were still unable to meet their total $50,000 contribution. A statement by Parking Authority Chairman Robert Novell at the time is revealing: "The $40,000 already subscribed represents the willingness of a relatively small percentage of downtown merchants and property owners."[377] No further details were specified. By March, the merchants' deficit was down to $6,000, but another problem had arisen: the possible assessment of the garage property for tax purposes. Additional appeals to the Borough Council's Finance Committee for assistance were unsuccessful.

By the end of the year, the original plan had changed. The proposed site had shifted to an adjacent tract at the corner of Lafayette and Swede streets (owned by Main Street merchant David Wachs, proprietor of Charming Shoppes at 8 East Main Street). A new financing arrangement was the key. This new version of the garage was projected to cost $487,000. Wachs accepted a $50,000 second mortgage to aid the project, on top of the $225,000 mortgage negotiated by the three cooperating banks. The remaining $212,000 was to be raised through "unsecured debentures and common stock," provided by local businessmen.

By April, the Pennsylvania Securities Commission had approved and authorized the necessary financing. The project would be incorporated under the name Lafayette Auto-Matic Parking Corp. The Keystone Parking Corporation was to operate the garage, with Taylor Pigeon-Hole Company providing the lifting and retrieval machinery. Formal groundbreaking took place in May 1960, 18 months after the project was first proposed. David Wachs, now President of Lafayette Auto-Matic Parking Corp., spoke in glowing terms of the project, saying that the new facility would give "the consuming public parking space within a few feet of downtown Norristown." John G. Schott, President of the Central Montgomery Chamber of Commerce, added to the plaudits, proclaiming "This will do an awful lot for downtown Norristown."[378]

Construction was slow and the expected spring opening date was not met. In the interim a *Times Herald* article attempted to address concerns about the technology with assertions that would come back to haunt the paper, which proclaimed the garage an "intricate but faultlessly efficient building," and "a veritable parking paradise for Norristown's downtown shoppers." Readers were assured that "entrance and exit will be a simple procedure. A trained staff will reduce the mere acts of placing and reclaiming a car to a minimum of time."[379]

A last-minute change that almost escaped notice was a note on June 13 that another firm had been engaged to operate the garage, Electronics Parking Inc., of New York City. The *Times Herald* assured readers that the company had erected and operated "many such parking centers throughout the East." Testing of the apparatus was to begin the week of June 22, "to eliminate any 'bugs' before the service is offered to the public," and the garage would to open July 13, 1961.[380]

The "Pigeon-Hole" Garage, rather gaudily painted in blue and gold with aluminum trim, did open on July 13. Its opening was the centerpiece of "Bargain Jamboree Sales Days," a two-day event sponsored by the Downtown Merchants Division of the Central Montgomery Chamber of Commerce; 46 stores were reported to be involved. The program included a "park and shop" component, whereby shoppers with parking receipts validated by a local merchant would park for free.

What happened next is uncertain. The "Pigeon-Hole Garage" simply disappears from the pages of the *Times Herald* until an article in December of 1962, almost 18 months after its much-lauded opening. The article quoted *verbatim* the text of a letter signed jointly by the three local financing banks and giving a history of the project. The article made no specific mention of any problem or malfunction—pure evasion, as rumors abounded of problems at the garage, mainly concerning malfunctions of the lifting machinery. Police officer Frank (Hank Cisco) Ciaccio fielded many complaints about delays in retrieving cars back. Bill DeAngelis claimed that at least one auto had to remain overnight until a mechanic arrived the next morning. The December 1962 *Times Herald* article explained that "the professional manager who had been employed 'walked out,' leaving things in great confusion." There was a reference to the elevator not having been properly serviced.

Judging from the *Times Herald* article, problems began quite early in the garage's existence, as "very shortly after the opening the revenue was insufficient to pay interest and debt reductions payments on the mortgage held by the bank."[381] The Lafayette Automatic Parking Corporation went out of business in May 1962. The local banks refused to accept the deed, and operated the garage themselves from June through November, at a loss. While the local banks, those most on the hook for the losses, were considered to be cautiously optimistic that the garage could be made profitable over a period of some two or three years, pressure was mounting from "banking authorities" who looked askance at banks operating a business. There were reports that the City of Reading was interested in purchasing the structure, removing it and re-erecting it there, but the reports came to nothing.

In terms of its effect on shoppers on Main Street, it does not matter what had *actually* happened at the Pigeon-Hole Garage. Everyone interviewed for this project who was an adult during that time remembers hearing rumors about damage to one or more automobiles, even though no one can name a particular incident, car owner, or evidence to substantiate the memory. But the rumors of problems spread quickly, and thereafter the garage was doomed, even if it turned out that reports of problems were exaggerated—which they may well have been. In any case, few shoppers were willing to take a chance on an apparatus that had quickly become infamous.

The Pigeon-Hole Garage was a financial disaster. The three local banks—The Montgomery County Bank and Trust Company, Peoples National Bank of Norristown, and the Montgomery Office of the Philadelphia National Bank—lost almost their entire $225,000 mortgage. The remaining amount (initially $212,000, and reported in the *Times Herald* article to be "over $200,000") raised by 53 local investors was also lost. In the interests of not-quite-full disclosure, the *Times Herald* article revealed that one of the local investors had been "the local newspaper." Although there was no mention of it, the $50,000 second mortgage to David Wachs most likely joined the other two in the loss column.

The psychological blow was even worse. In fact, it would be difficult to overestimate the extent of the damage caused by this fiasco. While such losses are usually calculated in dollars, what downtown Norristown lost in this affair was the one thing that mattered most at this critical point: confidence in itself. Main Street, its internal divisions as deeply set as those of Norristown itself, had this one time managed to come together and take what seemed like positive action to solve a problem. The reason for this supreme effort had been clear to all involved: parking, to compete with "the new type shopping centers being developed in the suburban areas to Norristown," as the *Times Herald* had expressed it. In response to what was fast becoming a crisis, local merchants and banks had conceived, financed, and constructed what all hoped would be the solution to their collective problem. They had also done so without any financial help from the borough government.

But they had failed, calamitously.

What was lost was far more significant than even the financial figures would indicate. Other garages, and other ideas, would be proposed, but the Pigeon-Hole Garage was the first time that the components of Norristown's Main Street shopping community had actually implemented a project aimed at their parking problem. It would also be the last. Badly stung, local banks would never again contribute that kind of favorable financing. Local businesses would be extremely reluctant in the future to commit funds to any project, at any point in the planning process. The *Times Herald* had signed on to the Pigeon-Hole Garage with both verbal and financial support. The newspaper would report all future proposals, but never again so fully endorse any of them.

The final, plaintive sentences of the report to the Borough Council revealed that this colossal public failure had torn the heart out of the Main Street business community. Private initiative to save Main Street had failed. The future, if there was one, must lie with the borough itself:

> The providing of adequate parking facilities, fundamentally, is a responsibility of the municipality and not of private enterprise. If, because adequate parking facilities are not provided and the value of mercantile property thereby is decreased, the municipality as a whole is the loser because of the loss of taxes.[382]

165

Thus was the responsibility for solving an intractable problem passed to a legislative body lacking both the will and the resources to perform what was being asked of it. The timing of the fiasco could hardly have been worse. Norristown's immediate suburbs were in the middle of an unprecedented expansion of population, thus providing more and more potential shoppers. Main Street had essentially wasted a decade of opportunity to attract this burgeoning new group of suburbanites, and now could not adequately serve them. Its suburban competition, by contrast, spent the decade in steady growth and development, and was ready to set up shop.

11

1962: Sesquicentennial Health Update

The prospects for downtown Norristown turned dramatically worse in 1962. Downtown's merchants had already begun to see their long-standing commercial dominance eroding, but until then the external challenges had come from individual stores and local shopping centers that had sprung up during the 1950s. The competition from those small but plentiful retailers would only grow in the following years, but even that would be overshadowed by two major events in 1962. The first was the opening of the King of Prussia Plaza, at the intersection of the Pennsylvania Turnpike and the Schuylkill Expressway just south of Norristown. The second was the announcement of another major concentration of stores, the Plymouth Meeting Mall, to be built at the intersection of the Pennsylvania Turnpike and its northeast extension, just northeast of Norristown. These two events would inaugurate a new era in the history of retail commerce, in Southeast Pennsylvania and beyond.

Of course, at this time Main Street still faced its internal challenge, which had literally cut the heart out of downtown between 1954 and 1961. In 1962, the four structures to the east of the Public Square that had for many decades housed a number of businesses, sat silent and shuttered. Everyone knew that more was to come, but not when or how much. It was not long before that uncertainty was resolved, and not in a way that would benefit Main Street.

Downtown's merchants had not been idle during all this time. They recognized and were eager to face full on their two fundamental problems, the same two they had faced since the end of WWII: how to get automobiles into and out of downtown efficiently, and how to accommodate those automobiles once they got there. These two closely related issues had by now been argued over for almost two decades, but neither had been solved, nor even abated significantly. The only physical result of their efforts was the virtually abandoned hulk of the Pigeon-Hole Garage.

Even the borough government can be said to have embarked on a new era in 1962, albeit over considerable resistance. In 1962, the Planning Commission began to function. The era that followed nationally would be a great era for the concept of "municipal planning," at least as measured by public and private interest, if not results. Municipal planning in Norristown would run into that ancient and deeply rooted American abhorrence of outsider oversight, and municipal planning would lose out because of it. The results would not be entirely negative, however.

For Norristown, and particularly for Main Street, 1962 started out hopeful, and ended with those hopes dashed as delays continued over proposed resolutions of the borough's by-now familiar challenges. The fate of the north side of Main Street's core block hung on the decision of Montgomery County government, over which Borough Council exercised little to no influence. That fate remained unresolved that year. Then, residents were hopeful that there would be at least a partial solution to the decades-old problem of getting vehicles into and out of Norristown expeditiously, when plans were floated for the long-desired construction of a second bridge over the Schuylkill River. Residents waited for most of the year while officials discussed the possible physical impact of such a bridge, only to watch their leaders rise up against the plan offered by the state. Finally, with respect to the ongoing issue of where people coming into downtown should park, residents were temporarily heartened when the Parking Authority was reactivated and new members were appointed to fill out its ranks. But again, the message from the Borough Council was clear: yes, there was a problem, but the Borough Council was not interested in spending any money to resolve it. Norristown turned 150 years old in 1962, making it an appropriate anniversary to contemplate the past, and residents marked the sesquicentennial year with the usual celebrations and speeches. As usual, too, leaders and residents both spoke bravely of better days ahead. What is less certain is whether many of them actually believed it.

Planning for the sesquicentennial celebration began a full two years before the event. The Borough Council, at its April 5, 1960, meeting, officially designated 1962 as "the year for special celebration of the Sesqui-Centennial Anniversary of the beginning of the borough."[383] A formal Sesquicentennial Celebration Committee was selected, which in February 1961 formed a corporation to coordinate all aspects of the event. Judge Alfred Taxis was appointed chairman and Robert McCracken, the editor of the *Times Herald*, was named president. The *Times Herald* played the part of booster during the entire run-up to the sesquicentennial, running articles from late February to the eve of the celebration about the plans being made for the celebration, and frequent and more detailed articles about the elements of the celebration itself while and after it took place.

A prominent component of Main Street's promotions for the sesquicentennial that had not been included in the centennial celebrations of 1912 was any specific effort to draw visitors from the suburbs during the festivities. Such efforts had been unnecessary in 1912. Then there were no suburbs proper, just town and country, and some transitional neighborhoods in between. Downtown Norristown had no competition; virtually all the residents of central Montgomery County shopped there. Additionally, Norristown's centennial had little competition from other leisure time activities— something that was very different in 1962, when people could travel wherever they wanted on their own schedules just by hopping in their cars.

The planners of the sesquicentennial celebration were all but desperate to attract not just the usual locals but new visitors to the borough, and to Main Street in particular. They invested a great deal of time, energy, creative thought, and money into pulling people into the area for the celebration. Publicity touted their efforts to combine the lure of shopping bargains, nods to history, and fun activities. The core of the outreach effort involved a series of automobile caravans through the region, spreading the word of the upcoming celebration. Norristown residents dressed up in period clothing from the 18th through early 20th centuries and rode in antique cars and trucks, journeying to locations throughout Montgomery County—even as far as Souderton, on the border with Bucks County. The first of these caravans took place on the first Saturday in April, and toured the communities to the northwest, including Collegeville, Schwenksville, Royersford, and Phoenixville. Caravans to other regions followed on each Saturday thereafter. The message was "come see us!" for the celebration planned to last a full week.

The sesquicentennial celebration kicked off in March, when the borough observed Charter Day, in recognition of the formal creation of Norristown as a borough. The ceremonies included Sesquicentennial Corporation leaders Judge Taxis and Robert McCracken accepting the official banner, along with speeches, songs, and a 25-minute skit portraying the Pennsylvania Legislature's original grant of the charter. The week of sesquicentennial events began on Thursday, May 3, with the opening of "Old Fashioned Bargain Days Sale," which was scheduled to continue through the weekend at each of the borough's three shopping areas. Friday saw the formal opening events, including the crowing of a pageant queen, and subsequent "Coronation Dances."

Many people offered comments about Norristown during this event so focused on history—some in formal speeches, some in newspaper articles, and some just to friends. Sadly, the one individual more qualified than most to comment on the history of Norristown was not able to do so. Edward W. Hocker, whose weekly column "Up and Down Montgomery County" had appeared in the *Times Herald* since 1922, lay dying in a nursing home in Chestnut Hill (he died on July 9). Hocker, a native of Norristown, had begun his newspaper career soon after graduating from Norristown High School. For decades he had written a column that featured tidbits about the county's past, and while these were sometimes viewed skeptically by other historically minded residents, his work propelled him to the position of authority on Montgomery County history. He wrote a county history that was never published as a book, but was the backbone of an enormous 104-page edition of the *Times Herald* in honor of Montgomery County's 175th Anniversary celebration in 1959. The *Times Herald* continued to recycle his columns for decades after his death. Had he been healthier, his presence would have contributed mightily to the sesquicentennial's history-laden celebration.

The 1912 centennial celebration had been built around parades, with one almost every day. The 1962 sesquicentennial offered just two. The Loyalty Day Parade, which began the events on Saturday, was a small preview of the one to come, and followed the same route, assembling at the intersection of Ford and East Main streets, then proceeding west on Main Street through the entire six-block downtown area, across Markley Street to Astor Street, where the parade turned right. The marchers then turned left onto Marshall Street and continued to Haws Avenue. True to its theme, it featured trucks bearing the Nike, Zeus and Polaris missiles, in addition to the usual assembly of bands, floats, fire trucks, and emergency vehicles, while the air echoed with the sounds of rifle salutes and the roar of planes overhead. A performance of "The Norristown Story" took place Saturday evening before an audience of 3,000 at Roosevelt Field, Norristown High School's athletic site, on Swede Street some blocks south of the high school itself.

Sunday, May 6, was designated "Faith of Our Fathers Day," and was celebrated in local churches in the morning and in a religious-themed musical performance, again at Roosevelt Field. Each day, Monday through Friday, May 7–11, featured a specific theme. Monday was "Homecoming & Senior Citizens' Day," and featured a social event at Elmwood Park, along Stony Creek north of the downtown area. Tuesday saw several local industrial plants open to the public for tours on "Industrial Progress Day." "Valley Forge and Audubon Day" fell on Wednesday. Thursday was "Youth Day," with festivities in local school and student representatives were temporarily installed in Borough offices. Friday was "Ladies Day." The sesquicentennial's climactic event, as with the centennial before it, was the official parade held on Saturday, May 12. The weather for the event was excellent, a rarity in Norristown history. Downtown was gaily decorated, and people lined the streets, often several deep, to see the marchers go by. The *Times Herald*, always generous in such situations, estimated the crowd at 50,000 people.[384]

To compare the climactic parades of 1912 and 1962 with the presentation of statistics, observations as to the extent of the decorations, or by virtually any method of comparison would be unfair to the later date. Much more than the primary means of conveyance from carriages to cars had changed. The nature of the Norristown community, as with communities across the nation, had changed mightily in the previous 50 years. Everywhere there was less interest in pomp and ceremony to mark official events, and less participation by the residents. The *Times Herald* placed the number of parade participants at 3,000. Some floats depicted historical themes, and some were sponsored by local companies, but many more were from local organizations, some of them clearly *ad hoc*, with whimsical themes. Men's beards made a ceremonial return, as the "Brothers of the Brush" had been active in the event promotions. Some of the hirsute marchers pushed baby carriages carrying their "Junior Fuzzy Brushes." Even Santa Claus put in an appearance, riding in a 1924 Chevrolet.

In one of the vehicles for honored guests rode Norristown Mayor Merritt W. Bosler, the elected burgess of Norristown since 1957. In 1961, state legislation changed the title of the office to Mayor, and Bosler assumed that title, effective September 1, thus becoming both Norristown's last burgess and first mayor. Bosler was re-elected as mayor in November 1961, but on that day in May 1962 he yielded primacy to the Sesquicentennial Queen, Susan Shannon, who was joined by Alice Evans, nee Meeh, the former Centennial Queen of 1912.

At the banquet honoring the Sesquicentennial queen, Pennsylvania governor David Lawrence commended the borough's "business stability." The *Times Herald*, deeply into its booster role, went much farther, with its lead article on May 3 proclaiming that "now, at long last, a confident and happy Norristown has begun its magnificent Sesquicentennial Celebration." In turgid, formal prose more befitting 1912's centennial celebration than one halfway through the 20th century, the *Times Herald* predicted that "it will be a Sesquicentennial time in every home, in every organization, on every street, in every place where citizens gather and in the hearts of every person who finds pride in the fact that he is a Norristonian, a citizen of one of the finest and most secure habitats on the face of the globe."[385] Both the prose style and the claim would have been justified in 1912, and perhaps even in 1937 despite the Depression. In 1962, the return of such prose might easily be excused, but the claim itself was open to serious question, and the more perceptive among Norristown's leaders understood this.[386]

The Friday, May 3, edition of the *Times Herald* that announced the opening of the festivities and listed the schedule of the next week's events also contained extensive articles on borough history and a number of old photographs. Its significance here, however, lies in the large number of commercial advertisements contained in this edition of the newspaper. These, combined with the articles on Norristown history, caused this particular edition to be 80 pages in length (plus a 32-page insert that contained solely historical articles). An analysis of these advertisements reveals a great deal about the changes in the Southeastern Pennsylvania countryside surrounding Norristown, and in the borough itself.

The 112 pages of the May 3 *Times Herald* contained a total of 386 commercial advertisements (those from, or to local political figures are not included), with 254 of the advertisements in this special edition from firms located within Norristown borough itself. Clearly, retailers' and residents' move to the periphery had altered the traditional relationship between urban and rural in Montgomery County. The days when Main Street, Norristown, was effectively local shoppers' only option for things other than the daily/weekly essentials were long over.

Only 68 of the 254 "local" advertisers in this edition were located within the Main Street survey area. This represents only 27% of the total advertisements from businesses within the borough and a mere 18% of the total number drawn from Norristown and the surrounding areas. Friedman's New York Store took a sizeable ad on the first page. Snyder's Jewelers went another route, sprinkling three smaller ads among the later pages. Gilbert's, whose owner Morton "Bubby" Weiss had been a prime mover in organizing downtown for the celebration, also took a full-page ad. Chatlin's, celebrating its 70th anniversary that same year, ran both a full-page ad and another large ad several pages later. For as long as many people could remember, Chatlin's and Block's had carried on a "war" that had long enlivened the advertisements of the *Times Herald*, with each laying claiming to the number one role. Ads had appeared for years proclaiming Chatlin's to be "Central Montgomery County's No. 1 Famous Brand Store," and Block's to be "Norristown's Only Complete Department Store." The 1962 ads were no different, although now both stores were just medium-size fish in a very small pond.

The *Times Herald* had a full-page ad, and Norristown's realtors had banded together for a full-page salute to the borough. The Norris Amusement Company advertised the Norris Theater, but also placed two ads for each of its drive-in locations. The Valley Forge Hotel contributed a medium-size ad. But 132 advertisements came from firms located *outside* the borough of Norristown, including one from the Hotel Taft in New York City; 15 advertisers were from the borough of Bridgeport across the river, and 12 were from the borough of Conshohocken a few miles downriver. Both were heavily weighted towards manufacturing firms.

Some of these advertisers were national firms, including UNIVAC in Blue Bell and Merck, Sharp & Dohme, Inc. in West Point, both in Montgomery County. Other employers of some size were spread out around Norristown, including Superior Tube in Collegeville and Steel Plant Equipment Inc. in Eagleville (both along Germantown Pike), Synthane Corp. in Oaks, Taylor Fiber in West Norriton, and Alan Wood Steel in Plymouth, the area's largest manufacturing firm.

Among Main Street's direct competitors, only Logan Square contributed a group advertisement. Its half-page ad listed the 22 firms located within it; three individual firms located in Logan Square added their own ads to the total. Across the river, three businesses in the Valley Forge Shopping Center contributed advertisements.

The large number of advertisements from commercial firms in the general area surrounding Norristown testify that as the houses and the jobs had moved to the suburbs, so too had the retail and service shops needed by the new residents and workers; such firms dotted the increasingly suburban area around Norristown. There were ads from 63 businesses in the surrounding townships of Plymouth, East Norriton, West Norriton, Lower Providence, and Upper Merion (exclusive of Bridgeport and Conshohocken). There were also ads from firms from as far away as Downingtown in Chester County, and Bryn Mawr in Delaware County.

There was one small advertisement, just one by two column inches tucked onto page 71, that may have gone largely unnoticed amid the many other large ones. Few people might have noticed the tiny ad for Anthony DiLucia, Builder, or recognized the name. But they would hear it again soon enough, especially those concerned about downtown Norristown.

Downtown in 1962

As the sesquicentennial day parade wound through downtown Norristown's six-block core, the decorations were far more restrained than in 1912. More significantly, the buildings behind the bunting—many of which also overlooked the 1912 parades—showed symptoms of downtown's flagging economic health. It is not possible to determine exactly how many vacant storefronts the sesquicentennial parade marched past on Main Street, but the 1963 directory suggests that it was 21. Thus, it is possible that more than 10% of the 193 storefronts in Main Street's six-block core were vacant. The number of storefronts in the 1963 directory represented an approximately 8% loss from the 209 storefronts reported in the 1951 directory. Such losses might have been more easily hidden had they been more evenly distributed. But 12 of the 21 were located in three clusters, one on East and two on West Main.

As the parade wended its way from the East End, past the first two of downtown's core blocks (counting Mill Street, which did not go north of Main Street) it passed by long-term survivors such as Chatlin's and Zummo's, along with other, smaller establishments that had been around for almost as long. These included Acme Markets, with its atypical roofline, but were mostly inhabitants of Norristown's traditional two-to-three-story brick structures, often still the original 25 feet wide. A few of these local establishments were Quinn's Paints, Gus's Steak Shop, Anthony Catagnus (who had shifted from books to novelties), Charles S. Bono's barbershop, and Joseph Discianni the shoe shiner. Between Arch and DeKalb the parade would have passed by perhaps five vacant storefronts.

The next block—numerically the first block of East Main—had been the core of downtown Norristown since Norristown had had a downtown. Here, the picture changed for the worse, at least on the north side of Main Street. At 67 East Main stood what had been the Grand Theater building . The elaborate marquee still jutted out across the sidewalk announcing its presence. But unlike in former years, it was now faded and peeling, and instead of trumpeting the name of the latest movie playing inside, the letters there spelled John's Bargain Store.

Just past that depressing sight, marchers in 1962 would have passed by the decrepit, shuttered and abandoned structures owned but unused by Montgomery County. When the centennial parade had passed that point in 1912, those addresses would have boasted perhaps the most varied array of tenants in the borough: 29 East Main Street was then the Boyer Arcade, host of the largest number of businesses at one location on Main Street; 35 East Main Street was still the private residence of the Mitchell family. While 35 and 37 East Main Street had housed retail outlets at street level and professional offices or residences above, now the buildings stood empty. Across the street, the Valley Forge Hotel presented a slightly better picture. It was still the site of many ceremonies and banquets. Unfortunately, its fortunes for this anniversary year cannot be determined; 1962 was another year for which the annual *Times Herald* summary article provided absolutely no financial figures.

As the parade approached Swede Street, it would draw near the hulk of the Pigeon Hole Garage, which sat a block to the south on Lafayette Street and Swede Street—thankfully out of sight, but hardly out of mind. As the parade crossed Swede Street and onto West Main Street, it would have proceeded past the still-imposing Montgomery County Bank and Trust Company at 1, then Block's at 11, and the ancient stone Corson Building at 33 West Main Street. Virtually all of Norristown's Main Street parades had passed by this building. At the time of that sesquicentennial parade it housed 11 entries, including John J. Corson, realtor, and Russell C. Corson, attorney. Once past the still-striking Norris Theater, as West Main Street descended toward Stony Creek in its third block, the parade marchers would have encountered not just vacant storefronts but raw openings where buildings had been razed. The first such gap, what had in 1950 been four storefronts at the site of the old Lincoln Hotel, was partially obscured as it was a lot used for parking and storage by the Firestone Store at 201 West Main Street. Across the street, the addresses from 212 to 224 West Main Street—the old Garrick Theater and adjoining buildings—stood empty, the buildings having been torn down years before. They now served as a parking lot for Melnick's Esso Service Center at 220 West Main Street. Just down the block at the site of the old Milner Hotel, the building at 231 to 237 West Main Street had also been torn down. None of these sites ever appeared in the *Polk City Directories* under Parking Lots. Their addresses simply ceased to be entered.

The crisp, fresh bunting and banners celebrating Norristown's sesquicentennial year of 1962 belied the truth: downtown Main Street was fraying and tattered. Had crumbling buildings been restored or replaced by vibrant businesses, the losses would not have been as painful. But this had not been the case; the failure of private enterprise to show any interest in replacing the missing buildings downtown spoke volumes about the declining property values of what had been for so long prime commercial real estate.

Downtown Norristown Inc.

By mid-1962, Main Street merchants had recovered sufficiently from the shock of the Pigeon-Hole Garage fiasco to create a little shock of their own. They decided to organize their own separate entity, Downtown Norristown Inc. Although Downtown Norristown Inc. claimed to operate as an independent subsidiary of the already-existing Downtown Merchants Division of the Chamber of Commerce, its decision to incorporate is suggestive of internal divisions between Main Street's merchants and the larger Chamber. The formal announcement of this new group gave as its purpose "to develop, protect and promote the interests of its members engaged in business, professions and industry and to foster, develop and protect the civic, commercial and industrial welfare of the Borough of Norristown."

Downtown Norristown Inc. held a dinner meeting in September—at the Valley Forge Hotel, of course—to introduce its "plan for Norristown." It was quite a gala event, but one that delivered a sobering, almost depressing message. Entertainment included a performance of the new organization's theme song, "Everything Good That's Going On is Going On in Norristown," and a mini pep rally by cheerleaders from the high school. The *Times Herald* summed up the evening, saying "All in all, it was a gala social evening combined with a description of the hard-headed facts of life facing the downtown businessman in his immediate and long range future." The article's opening sentence employed a term borough or association officials—as well as the *Times Herald*—had been loathe to employ thus far: "revitalization." Despite the verbal cheerleading in the speeches that accompanied this and subsequent events, it is clear that by Norristown's Sesquicentennial year Main Street was not only dying but its civic and business leaders were well aware of the fact.

A New—and Newly Mobile—Population

Montgomery County during the 1950s experienced an unprecedented increase in population. The Bureau of the Census had established the 1950 population of Montgomery County at 353,068. This was already an increase of 22% over the 1940 figure of 289, 247, and the pace was quickening. As early as 1954 the Chamber of Commerce of Greater Philadelphia was predicting that the county's population would increase by more than 35% during the decade then under way. In August 1956, the Montgomery

County Planning Commission estimated that the county's population had increased by 122,628 since the 1950 Census, pegging it at 475,696. That was just about a thousand people shy of what the Census Bureau had expected the county's population to be by the time of the 1960 Census. The Montgomery County Planning Commission concluded that the bulk of this unprecedented population influx was being absorbed by the previously rural areas of Montgomery County, and was very clear as to the reason:

> Mobility afforded by the automobile and the septic tank has permitted a widespread scattering of small developments over most of the Southeastern and Central areas of the County.... Nearly all of the new developments are dependent upon the automobile for transportation. More than 400 miles of wide-paved, residential streets have been added to the road system inherited from the past. The limited capacities of the old, outmoded road network area are strained even before the full development occurs.[387]

The 1960 Federal Census revealed that the population of Montgomery County had reached 516,682, an increase of 46% over the 1950 figure. The "greater Norristown area," defined as the borough itself, Bridgeport, plus the townships of Upper Merion, Plymouth, East and West Norriton, and Lower Providence, saw its population increase by 29,128 during the decade. Within this area, only Bridgeport showed a population loss, of 542 residents. The Borough of Norristown showed an increase of 701 residents. The remainder settled in the townships, producing growth rates exceeding 100% in Plymouth and East Norriton, and just under that number in West Norriton and Lower Providence. This was spectacular growth by any previous standard, but even this was dwarfed by the growth of Upper Merion Township, on the south side of the Schuylkill River.

In 1950, the population of Upper Merion Township had been 6,404; the number had been virtually static for years. Upper Merion conducted a special census of township residents in 1957, finding 13,142 residents—an increase of 105% in just the seven years since 1950. The 1960 Census revealed not just a higher number, but a substantial increase in the rate of increase itself. Upper Merion in 1960 possessed 17,096 residents—a rate of increase of just over 265%.

In addition to their numbers, these new residents of the central Montgomery County area exhibited another unprecedented characteristic: they all possessed automobiles. This new fact—and what it implied for the Norristown area—was noticed early in the decade. The *Times Herald* published a two-part series in August 1953, on the changes already under way in King of Prussia:

> Statistics on automobile registrations and data from the survey of selected subdivisions indicate the primary role of the automobile in outlying areas, as contrasted to its lesser importance in urban centers. The flexibility of location of home with respect to place of work, which the automobile makes possible, will continue to exert a powerful impact on the pattern of residential and industrial development in the outlying sections of the metropolitan area.[388]

We tend to take that simple statement for granted today, in the early part of the 21st century. The 1953 statement says, in essence, "People have cars, so now more of them are choosing to work and live—and *shop*—farther away from the downtown areas." Montgomery County had gone from 76,520 registered automobiles in 1945 to 124,776 in 1952. Put another way, Montgomery County in 1952 possessed just over 120 automobiles per 100 households, or more than one per household. By 1960, not just the number, but the very standard for the number had to be changed, when the residents of Montgomery County possessed 125 automobiles per 100 *persons*, not households. The result of this could be seen in the spectacular growth of peripheral shopping centers, all constructed at the intersections of local roads.

The County Comes to Main Street—Again

The county's ambitious plan to construct its new administration building by the end of 1963 got off to a reasonably on-time start with the call for demolition bids. The county judges began to raise questions about the project, however, and more squabbling between the two branches of county government began. (The nature of the disagreement lies beyond the scope of this work, and thus only its effect on Main Street will be discussed here.) The dispute stretched through the summer, delaying the demolition work for which the April demolition bids had been solicited.

The dispute between county commissioners and the court dragged on for the remainder of 1962. At one point, the county judges even sent a letter to the county commissioners suggesting that the courthouse itself be torn down to accommodate the new administration building on the site. This proposal, whatever the facts of its origin, was greeted with shock by the commissioners, and nothing more was heard of it publicly. Thus did the sesquicentennial year of 1962 proceed for downtown: hope amidst delay and decline.

Along with all the other signs in 1962 that times were changing, the Borough Council now included three Democrats, along with nine Republicans. Regardless of party affiliation, each council member had to confront the fact that Norristown was in financial difficulty. The Borough Council's annual January quest for a budget saw an at least tacit admission of problems, and sometimes more. Revenue was always an issue, and that year was no exception. It was clear by then that the county's acquisition of properties on Main Street had cut into the borough's tax revenues. Old issues such as the policies for parking tickets were rehashed, and newer issues raised, such as eliminating the meter maids. That such an action was proposed less than three years after the program was put in place is suggestive evidence of decline. The revenue from parking meters had, in fact, been falling. The *Times Herald* revealed in August 1961 that meter revenues had fallen over the first seven months of that year from $38,253.81 in 1960 compared to $34,299.63 over the same period in 1961. Figures from the final five months of 1961 were never made public, but the Borough Council's debate over meter maids suggests that the situation had not improved.

With revenues falling, the overhead of the Meter Maids program was costly. Police Sergeant "Hank Cisco" Ciaccio, who had created the corps, remained their staunchest defender: they covered Norristown "like the dew," he argued. He conceded that the meters and the enforcers may have contributed in some small way to hastening downtown's decline, since shoppers will always prefer not having to pay to park, and they especially don't enjoy paying fines for overstaying their meter time, so "they went to the malls."[389] However, since the parking situation in downtown Norristown was now acute, declining revenues could hardly be attributed to too many empty parking spaces, so the Borough Council blamed the deteriorating condition of the meters themselves, and the Meter Maids Program survived for a while longer.

The Second Schuylkill River Bridge

Residents, businesspeople, and political leaders had discussed building a second bridge over the Schuylkill River since the closure of the Ford Street Bridge in 1939. The project had seen previous false dawns, as proposals to locate it either to the east or west of the DeKalb Street Bridge, usually as a component of the chimerical proposed Norristown Bypass, provoked opposition. Norristown citizens, seeking reasons for optimism in their sesquicentennial year, found one when plans for a new bridge finally obtained legislative approval. In September 1962, the state presented its engineering plan. This, of course, led to new controversies, and Norristown's optimism fell victim to long delays in both design and construction.

While the efforts to build a second bridge had never actually ceased, the push that would finally bring success began in 1958. The *Times Herald* can be said to have inaugurated this latest attempt with an editorial in early June of that year calling again for a new bridge. Interestingly, the editorial's argument rested on the contention that most of the traffic in the jams on Route 202 was of local origin, not people using the highway as a long-distance route. This was a fundamental departure from all previous claims about traffic on Route 202 and the DeKalb Street Bridge. The Borough Council followed in July by unanimously adopting a resolution to be sent the state government asking for a second bridge between Norristown and Bridgeport. When the state assembly reconvened in January 1959, local state representative Walter C. Fry submitted a bill for the second Schuylkill bridge. The bill initially made good progress, and was introduced in the upper Assembly house in February. Then the delays began.

The Pennsylvania Legislature in July 1961 finally passed the bill authorizing a second Schuylkill River bridge. Governor David L. Lawrence signed the bill into law on July 26. With the political process complete, the next step would be engineering. The central issue, as always, was whether to locate the new bridge to the east or west of the existing DeKalb Street Bridge. The state chose to locate it to the west, and the proposal for the new Schuylkill Bridge was announced in September 1962. The design was for a high bridge that would begin at Rt. 202 in Bridgeport and cross over the railroad lines on the Bridgeport side, span both the river itself and Norristown's water purification plant at the river's edge, pass over the Pennsylvania Railroad tracks on the Norristown side as well as over Lafayette Street and Main Street, and finally touch down at Marshall and Markley streets.

Both borough officials and Main Street merchants looked this gift horse directly in the mouth and did not like what they saw. The new bridge's roadway would loom directly over the intersection of Main and Markley streets, they pointed out, not unlike how the old P&W Bridge had loomed over the Public Square. This would, they said, "cut the town in half," and be a death blow to the downtown shopping area. The Borough Council protested the plan, and suggested having the new bridge touch down at Main and Markley streets. A public meeting the next day endorsed the suggestion, with the *Times Herald* adding editorial support the day after that.

Their complaints had the desired effect. By March 1963 the state had agreed to change the bridge's touchdown point from Markley and Marshall to Markley and Main, as local authorities had requested. It was a prime example of "be careful what you wish for." The redesign did dramatically change things. It dumped all northbound traffic at the intersection of Main and Markley streets, which added to ongoing traffic congestion problems rather than solutions.

While the wishes of Norristown were accommodated, those of Bridgeport were not. Bridgeport's citizens and government had opposed the bridge in its entirety, and with good reason. The bridge would cut through the western end of their borough, thus uprooting residents (and removing properties from the borough tax rolls). Its southern end was at a high point in the terrain just before the substantial descent into the valley of the Schuylkill and, as an elevated roadway over Bridgeport, would casting its shadow over the land below. The visual and physical obstruction of a high bridge was substantially (although not entirely) reduced for Norristown, but not for Bridgeport. The Bridgeport Borough Council went on record as unanimously opposing the bridge, but to no avail. The design of the bridge had also increased its scope, which added to the portion of Bridgeport it was going to erase.

The Borough Planning Commission

Yet another fundamental change occurred in 1962. The proposal to create a Borough Planning Commission, after almost a decade in abeyance, had been narrowly approved in late 1961. As 1962 dawned, this seemed to some like another ray of hope in an uncertain time. With its personnel in place by December 1961, Norristown's newly appointed Planning Commission set to work in 1962. The commission found a firm supporter in Arthur F. Loeben, director of the Montgomery County Planning Commission. By early spring the commission had prepared a proposal for a comprehensive survey of the borough to assess its planning needs. Loeben participated in a joint meeting between the Borough Council and the Borough Planning Commission on April 17, seeking support for the proposed survey.

The survey, which would take two years to fully accomplish, would be funded by contributions from the borough, county and federal governments. The bottom line—understood by all involved—was that should the borough seek state or federal funding for future construction projects, such a comprehensive survey would be a necessary part of the application process. Equally well understood was that any possible state or federal funding would also hinge on the borough's hiring a full-time planner. The underlying issue was ideological: the potential loss of local authority. The most visible issue, however, was that of financial cost to the borough, particularly for any full-time personnel that would be required. The proposal finally came to a vote at the Borough Council's regular July meeting. The resolution calling for the planning study received a tie vote (Paul Santangelo voted no). Mayor Bosler wasted no time, and immediately vetoed it. For the time being, Norristown continued to possess a Planning Commission, but one with little to do.

The *Times Herald* published an article by Arthur Loeben during the effort to rally support for the comprehensive planning survey. His topic was the Norristown of the future; his purpose was to promote municipal planning of that future. He conceded that specific instances of planning could be found in Norristown's history, but "taken as a whole, Norristown had developed over 150 years in a general uncontrolled and unplanned manner, with dependence upon the free forces of the market and individual enterprises." In this, its sesquicentennial year, the borough of Norristown faced many problems. Among them, he wrote, "many of the buildings in Norristown are old, run-down and ugly"; the economic base was undergoing transition, and while the old was clearly in decline, the shape of the new was not yet clear. Many families had moved from the borough, resulting in declining tax revenues. Loeben did not neglect the traditional laments, noting, "There is traffic congestion and inadequate circulation of automotive vehicles."

Loeben's wish list for the future was comprehensive and borough-wide, but was headed by projects with a downtown focus, including a revitalized downtown area, a new bridge across the Schuylkill and a revised plan for circulation of automobile traffic. Among the other proposals was one that would persist, and eventually dominate downtown planning: the integration of the railroad, P&W trolley line, and bus lines into a regional transportation center. Loeben argued that the best course toward the uncertain future lay with comprehensive municipal planning. "By 1987 the Borough will be different, and if developments are guided and controlled in a planned fashion, Norristown can be a far better place than it is today."[390] Subsequent events would prove that the Norristown Borough government did not exactly share his view of how the future should proceed.

Part III

Decline and Fall

12

If You Build It, They Will Come—And Shop

As the borough of Norristown entered its 151st year, the external challenge to Main Street was on the verge of maturing. The King of Prussia Plaza would officially open in 1963, the Plymouth Meeting Mall in 1966. The 1960s would see the multiplication and expansion of smaller malls all around Norristown. Their numbers, variety, and free, ample parking steadily expanded their appeal. Whether such an external challenge to Main Street could have been surmounted even by an aware, active, and supportive borough government is highly uncertain. It is also academic; Norristown did not possess such a government.

The internal challenge from the government of Montgomery County that had torn out the heart of Main Street by the time of the sesquicentennial continued its damage during this period. The businesses were gone and the old buildings would follow, but controversy and delay dogged the county's expansion onto Main Street. Between 1963 and 1969 the Borough Council repeatedly tried to deal with the long-standing issues of traffic congestion and parking. The one fundamental change that they did enact was yet another serious injury to downtown. In making Main Street one-way, and finally fulfilling the "Comprehensive Plan" of the early 1950s, they once again placed the need for parking second to expediting traffic flow, to the direct and immediate detriment of Main Street merchants.

The Borough Council also spent a great deal of time debating broader responses to a changing reality. These would include the by-now familiar issue of municipal planning, plus newer ones reflective of the national mood, such as proposals for massive urban renewal. The Borough Planning Commission would have a quasi-existence, but progress would be hard-fought and ultimately reversible, in the Norristown tradition. Amid all this, downtown's decline began to accelerate.

Critical Condition: By the Numbers

Summarized on the following pages are net changes in the 1951, 1963, and 1970 editions of the Norristown city directories. Number and percentage changes for each periods' categories are included. The numbers for Main Street's peripheral categories (e.g., Manufacturing, Other/Unknown, School and Wholesale) show contradictory trends that the percentage column exaggerates due to the small numbers within each category. The more central and more numerous categories (e.g., Retail-Department

Store, Retail-Specialty, Service-Trades, Financial Service and Food Service) demonstrate that Main Street's decline had not just continued but intensified.

	1951			1963			1970		
	#	# Change	% Change	#	# Change	% Change	#	# Change from 1951	% Change from 1951
Total Entries	524	-64	(12%)	460	-82	(18%)	378	-146	(28%)
Storefronts	209	-16	(8%)	193	-13	(7%)	180	-29	(14%)
Auto Service	4	-2	(25%)	2	0	—	2	-2	(50%)
Bank	4	+1	25%	5	+3	60%	8	+4	100%
Company Office	17	-5	(29%)	12	-2	(17%)	10	-7	(41%)
Financial Service	15	+1	7%	16	-5	(31%)	11	-4	(27%)
Food Service	19	-4	(21%)	15	-4	(27%)	11	-8	(42%)
Government-County	2	-1	(50%)	1	-1	(100%)	0	-2	(100%)
Government-Federal	2	0	—	2	+2	100%	4	+2	100%
Grocery/Market	9	-6	(67%)	3	0	—	3	-6	(67%)
Hotel	4	-2	(50%)	2	0	—	2	-2	(50%)
Manufacturing	2	0	—	2	1	(50%)	1	-1	(50%)
Other/Unknown	4	-2	(50%)	2	-1	(50%)	1	-3	(75%)
Parking Lot	1	0	—	1	0	—	1	0	—
Professional Office	50	-13	(26%)	37	-23	(62%)	14	-36	(72%)
Retail-Dept. Store	15	-8	(53%)	7	-3	(43%)	4	-11	(73%)
Retail-Specialty	114	-12	(11%)	102	-29	(28%)	73	-41	(36%)
School	3	-2	(67%)	1	+2	200%	3	0	—
Service-Professional	14	-12	(86%)	2	0	—	2	-12	(86%)
Service-Trades	26	-6	(23%)	20	-11	(55%)	9	-17	(65%)
Tavern	4	+3	75%	7	-3	(43%)	4	0	—
Theater	3	-2	(67%)	1	0	—	1	-2	(67%)
Transportation	3	-2	(67%)	1	0	—	1	-2	(67%)
Wholesale	1	0	—	1	+1	100%	2	+1	100%
No Return/ Vacant*	14	+22	157%	36	+27	75%	63	+49	350%

†*Adjusted number, accounts for addresses disappearing from Directory, but not torn down.

The above table starkly demonstrates Main Street's accelerated decline after the opening of the King of Prussia Plaza. Only five categories demonstrated net gains between 1963 and 1970. Of these, only the Bank category had also shown a rise between 1951 and 1963.

The largest gain during this second period showed up in the least welcome category, No Return/Vacant. The nine entries in this category in the 1951 directory represented just over 4% of the survey area's total storefronts in 1951. By the 1963 edition, the 21 No Return/Vacant storefronts represented fewer than 11% of the total. In the 1970 Directory, the grim news would be 63 No Return/Vacant entries, 36 of which were storefronts—a full 20% of the survey area's remaining storefronts.

Seven categories registered neither an increase nor a decrease between the 1963 and 1970 directories. The Parking Lot category continued to be inaccurate and thus irrelevant as an indicator. Buildings were torn down and converted to parking lots but never counted in the directories. The Acme grocery store lot disappeared from the directory after the 1962 edition, although it continued to exist. The Acme store itself, however, would change hands, and in 1970 appear as Fiore Super Market, with its parking lot presumably in place but not listed. The lot that was listed in 1970 was adjacent to the Continental Bank, which for a period of two directories would be referred to as the Municipal Parking Lot, even though it was owned by the bank. (The story behind this lot's availability would be that of another major loss to Main Street.) Overall, 11 categories showed net losses from 1963 to 1970.

The net decline of Professional Office and Service-Trade entries between the 1963 and 1970 directories, at 62% and 55% respectively, would be the worst performances statistically among the significant and numerous categories. It would be the less significant statistical declines in both Retail-Department Store and Retail-Specialty, however, that would supply the most telling evidence that by 1970, Main Street's condition was close to terminal.

Main Street's department stores had lost over 50% of their number by the 1963 directory. These included some "department stores" in name only, small shops of little direct competition to their larger brethren. The late 1960s would see two more of the smaller department stores close, but the big blow would hit in 1968, with the closing of two of Main Street's remaining major department stores.

Retail-Specialty stores had peaked at 122 entries in the 1953 directory, and then began a steady, year-by-year decline. The 1963 directory closed the period with 102 Retail-Specialty listings, a net loss of 12 stores or 11% of the 1951 total of 114 stores. The later 1960s would see this trend intensify: by the 1970 Directory, the Retail-Specialty category had lost 29 of the 102 listings in 1963, or 28%, finishing the period with 73 stores. The ominous, continuous and accelerating decline of this category, combined with that of the larger stores and that of the other significant retail and service categories, provides conclusive evidence of Main Street's woeful decline by the end of the 1960s.

How the Professionals Saw Things

The accelerating decline of the Borough of Norristown—and not just its downtown—received the attention of the Montgomery County Planning Commission through the 1960s. Since the Norristown Borough Planning Commission existed but lacked any resources, it developed a close working relationship with the County Planning Commission. The results of this partnership would be two reports, the *Comprehensive Plan Report for Norristown Borough—1965*, issued in four volumes by the county planning commission, and the *Norristown GNRP [Greater Norristown Redevelopment Project] Interim Report: Existing Conditions, Analysis and Preliminary Recommendations*, issued in two volumes in December 1969 and February 1970 by David M. Walker Associates Inc. Possessing different though sometimes overlapping information, taken together these two reports offer a professional view of conditions in Norristown—one at mid-decade, and one at the decade's end. They offer successive pictures of downtown decay, and serve as informative additions to the statistics in describing the rapidly declining state of downtown.

The 1965 report originated in a 1963 request by the Borough Planning Commission, together with its County counterpart, for urban planning assistance funds under the provisions of Section 701 of the Federal Housing Act of 1954. A contract was signed in January 1964, and the final report was published in five volumes in 1965. The Planning Commission report painted a realistic (that is, grim) picture of Norristown's condition at mid-decade. Two quotations impart the overall message:

> The most important shopping area in the Borough is the Central Business District. It is an older shopping area typical in appearance to the Main Streets of many medium sized cities.... In recent years, however, its impact has begun to diminish because of competition from major shopping centers. Both Plymouth Meeting Mall and King of Prussia Plaza and several smaller shopping centers have adversely affected business in the downtown area. Many stores in the Central Business District are now vacant. Several buildings, because of age and original design are clearly unsuited to modern shopping practices....[391]

> One of the major deficiencies in Norristown is an insufficient number of off-street parking spaces. This lack has resulted in a great reliance on on-street parking which contributes to traffic congestion, particularly in the downtown area. The insufficient number of parking spaces is one of the prime causes in the decline of the business district. Many stores have relocated outside the community and others are of a marginal character, giving the business district a blighted appearance.[392]

A brief overview of the borough's commercial history argued that between 1948 and 1954, retail trade in the borough grew at the same rate as that in Montgomery County as a whole. There was a small increase in the borough's retail trade between 1954 and 1958, but, as the report observed, "Note the small increase in retail sales in the Borough between 1954 and 1958. If inflation were considered, this would be a decline. This happens despite the rapid population expansion in the surrounding townships." The report identified an additional threat in "the growing suburban shopping centers," citing the King of Prussia Plaza and the Valley Forge Shopping Center. Warning that this growth could be expected to continue, the report also cited a pending threat, the Plymouth Meeting Mall.[393]

The report's recommendations to increase Norristown's population and retail trade were typical of the 1960s: "A vigorous program of urban renewal is needed in Norristown for both residential and non-residential uses. Such a program is needed not only for clearance of blighted structures, but also for the arresting of blight in otherwise sound areas." It recommended securing federal and state aid to raze nearly all the existing buildings in the designated Central Business District (CBD), especially Main Street, and much of the surrounding the area. In the place of these 19th-century buildings were to arise that quintessential 1960s solution to urban decay: blocks of high-rise apartment buildings. The report specifically recommended altering the borough zoning ordinance to allow such structures.[394] Its accompanying map placed them in an arc surrounding Main Street, largely on the north side.

As for Main Street itself, the report produced only a vague drawing, obviously of a mall-like concept. There were tables and benches, and something rather like a tram in the background, and open sky all around. No further details were provided as to what would be constructed after the buildings on Main Street had all been torn down. There is no record in the *Times Herald* that this floating of the mall concept initiated any tangible response.

The borough's only response to the 1965 report—if it was, in fact a response—was the preparation of a borough resident questionnaire, which was distributed in 1966. The results should have given pause to anyone advocating municipal planning. Everything about the borough resident questionnaire brought into serious question whether local residents were even interested in renewing downtown Norristown. Of the 3,000 questionnaires distributed, only 1,047 were returned. More than half of these were the result of distribution via students in the high school, where the social studies department made their distribution a class assignment. This was a "last resort" measure, invoked late in the process, when it became clear that few completed questionnaires were being returned. The nature of the responses rendered the results statistically invalid, but of those who did respond, few appeared to hope for anything resembling concrete results. A November article in the *Times Herald* summarized the unpleasant facts gleaned from the survey. The survey had highlighted some of the attitudes that were prevalent among Norristown residents: one, apathy and indifference to the planning process in the borough; two, suspicion about how the data would be used; and three, cynicism, as expressed in such comments as "nothing ever gets done in Norristown anyway." More specific issues also came under criticism. "Many of those who answered the questionnaire also voiced objection to many facets of downtown Norristown, including merchandise selection, unattractive stores, traffic problems and poor accessibility." But perhaps there was still hope for downtown, since according to the questionnaire, "nine out of ten respondents shop within Norristown for their drug items and daily groceries.... Lesser numbers, but still a significant percentage, shop for major items such as clothing and appliances...."[395]

By the time the second joint planning commission report appeared in late 1969, that could no longer be said. Evidence of downtown's decline was beyond dispute. There was much council resistance to accepting even a portion of the total expense for this second report, but D. Rae Boyd and J. Harvey Shillingford, who was then executive director of the Montgomery County Redevelopment Authority, fought for it. Shillingford was particularly blunt, arguing that the borough had reached "the point of no return. Norristown's future is in jeopardy if nothing is done."[396]

The report was issued in two volumes, in 1969 and early 1970, and was a more expansive and detailed affair than the first. Still, both volumes essentially built on the previous report within the specified survey areas, which included the West Marshall Street shopping district in a separate discussion. Volume 1 of this second report contained yet another traffic summary, which despite its specific numbers, produced no more information than was already well known to the average Norristown resident. Volume 2 included the results of a survey of Norristown merchants, which unsurprisingly found that parking was the major issue for 68% of them, with 81% claiming that there were an insufficient number of spaces. Curiously, only 4% cited the outlying shopping centers as a major problem.[397] Despite this, the second report was in general continuity with the first as to the reasons for Norristown's condition:

> Recent trends in suburban shopping have tended to take shoppers away from Downtown Norristown. Of particular significance is the growth of modern indoor shopping malls at Plymouth Meeting and King of Prussia Plaza. They are both located within the trading radius of the borough Central Business District, and, both have registered significant increases in retail trade. Retail trade in the Borough Central Business District, on the other hand, has been declining. Vacant store fronts and empty lots attest to this recent decline in the commercial significance of the Central Business District....These two shopping centers, within a four mile radius of Norristown, have between them five department stores and more than two hundred other shops and have contributed to the decline over the past five years of the Norristown CBD as a major retail outlet.[398]

The report did not blame the new shopping centers for Main Street's woes:

> Although these two shopping centers have taken many potential customers away from the CBD, they are not the main cause of the decline in the level of retail sales in Norristown. This is due primarily to the actual physical features and appearance of the Central Business District.[399]

The report then painted a considerably grimmer picture of Main Street in 1969 than its predecessor had in 1965:

> It is insufficient to refer to the condition of structures without pointing out other and equally blighting influences. These are a source of concern in downtown Norristown. Firstly, a survey of the area shows the presence of a substantial number of vacant stores and structures. They are obviously detrimental to the environment both from a psychological as well as a business point of view. They indicate an outmigration of business and adversely influence neighboring stores. In addition empty stores are visually unpleasant due to aspects such as shop windows and cluttered interiors. Next, there are scattered throughout the Central Business District, a significant number of vacant lots. No logical reuse has yet been found for by the present reverse of some of these lots. They are visually undesirable, tend to accumulate rubbish and interrupt the continuity of store fronts. These also have a negative influence on shoppers and business alike. In some instances, a number of these lots have been converted into parking lots. These are situated haphaz-

ardly and are often environmentally unsatisfactory. They definitely have blighting influence upon the area.[400]

Several photographs of deteriorated buildings and related conditions were included in the report. One of the most striking was of the brick façade of a Main Street building, taken from across the street. Bricks left exposed by fallen stucco and peeling paint spotted the second floor, while the first was defaced by faded wood shutters. The building was part of Chatlin's.

While continuity generally characterized both reports, the second report differed sharply on the subject of Main Street and its future. While the first report had argued for commerce continuing to be a feature of downtown, the second report argued the exact opposite, saying this:

All indicators at present point to a changing role for Downtown Norristown. Commercial activities are declining, governmental and office related white collar type of activity, on the other hand, is increasing. This changing character of the Central Business District calls for the conversion of one type of use to another, and the replacement of obsolescent facilities with new and relevant ones.[401]

The second report pitched otherwise similar zoning, clearing and construction plans to implement this new direction. The concept was not to eliminate commerce in downtown, but to eliminate the old downtown. The recommendations included the "Removal of all obsolete buildings," "Condensing the physical area (length) of the CBD, naturally requiring removal of all marginal commercial development," and "Possible closing of Main Street between Swede and DeKalb to traffic and converting that area behind the County Courthouse into a mall."[402] This was a clear declaration that retail commerce would not play a major role in Norristown's future. Downtown as a shopping center was on its deathbed, and the treatment proposed was euthanasia: put it out of its misery by bulldozing it out of existence.

A document entitled "Comprehensive Plan 1969, Norristown Borough, Montgomery County, Pennsylvania" followed the publication of the two volumes of this study. This summary of the proposed plan was published by the County, stripped of much of its detail and statistics and focused on recommendations for the future. The plan clearly recognized the centrality that Norristown's relationship to the automobile was playing in the drama:

All around Norristown there are high speed highways. In the future there will be more. But people in Norristown have to travel through traffic or over narrow back roads to get to these highways.[403]

Its recommendations contained specific measures to correct this problem, including connecting the Schuylkill River Bridge to what the report referred to as the "Schuylkill Spur," a highway to carry traffic north from the bridge's end at Markley

Street (similar to the old "Norristown Bypass"), and a "North Shore Expressway" to connect to the Betzwood Bridge. Specifics were in short supply. The plan merely recommended the conversion of Main Street into "a mall," ignoring the primary appeals of real malls: space, and the all-important free, ample parking. The dominance of retail commerce was past, and the report made that clear: "For the future, Norristown can expand its role as a center of government, finance and medical services." There were to be many new residents of this new center, and they were to be housed in high-rises surrounding Main Street and the courthouse complex.

A brochure outlining a simplified Comprehensive Plan was mailed to all borough residents in 1969; it summarized the plans undertaken since the first application for federal funding in 1963, and outlined the new proposals. The Borough Council voted to adopt the Comprehensive Plan in July 1970.[404] As the vote was unanimous, the obvious question was whether such an action by a council with several staunch opponents of municipal planning in general sitting on it was more than a *pro forma* action. Subsequent events suggest that the Borough Council's action was just that, and that no actual attempt to implement the plan was contemplated.

Whether or not action based on the plan was ever contemplated, at least one prominent Norristown resident—and later mayor—pointed to the plan as contributing to the exodus of long-standing Norristown residents. While this movement had been under way for some time, publication of the plan for Norristown actually spurred it, he claimed. "The fear was that, whatever was decided, now was the time to move, before they were made to by redevelopment."[405]

The proposals contained in the two county planning documents provide strong counterargument to those who claim that during this period a primary reason for the decline and collapse of downtown was the consistent and sustained failure of Norristown Borough Council to seek federal funds. From the perspective of decades, it is clear that assumptions underpinning the report concerning new residents and high-rise apartments were invalid. At this distance, the idea that a sufficient—and, of necessity, quite large—number of new residents could be enticed to leave the suburbs and move into high-rise apartments overlooking a decayed riverfront seems ludicrous. The result of accepting federal funds for urban renewal demolition would have been the destruction of the old "Town of Norris," and with it a great many of Norristown's trove of period buildings. What would have replaced them—and when—is purely conjectural, but it is unlikely that the change would have constituted any improvement.

The Sincerest Form of Flattery

In 1963, with the King of Prussia Plaza not yet officially opened, Main Street's merchants, through their advocacy organization Downtown Norristown Inc., effectively conceded defeat. The group sponsored a meeting in July to present its plan for turning downtown into a "colonial-style shopping center," thus anticipating the County Planning Commission by two years. The four-phase plan would initially remodel the shops along the north side of Main Street between the Public Square and DeKalb Street. The appearance of the buildings in this stretch would be altered so that they conformed to a faux-colonial style, with the "hodge-podge of colors" replaced by a unified color. The centerpiece of the project was a seven-foot wide metal canopy extending over the sidewalk, under which shoppers could stroll relatively safe from the elements. Virtually all of these features were to be found across the river at the Plaza. No more striking evidence of the growing despair among merchants along Norristown's Main Street can be found than this plan to remake the downtown into a shopping-center lookalike. Those promoting the project minced no words:

"Downtown Norristown's fate as a trading mart hangs in the balance," said Howard Custer, president of Downtown Norristown Inc. "Millions of dollars will be poured into new shopping centers within the next three years…. You must make your decision now."

For T. Allen Glenn, president of the Peoples National Bank and Trust Co., the enemy was clear. "We must combat this movement to take both the shopper and the shop to places outside of what has been an historic shopping center."

Architect Louis A. Goldberg warned of the cost of inaction: "If there is deterioration and decay—and we must admit there is—the next step, if no remedial action is taken, is a slum."

This was an admission of the defeat of the traditional urban downtown shopping area. Having lost to "the malls," the plan was to imitate them. Yet for all of the supposedly frank talk about deterioration and decay, and the dramatic calls for action, the proposal failed to address the real problems: traffic and parking. Banker Glenn was noticeably sanguine nonetheless, declaring that Main Street's pending switch to one-way on Main Street would solve the traffic problem and that the parking situation "was being worked out."[406]

There was polite initial reception, but the plan went nowhere. The second dinner meeting of Downtown Norristown Inc., held in September, featured no mention of the plan at all. This second meeting may have been conspicuous for its lack of follow-up to the "mall" idea, but there *was* much discussion over the reality of Main Street. That talk centered on a word rarely heard previously: "decay." Ominously, joining decay as a subject was lethargy within the business community, a tacit acceptance of decline.

While Downtown Norristown Inc. was proposing the destruction of downtown with one hand, it continued to promote its existence with the other, sponsoring sales events and acting as the merchants' voice to borough government. It would continue to organize and promote downtown events through the end of the decade. Its annual summer event, "Old Fashioned Bargain Days," was still held every July. Specific events included a "Lucky Bucks" promotion in the fall of 1964, "Hospital Day" in 1967 (during which 10% of downtown sales were pledged to Norristown's three hospitals), a "Bunny Money" promotion in March of 1968 (shoppers were to receive this money according to the amount of their purchases), and a "Moonlight Sale" in August 1969. Other, separately organized events would take place, with perhaps the largest in geographic area—if not in scope of products offered—taking place during the first two weeks of May 1965. Although its formal title was the "Spring Appliance Spectacular," it included Main Street stores as diverse as Baer's Home Furnishings, Block's, Chatlin's, and Firestone Tires, and included stores from Logan Square, Bridgeport, Norriton Square Shopping Center, the Valley Forge Center and as far away as Collegeville. Each of these promotions were accompanied by lists or advertisements by the retailers participating in the event, Such publicity benefited the merchants who joined in, but also provided evidence that Downtown Norristown Inc. did not enjoy unanimous support, even in the core of downtown.

The specter of abandoned buildings had by this time been added to the growing evils against which Downtown Norristown struggled. The organization's 1964 annual meeting saw yet another plea to the county to raze its long-vacant and by-now "eyesore" buildings on Main Street. Yet formal denial was still the order of the day. In November, organization stalwart Morton Weiss—using Gilbert's Clothes as his only title—used the *Times Herald*'s Letters to the Editor section to address a quote from an unnamed council member that "Downtown Norristown consists of many empty stores." Nothing could be further from the truth, Weiss claimed. "With few exceptions, there are no desirable store locations empty at this time…. Despite the recent areas of competition, most of the stores are holding their own, and many are showing increased sales."[407] Such careful wording hardly constituted a refutation.

In April 1965, Norris Entertainment announced the sale of the Norris Theater to Budco Quality Theaters. Any lamentation over the loss of local ownership was muted by the fact that local ownership had let the theater get quite run-down in recent years. The new owner duly promised to make the Norris the "theater showplace it once was in the Norristown area." Budco did install badly needed new seats, but only covered the wall decorations, mirrors and murals with drapes, and placed fabric over the marble columns in the foyer.

The abandonment of Main Street was the consistent theme of these years. It even played out within the younger generation, those lacking memories of the way things used to be. Jack Coll was a boy living in King Manor, adjacent to Bridgeport. When he decided to spend the money he earned on his paper route, he went first to downtown Norristown. King Manor was (and still is) a stop on the P&W trolley line between Norristown and 69th Street, Philadelphia, which allowed Jack to begin spending his Saturdays on Main Street in the early 1960s. As with many other boys and girls at this age, his world then was divided into two components: music, and everything else. This made his sojourns onto Main Street quite focused: he went seeking 45 rpm records and his special interest, transistor radios. Even focus could wait for refreshment, however, so after descending from the second floor terminal at Swede and Main streets, Jack would go directly to Woolworth's, where he patronized its famous soda fountain. His next stop was Chatlin's, then it was on to John's Bargain Store, both of which sold the items he desired. He clearly remembers the creaky wood floors of both Woolworth's and Chatlin's. John's Bargain Store was not well kept, but Jack knew that the best bargains were displayed at the rear, where tables of mismatched and otherwise defective merchandise awaited those with either patience to look or little to spend on such things as clothes.

Jack Coll's sojourns on Main Street did not last long. By 1966, the "happening thing" was to meet one's friends at the King of Prussia Plaza on Friday and Saturday evenings. It was a safe haven from the weather, complete with food sources. In the winter he would put his coat in a locker there and spend the evening enjoying the indoor temperatures. There was no rail connection to the Plaza, so hitchhiking was common among the young. The contrast between hanging out on Main Street and hanging out at the King of Prussia Plaza was known to all: "It was the difference between major league and minor league, no doubt about it."[408]

Those who had worked downtown felt the result of those decisions. While Fran Zummo was in college in the late 1950s, she still got phone calls from Chatlin's asking if she was available to work that coming weekend: "We need you." But after graduating she began to feel "something was not right." She married, and her children were born in 1963 and 1965. By the time she was raising her own family, she had a car and did her shopping at the malls, despite her dislike of the mall environment. Logan Square was near, so they often went there, usually to Sears. "That was where you went; there was no place left [downtown]." Her children never spent any time downtown.[409] Still, some clung to old habits, among them Mary Early. She too had a car by now, but she did not like to drive, and had long ago gotten accustomed to walking. In the winter, she pulled a sled to carry her purchases.[410]

In 1967, an event occurred that brought a foretaste of what was to come. Kerson's Ladies Wear had closed its store at 64 East Main Street in 1966 and abandoned the property. In March 1967, it burned down, and remained an eyesore for seven months before it was finally torn down in mid-October. The lot was offered to the borough for a parking lot at an asking price of $50,000. The Borough Council declined, citing the lot's long, narrow shape as inconvenient for parking. The lot remained, another open gap on Main Street's core block, and the address disappeared from the directories. In the years to come, such fires "of suspicious origin" would become a recurring event on Main Street.

Another Norristown retail institution abandoned Main Street in March 1968 when B. E. Block & Bros. announced the sale of its building at 11 West Main Street to the Continental Bank & Trust Co. Like Sears before it, Block's moved to Logan Square. The transaction was handled by Harry and Joseph Butera. The firm's formal notice repeated the by-now familiar refrain:

> Our need for more modern facilities, better merchandising and in-store traffic patterns, additional and convenient parking space, plus greater overall shopping convenience makes the Logan Square Shopping Center a wise choice for us. It offers Block's a new up-to-date and convenient location without severing the strong ties the store has with the Norristown area and the many friends it has made through the years.[411]

Block's last day on Main Street was Friday, May 10; the new store opened at Logan Square on May 23. The firm immediately began a heavy advertising campaign in the *Times Herald*. The headline on its advertisement in Tuesday's paper succinctly summed it up: "We Moved to Give You What You Want: More Convenience, Easier Parking, Bigger Selections, Lower Prices!"[412]

Continental Bank announced plans to raze the Block's building for use as a parking lot, but insisted that its long-term plans were to use the lot for expansion of their own building. This is the lot that appeared in the 1970 and 1972 directories as the Municipal Parking Lot. It would remain a parking lot; no building expansion would take place on it. Thus, another significant gap was added to those already existing among Main Street's buildings. The address disappeared from directories after 1972.

An identical fate befell a diverse structure known as the Wildman Building, which spanned 105 through 121 West Main Street. Norris Entertainment sold the Wildman Building and a lot adjacent to the Norris Theater to the Commonwealth Federal Savings & Loan Company at 104 West Main Street in June. The Wildman Building housed seven individual stores or services, including Pep Boys Auto Supplies, as well as apartments on the upper floor. All seven—plus the apartments—were lost when the Wildman Building was demolished and replaced by a parking lot for Commonwealth customers. All seven addresses disappeared from the directories beginning in 1970. Meanwhile, at downtown's very west end, preparations were finally under way for the second Schuylkill River bridge, and meant the destruction of three more buildings.

Novell's left Main Street in 1968, becoming the only significant Main Street store to relocate to the King of Prussia Plaza. Wanamaker's at the Plaza announced in March that it had purchased the entire stock of menswear from Novell's downtown store. Novell's found no buyer for its building, and abandoned it.

Less than 18 months after the blaze that destroyed Kerson's at 64 East Main Street, three almost simultaneous fires broke out downtown in the morning hours of November 8, 1968. One fire destroyed the vacant Novell's building at 54 East Main Street, damaging the W. T. Grant store at 58 and the C. R. Jennings jewelry store at 52. There were reports that all three fires were caused by "Molotov cocktails."[413] The W. T. Grant store had also been damaged in the blaze that had destroyed Kerson's, and this second fire was the last straw; after that, the W. T. Grant store closed for good. While Grant's was not in the same class as Block's, its departure contributed to the bleak condition of Main Street that was becoming graphically apparent by 1969.

"Blight"

By 1969, people who had been observing Main Street's decline, from professional planners to casual shoppers, had ceased to mince words. The second of two planning reports for the Greater Norristown Redevelopment Project mentioned earlier made the point in the starkest possible terms: "However, in the case of Norristown, we are dealing with a declining, economically dying central business district."[414] In support of this claim, the report included a summary entitled "Estimated Sales Structure of Major Shopping Centers and Other Areas of Retail Activity Forming Part of the Retail Market Surrounding Norristown, Pennsylvania, 1968/9." The basic results (expressed in $000) demonstrated the complete nature of the turnaround in the traditional retail relationship between Norristown and its environs:

194

Norristown

Central Business District*	$ 11,950–15,600
Logan Square	$ 22,720–26,370
West Marshall Street	$ 3,300 –4,200
Plymouth Meeting	$ 36,000 –40,200
King of Prussia	$ 55,000–61,500 [415]

CBD, substantially larger than the survey area

Logan Square's gross sales were almost twice that of the entire Central Business District. The Plymouth Meeting Mall, which had only opened in 1966, posted sales of more than three times that of the CBD, while the King of Prussia Plaza had assumed a considerable leadership position, with gross sales almost five times as large. A letter to the editor of the *Times Herald*, printed on May 21, 1969, expressed the same view but from the shopper's perspective, using a distinctly unpleasant metaphor. The anonymous writer, claimed to be a newcomer, but pulled no punches:

> Blight has set in. The consumers, including the downtown residents, have fled with their dollars to the sprawling malls in the suburbs. Exit the dollar and exit the shops and service establishments that catered to the Norristown community and dollars. Stores were closed down and were knocked down so that Main Street now has a very grim countenance. It has the look of a German city with gaping voids, yawning in ugliness. The only difference is the buildings over there were bombed out and in Norristown they were driven out by lack of trade.[416]

The Valley Forge Hotel followed an increasingly downward economic course in the years after Norristown's sesquicentennial celebration. By the end of the decade, the corporation had begun to lose money again. The following financial summary uses the figures made available in the annual *Times Herald* articles. It demonstrates the hotel's quickly deteriorating status by the end of the 1960s.

Year	Income	Expenses	Net Profit
1951	$383,334.46	N/A	$33,404.94
1952	$394,529.34	N/A	$31,710.74
1953	$356,986.72	N/A	$30,094.09
1954	N/A	N/A	$30,064.72
1955	$350,156.00	N/A	$28,770.46
1956	$359,787.07	$277,272.10	$27,619.12
1957	$367,794.00	$288,877.00	$22,361.00
1958	$356,647.82	$288,321.13	$18,668.75
1959	$347,958.00	$279,873.00	$19,326.19
1960	N/A	N/A	$20,278.96*
1961	$376,016.02	$301,193.91	$25,100.97
1962	N/A	N/A	N/A
1963	N/A	N/A	N/A
1964	$354,999.12	$318,917.79	$8,565.76
1965	N/A	N/A	"slightly in excess of $3,000"

1966	$423,727.32	$362,075.21	$18,095.43
1967	($4,365.96)		
1968	$397,696.43	$369,686.63	($5,324.03)
1969	N/A	N/A	N/A

* *As extracted from 1962 report. Result was partly earnings from operation and partly from non-recurring capital gains on the sale of securities.*

The hotel suffered a major non-financial loss in September 1964 when hotel manager Andrew Malone resigned. He had begun at the hotel as a bellboy in 1935 and, except for a stint in the army during WWII, had worked there ever since. He was named assistant manager in 1950, and manager in 1955. The annual summary articles in the *Times Herald* are replete with compliments for his management skills. It does appear, however, that the verbal support given him was not equaled by the financial support. (As Horace Davenport put it, Malone was "manager in title, but never manager in salary.") He left to become manager at the much newer City Line Marriott, at the intersection of City Line Avenue and the Schuylkill Expressway. He was replaced by his assistant manager, who lasted only one year before resigning. His replacement lasted until 1968, when he also resigned. His replacement, in turn, resigned in January 1970.

The year 1966 would be touted in the annual article as an exception to the steadily worsening financial picture, as the figures supplied to the corporation's stockholders and to the *Times Herald* indicated a reversal of the declining profit picture of the previous two years. Those figures indicated the largest net profit since 1961, in 1967 the hotel posted a net loss, which was blamed on the need to replace the entire 40-year-old heating system. Clearly the question of an annual profit or loss depended on the amount of maintenance the aging facility required. That same year, an unnamed resident of the Valley Forge Hotel who had lived there since July 1966, after his release from the Norristown State Hospital (a mental facility), hung himself in his room.

Income and expenses for 1968, and the resulting net loss, were listed in the annual article in the *Times Herald*, which mentioned "major improvements" completed during the year and a declaration by the president of the board of directors that prospects for a dividend in 1969 looked "good." The headline for the article also demonstrated confidence, or at least boosterism: "Hotel Girds for Key Role in Downtown Renewal Plan."[417] As it turned out, 1969 did not deliver on its perceived promise. The annual article in January 1970 listed no financial figures, but contained an admission that the hotel "has been financially unsuccessful this year." The reason was the one that had always plagued the Valley Forge Hotel, but the proposed solution was new, and a clear sign of desperation. According to the president of the board of directors, "The reason we have been losing money is the fact that our room occupancy has been rather low. In order to improve this situation, we have started renting office space." Despite this, and an admission that the hotel had no space to expand its utterly inadequate parking situation, the president still managed to close with the usual optimism: "We feel our location is tops and we are looking forward to a much better situation."[418] They can be forgiven for that hope, since they might have imagined that things could not get much worse. And yet they did.

Assisted Suicide? The Role of Borough Council

By now it should be clear that as the sesquicentennial year of 1962 receded into history, the merchants of downtown Norristown were fully aware of the challenges they faced, both internal (i.e., traffic congestion, lack of parking, and the county's plans for its downtown properties); and the external issues (i.e., proliferating local shopping centers and large malls with free, ample parking). In response to these well-known problems, the Borough Council, local business leaders, and residents would, throughout the 1960s, play out a sad sequence of proposal, discussion, delay, disagreement, and controversy over and over again, all against a backdrop of increasing downtown business decline. Norristown Borough Council would, in particular, continue its traditional ways, with the level of personal rancor perhaps even somewhat elevated. Such institutional behavior was as routinely excoriated both in public and in private then as it had been previously, but it must be remembered that Borough Council and its behavior had been sustained in 1960 when Norristown voters overwhelmingly rejected the "City Plan" in a referendum.

The Borough Council's torturous path to any decision was repeated in its attempt to finally make Main Street one-way. This conversion had been theoretically pending since the original "Comprehensive Plan" had been issued in 1951, but the struggle to convert DeKalb and Markley streets had been so acrimonious that converting Main Street, the second step in the plan, had been quietly buried. Council's revisiting the issue once again in 1963 began a roller-coaster ride that was excessive even by the council's considerable standards. The Borough Council's tradition of local control and fiscal conservatism would during this period be further tested by the increasingly liberal national mood, as symbolized by the "Great Society." To borough leaders facing declining local tax revenues, the quickly increasing level of federal funding being made available to municipalities through a plethora of programs provided considerable incentive to seek a share of that funding. Unfortunately, these national programs carried with the welcome funds the utterly unwelcome requirements, restrictions, and oversight. Thus, the real cost of these projects to the elected leaders of the borough lay in the ceding of authority to outside sources—a cost that the Borough Council members were not willing to pay.

Resurrecting the Comprehensive Plan

Theoretically, the conversion of Main Street to one-way had been pending since the original Comprehensive Plan of 1951. This second step in the plan had been quietly buried, without any announcement. The Borough Council reopened the issue in 1963 in conjunction with the pending purchase of new parking meters by asking the police chief to investigate the change to one-way for both Main and Airy streets. By this time, the state of Pennsylvania had assumed overall authority over Airy Street in addition to Main Street; this would further complicate the situation.

The actual ordinance directing the change was not passed until August, and then only for a 90-day trial period to begin on October 1. As the three-month period drew to a close, 43 Main Street merchants, citing loss of business, presented a petition to council asking that the one-way experiment be reversed. Council, however, opted to continue with the one-way plan for an additional three months. By the time three-month review arrived, the one-way arrangement had received support from the chief of police, the Central Montgomery County Chamber of Commerce, and the Norristown Planning Commission—not to mention an editorial from the *Times Herald* that offered the rather backhanded praise that by doing nothing to alter the one-way arrangement despite local pressure, the Borough Council had actually taken a progressive step. Despite such support, the council voted 8:4 to abandon the one-way plan. The *Times Herald* rapped the decision editorially, and the Norristown Planning Commission reiterated its support for the one-way arrangement. Councilman Leonard Deloplaine, the one-way project's primary supporter, condemned his fellow council members for abandoning the plan. The logic of his letter, printed in the *Times Herald*, was simple and clear, if unpalatable to Main Street merchants:

> Typical of many old towns, we are plagued with streets that are not designed to handle the traffic flow of 1964. These streets just cannot handle the volume of local and through traffic which uses our streets without a considerable amount of delays…. It is impossible to increase the width of our streets unless we move to the ridiculous and eliminate the sidewalk areas…. Norristown streets were designed many years before the advent of mass private motor transportation.[419]

Deloplaine denounced the alternatives offered by the plan's opponents, in particular the proposal to ban parking on the north side of Main Street during peak traffic hours. Terming this the "Paul Plan," he pointedly observed that it was being offered by the same council member who had led the fight against borough funds for "much-needed municipal parking."[420]

It became a moot point. The State Highway Department denied the borough's request to abandon the one-way layout on Airy Street. This led to a Borough Council meeting in May that was chaotic even by Norristown standards. Lost in the heated arguments was a resolution to rescind the one-way plan; it never made it to the floor. Paul Santangelo, for one, did not even see the reason for such a resolution, as the original resolution had been for only a three-month experiment. Informed of the state's wishes, he bellowed, "Who's running this town, the state or council? I see what is happening here. The majority is not ruling, it is the minority ruling." Emotions ran so high within such a badly divided council that even the motion to adjourn received a tie vote until interim mayor Oler broke the tie.

In the end, Main and Airy streets remained one way, although some minor modifications were later enacted. That decision has been harshly criticized, then and since. Two Main Street merchants interviewed for this work brought up the 1963–1964 struggle over making Main Street one way, and condemned the Borough Council, but neither linked it to the 1951 dispute, despite one of them having been present for both.[421] Upon examination, the motive involved was most likely the obvious one: to move automobiles into and out of the borough more expeditiously. Before, then and since, the Borough Council consistently elected to expedite traffic flow rather than prioritize the needs of downtown merchants. This did not necessarily involve malice on council's part; it was just that, as one interviewee put it, "The preservation of Main Street was not even on their radar."[422]

A Bridge Too Late

Norristown may have been divided over whether to make Main Street one-way, but it was unanimously in favor of a second bridge over the Schuylkill, if not exactly on where to locate it. Such a bridge had seemed to be close to approval before, but this time Norristown had a state elected official firmly on its side. Drafting the engineering plans and securing funding at the state level required a considerable expenditure of time and effort, but the man who chose to spearhead that effort was extremely motivated: state representative Robert (Bob) Butera, successor to Walter Fry and the oldest son of Harry Butera. The elder Butera's desire for and efforts on behalf of a second Schuylkill bridge made Robert Butera determined to fulfill what he believed to be his father's legacy. He made the project a priority, and constantly nudged the process along—work that didn't earn headlines, but made sure that this time a bridge actually resulted. Butera's vision for the bridge did not stop at providing a second crossing of river between Bridgeport and Norristown. He envisioned it as part of a master plan to connect this span with the modern new span then under construction across the Schuylkill to the west, at Betzwood, just east of Valley Forge Park. This span was, in turn, to spur construction of a limited-access highway to Pottstown and Reading. The connection between this highway and the Schuylkill Bridge, known as the Schuylkill Parkway, was to be a limited-access highway along the south bank of the Schuylkill between the two spans. The idea was to route traffic from Norristown and King of Prussia toward Reading on these interconnected bridges and highways.[423]

In June 1966 project consultants publicly estimated that construction would begin within 18 months. This announcement also finally gave Norristown residents details of the bridge's termination at Main Street. The scaled-down design greatly lessened the physical changes required in the borough. Lafayette Street would be terminated just short of its intersection with Markley Street, to accommodate the bridge's descent from its crossing height down to Main Street. Markley Street itself would be expanded to two lanes in each direction from Main Street to Marshall Street to handle the influx of traffic coming off the bridge.

The engineers' estimate of the project's starting time proved to be accurate. Construction preliminaries began, after a brief ceremony, on December 8, 1967, with the razing of ten houses in Bridgeport and Upper Merion. *Then* the delays began. The contract for the construction itself was not awarded until August 1968. Alas, for Norristown, the construction of the bridge took longer than expected, for reasons not pertinent here, and it would not be even partially open until October 1973, when the two southbound lanes began carrying traffic. Even then the delays did not end. When the two southbound lanes opened, completion of the full project was predicted for late 1974, but the final two lanes did not open until June 1975. Nevertheless, the Judge

William Dannehower Bridge, as it would be christened (there had been support for naming it after Harry Butera), was welcome to Norristown and (most of) Bridgeport, and continues to be so.

None of the associated plans—either Robert Butera's Schuylkill Parkway, or the Planning Commission's Northern Spur—ever came to be. The south end of the bridge still has two sweeping roadways that turn upriver, then abruptly terminate. Given the subsequent residential development in those areas through which these extensions were to pass, it is safe to conclude that they will never be built.

What? No Free, Ample Parking?

In 1963 the question arose of what to do with the old Pigeon-Hole Garage. In March, the Parking Authority formally asked the Borough Council to purchase the garage for $250,000, proposing that they float a bond issue that would, in turn, be purchased by the three banks still trying to operate the garage. They presented figures to show that the garage would produce an operating profit within three years.

The proposal provoked a firestorm at the March meeting. The memorable and melodramatic evening saw various council members leaping to their feet to deliver passionate views, but fortunately no direct physical confrontations. Council member Leonard Deploplaine tried to plead the case for taxpayer support of the garage, noting that the local banks had already lost $200,000 on the garage, and needed help. "You have to consider the plight of the downtown merchants; if you fail to cooperate with them, then the borough will eventually lose tax dollars when the stores close."

Council member Deem interjected, "What are they going to do? Tear down the buildings on Main Street? The properties will still be there. Suppose we go along and in five years Main Street becomes obsolete. We'll have a garage and nothing else." There was both blindness and prophecy in these observations. Main Street was already obsolete. The confident prediction that the buildings would remain proved to be quite wrong. The vision of a Main Street with a parking garage and nothing else was more accurate, but that would happen more than 40 years in the future. Council member Francis Orr denounced Deploplaine for arguing that revenue from parking meters should be channeled to fund the garage, calling him "worse than former Philadelphia Mayor Dilworth" (whose proposal for downtown parking fees had recently drawn vehement opposition). Stung by the *ad hominem* attacks, Deploplaine withdrew from the meeting, and from any further advocacy of parking.

The result was a tepid motion to have the Finance Committee discuss the idea and report back. Even this was too much for Paul Santangelo, who cast the only vote against the motion. Santangelo ranted that not only should the council reject the Parking Authority's proposal, it should reject the Parking Authority. "I have said before a Parking Authority is not in the best interest of the taxpayers of this borough. I have said in the past there is no need for a parking garage in this town. We wasted $7,500 of taxpayer's money years ago with a Parking Authority. And for what? It just went down the drain.... I don't want this borough to have anything to do with a Parking Authority or the Pigeon Hole Garage."

The more moderate majority view was best expressed by veteran council member Ciccarone. "We can't tax the entire town for the convenience of downtown parking facilities."[424] The issue was raised again at the March and April meetings, but did not come to a decision until a special meeting in May when the council, concluding that the garage would never turn a profit, rejected the proposal. Disappointed but unsurprised, the three local banks continued to operate the garage while looking for ways to dispose of it. The Pigeon-Hole Garage took a long time to go away. It formally ceased operation in April 1964, and continued to sit as a rusting hulk for decades.

One of the objectives of the sesquicentennial celebration in 1962 had been to bring shoppers "back to Norristown." January 1963 brought alarming evidence that they had not returned, even for the Christmas season, traditionally downtown's biggest and most crucial shopping time. December 1962 revenues were second only to February in the year's monthly parking meter revenues. The council still blamed the revenue decline on old meters. The question of whether to buy new ones in turn raised the issue of whether to retain the traditional rate of 12 minutes for a penny. In true Norristown fashion, this issue generated controversy far in excess of its importance. Sentiment at first seemed to favor eliminating the penny option, but in October the council voted to keep the penny option when it installed new meters. It then reversed itself a week later. Nearly 800 new meters authorized in September 1963 were delivered two months later by the manufacturer, and were installed in November without the penny option.

The proponents of the penny option did not give up, however. A July meeting of a previously unknown (and short-lived) organization known as the Norristown Citizens Committee claimed that 5-cent meters drove business from downtown, and that restoration of the 1-cent rate would actually make more parking spaces available for "short-stop" customers. The issue of how to treat short-stop customers revealed the same old dichotomy: on the one side were residents and merchants trying to address new problems using the traditional solutions, and on the other side was the Borough Council, less interested in solutions than in maintaining the *status quo*—especially with respect to taxes. The result was a year of pointless declarations by people in favor of accommodating short-stop customers and more than the usual "split the baby" pontificating by the *Times Herald*.

In July 1965, those nostalgic for the 1¢-meter option found their champion. Jeffersonville resident Francis Mullinson, secretary to the pastor of Norristown's First Presbyterian Church, had stopped briefly to pick up a "zep" on East Main Street. She did not deposit five cents in the meter, and when she returned she found a ticket fining her $1. She refused to pay the fine, and was summoned to a hearing, where she pleaded guilty. Given the alternative by the Justice of the Peace of either paying a $5 fine (plus an additional $9 in costs) or spending five days in jail, she chose the latter. In her statement, she made it clear that the cause of the short-stop shopper had been her motivation. She proclaimed that provisions should be made for those desiring to make quick drop-offs/pickups. "If this courtesy cannot be accorded shoppers, then the borough ought to return to penny meters." She was willing, she said, "to become a martyr to bring this matter to the attention of the public and to borough council." Her pastor said he supported her fully, pointed out that the lady in question had no criminal re-cord, and added that, "the five-cent parking meters are strangling the business inter-ests."[425] In any event, the young lady ended up serving only about ten hours of her five-day sentence. An "anonymous friend" paid the woman's fine and costs before she actu-ally had to spend the night in jail.

Francis Mullinson's stand in favor of the penny parking option moved the *Times Herald* to one of its long, homily-filled editorials. "That woman in jail is the image of a long controversy here and everywhere about parking meters, especially those that don't sell less than an hour of time," it said. "Five cents for two minutes is too much. A dollar or five dollars for a violation is too much." Ever short on solutions, the edito-rial concluded with a predictably vague, please-all declaration that "a lot of thought and some kind of action is needed so that the meters will be more acceptable to busi-nessmen, their visiting business associates and their customers."[426]

Less than four days later, the Borough Council, in session as the Finance Commit-tee, demonstrated what it thought of all this. The Finance Committee offered a pro-posal to convert the 380 parking meters in the immediate downtown Norristown business district, which included Main, DeKalb, Cherry, Penn, and Swede streets, from a one-hour capacity to a two-hour capacity; the cost would remain a nickel an hour, but the meters would accept a second nickel. The penny option was not even ad-dressed. In August, the council formally received the recommendation. Discussion re-vealed that the time extension had been the initiative of Gerald A. Salatino, executive director of Downtown Norristown Inc.—evidence that local merchants were focused not on the short-stop shoppers, but on those concerned that one hour was not long enough. The two-hour meters were in operation by October.

And what of the self-proclaimed short-stop martyr whose need had so moved the *Times Herald* three months earlier? Francis Mullinson wrote a single letter to the Borough Council while it was considering the time-limit extension, asking for "some provision for the in-and-out, the five-minute shopper." After that, neither she nor the "five-minute shopper" was heard from again.

In acting as it did, the Borough Council failed to address the fundamental difference between parking in the downtown area and parking at the new malls; the latter was "free." The (admittedly few) letters on the subject of parking meters published by the *Times Herald* during this period appear to reflect concern about this central difference. In February 1965, a King of Prussia resident said the wish to visit downtown Nor-ristown more often to shop was discouraged by the "lack of convenient free park-ing."[427] A letter in July from someone who claimed to shop exclusively downtown la-mented the parking situation, and in particular having to go to City Hall to pay a fine. "I want to continue to do my shopping in Norristown but, please give the shoppers a break and don't penalize us for coming to Norristown."[428]

While this longing for a relic of a vanished past decorated the pages of the *Times Herald* for several months, the issue of parking meters once again became caught up in a renewed effort to obtain off-street parking in the borough's shopping areas. This long-simmering issue came to a head again during the second half of 1964, and lead to a formal legal challenge in early 1965. Downtown business owners circulated two petitions in 1964, and presented them to the Borough Council in July, signed by over 200 local business and professional people. The petitions asked for borough support in obtaining off-street parking. The *Times Herald* article pointed out that the immediate spur for the effort was the construction of the Plymouth Meeting Mall, which the article identified as "the sixth in the area immediately surrounding Norristown" (the others were not identified, nor were the criteria for their inclusion).[429]

A special meeting to receive the study and discuss the issue was called for July 21. On July 20, a *Times Herald* editorial was starkly clear about what was happening: there was no longer a threat facing downtown—the threat had materialized. The problem was clear and local: the lack of parking. "Many of the people now shopping in the suburbs would shop in Norristown instead if they could only find a place to park. Absent action by the Borough—and quick action at that—the outlook was for a further decline in business, store closings, and fewer retail job opportunities."

The villain of the story was *free, ample parking*.

The editorial acknowledged the failure of the Pigeon Hole Garage, calling it "an apparently unpopular central parking arrangement," and called for the borough to obtain several small parking lots. Having gone this far, it would go no further, urging only that the Borough Council take the lead in obtaining the lots, but not necessarily in paying for them.[430]

A committee of local merchants and professionals had prepared a nine-page study of the parking problem, with proposals for its resolution. Representatives of this group included Morton Weiss, of Gilbert's Clothes (and president of Downtown Norristown Inc.); Arthur Cooper, general manager of Chatlin's; David Kogan, of the Paris Linen Shop; and Dr. Irving Segal, president of the West End Business Association. They presented the study and its proposals to the Borough Council on July 21 and called for the borough to provide off-street parking facilities in both the downtown and West End business districts through bond issues to be backed by revenue from parking meters. In making the presentation, Cooper made the feelings of Norristown merchants crystal clear:

> All of us who signed the petition, many of whom are here tonight, feel that this is a time of crisis, that if positive steps are not taken to alleviate the parking problem as it is today, tomorrow will find a run-down, defeated business community. There are some business firms in Norristown now who are seriously considering giving up their stores when their current leases expire. A positive approach to the parking problem might influence these firms to remain in Norristown.[431]

The council listened politely, and president Tyson promised that the council would study the request, and respond. But there was no formal response. Amid all this, the Parking Authority reorganized once again, with largely new members. This newest version then requested an operating allotment of $10,000 be included in the borough's 1965 Budget. An identical sum had been requested by the earlier version of the Parking Authority for inclusion in the 1964 Borough Budget. The request had been cut to $5,000 in initial discussions, and then had disappeared altogether.[432] This new request appears to have met a similar fate, as nothing more was heard of it.

Months passed with no agreement among council members, and therefore no response to the merchants. In early January, in a desperate measure Downtown Norristown Inc. and another group of local businesses, including B. E. Block Brothers and Gilbert's Clothes, filed a lawsuit in county court. The suit asked the court to prohibit the Borough Council from placing revenue from parking meters in the General Fund, to order the revenues to be placed in a Special Parking Meter Fund, and to decree that all future meter revenues be placed in this fund to be administered by the Parking Authority solely to finance off-street parking. The suit also sought an accounting of all parking meter revenues since 1940, with any amounts found to be in excess of operating costs to be placed in the Special Parking Meter Fund. The Parking Authority was not a party to the suit, but two of its members were. A county judge dismissed the suit in June. Legal options did remain, but by that time Norristown was buzzing with news of a "top secret" report in the hands of the county commissioners. Ironically, not only its subject (a parking garage) but its author, National Garages Inc., were commonly known. This news ended whatever chance remained to continue the legal challenge.

The County Comes to Main Street, Part Three

The county's expansion plans—at least with respect to Main Street—languished between the last burst of planning in 1961 until mid-1965. The buildings on Main and Penn streets remained boarded up and empty. By spring, word circulated that the county was considering allowing the site to be used for construction of a major parking garage, an idea that met with considerable local anticipation. By the end of August, the outlines of the proposal had emerged. This latest manifestation of plans for the properties was a curious hybrid. The structure was to be a multilevel garage fronting on East Main Street from the Public Square east to Peoples National Bank at 42 East Main Street, but would also include some 7,500 square feet of new retail space. There were even vague references to the county retaining "air rights" above the structure to accommodate future upward construction. There would be an entrance on Main Street, and an entrance and exit on Penn Street. The proposal was careful to point out that the garage would be self-service, not a "mechanical type"—a not-so-veiled referenced to the Pigeon-Hole Garage—and would have 450 parking spaces, of which 100 would be reserved for county personnel, with the remainder available for use by shoppers.

Curiously, the authors pitched the plan to the county as a project to be administered by the Borough Parking Authority, which would borrow the money to construct the garage/retail space. This did not sit well with borough officials, of course, and the pages of the *Times Herald* for the next few days featured articles about different officials discussing the plan, virtually all unfavorably. To these officials, the plan seemed to require that the borough underwrite the entire project. By late September, the Borough Council formally rendered its "no" verdict. Included was a statement of even broader significance that "Councilmen felt that taxpayers of Norristown were against the expenditure of money for parking facilities."[433]

The county commissioners withdrew the proposal and by February 1966 had hired an architect to design a new version of the plan, a self-service parking garage and a multistory county administration building, also between Main and Penn streets. The self-service parking garage remained the centerpiece, but this plan still contained new storefronts along Main Street. Parking capacity had been lowered to "more than 350" spaces, though that would change again as the design evolved. Initial response from council members and the *Times Herald* was tepidly favorable.

By year end, the Borough Council's support for the project had increased. In December, they voted unanimously to vacate a portion of Penn Street to accommodate the county's construction plan.[434] What seems to have won over the council were assurances by the county that at least 100 of the proposed parking units would be reserved for general public use during courthouse business hours, with all spaces generally available after business hours and during holidays.[435] The *Times Herald* gave strong editorial support to the project on December 12, imagining the good the new courthouse complex could do, even arguing that it "could provide the spark, the catalyst, if you wish, for a community-wide refurbishing program which might project Norristown's central area to the position of prominence it deserves."[436] County Commissioner A. Russell Parkhouse repeated the refrain to an April 1967 meeting of Norristown area's Republicans, calling the county's expansion program "the anchor for a rejuvenation of downtown Norristown."[437]

The first step in the project was the demolition of the existing buildings, which began in August 1967. One by one, buildings that had long graced the core of downtown fell to the wrecking ball, among them the Montgomery Trust Building, with its Roman-style façade with columns, the Montgomery Trust Arcade Building (originally the Boyer Arcade), and old Mitchell residence, commercial since 1952. Once the demolition was complete, the county made an immediate gesture toward downtown's parking problem by grading the lot and laying stone over the dirt, thus providing a makeshift but serviceable parking lot, leased to the Parking Authority for $1. This served a useful, if informal (it never appeared in the directories, naturally) role in addressing the downtown parking situation. It was known and accepted by all that the lot was temporary, existing only until construction began on the expansion project. Construction was expected to commence in early 1968. True to tradition, that date was not met. Formal construction did not begin until May 1, so the temporary lot was still available for the 1968 Christmas shopping season. Morton Weiss, speaking as chairman of the Parking Authority, was properly grateful, and attributed a claimed increase in business downtown to the lot's existence.

An artist's rendering of the garage portion of the plan in the December 4 edition of the *Times Herald* showed that changes had been made. The garage was now part of a larger, multiuse complex that would extend past a to-be-demolished portion of Penn Street to the existing administration building on Airy Street. Gone was the structure's frontage along Main Street, and the potential retail sites. The structure was largely set back from Main Street, and its only frontage there was the entrance, set between stepped concrete side walls like the paws of a modern Sphinx, between which supplicants would enter on a daily basis. Thus died Main Street's last hope of retail shops replacing those torn down by the county. The garage itself would not appear for several more years, and by the time it was usable, its use by downtown shoppers would be too little and too late for it to contribute anything to Main Street.

The Struggle Over Municipal Planning

The Borough Planning Commission spent the years prior to 1970 generating far more headlines than results. There was plenty of fault to go around, and commission chairman D. Rae Boyd became the lightning rod of much of the criticism leveled at the commission. The fundamental problem, as always, was money—rather, the lack of it. The Borough Council created the commission and staffed it with volunteers, but had not provided any funding for projects.

D. Rae Boyd was a large, open-mannered and good-hearted man, always available to volunteer time as well as money to local causes. He truly loved Norristown, and tried to use his position as chairman of the Planning Commission to influence the borough toward goals he perceived as desirable. Absent any funding, however, his options were limited. He was a good speaker, always ready with a quote, and talking was about all he had the resources to do. Over the remainder of the decade, Boyd made numerous speeches and issued annual predictions of Norristown's bright future. By the late 1960s, these latter had evolved into annual *Times Herald* articles published in early January. Boyd played the role of booster in both his speeches and articles; he could be critical, but always tried to put the best face on things.

Still, the Borough Council reined him in frequently. In 1963, Boyd voiced opposition to demolishing the Montgomery Trust and adjacent buildings for the county's expansion plans. After "discussions" with county officials, he issued a statement of support.[438] In 1965, Boyd, enraged that several builders were not following plans they had filed, took it upon himself to issue stop work orders on Planning Commission stationery. The builders' protests had the desired effect: the Borough Council rebuked Boyd for his actions, and reminded everyone that the Planning Commission was purely an *advisory* group. That is, they had zero power.

Each Boyd's speeches during this period individually made positive claims; an examination of them in sequence through 1969, however, reveals each article to be couched in less positive terms than its predecessor. In a 1964 speech to the Norriton Lions Club, he buoyantly predicted that "if we carry out all the projects now either begun, awaiting approval or contemplated, by 1985, nobody can imagine what a fine place Norristown will be." He foresaw Main Street as a tightly concentrated center for business, with banking, financial, and professional firms. In a *Times Herald* article the following month he waxed philosophical, admitting that Norristown, "like Topsy, has just grown," adding that municipal planning locally had begun "about 10 years too late." He based his optimism on a curious, and questionable, belief about the times: "There is a change gathering momentum every day, quite the opposite of the post-

WWII years. People are flowing back to the cities. Now, Norristown has all the facilities that make a first-class city and we should adapt them."[439]

By 1967 Boyd's formula for success boiled down to a plea for help through local cooperation: "The future of Norristown also rests on the 'new city' concept. 'New city' means that the townships surrounding Norristown will blend together with the borough to form, if not one political unit, at least a system for solving area-wide traffic problems, land-use problems, economic problems and the many other conditions which spread over municipal boundaries."[440] Boyd's 1968 annual article returned to the upbeat attitude, if more restrained in expression. And in January 1969, his article managed to include the word "progress," but used the word in a manner that recognized the general decline: "Progress is being made in the revitalization of Norristown."[441] By 1969, even the rose-tinted glasses of D. Rae Boyd could not hide the signs that were all around him.

To the Periphery

The shopping choices for customers in the areas around Norristown continued to expand and multiply during the 1960s. Logan Square was growing. In late 1964, Sears began construction on its new store, triple the size of the existing store, with over 157,000 square feet of indoor space and a 7,000-square-foot garden section outdoors. It opened in August 1966.

Soon, however, signs increased that even Logan Square, a pioneer in the movement to the periphery, might not have moved far enough and was destined to suffer the fate of Main Street. The plans for enclosing the entire center under a roof never materialized, Santa ceased to arrive in a helicopter, and in 1966 the annual automobile show decamped for the spacious and temperature-controlled interior of the Plymouth Meeting Mall. Block's Department Store never regained its importance after moving to Logan Square, and disappeared from the directories in the mid-1970s. Logan Square will be mentioned again in the context of another move by a major Main Street retailer, but its story effectively ends here.

By 1963, the Plymouth Meeting Mall at the intersection of the Pennsylvania Turnpike and its Northeast Extension was becoming a reality. The project broke ground in October 1964 and opened on February 22, 1966. At first, the enclosed building contained 60 stores open for business, including the Strawbridge & Clothier branch store, which was soon joined by Woolworth's and Lit Brothers. By midsummer the mall was expected to encompass 800,000 of space and 90 stores, banks, and restaurants—all of it indoors, sheltered from the unpredictable Pennsylvania weather, kept at a temperate 72°F year round, and artfully "landscaped" with flowering plants, shrubs, and even caged tropical birds. A visual metaphor of the times was the display of a cross-section of a local sycamore tree, in excess of 200 years old when it was cut down to widen the Germantown Pike to accommodate the mall. Even a major fire in 1970, which damaged at least 90% of its 128 shops, did not slow the mall's momentum. A majority of those shops reopened within days.

The Plymouth Meeting Mall also ends its place in this narrative at this point, for the same reasons as Logan Center. The Mall would outperform Logan Center by far, and continues to offer an attractive alternative to Norristown shoppers to this day. But even the Plymouth Meeting Mall would never create the kind or the size of the development that occurred across the river in King of Prussia.

Meanwhile, Across the River

An announcement in June 1963 by the U.S. Post Office encapsulated the sweeping changes then under way in Southeastern Pennsylvania. Rife with symbolism, it testifies to the underlying thesis here, that a change in the dominant mode of transportation—Americans' love of the automobile—changed Norristown forever. Norristown had been the regional distribution center for the mail in its immediate area since the Reading Company had been given a contract to service southeastern Pennsylvania during the Civil War. The procedure had been to send mail from Philadelphia to Norristown via the railroad's Schuylkill branch line. Upon arrival at the DeKalb Street Station, it was shipped to the borough's post office, first in horse-drawn wagons and later in trucks, then sorted and then distributed throughout the region. It was a big deal, then, when the USPO announced that effective July 1, 1963, a new site in King of Prussia would replace the Norristown Post Office as the regional distribution center. Mail would arrive from the new post office annex at 30th and Chestnut streets in Philadelphia via trucks, which would travel the Schuylkill Expressway. The King of Prussia site became the distribution center for the region, sending mail to Norristown as it did to other localities. An article on the day of the switchover itself described the nature of the change: "Effective today, 68 truck routes with 170 departures daily take over the mail service formerly provided by the six to eight trains in daily service."[442]

At the time, it seemed that all the big news was coming out of King of Prussia. The retail behemoth known as the King of Prussia Plaza was formally dedicated on August 22, 1963. The dedication was something of a technicality, as a number of stores had already opened and the ceremony was the second part of a two-part event. Fifteen stores opened on August 15, kicking off a three-day celebration, followed by the opening of six more stores and the official dedication August 22, which started another three-day celebration. King of Prussia Plaza at that initial point contained more than 50 stores totaling some 1,300,000 square feet of retail space. But it was much more than a group of stores. It was more like a miniature city, with benches, an amphitheater, and landscaping with live plantings. Adjacent to all this was the big draw, the inevitable *free, ample parking*—spaces for 9,000 cars at one time.

Even before the Plaza opened it announced the inclusion of another major store: famed Philadelphia retailer John Wanamaker would open a 200,000-square-foot store. The company cited the by-now familiar reasons for the move: "We feel the geographic location of King of Prussia is of prime importance as a merchandising area. The great expansion of population in this area and the excellent road artery situation makes this a good place to locate for business."[443] When the John Wanamaker store opened its doors on August 16, 1965, the *Times Herald* recorded the public's response in awed tones: "A huge crowd, much larger than expected, swarmed through the main entrance...seconds after the opening day ceremonies were completed."[444] By 1965, there were no crowds of any sort, at any time, to be seen on Main Street across the river.

While Main Street emptied out, the mall filled up. In 1965, Gimbels Department Store became the fourth major department store to open at the Plaza, opening a 229,000-square-foot store. At the same time, the Plaza announced its own expansion plans: to accommodate its immediate popularity, the site was building an enclosed two-story mall addition to the open "Colonial" section. When that expansion was completed in 1966, the Plaza would have more than 100 stores and service establishments and four major department stores.

A *Times Herald* article on the new Gimbels showed how the automobile had completely re-defined "marketing area." King of Prussia Plaza had by then become the retail center for an area that reached well beyond Norristown. Thanks to the Plaza's location at the center of a network of highways, its marketing area included "Pottsville, Reading, Allentown, Bethlehem, Lebanon, Harrisburg, Lancaster, York, Pottstown, Coatesville, Phoenixville, Chester, West Chester, Norristown, Philadelphia, and a multitude of smaller cities, towns and boroughs."[445] During the railroad era, each of those cities and boroughs had boasted thriving downtowns of their own, but their marketing areas had been largely restricted to the immediate vicinity, although some of those areas had been quite sizeable. Still, none compared with the reach of the King of Prussia Plaza in the new era of the automobile and the superhighway.

The King of Prussia Plaza is today known as the King of Prussia Mall, and is the largest mall in the eastern United States (and the largest anywhere in terms of actual retail space). In this, Norristown's bicentennial year, the King of Prussia Mall is planning to expand yet again, after which it will eclipse even the Mall of America in Minnesota as the largest mall by any accounting. But for the purposes of this narrative, its story will end here in the mid-1960s, when it was just beginning its ascent to retail fame. For in the future it would go from success to success, while the protagonist of our story—downtown Norristown—would go from failure to failure. By the end of the sixties, the large malls and shopping centers outside Norristown inhabited a far different conceptual world from Main Street, Norristown. The superhighways had made the malls and the downtown into two different modes of shopping. Yet they might just as well have been two different planets, so alien were the experiences.

13

Establishing the Time of Death

This book began with the logical starting point: the establishment of what became the borough of Norristown. It then covered the early century of steady growth and success engendered by advances in transportation—followed by an equally steady decline due fundamentally to another advance in transportation, the automobile. It talked about the life of Main Street, noting significant events both in the borough and in the region and the country as a whole, and offered some insights into how Norristown was faring with stories framed against the backdrop of city directories and anniversary celebrations.

The statistical study began with the *1951 Polk City Directory*, which painted a picture of downtown Norristown in 1950, a year of post-war prosperity. Most important, 1950 marked the arrival of the Pennsylvania Turnpike just across the Schuylkill River from Norristown, which clearly set many things in motion. Choosing a logical end date, however, was difficult. When had its heart ceased to beat? Research told me that for some time Main Street continued on life support, so the actual time of death could not be pinpointed. The study was based on the assumptions that the commercial decline of downtown Norristown could be examined, and that data could be extracted and analyzed to form conclusions about what happened to the once-thriving downtown—conclusions with broader relevance for similar downtowns nationwide. That proved possible for the years up to 1960, but after that things became much more complex.

It grew increasingly clear to me that Main Street's commercial decline after the 1960s could no longer be examined accurately as a standalone phenomenon. Norristown's downtown was clearly being buffeted by broader social forces sweeping the United States. By the 1970s, downtown—not just Norristown's downtown, but generic urban settings across America—was no longer the place where people wanted to move into but the place they wanted to flee. There were exceptions, of course. But across the nation, including in Norristown, the geographical trend was eerily in step with the political trend: people were moving away from the center.

Any date indicating downtown's time of death would be both arbitrary and imaginary. Thus, the study employed two "end" dates. For the first, 1978 marked the last publication of the *Polk City Directories* that had provided such rich data for examining downtown Norristown, so the final analysis of decline on Main Street makes use of the data through the final edition, effectively pinpointing the situation in 1977. For the second, as readers will soon see, I chose to end the narrative at 1975, for both symbolic and substantive reasons. It was clear that by that time, in the face of greater social forces sweeping the United States, specific local issues—in this case traffic congestion and parking—would effectively become subsumed as the 1970s progressed. The directories for the few short years after 1975 contained nothing, not even a hint, that to suggest that anything had changed that would affect the narrative's end.

Downtown Norristown continued to technically exist, of course, and is still there today as this is written, in the bicentennial year of 2012. The final chapter of this book will be, then, something of an obituary. And in that metaphor, the section that follows details the results of the patient's final years in the early 1970s, as death approached. People more interested in the final certificate of death than in the deathbed details might be excused for skipping ahead to the end, but those who want the full story, and those whose memories of downtown Norristown trying desperately to cure itself are bittersweet and something worth remembering, should read on.

Broad Social Forces

In Norristown, as in other urban centers across America, the demographics had changed by the 1970s. Many of the long-time residents—led by the better-off Italians this time and including a substantial portion of the Jewish community—had abandoned Norristown for the suburbs. The new residents were a varied lot, but tended to have darker skins and/or lower incomes. Part of the increasing divide during this period was the inevitable differences between old and new, and between old-timers and newcomers. Part of it was the shifting proportions of people who could contribute financially to the borough and people who, in contrast, needed to draw on the borough for services, while the Borough Council fretted over an eroding tax base. In the vacuum left behind by people of means fleeing the downtown for literally greener pastures (that is, suburban lawns), others moved in—people who before would never have been able to afford downtown addresses, people who were never part of the boosterism and community efforts of the past.

These were not the same people who moved into such areas decades later when downtowns began the process known as "gentrification." No, these were the nation's urban poor—both the working poor (often people struggling on minimum-wage incomes), and the unemployed poor (the sick or disabled, the elderly, the war vets, the unstable, the addicts, and yes, some predators). Main Street was not a complete ghost town. It had a handful of commercial holdouts hanging on for a variety of reasons, mixed in with the ever-changing dime-a-dozen shops there because the rents had dropped so low. But it was not the bright, lively destination of the 1950s. Downtown in the 1970s was, at least in the minds of many Norristownians, "scary." It was dark, crime-ridden, plagued with drug users and muggers. It doesn't matter whether you could walk down the street at midnight or even noon without having your wallet stolen: the perception of people was that you could not, that to go "downtown" was to descend into some sort of thieves' den where you would certainly be set upon by thugs and relieved of your money, your dignity, and possibly your life.

This, then, is downtown's obituary.

The "conventional wisdom" was exaggerated, but by 1970, Main Street had the gap-toothed appearance of an old panhandler. Many buildings had been demolished and never replaced, and vacant and boarded-up storefronts appeared on both sides and both ends of the street. Many of the stores that had managed to stay in business had peeling paint, dirty windows, and the musty air that suggested a general lack of maintenance. Street crime was on the rise, leading the borough to organize a special "anti-pickpocket and purse thieves unit," with by-now Sgt. Frank "Hank Cisco" Ciaccio as its head. Gang activity had picked up, too, and the police began more strictly enforcing the juvenile curfew ordinance that had been passed in 1958.[446]

One interviewee, Norristown stalwart Fran Doyle, described things in the 1970s:

> It went downhill, and that's all there was to it.... It looked like they just lost interest. It got depressing-looking.... Years ago, the first thing they did when they opened up their stores, showed up with a broom, swept their pavement, washed their windows...they didn't do that anymore. It was dirty, that's what it looked like; nobody seemed to bother anymore—a few, but not many.[447]

Main Street had lost its luster; even the lights over the street during the Christmas season had disappeared. In July 1970, former Borough Planning Commission chairman D. Rae Boyd reminisced to the *Times Herald* about how things had changed since he had first arrived in Norristown. "On Saturday night we used to just sit down on Main Street and watch all the shoppers go by. Now you could fire a shotgun down Main Street on any Saturday night and not hit a thing."[448]

Still, Main Street merchants struggled to lure customers back. Sometimes there were individual efforts, sometimes joint efforts with one or two other stores and often through Downtown Norristown Inc. From 1970 to 1975 there was a continued advertising effort by these merchants in the pages of the *Times Herald*. Downtown Norristown Inc. offered an array of promotions, including regular sales events such as George Washington's birthday and the annual sidewalk sale in July. Three of the strongest stores within Downtown Norristown Inc.—Chatlin's, Gilbert's, and Charming Shoppes—on occasion coordinated joint advertising among themselves. In October 1970, their joint ad proclaimed them as "Norristown's largest women's store (Charming Shoppes, 8 East Main Street), department store (Chatlin's, 236 East Main Street) and men's store (Gilbert's, at 132 West Main Street)." And they were the largest...of those left downtown. In March 1974, they were jointly offering a "Come Back to Norristown!" sale, but their two-page advertisement was seriously overshadowed by an immediately adjacent six-page insert from one of their non-downtown competitors, Atlantic Stores. The insert listed nine outlets in the Pennsylvania/New Jersey/Delaware area, including one on DeKalb Pike in East Norriton. Chatlin's made a serious individual effort to re-invent itself in 1973, clearing out old merchandise in June, and opening a "His & Her Jean Shop" within the store in August, and a month later proclaiming itself "The New Chatlin's" as it celebrated its 81st anniversary with a sale. Friedman's New York Store soldiered on.

Another downtown institution disappeared as the decade of the 1970s began; the Curren Arcade at 51 East Main Street. Once the Curran and the Montgomery Trust Arcade had provided small businesses with a prime location they likely would not otherwise have been able to afford. After the takeover of the Montgomery Arcade by the county government in 1954, the Curren had become the only downtown location that grouped such businesses. But in 1972, the Curren went under the wrecking ball. Its old footprint became part of the parking lot for the American Bank & Trust Company at 43 East Main Street, the old Peoples Bank building. What had once been Main Street's most prosperous block had lost another old friend.

The downtown did still have a theater, at least. But that fact was no longer seen by everyone as a good thing. By 1970, the Norris Theater was badly in need of interior renovations, but was receiving none. The fountains had ceased to flow and the once-beautiful maroon carpet was permanently stained. But the worst of it, to the people who remembered better days, was that the Norris Theater was now showing X-rated films. Longtime residents like Fran Doyle, despite having fond memories of heading to the Norris when she was young, now had to load her children and the neighbor kids into her station wagon and drive away from downtown if they wanted to see a movie.[449] Public dissatisfaction with having an X-rated theater on Main Street led Mayor Frank I. Caiola to contact the company that held the operating lease, Fox Enterprises, to express concern. The reply from Fox Enterprises pointed toward the unpleasant economic reality of a traditional movie theater on *any* traditional main street by the 1970s: not enough people showed up to cover the costs of renting the films. Fox Enterprises reminded Caiola and others that they had shown GP-rated films, and even an all-Italian double feature.

"For the GP-rated film we had 10 people show one day and 12 the next. The turnout was just about as poor for the double feature." Then management had begun to schedule live concerts and shows, including *Jesus Christ Superstar*—and again lost money. Mayor Caiola reluctantly admitted the truth of what the theater operators had said. "The economic facts are that when 'name' pictures were being shown, the management lost a considerable amount of money. What they show now is the cheapest possible film. Unfortunately, it's part of the general economic trend."

Even police chief Joseph Interrante noted that when the theater tried to show Saturday childrens' matinees, there was a considerable problem with mischief, slashing of seats, and even assaults. "There's no doubt the dollar value wasn't there, even for repair bills, for the management to continue showing other types of films." Fox Enterprises was uncertain whether it would renew its current lease when it expired.[450]

The banks downtown at least has seemed resistant to the overall decline. Negotiations had long been under way between the borough and Continental Bank, headquartered at Main and Swede, to construct a "major operational complex" in Norristown. Continental Bank had acquired the Block's lot as a component of this expansion and razed the old structure. After temporarily allowing the space to be used as a municipal lot, Continental Bank had reclaimed control of the lot for the sole use of its employees and customers. That was bad enough, but the worst was yet to come. In April 1970 Continental Bank announced that it was closing its downtown branch entirely and moving to Upper Merion. The villain was identified as a zoning ordinance that prohibited high-rise buildings of the size and scope Continental wished to build on the empty lot. Roy Peraino, the bank's president, announced, "the zoning ordinances here do not permit the type of structure Continental feels it must have for its future needs," and added that unless the town wanted to see more such departures, "something must be done" about zoning in Norristown.[451]

The situation continued to deteriorate. In May 1971, fire consumed 82 East Main Street, once occupied by Hanscom Bakery but abandoned a year or two earlier, and damaged the Golden Dawn Shop next door. A November *Times Herald* editorial on street crime added to the by-now common belief that it was dangerous to go downtown. "The deserted downtown section on almost any night of the week is excellent testimony to the fears held by these many citizens. So too the deserted churches, stores and other business places."[452]

William Walkup, president of Downtown Norristown Inc., opened 1972 with a decidedly mixed forecast of the future, and a curious take on one of the side issues involved in the downtown-versus-mall dichotomy. He managed to produce some measured enthusiasm, saying "I don't think we are going to have a boom but, generally, there should be better business conditions for Norristown this year." Such conditions, however, would require "work, creative thinking, imagination and vigor." His target was "local customer apathy." He saw the root of this apathy in the customers being "bored of having to walk greater distances to reach a Main Street store than in malls." He argued that changing this alleged attitude would require "conditioning people to shop on a shopping street." Walkup did not comment on the irony, and offered no suggestions as to how such conditioning was to be achieved.[453]

Two couples will serve as examples of people who perhaps needed such conditioning. Both were new borough residents. Karen McCurdy Wolfe had been a child of the suburbs, born in 1949 in East Norriton. Her parents had been raised in Norristown, but had moved to the suburbs when it was economically possible. In 1972, after Wolfe had secured what was to be a "temporary" job at the county courthouse—her employment there would last 36 years—she and her husband moved into the apartments along the north bank of the Schuylkill, between the DeKalb Street Bridge and railroad station. Their timing was not good. They had moved in during February, and in June they had to evacuate the apartment because of the rising waters of the Schuylkill River. They did settle back in, however, and remained borough residents for six years.[454] Nevertheless, though Wolfe worked downtown at the courthouse, she limited her Main Street shopping to small items she purchased over her lunch hour. Everything else she bought elsewhere, far from downtown.

Richard Schmoyer and his wife also moved to Norristown during 1972, although after the flood, taking up residence in the borough's north end. He arrived to take up a job as a community planner with the Montgomery County Planning Commission.

His professional eye saw immediately that Main Street had declined, and was still in decline, particularly at each end of downtown. Despite the several vacancies and even the buildings that had been torn down, he immediately concluded that Norristown had fared better than its sister borough downriver, Conshohocken. Conshohocken's downtown had been removed by this time. The plan had been similar to that offered to Norristown in the studies of 1965 and 1969–70: remove the old buildings and build a "mall" downtown. Conshohocken had taken this option, and the old buildings had come down. Unfortunately, the new downtown was taking a very long time to appear. The only thing visible in 1972 was a string of fences surrounding the demolished area. Schmoyer had seen much the same thing in Reading, upriver from Norristown. To Schmoyer, with his love of period architecture, Norristown was the more attractive of the two. "[Norristown's Main Street] did not have that governmental intervention that downtown Conshohocken had…. I knew right away this place wasn't touched by the urban wrecking ball of the Urban Renewal Program."[455]

Although both the Wolfes and the Schmoyers lived in Norristown, neither couple went shopping on Main Street. Schmoyer patronized a few of "the stragglers," as he termed the remaining stores, but he and his wife shopped at the malls. Both couples had cars, which gave them many alternatives within a radius of a few miles. The Schmoyers even shopped at a brand new mall some distance away in Exton, Chester County, because they liked the layout and store offerings.

One Montgomery Plaza

Amid the increasing cacophony of bad news, downtown Norristown actually received some good news in July 1972—that is, good news for county government employees; whether its effect on Main Street overall was positive is debatable. In late November 1965, an article in the *Times Herald* had announced plans for a high-rise office building with subterranean parking to be located at the corner of Swede and Airy streets, directly across from the county courthouse, at the site long occupied by the Rambo Hotel. Residents were skeptical: Norristown was accustomed to hearing about promising projects that never came to anything, and this project seemed to follow the pattern, as nothing more was formally announced for many years. In July 1972, however, came official word that the rumored high-rise, One Montgomery Plaza, was actually going to be built. It would feature two towers of ten stories each, with a facing of brick and stone, and a subterranean parking garage. Together the two towers were to possess 186,000 square feet of office space, which would make it the largest commercial project ever built in Norristown. The developer was Anthony M. DiLucia—the same successful local builder who had placed a tiny advertisement in the sesquicentennial edition of the *Times Herald* 10 years earlier. Norristown was overjoyed. The usual strident public opposition and threats of legal action were overcome, and the formal groundbreaking ceremony (for a modified design) took place on March 22, 1973. One Montgomery Plaza officially opened on July 16, 1974. By that date it had become apparent that DiLucia had additional plans for downtown Norristown, encouraged by the success of One Montgomery Plaza.

215

Dark Days

As the 1972 Christmas season began, concern over crime in the downtown shopping area led the borough police department to begin K-9 foot patrols on Main Street and West Marshall Street. Police dogs had formerly been used only in patrol cars at night. This very visible gesture was intended to have an equally visible and positive purpose: "To give shoppers a stronger sense of security in business districts, which in past Christmas seasons have seen a rise in petty thefts and muggings; to offer merchants added security, and to put a spotlight on the K-9 Unit."[456] It was also an admission of sorts by the borough that the problems downtown were now more serious than traffic congestion and lack of parking.

In March 1973, the *Times Herald* reported an incident that, while minor, was symptomatic of what was beginning to happen a large scale in Norristown. Two un-named buildings in the 200 block of East Main Street were discovered to have illegally "sublet" the upper floors to tenants as living quarters, in violation of zoning ordinances. This was the first reported instance on downtown Main Street of what had already become a borough-wide problem. The general abandonment of Norristown had led to a great many properties being left vacant. These could be purchased for very little, then subdivided and "rented," usually without reference to any ordinance or health requirement—let alone a public record of the process. The result was the growth of what amounted to slums in what had once been vibrant neighborhoods all around the borough. Such cheap and "under the radar" housing would steadily increase all through the 1970s.

In that same year, the decaying hulk of what had once been the Grand Theater at 67 East Main Street suffered its final indignity. When John's Bargain Store had occupied the premises, it had simply hung a suspended ceiling over the entire theater, to cut off any view of what once been the spectacular walls and the original ceiling. In October 1973, the suspended ceiling collapsed. The store was shuttered, and a *Times Herald* article indicated that John's Bargain Store would be closed for at least a week. In fact, it never reopened. The store was vacated, and then finally the theater itself was demolished. The only department stores left in Norristown were Woolworth's, Chatlin's, and the persistent little Martin's Department Store.

The moribund Valley Forge Hotel limped toward bankruptcy during the early 1970s. A complete management shakeup in 1971 led to a last-minute attempt to remake the always-unsuccessful hotel portion of the business into office rentals. While this had been done earlier on a small scale, this was the first time that management would all-but-abandon any further attempts at operating the building as a hotel.[457] The new management pursued this makeover with vigor—and with funds from mortgaging the property. It would barely have time to get under way before the end arrived. The policies adopted during this brief period give rise to questions, in view of the financial figures divulged in 1974. Given the lack of reliable figures, and the known tendency of the hotel's directors—regardless of time period—toward optimistic statements, judgment must be suspended at this point, beyond that of recognizing an obvious death spiral.

The income, expense, and net profit figures that appeared previously about the hotel are continued below for the period after the sesquicentennial. Incomplete and of questionable reliability, they nevertheless demonstrate the increasingly dire financial straits of the hotel corporation.

Year	Income	Expenses	Net Profit
1963	N/A	N/A	N/A
1964	$354,999.12	$318,917.79	$8,565.76
1965	N/A	N/A	Profit "slightly in excess of $3,000"
1966	$423,727.32	$362,075.21	$18,095.43
1967	($4,365.96)	N/A	N/A
1968	$397,696.43	$369,686.63	($5,324.03)
1969	N/A	$60,000+ *	N/A
1970	N/A	N/A	N/A
1971	$366,363	$436,948	($102,111); includes $28,000 debt writeoff
1972:	($85,887)	N/A	N/A
1973:	N/A	N/A	N/A

TH 3/19/1971

No financial figures were reported for 1969 beyond an admission that the year had been financially unsuccessful. A *Times Herald* article in March 1971 reported that the actual loss for 1969 had been in excess of $60,000. No financial figures were printed for 1970, and the annual meeting in January 1971 produced a wholesale change in management, along with a reduction in seats on the board of directors from nine to five and a reduction of the directors' tenure of office to one year. The short article indicated that the hotel had run through two managers during the year.

The new management wasted little time before sending a letter to the corporation's stockholders revealing that losses in recent years had "seriously impaired the working capital position of the company." Management planned physical changes "to increase the hotel's usefulness to the community, and diminishing working capital make it imperative to borrow a large sum of money by mortgaging the property." The letter also advised the stockholders that anyone wishing to sell shares of preferred stock would receive $35 a share, but that common stock could only be "turned over at no cost."[458] A meeting of the stockholders in March approved the request for the mortgage, but no figures for the mortgage amount were printed.

Management pressed forward with its plans in 1971 to renovate rooms for their new use, and even physically expand the hotel to turn it into an office complex. This expansion would occupy the small existing parking lot, so adjacent plots of land were purchased for the new lot. At the annual meeting in 1970, the corporation's managing director announced that six office tenants had moved in, and that a 15-year lease had been negotiated with First Pennsylvania Banking & Trust Co. to establish banking facilities on the first floor, perhaps including a drive-in window. Renovations were scheduled to begin soon, with occupancy by September. Although it was not reported at the time, this renovation would require evicting the 10 tenants then occupying the building, who were asked to move in late 1972. One of the remaining business tenants was Bill Giambrone and his barber shop. His lease, however, could not be broken, and he remained at his shop until the very end.[459] Another announcement hinted at internal disagreement over new policies, informing readers that the publisher of the *Times Herald*, Robert I. McCracken, had resigned his longtime membership on the hotel's board of directors, though he remained a stockholder.

The *Times Herald* published an article in February 1972 that highlighted how insignificant the Valley Forge Hotel had become. Tourism and business had continued to expand in the Valley Forge area, and the motel industry had adapted to the change in both numbers and purpose of room rental. These newer ventures were both larger and more ambitious in their marketing than first motels built along the turnpike: along with rooms, they offered banquet facilities and rooms (often of expandable size) for business meetings. By 1972, motels in the Valley Forge area were estimated to possess more than 1,650 guest rooms and meeting space for over 5,000 people. These included such names as Hilton, Sheraton, Stouffer's, Holiday Inn, and Howard Johnson, as well as the now-expanded George Washington Motor Lodge. Should even that number prove inadequate, there were "back-up facilities," said Raymond L. Posey, executive vice president of the Valley Forge Chamber of Commerce, mentioning such locations as Fort Washington, St. David's, Kulpsville, and even Downingtown, all several miles distant. Posey did not mention the Valley Forge Hotel. The writer of the article, however, tacked it on: "Primary or back-up status must, of course, also be given to such hotels or motels as the Valley Forge in Norristown, the Colonial Motel, the Crossroads and a number of others."[460] The once-mighty had fallen far indeed.

The annual meeting in January 1973 revealed another management change, installing a new corporation president. It also hinted that reports of a fully negotiated lease with First Pennsylvania Bank & Trust Co. had been premature; the 1972 annual report mentioned only that negotiations with "a major Philadelphia bank [were] in abeyance." The corporation's general manager was more direct: "Drastic measures must be taken quickly to turn the profit picture around." No specific drastic measures were mentioned, a lack of decisive intentions that spoke volumes.

They (Finally) Built a Garage…and Nobody Came

For both downtown merchants and shoppers, the most significant component of the new county government complex was the parking garage. The first part of the renovation project to formally open, on June 21, 1971, it still lacked what were described as "finishing touches," but that did not deter the speechmakers. Commission chairman Russell Parkhouse proclaimed it a "landmark in Norristown History made possible through cooperation of county and borough officials," and repeated the by-now ritual mantra that the garage would be a "stimulus for the downtown shopping area"[461]

An announcement right before the opening of the garage reminded Norristown that the "modern 415-car parking garage was constructed by the county for the convenience of the general public and Court House needs."[462] The emphasis on the public over the courthouse as the primary beneficiaries was quickly questioned. People who parked in the new garage discovered that it was far more convenient for courthouse personnel than for anyone else: people accessing the courthouse could use the elevator, while those exiting on Main Street had to use the stairs. Nevertheless, downtown had its long sought-after central parking—at least until the new county office space opened up and increased demand for parking. Although 100 spaces or so were set aside for select county employees, the rest was available to the general public.

Looking to give Main Street a badly needed economic shot in the arm, Downtown Norristown Inc. organized a shopping promotion using the *Times Herald*. The June 19 announcement of the garage's imminent opening offered shoppers free garage parking for the first half hour for anyone with a validation stamp from a local store. The downtown merchants waited for the waves of customers to flood into Main Street, those who had been holding back out of frustration from the days when shopping downtown meant having to circle the block several times to find a place to park. The downtown merchants waited...and waited.

The wave turned out to be, at best, a trickle. Usage of the garage by the general public during this initial period was shockingly low. A September *Times Herald* article revealed that an average of just 125 to 150 spaces per day had been occupied since the garage's June opening. Of this number, 91 spaces were monthly rentals. It was unclear whether the 91 spaces belonged to the 100 county employees, but they were certainly not shoppers. This left only just 35 to 50 being used on an average day by downtown shoppers. Pat Giannone of Downtown Norristown Inc., in a grand understatement, admitted in September that public response to the parking garage, including even with the free half hour, "has not been tremendous." The books of parking validation stamps distributed to downtown merchants went almost unused.

Both county officials and downtown merchants professed to be puzzled by the low rate of use. One opinion was that the "finishing touches" had scared away prospective users; another blamed the lack of a flashing light over the garage entrance. Another simply attributed the low number to the fact that fewer people shopped during the summer. While such considerations may have contributed in minor ways, the truth was unspoken but obvious. Given the decades of decline on Main Street and the many new, beautiful stores and shopping centers away from downtown, people were going elsewhere to shop. The reputation of Main Street as a shopping destination had completely collapsed. This was clear in the message of the ad campaigns: come *back* to Main Street. Once again: too little, too late.

A Tumultuous Term

The 1969 election breathed fresh air into Norristown politics: the new mayor was young, vigorous, and progressive, especially by Norristown standards. At 28, Frank L. Caiola was the youngest mayor (or burgess) ever elected.[463] He was a perfect combination of local product and national mood: a Republican who regarded Robert Kennedy—whom he had met—as an inspiration. Caiola took office in January 1970, just as social forces far beyond the control of any one individual would begin to coalesce within Norristown. In his one term, he labored mightily to enact fundamental change, but his plans would run afoul of the innate conservatism of Norristown residents.

Caiola believed he possessed a mandate to bring about change, and understood full well that resistance to change lay foremost with the borough council. Unfortunately, as mayor in 1970 Caiola possessed no more power than had Merritt Bosler as burgess in 1950. As a newcomer among many old hands, he probably possessed less. The makeup of the Borough Council of 1970 differed from 1950. Five of the council members were Democrats, one of them the first woman ever elected to the Norristown Borough Council, Marion Brandon. The council was still the locus of political power, and likewise the source of the borough's paralysis in meeting the challenges it continued to face. No surprisingly, Frank Caiola came into office convinced that change for Norristown required changing its form of government.[464]

Caiola quickly realized that, even in the exercise of his limited power over matters that were not controversial, he was still confronted with an old issue that had faced not only Bosler, but was older than the 20th century itself: Norristown's ethnic and religious divide. Other groups, most notably Norristown's African-Americans, whose numbers had begun to translate into electoral clout, made the divide more complex, but in 1970 the epicenter of the was still the borough's Italian-American residents. Italian-Americans had long since come into local power, and Caiola was living testimony to that fact. The issue of their proportion of representation would nevertheless dog Caiola's appointments to boards and volunteer committees. He had to perform a very delicate balancing act, and rarely satisfied everyone. He recalled that he once received a complaint that there were no Italian-Americans appointed to a particular committee. The complainant was less than mollified when Caiola pointed out that he, the mayor and chair of the committee, was Italian.[465]

The 1970 Borough Council found financial issues, as always, to be the most pressing of the many on its table. The need for revenue, in turn, led the list of financial issues. By this time, however, questions about the borough's official records were casting strong doubt on the numbers that had been produced and relied upon for decades. A major altercation arose in April over whether the borough's financial records had followed proper accounting standards. An extensive *Times Herald* article related the numerous charges and countercharges, adding to the perception of confusion and incompetence more than anything else. More investigations would ensue, and the bad news would become public, but not fully until 1974.

The Borough Council at this time was between the proverbial rock and a hard place in regard to its own headquarters on the corner of Airy and DeKalb streets. The building had housed the borough government since 1896, and by this time it was literally falling down around its occupants' collective ears. Council had first tried to fund a new building on its new property to the east on Airy Street back in 1959, but voters had decisively defeated the necessary bond issue. By 1971, the need for a new headquarters had become desperate, budget crisis or no. In November 1971, the Borough Council voted to build a new borough hall on its East Airy Street property.[466] Given the strained financial situation, however, it was not until March 1972 that the council was able to award the first construction contracts, and not until February 1973 that the official groundbreaking ceremony took place.[467]

The decision in April 1970 by Continental Bank not to build a new complex in downtown Norristown had been a serious blow to the borough's hopes for revival. The bank had blamed Norristown's zoning ordinance, which in 1970 was already 43 years old. This loss, added to the strong criticism of the ordinance in the recently issued report from the County Planning Commission, led to efforts to rewrite and update Norristown's zoning. Such an effort led, quite predictably, to extended political infighting. Paul Santangelo, equally predictably, was at the center of the dispute.

In July, the Borough Council passed a new zoning ordinance.[468] Close examination unfortunately revealed that the ordinance had some conflicts with the just-adopted Comprehensive Plan. Some argued that these disagreements did not matter, as only the zoning ordinance had legal status: "A plan is all it is, a guide for future development. It is not compulsory. It is not binding. No one has to heed its recommendations. It can be filed in an empty drawer and gather idle dust."[469] Unfortunately for this argument, the Pennsylvania Municipalities Planning Code, newly effective in 1969, required all local zoning ordinances to be based on a comprehensive plan.

This signaled the beginning of an extended mayor-council battle, and the question of the Comprehensive Plan's influence was lost in the bitter dispute that followed. Caiola refused to sign the zoning ordinance, citing an amendment offered by Paul Santangelo that the Borough Council had included in the final text that granted Santangelo virtually "carte blanche" (Caiola's words) power over zoning in his ward—including a number of changes that Santangelo had written and the Borough Council had approved without reading. Caiola's break from the traditional deference to Santangelo became a challenge to council itself, and the response was predictable. The Borough Council again passed the zoning ordinance in December, with Santangelo's amendments, and Caiola again vetoed it. Council attempted—but failed—to override his veto on January 5, 1971. A compromise was then reached that deleted most of Santangelo's specific changes. The Borough Council finally passed this final version of the zoning ordinance on January 14, by a 9:3 vote. Santangelo voted no. This time, Caiola signed it.[470]

While the town's bloodbaths had been up until then largely figurative, things changed for Norristown in October 1970 that added to Norristown's growing reputation as a dangerous place. Racial skirmishes broke out in the borough, and after a second night of clashes, Mayor Caiola declared a state of emergency and ordered a curfew. The violence ended, but the issues remained, in true Norristown tradition, largely ignored and unaddressed. There were "demands" issued by "spokesmen for the black community," and a few people started the "Norristown Committee to Support Your Local Police," but racial, ethnic, and religious tensions continued to bubble under the surface in Norristown as they did nationwide. Events of the past century and a half had shown that when there were problems in the borough, it was always easier to point fingers or, better yet, look away from the issues altogether, than to pull together in anything approaching constructive debate or polite discourse.

And yet, Norristown did have times when its residents were forced to work together, and they did so without reservation. This was the case in June 1972 when Tropical Storm Agnes, demoted from hurricane status and late into its meandering course, passed over central Pennsylvania dumping considerable amounts of rain, then returned to dump even *more* rain. One result was severe flooding in the Susquehanna River that inundated the state capital at Harrisburg. Agnes also produced the highest flood level on the Schuylkill River ever recorded. On June 23, Mayor Caiola declared a state of emergency in the borough. Floodwaters rose above the Norristown end of the Dekalb Street bridge, completely filling the DeKalb Street underpass below the railroad tracks, and then flooded Lafayette Street itself. The water forced the evacuation of apartments along the river's edge, sending many dwellers—the Wolfes among them—to higher ground. Saw Mill Run backed up and flooded the intersection of Main and Arch streets. While the borough had experienced flooding before, in past such surges had always been caused by the volume of water coming down Saw Mill Run itself. This time the problem came from below. Stony Creek backed up also, but its relatively sizeable floodplain close to the Schuylkill diminished the effect, and it flooded only below the Main Street bridge.

The National Guard arrived within 48 hours and dispersed into the flood zone. They were there partly to prevent looting, but more important, they brought in and supervised the distribution of potable water, as the borough's plant had thoroughly flooded, as had its sewage treatment plant. Stores were ordered closed and a curfew established, but as the waters receded the borough began to recover quickly. By June 24, grocery stores, gas stations, supermarkets, and pharmacies near the affected area were allowed to open. Water pressure had begun to be restored by June 26, and by June 28, things were pronounced "almost normal." It would be considerably longer before the sections of Norristown below Main Street were anything close to normal, as even basic cleanup there would take months. And for long after that, anyone who traveled across any of the area's bridges, whether across rivers, creeks or streams, could see ample evidence of Agnes's wrath jammed against their foundations.

Although beset by the furies of both man and nature, Frank Caiola had campaigned on a program of fundamental change, and in 1971 he spearheaded an effort that offered to the residents of Norristown the clearest choice to date between the past and the future. To a public whose cynicism and apathy had been pointed out in surveys, derided in letters to the editor, and which allegedly despaired of borough government accomplishing anything significant, Caiola's governmental reform movement offered fundamental change as the answer. The movement to change Norristown from a Borough to a City of the Third Class under the Pennsylvania Municipalities Code took direct aim not just at the Borough Council itself, but at the basic principle that had caused the council to be so ineffective in the past: the election of council members by separate wards. In the new "Mayor-Council" form of government, the residents of the City of Norristown would elect not just the Mayor but all members of Council on a citywide basis. While much rhetoric would be employed concerning other issues, both sides realized that *this* was the crux of the matter. The Borough Council symbolized the recent unhappy past, while the City movement's backers labored to sell the idea that a Mayor-Council elected by everyone affected was the path to a happier future.

Mayor Caiola used his powers of appointment to create "The Norristown Charter Commission," a group invested with the task of examining the borough government and recommending changes. There was never any real question that the committee's final report would recommend replacing the borough form of government. The result of these deliberations was the *Report and Recommendations of the Norristown Charter Commission*, formally released to the public on April 2, 1971. The opening sentence itself tackled the basic issue head-on:

> The Charter Commission hereby files its report and recommends the adoption of the mayor-council form of third class city for the Borough of Norristown, with a mayor and a seven-member council, a treasurer and controller, elected at large.[471]

The commission's conclusions regarding the continued suitability of the borough form of government followed shortly. They also were clear:

> Norristown has a population of over 40,000 inhabitants.... The present annual operating budget exceeds $4 million. Yet this vast municipal complex is governed by part-time officials, each of whom is paid $100 per month.
>
> Under the borough type of government the councilmen enact, and through committee appointments, implement their own laws. Additionally, they exert a commanding influence over the various departmental personnel. Since no central authority exists, there is no coordination of activity or sense of direction.
>
> Our studies and deliberations have convinced us that the present borough form of government is incapable of meeting the essential needs of the people. We have also come to the conclusion that genuine reform within the system is unattainable.[472]

The report dealt equally clearly with the objections that the commission knew were coming. Previous attempts to adopt a city form of government had foundered on the specific concern that a city meant a paid fire department, and thus the abolition of the borough's treasured volunteer departments, and on the more general belief that becoming a city would bring about an increase in taxes. The report addressed them head on, denying both charges and asserting that the fire companies would remain unchanged and that taxes would not rise. The core objections lay in the change to "at-large" election of municipal officials (and the overall reduction in the number of members), and the report took pains to address these objections, too. The proposal received enough signatures to put it on the ballot, and was the subject of a special referendum in June. While not the first such proposal, the 1971 referendum was the first one supported by the incumbent mayor. The campaign featured literature and even buttons, all calling for the change to a city.

Opposition, as expected, centered in the Borough Council. A change to at-large elections would strike the members of the Borough Council at the very heart of their political being—their neighborhood base of support. The *Times Herald* editorially supported the proposal as the vote approached, and urged Norristown voters to approve the change. It printed several letters to the editor in the run-up to the vote, from both sides, addressing the issues. These letters were not numerous enough to warrant much extrapolation, but the underlying concerns seemed to be economic, not political. Despite being assured that the changeover did not automatically mean higher taxes, people continued to believe that taxes would go up.

Norristown's voters decisively defeated the Third Class City Proposal in the June 1971 referendum, 3,431 to 2,472. That is, 42% voted for the opportunity for governmental change, and 58% voted to keep things as they had always been. The *Times Herald* article about the vote revealed that opposition to the proposal was widespread, but clearly identified the central player in that opposition:

> Councilman Paul Santangelo's Fifth Ward proved the most decisive. Santangelo was extremely active against the change to Third Class City. His work paid off. Voters in his ward went 454:87 against change.[473]

It is human nature to resist change, though most people adopt it when they believe it is in the best interests of themselves or, more rarely, the greater good. Most people do not live in Norristown, where tradition trumped everything. Offered a glimpse of the future, the voters of Norristown chose to remain with the past.

Interviewed for this work some 35 years after the event, Frank Caiola offered that the campaign had been doomed from the outset by its adoption of and frequent promotion of the virtues of a "city." To the residents of Norristown, city meant Philadelphia—and Philadelphia in 1971 was afflicted with serious problems, ones that were widely publicized. Many people could see no sense in becoming a city if meant that Norristown would end up experiencing the same problems they were reading and hearing about Philadelphia.[474]

Another likely contributor to the referendum's defeat was the by-now firmly accepted apathy of Norristown residents. The feeling that "nothing ever gets done in Norristown" undoubtedly spurred many of the proposal's activists to prove the naysayers wrong, but may have also contributed to the "no" votes. If nothing is going to get done, why take a chance on change? In the end, apathy's biggest effect was demonstrated in the turnout numbers: the 5,903 votes cast showed that only 44% of those eligible to vote bothered to vote at all.

The End of the Borough Planning Commission

Any dreams about whether the borough would follow through with the Comprehensive Plan produced by the County Planning Commission were quickly disabused by the treatment the Borough Council meted out to the always-controversial Borough Planning Commission in the early 1970s. It made no difference that D. Rae Boyd, the lightning rod for planning controversy, had resigned in November 1970 as chairman, ostensibly for reasons of health (though he remained on the commission).

The Borough Council election in November 1971 led, somewhat indirectly, to the Planning Commission's demise. In that election, council member Augustus R. Dimino was defeated in his reelection bid. Dimino had been a consistent opponent and critic of the commission, and when the council convened in November, the now lame-duck Dimino introduced an ordinance abolishing the Planning Commission entirely. In December, he laid out his accusations against the commission, charging it with actions "not cooperative with the legislators and not in the best interests of Council." He specifically charged the commission with using county government planners who lived outside the borough, seeking too strict compliance with building regulations, and insisting on an "unrealistic" adherence to the Comprehensive Plan, "which is supposed to be a guide and not an inflexible plan." To support his charges of actions not in the Borough Council's best interest he reminded members that the commission's chairman had been active in the Third Class City movement, which would have eliminated the Borough Council. Council duly voted 7:4 to proceed with the ordinance abolishing the Commission, with Paul Santangelo, naturally, voting in favor.[475] Borough Council moved swiftly. At a special meeting on December 2, it formally abolished the Borough Planning Commission by an 8:2 vote.[476] Mayor Caiola vetoed the action, but the council (including Santangelo) overrode his veto by 9:3 in February 1972.[477]

Thus ended the stormy, slightly-more-than-a-decade life of the Norristown Borough Planning Commission. Controversy attended its creation, short life, and death, and the few results it produced were decidedly mixed. Perhaps the final statement on its existence came from borough manager D. Richard Wenner, during his exit interview with the *Times Herald* in July 1973. He judged the former commission "not impressive," and opined that "it may in a sense have gotten what it deserved."[478]

The Pursuit of Parking (Again)

Between 1970 and 1975, financial considerations began to override or intrude openly on virtually all borough issues, including parking. Main Street merchants had been greatly thinned out, but those that remained girded themselves for one last effort to obtain their holy grail, a downtown parking garage. Yet the underlying premise for most of the events relating to parking had clearly undergone a fundamental transformation. Historically, discussions about parking had focused on the need to accommodate shoppers, including such exercises in nostalgia as "the short-stop shopper." By 1970, and increasingly through this period, the dialog over downtown parking reflected a very different reality. The decline of downtown, combined with the steady increase in county government functions—and its attendant increase in law-related support services—had fundamentally altered the reasons that people in the 1970s drove to downtown Norristown in the first place. Very few came to shop; most now came for governmental, legal, or professional reasons. This meant that the garage in the county office complex was not adequate to meet the overall parking demand. This was not news: the county planners had pointed this out in their 1965 and 1969 publications.

Yet true to form, Norristown had made no changes to adjust to this new reality. The rhetoric surrounding the age-old issue of on-street parking and the struggle over the need for a parking garage illustrated the painful truth that downtown Norristown as a shopping location was already on life support, and at death's door.

Morton Weiss, chairman of the Norristown Parking Authority, recognized as much in an article in the *Times Herald*. Weiss cited the previous studies as demonstrating that the nature of downtown was changing, "namely the growing importance of government financial and legal segments, and the diminishing of the retail trades.... Parking in central Norristown is no longer just a retail problem. It has begun to affect every type of enterprise, activity, and occupation. Banks, loan companies, public utilities, lawyers and professional services all lack parking facilities for their employers, employees and customers."[479]

What Weiss did not mention was that as people's reasons for parking downtown had changed, so too had the length of time they need to occupy a space. Borough government did recognize that change, however, and acted as best it could to deal with— and exploit—the changed situation. Seen as villains now were people staying too long in a space—the "meter feeders" or "meter squatters" who took up spaces all day. In May 1970, Mayor Caiola assigned an officer specifically to patrol the streets around the courthouse to ticket such offenders. In his announcement of this singular duty, the mayor took pains to stress that such people were a result, not a cause, of the borough's downtown parking problem. His identification of the courthouse area as the sole area to be specially patrolled reflected a harsh reality, not parochial spite against a more significant neighbor immune to any influence. County government's growth after WWII, a local manifestation of the nationwide revolution in expectations about all levels of government, had been substantial. Downtown Norristown now played host to a plethora of individuals with legal or other appointments at the courthouse complex, all of them arriving by car and needing a place to park.

Weiss also called attention to the worrisome fact that despite this increased demand for curbside parking spaces, revenue from the borough's parking meters had continued to decline. Weiss's figures indicated that revenue from meters had peaked in 1964 at approximately $72,000 and steadily declined since, to a 1969 total of only $50,000. Weiss further noted that there had been a "complete breakdown in meter enforcement." While the Borough Council responded to the budget problems in part by eliminating those charged with meter enforcement, the corps of so-called Meter Maids, their organizer and supervisor, Sgt. Frank "Hank Cisco" Ciaccio, always contended that the problem lay with the meters themselves, not with his enforcement cadre. There is no evidence that their departure caused any sorrow among those parking on Norristown's streets, which indirectly supports his point.

In March 1972, the Borough Council moved to gain what it could from "meter feeders" by doubling the meter fee from five cents to ten cents an hour, promising to deposit half of the revenue from the meters in the West Marshall Street area into a special fund for obtaining off-street parking lots, as a salve to partially ease the pain the increase would inflict.

In early 1970, the *Times Herald* asked readers to submit letters offering their opinions on parking in Norristown, and the results of that plea appeared in many editions in the coming months. The letters presented many different perspectives. The majority focused on parking problems in front of homes, not downtown, evidence that the switch to the automobile had created another enduring problem for urban dwellers. One letter did complain that borough police were too zealous and "vindictive" in enforcing the meter's time limits. The following letter is worth quoting at length. Its author, identified as J. Max, of Bridgeport, not only went beyond parochial concerns and addressed the more fundamental issues, but offered a summary of the situation that would do credit to someone researching the issue at a much later time:

> Is Main Street still around? No, it has moved from the Metropolis and into suburbia.... What has caused the exodus of downtown business to the suburbs and beyond? Obviously the automobile, and greed and shortsightedness of city officials everywhere, in not building adequate parking facilities for the millions of cars now crowding the highway. Also the parking meter traps and consequent overparking fines imposed on law-abiding citizens who heretofore have never had a record of law violation.

> The shopping center has taken over; the big downtown stores have moved there, the movies, the smarter than smart specialty shops, the chain store giants, banks, etc., all have seen the light, and to stay alive have taken to the suburbs where shopping centers provide parking for over 5,000 cars and customers can step out of their cars, into the stores free from parking meters and subsequent overparking fines, police abuse and harassment.

> Buy a piece of land adjacent to a criss-cross of highways, which lead in all directions to say highly populated suburban area; pave a lot to provide parking for 5,000 or more automobiles and the merchants will build a path to your door. Presto, another shopping complex has been born. Another Main Street has passed.[480]

The Last Gasp Garage

Downtown merchants, however, were *still* not ready to admit that the commercial draw of Main Street had passed. In October 1970, Downtown Norristown Inc. approved spending $4,000 for a downtown parking "review and feasibility study" to be performed by a firm titled Parking Unlimited. In a November *Times Herald* article, Douglas Howe, the company's president, pointed out that by 1970, Norristown—the entire borough, not just downtown—accounted for only about 7% of retail sales in Montgomery County. He was ambivalent about whether shoppers would ever return. In fact, as the article concluded, "Howe foresees Norristown's future, with its courthouse, many banks, law offices and the like, as being more of a service than a retail center."[481] Main Street's merchants were not deterred by this grim assessment, and proceeded to hire Howe and his firm to design a parking garage for downtown. Thus began the last, quixotic quest by downtown merchants for a parking garage. Howe, in

227

his new role of pitchman for a parking garage, made his plea to the Borough Council on May 10, 1971. After offering statistics about the need for parking, Howe outlined plans for a $1.3-million multilevel, 300-space garage to be built at the corner of East Main and Green streets. He was more positive and encouraging to the Borough Council than he had been to Downtown Norristown Inc., insisting that the garage would bring people downtown to shop and help Norristown grow. The council voted 9:1 to explore the proposal, with Santangelo casting the only no vote.[482]

The most significant aspect of this project—seen in retrospect, if not by the people involved at the time—was the location. The corner of East Main and Green streets had been occupied by the Humane Fire Company since 1888. The company was conveniently considering relocating, and was thus receptive to what would previously have been an almost unthinkable action: demolishing the old firehouse. Downtown Norristown Inc. gave its formal endorsement to the plan, and the Borough Council formed a special committee composed of council members, the chair of the Parking Authority and the borough's solicitor to expedite planning for the garage.

The Norristown Planning Commission did not fall into line, however, delaying any action until October 1971, at which point it issued a report prepared by the staff of the county planning commission. The report faulted the garage's proposed location. Clearly the commission did not see the garage as a potential draw to bring shoppers back to Main Street. An article in the *Times Herald* quoted the report: "We maintain that the parking facility should serve the needs of not only shoppers, but commuters and local employees. The site selected, at Main and Green streets, would only serve shoppers and is too distant to serve commuters and the greater bulk of local employees." The report also saw the still-pending Borough Hall complex on Airy Street, which was to contain a 100-space parking lot, as taking away revenue from the proposed garage. This conclusion raised concerns whether the proposed garage would produce enough revenue to finance its costs. The council deliberated the garage issue at some length at its November meeting, finally voting 8:3 to accept the recommendation for a parking facility at Main and Green streets and to sign a contract with Parking Unlimited Inc.. The size of the majority was surprising, but even more so was the fact that Paul Santangelo *supported* the proposal.[483] The Contracts with Parking Unlimited and Conrad Associates Inc., of New York, who were to provide architectural and engineering services, were signed by December.

The inevitable opposition appeared. A group calling itself Citizens Opposed to the Parking Facility claimed that the garage would never pay for itself and have to be tax-supported for a considerable time. Ex-council member Leonard Deloplaine, who had supported previous garage proposals, was prominent among the opposition, and his about-face led weight to the arguments in opposition. To counter the charges, Parking Unlimited's Howe released a statement to the *Times Herald* in April 1972. He pegged the garage's cost at $1,344,095, and claimed that demand for downtown parking was so intense that the garage would earn revenue sufficient to cover not only its operating expenses and debt payments, but turn a surplus in its first year—even it was used to only 50% capacity. At the same time, Howe continued to question whether downtown

Norristown would ever see a rejuvenated retail status, but he was safe in making this following argument for building the structure: "But if Norristown does nothing, I can tell you this—parking and the business district can only get worse."[484]

Leonard Deloplaine replied in a letter to the editor within a week. He reminded his readers that not only had he been a consistent supporter of off-street parking while he was a member of the council, but that "Council has historically refused to recognize its responsibilities in this area.... Meanwhile severe deterioration has taken place and the odds are heavily weighted against a rejuvenation in downtown Norristown which can overcome the financial loss which this parking facility is bound to incur."[485]

This financial argument—a good one, then and in retrospect—underlay the opposition to the garage, but the project also ran afoul of the always-controversial zoning ordinance. This struggle lasted until November 1973, and included legal proceedings. It was not until December that the opposition decided against any further court challenges. The legal process added substantially to the costs the Borough was incurring for the project. Confident that legal objections would fail, the Borough Council's Municipal Projects Committee in May approved the demolition of three houses on Green Street, and directed the borough solicitor to proceed with the condemnation process.[486] By the end of 1973, the council had approved acquisition of the remaining properties needed and a plan to finance its construction.[487]

However, additional financial difficulties had arisen while the legal effort against the garage was working its way through the court system such that by late 1973, support for the garage began to wane. Council members began to refer to phone calls and letters they were receiving opposing the project. The project appeared to be in jeopardy. On April 4, William Walkup, representing Downtown Norristown Inc., made another impassioned appeal, and in so doing underlined the grim reality that was Main Street by the mid-1970s:

> We [Downtown Norristown Inc.] have been taking a look at the situation for some time, and what we see is not good. We have had a variety of stores close up recently, in most cases the closings are due to a parking problem. We feel we are witnessing, at a very rapid pace, the distruction [sic] of the town. We have a nucleus of stores in the downtown area which are needed by everyone but the problem is the people cannot get to them. It is our firm conviction that what we see happening now is just a forerunner of what will happen in the future if something is not done now. We are witnessing the deterioration of the core of the community. In the past, I think everybody agreed that the central business area was a classy upcoming situation. What we see now is a completely opposite thing.... At some point a business reaches a point where they say we can no longer operate under the conditions as they are, and they go out of town.... Chatlins and Woolworths are two stores that are thinking seriously of going elsewhere. There is no prestige in representing a town that is dead.... Now is the time for the council to make a decision, time is running out.[488]

Council member Thomas Tornetta's remarks stated the fundamental reason for the Borough Council's growing reluctance to move forward, saying it was just following the wishes of the people, as shared in the "many communications" he had received from constituents opposing the garage: "They don't want more taxes."[489]

Nevertheless, in May the council approved purchasing the last lots needed for the garage, but the 6:6 vote demonstrated how support on council was dropping; the tie was only broken when new mayor John Murray voted in favor. Curiously, Paul Santangelo persisted in his support for the project by voting in favor.[490] The *Times Herald* called the garage proposal "easily the most controversial project before council in a number of years."[491] Given the recent history of Norristown Borough Council, this was indeed saying something.

The final confrontation came at a special Borough Council meeting on November 12, 1974. A flyer that circulated asking people opposed to the garage to attend the meeting put the case this way: "With inflation at an all-time high, we sure don't need our taxes raised to build a parking garage to serve downtown businessmen." At this point, the mayor switched from support of the garage to opposition. Citing the many letters and telephone calls he had received, Murray declared that it was now evident that Norristown's taxpayers opposed the garage. His reversal made the November Borough Council meeting almost anti-climactic. Before a packed audience, the Borough Council voted to kill the parking garage proposal, 9:3. This time Paul Santangelo switched from his previous position, and voted against the project. The *Times Herald* article about the meeting provided an interesting, if uncorroborated, statement from those who supported the garage, which claimed that in the past (unspecified), the central business district had provided nearly 50% of the borough's total real estate tax revenue, whereas by 1974, it provided only about 15%.

The quest for this last-ditch attempt to address a decades-old problem consumed 3½ years and many thousands of dollars in legal fees for litigation and condemnation procedures. No garage resulted, and the borough was left owning properties it had condemned and obtained while the court process proceeded. The Humane Fire Company remained standing in its East Main Street location, and does to this day. While any judgment about whether the garage would have been successful or not would be decidedly academic, the decline in support for the garage had a real and substantial economic basis. The process also revealed that finally both the political and business leaders of Norristown were realizing the depth of the trouble that not just Main Street but the borough itself were in. By 1975, the true state of downtown's businesses—not to mention the effect of a parking garage—no longer mattered.

Governmental Change Redux

In 1973, a sadder-but-wiser Frank Caiola assessed the events and results of his first term, then in its last year. He was no quitter, but he was a realist, and the events of his first term had demonstrated the implacable opposition within Norristown to change in any form. He factored in the effect of another term on his legal practice and came to the rational decision not to run for mayor again. Before he left office, however, he bequeathed yet another attempt to change the borough form of government.

The opportunity arose because in 1972 the Pennsylvania Legislature passed Act 62, known as the Home Rule Charter Law. This law gave those seeking a change from the borough form of government more options from which to choose. This in turn inspired the election of a Government Study Commission in the May 1973 primary election. Unlike the 1971 Charter Commission, whose members had been appointed, this group was made up of members elected in the primary, which meant that it included people with many different views. In July, the study commission held several meetings, including a formal presentation from both sides of the basic issue. Caiola spoke for change, arguing again that election by individual ward was a problem. This time, however, he shifted his argument to address the sentiment in favor of this principle that had scuttled the previous attempt: he spoke for a compromise allowed under the new Home Rule Charter Law, with both locally elected and municipality-wide seats on council. Council president Francis Orr spoke for the viewpoint that the existing borough structure based on election by individual wards worked well enough that no change was needed.

The formal results of the study—a proposed "Home Rule Charter" of 40 pages accompanied by 67 pages of documentation—was made public in March 1974, with the vote scheduled for the May primary. The proposal was for a "mayor-council" form of government with an appointed managing director. Council would be reduced to nine members, of whom six would be elected from an expanded six-ward division of the borough and three elected at large. The position of tax collector, previously an elected position, was eliminated and recast as an administrative position.

What was remarkable about the commission's report was that the study commission unanimously endorsed the proposal. Such an occurrence had little precedent in Norristown history—and in this case quickly proved to have no foundation. Within a week, all pretense of unanimity had disappeared. Commission member Thomas Tornetta presented what he termed a "minority report" that questioned several of the commission's conclusions and recommendations. When asked about the "unanimous" concurrence to the report, he claimed that his acquiescence was only due to a "gentlemen's agreement" among the commission members.

The attempt at compromise that the new proposal represented did not sway the Borough Council in the slightest. At the April 1974, Paul Santangelo delivered a lengthy statement against the plan, and moved for a "no" vote. Council responded overwhelmingly, supporting Santangelo's motion by 10:1:1.[492]

The stage was set in the familiar way, and the campaign played out along familiar lines. The charter's opponents were as implacable as ever, but the campaign never achieved anything like the organization and thrust of the 1971 effort. This made for an equally familiar result: the "mayor-council" Home Rule Charter proposal lost 2,290 to 1,346. Voter turnout, low enough for the last such effort, had dropped by 62% from the 1971 vote, showing that the real victor, once again, was apathy.

The End of an Era

Two losses in 1974 and 1975 can be said to have formally announced the death of downtown: the Valley Forge Hotel and Chatlin's. By this time, their loss was not so much physical as psychological, but their departure was the final blow to Norristown's traditional downtown. Individual stores remained, and always have, but Main Street, Norristown, as a shopping mecca was no longer. Of course, 1975 was not the end of Main Street, nor the greater downtown area, or of the borough of Norristown itself. Nothing ended, as the coming years would demonstrate to everyone's satisfaction. What had been made absolutely clear by that time, however, was that downtown Norristown as a commercial destination was dead. It was no longer merely comatose and on life support, awaiting a miraculous cure. It could not be resuscitated. There was no heartbeat. The corpse would linger, but the ensuing decades would see not resurrection, only further deterioration.

The Valley Forge Hotel

After years of languishing in ill financial health, the Valley Forge Hotel ultimately expired rather quickly. On February 20, 1974, the board of directors of the Valley Forge Hotel Corporation voted to declare bankruptcy. The dining room closed within two days of the announcement. An auction of all interior furnishings was scheduled for March 9. The Forge Room bar, the location of so much Montgomery County political history, closed its doors on March 10. Bill Giambrone finally had to abandon his barbershop (though a county commissioner whose hair Giambrone cut pointed him toward another one at the county retirement center).[493] Corporation stockholders had not been told in advance of the decision nor even of the auction, nor was their approval ever sought. The announcement simply stated that the board had "for months sought to solve its financial problems which have climbed to an approximate $250,000 debt." No details were offered on how long this debt had been accumulating.

While debt underlay the bankruptcy decision, its timing was largely a question of unpaid taxes. The haste with which the social heart of Norristown was to be dismantled stemmed largely from the demands of the Internal Revenue Service. As the *Times Herald* delicately phrased it, "[the IRS] has told the directors that no criminal prosecution will be undertaken if something is done in the immediate future. Through the closing of the hotel and the sale of its assets the IRS will be able to collect some of the taxes due."[494] No further details were offered.

At the auction of interior furnishings (postponed until March 30, just before the final stockholders meeting on April 3), thousands thronged to the site to bid on virtually everything that could be carried away, from wall hangings to silverware. Auctiongoers dined on hot dogs and sauerbraten sold out of the part of the building that had once housed the Bud White haberdashery shop. By the end of the day, the hotel had been stripped bare, down to the bathroom fixtures in the rooms. The lead phrase in the *Times Herald* article that described the event would began with a ruefully appropriate epitaph: "The Valley Forge Hotel was never so crowded..."

Fewer than 30 stockholders attended the meeting four days later, but those few members' holdings, strongly reinforced by proxy votes and shares held by the members of the board, together accounted for 3,862 of the 6,123 shares of record, a voting majority. Several stockholders posed questions that corporate counsel Sidney DeAngelis did his best to answer, and in the process filled in a few more details about the hotel's demise. The hotel had closed "abruptly," said DeAngelis, "because of pressing demands by outstanding creditors." Total claims by creditors amounted to $306,000, with American Bank and Trust Company of Pennsylvania still owed $19,422 on the mortgage. The corporation owed $15,000 in taxes to the state, and about $29,000 to the borough and the Norristown Area School District. The firm had not paid its school district taxes for the second, third, or fourth quarters of 1973, nor the first quarter of 1974. The federal government had placed a $52,000 tax lien on the property. The auction of furnishings grossed $39,000, of which $33,000 would be paid to IRS after deductions for the auction expenses. This would leave the corporation still owing $19,000 plus penalties to the IRS; the penalties would be assumed by the directors.

Many of the questions came from prominent individuals in the community, including D. Rae Boyd, William Walkup, and Robert McCracken. Each tried to find out what happened. Corporation President Natoli tried to explain. He spoke of the struggle for revenue given the advanced age of the Valley Force Hotel compared with the dozens of spotless and new hotels and motels in the area. With a room occupancy rate averaging around 18%, the hotel's revenue had fallen from $345,000 to $276,000 during the hotel's last year in operation. No financial statement had been issued in 1972 and 1973, although DeAngelis apparently made the 1973 statement available at the meeting. The most recent appraisal, made two years earlier, listed the site's value at $200,000, including the parking lot. The stockholders were promised a meeting before the final sale of the property and distribution of funds. Thus advised, the stockholders approved the intention to sell off the property.

They did not have long to wait. On July 10, the promised meeting ratified the sale of the hotel property to none other than Anthony M. DiLucia, the developer of One Montgomery Plaza. DiLucia paid $235,000 for the property, which was $39,000 less than the corporation's total debt in both recorded liens and unsecured debts, so there would be no transfer of funds to stockholders. Nonetheless, the board said, DiLucia's offer should be accepted, as two Philadelphia real estate firms (not named) had advised the board president that the property was "not marketable." Alonzo Sinclair, a past president of the board until the 1971 shakeup, asked how the price could be so low when back in 1924 the site had been purchased for $225,000 [in 1924 dollars]. The reply he received spoke volumes, not just about the Valley Forge Hotel, or even Main Street itself: "Half of Norristown is for sale." The sale was approved. DiLucia took formal possession of the hotel on August 20.

Before the sale of the Valley Forge Hotel was finalized, Norristown residents learned that DiLucia had purchased other properties on Main Street's core block as well, including the retail store adjacent to the hotel at 18 East Main Street, and a number of other properties, mostly on the north side of the street: 67 East Main Street (the old Grand Theater/John's Bargain Store); 71 and 73 East Main Street (vacant lots); 75 East Main Street (which housed a tavern called Nate's Other Place, whose lease continued); and 81 East Main Street (a vacant building). Tucked between those purchases were long-time Main Street stalwarts Feder's Women's Clothing at 77 East Main Street and Brockton Shoe Store at 79 East Main Street.

As for the Valley Forge Hotel itself, DiLucia was frank. "The public auction held at the hotel a few months ago virtually gutted it. All the furnishings, fixtures and equipment of any value were sold. Replacing these at today's costs could be prohibitively expensive." He allowed, however, that "the Valley Forge Hotel has been an important part of the history of our town and we're going to take a good look of possible continuation of this in some way."[495] The first of these two statements was true; the second was not. There is evidence that DiLucia's entire purpose in buying the Valley Forge Hotel from the start was to raze it and build a parking garage.[496] The timing of events surrounding the demise of the Valley Forge Hotel supports this belief. The idea had apparently been in gestation since the construction of One Montgomery Plaza, when its occupants realized that the building's internal parking garage was inadequate for the people working in the building itself.

One September 23, the Valley Forge Hotel and the adjacent building started to come down. Many residents and office workers on their lunch breaks took in the sad event.[497] In keeping with the latest Norristown tradition, after demolition was complete the site was bulldozed flat to provide temporary parking, primarily for county workers though shoppers could park there on weekdays and have their cost refunded if they showed a validated receipt. Parking was free on weekends.

The Valley Forge Hotel had never been a major economic contributor to the community. It came into being as a physical testimony to Norristown's attitude toward itself: "A first class borough needs a first class hotel." The initiative to build it had come from within Norristown, as had the stockholders who had backed their faith with an initial purchase. It had never been a success as a hotel, but it had from its inception been Norristown's social and political heart. Generation after generation of Norristown residents grew up with memories of the hotel—proms, wedding receptions, fundraisers, business meetings, and every other type of get together. By the end of September 1974, only memories were left.

Chatlin's

A second loss rocked the downtown shortly afterward. Morris Chatlin died in May 1974 at his home in Miami. He had not been active in local affairs for some years, but made sure that the firm's general manager stayed involved in Downtown Norristown Inc. Chatlin's death but left no heir interested in running the business, and that task devolved on his widow, the former Cecele Stein, who became president of the firm upon his death. Within two generations, history had come full circle for the women who married into the Chatlin family. The insistence by Samuel Chatlin's fiancée on a physical business location, not life as a peddler, had motivated the store's founding. Upon the death of their son, it would be his widow who became responsible for rescuing a firm from ruin, and she chose to move and start anew.

On January 31, 1975, still identified as Mrs. Morris Chatlin, but now president of the company, she announced that Chatlin's was moving to Logan Square. The specific site was to be the building first occupied by Sears before it built its new, larger building. Chatlin's signed a lease in February, hired a store designer, and planned many renovations to the old building. By July, Chatlin's was advertising that after 83 years in downtown Norristown, it would be moving to a "sparkling new store" in Logan Square. Different news followed in September. Chatlin's was not moving, it was going out of business. The renovations at the Logan Square store were discontinued; the new merchandise was added to the remaining stock in a final "Going Out of Business Sale" over the next few weeks. It closed it doors on November 1, 1975. The party for employees honored three who together possessed 99 years of service at the store. The *Times Herald* offered a modest epitaph, but one that rang true to all who remembered what Chatlin's had been to Norristown;

> It has enjoyed the patronage of generations of Norristown and area shoppers. The success of the store was attributed to its friendly service, nationally advertised brands of clothing for the entire family, and a courteous sales personnel.[498]

The End of the Beginning

The *Polk City Directories* for the Norristown area that provided so much rich detail for this book ceased publication after 1978, further evidence of downtown's demise. Little changed between 1975 and 1978. The death of downtown Norristown chronicled above was just one part of what would happen to the borough as a whole—a decline that continued for decades, and in some ways may not have yet concluded. The collapse of downtown began before the additional components of that decline had made more than a token appearance, additional components that would strike in full force before the turn of the 21st century. Yet to adapt a famous quote by Winston Churchill, for Norristown the collapse of its downtown by 1975 was not the end, nor even the beginning of the end. It was merely the end of the beginning.

Few, if any, of Norristown's residents who lived through this period would see 1975 as any sort of boundary. Those interviewed for this work saw the decline of Norristown as a seamless whole, which in their experience it was. Yet the statistics contained in this study demonstrate that by 1975–1977, downtown as a commercial location was dead, and a lifestyle that had existed for decades was no more. The Friday night crowds had disappeared along with the stores, theaters, soda fountains, and specialty shops those crowds had thronged to patronize. Main Street over the Christmas holiday was a hollow mockery of its appearance 25 years earlier. Building after building was boarded up, or simply abandoned. The remaining shop owners no longer stood outside their stores, enticing passersby to enter. There were no passersby or, if there were, they were people with other business to attend to scurrying past to escape the unwelcoming downtown as quickly as possible. The men who now lingered singly or in groups along Main Street were no longer the retired, senior citizens of the community laughing and arguing over the latest town gossip: they were vagrants. The sidewalks and front steps were no longer washed or swept each morning; many smelled of urine. The police still made visible foot patrols downtown a priority, but the officers no longer stopped to chat with the shop owners who were no longer out-side their stores, and there was no longer any point in checking the locks on the rear doors, which were now as permanently in place as those on the front doors. All this was visible to those rare intrepid shoppers who still ventured downtown, and most of it was visible to those just driving through in their cars. There was no need to spell out the numbers to the remaining old-time residents, but the numbers drive home the story to everyone else.

Death Certificate: Norristown By the (Final) Numbers

The following summary compares the city directories from 1951 with those in the last directory, published in 1978. As before, these are net numbers grouped into categories and do not take into account the exit or entry of individual businesses.[499] Even allow-ing for the likelihood of directory errors, the numbers show that downtown suffered a stunning collapse between 1950 and 1978. The 1951 directory listed 312 "for profit" businesses on the six-block core of Main Street. There were only 110 such businesses listed in the 1978 edition—a net loss of 65%.

And the real losses, in terms of what was lost, are even greater. Closely examined, the numbers reveal a shocking loss, both broad and deep, with depressingly few excep-tions to the general trend. Of the 25 categories followed here, 17 fell between 1950 and 1978. The ones most central to downtown Norristown, both in numbers and impor-tance, fell the most.

	1951	Highest # in year	1978	# Change from 1951	% Change from 1951
Total Entries	524	533 in 1960	361	-163	(31%)
Storefronts	209	215 in 1955	177	-32	(15%)
Auto Sales	1	No entries after 1951	0	-1	(100%)
Auto Service & Parts	4	4 in 1951	1	-3	(75%)
Bank	4	8 in 1970, 1972	6	+2	50%
Company Office	17	17 in 1951	7	-10	(59%)
Financial Service	15	21 in 1955, 1960, 1962	3	-12	(80%)
Food Service	19	19 in 1951	8	-11	(58%)
Government-County	2	15 in 1960	2	0	—
Government-Federal	2	4 in 1968, 1970, 1972, 1974	3	+1	50%
Government-State	1	No entries after 1957	0	-1	(100%)
Grocery/Meat Market	9	9 in 1951	2	-7	(78%)
Hotel	4	4 in 1951, 1953, 1955, 1957	1	-3	(75%)
Manufacturing	2	2 in 1951, 1962, 1963, 1968, 1972, 1974	1	-1	(50%)
Other/Unknown	4	6 in 1962, 1977, 1978	6	+2	50%
Parking Lot	1	6 in 1977	5	+4	400%
Professional Office	50	51 in 1960	18	-32	(64%)

	1951	Highest # in year	1978	# Change from 1951	% Change from 1951
Retail-Dept. Store	15	15 in 1951	2	-13	(87%)
Retail-Specialty	114	122 in 1953	48	-66	(58%)
School	3	3 in 1951–60, 1966–70	2	-1	(33%)
Service-Professional	14	14 in 1951	8	-6	(43%)
Service-Trades	26	27 in 1953	1	-25	(96%)
Tavern	4	8 in 1960	5	+1	25%
Theater	3	3 in 1951	1	-2	(67%)
Transportation	3	3 in 1951	1	-2	(67%)
Wholesale	1	3 in 1968	1	0	—
No Return/Vacant	14 (9)*	111 in 1974	99 (71)*	+85	607%

*Adjusted number, accounts for addresses disappearing temporarily from Directory, but not torn down.

The 1951 directory for Norristown and its surroundings listed 524 total entries in the six blocks of downtown Main Street; by 1978, that dropped to 361, a loss of 163 entries. While businesses have been the focus here, that 31% drop included residences and non-profit entries. The disease that ravaged downtown was not fussy.

The numbers show that Main Street's decline began early. In most categories, 1951 was the peak year, including several core categories: Food Service, Grocery Store, Professional Office, Retail-Department Store, and Service-Professional. Retail-Specialty entries peaked in 1953, as did Service-Trades. By 1960, another four categories had peaked; five more peaked during the 1960s, one of them Financial Service, which repeated its 1955 peak. (Not every category is called out here, only those whose numbers enrich understanding of the story overall.)

Storefronts between 1951 and 1978 suffered a net loss of 32, from the 209 in 1951 to 177 in 1978. On the surface this seems a modest decrease, at 15%. But the number hides the real stories: long-time stores struggling to hold on but unable to stay alive; optimistic merchants starting up as others moved out, only to see their ventures fail before the paint on their signs had dried; store owners refusing or unable to relocate, digging in and hoping for the best; close-fisted retailers taking advantage of lowered property values to hawk their shabby wares alongside those of proud stalwarts. The net numbers mask the human side of the turnover.

A few distinctions need to be drawn with respect to declining storefronts. First, the net decline includes storefronts that became the expanded space of a neighbor who bought them. This might remove an address though the building itself may have remained (e.g., Zummo's purchase of the former Lutz Tire property at 261 East Main Street, or the removal of the ancient Lincoln Hotel and subsequent expansion of the Firestone Tire Store between 205 and 213 West Main Street). These types of changes helped maintain the visual façade of a healthy Main Street. Other storefronts disappeared because the buildings housing them were torn down, like those storefronts between 25 and 37 East Main Street, although these particular addresses were replaced by the sphinx-like entrance to the county parking garage. For most of the razed storefronts, however, the replacement was little more often a cursory grading and a shallow application of stone or asphalt to allow parking. In fact, four of the five parking lots listed in 1978 were once storefronts; two of those had each contained more than one storefront. Other addresses simply disappeared from the directory.

This raises the actual loss of storefronts from 1951 to 39, a figure reached by a manual tabulation from the directories and other sources, cross-checked wherever possible by articles in the *Times Herald*. The missing storefronts gave Main Street a ragged, gap-toothed appearance in 1978. The widest such gap was on East Main Street across from the county garage entrance, at the site of the former Valley Forge Hotel. Other gaps included the buildings east of the surviving bank at and the smaller but uglier gap caused by fire next to Woolworth's.

West Main Street presented an even more ragged appearance. The first block had the bank parking lot where Block's had once proudly stood; in the second block were the missing buildings east of the Norris Theater, by now another bank parking lot. The third block still showed the effects of the demolition of the Milner Hotel, and had been truncated on its south side by the removal of the buildings east of Markley Street for an off-ramp from the Dannehower Bridge.

The overall impact of business exits from Main Street from 1950 to 1978 was that 40% of the once-thriving retail center's storefronts stood empty. That is a stark and depressing fact. But there is still more to be learned from digging deeper into the numbers and analyzing the categories into which Main Street businesses were divided. These results reveal the full extent, the true depth and width, of the loss that Norristown suffered. The directories tracked 25 categories mostly "for profit" businesses and government entities. Of those 25, only six posted a higher net number in 1978 than in 1951; two posted neither a net gain nor a net loss over the period; and 17 recorded a net loss ranging from 33% to 96% of their 1951 net totals.

Bank was the only category important to Main Street that rose from 1951 to 1978, from four to six. The Continental Bank still maintained its imposing presence at 1 West Main Street, as did its drive-in office location at 222 East Main Street, which in 1951 had been Walter D. Wood auto sales.

Ironically, the directory entries for the category of Parking Lot proved to be increasingly unrepresentative of the reality on Main Street as buildings disappeared and were replaced with asphalt. The 1974–1975 directory belatedly recognized some of the long-existent lots, and the numbers suggest that category rose from one in 1951 (the parking lot for Acme Market at 218 East Main Street)—to five in 1978. But those numbers are suspect.

Main Street listed four taverns in 1951, and number that climbed to eight in 1960 before dropping to five in 1978. The entries noted several different names and thus presumably different ownership, but the physical requirements of such establishments meant that the locations of these taverns remained largely the same. One of the 1951 entries that disappeared was the bar in the Valley Forge Hotel.

Perhaps the single most compelling statistic is that provided by the category of No Return/Vacant, that reverse indicator of a commercial center's health. This category demonstrated by far the largest net change—increase or decrease—of any category during the period. In 1951, there were 14 entries in this category, of which 9 were vacant storefronts, and those 9 represented 4% of those in the six-block core area. In 1978, there were 99 No Return/Vacant, of which 71 were storefronts, and those represented a full 40% of downtown's still-remaining storefronts.

Only two categories demonstrated neither a net increase nor decrease. Wholesale entries spent almost the whole period at one, with a rise to three in 1968 before a return to one in 1978. This category was of no significance to Main Street. The second category demonstrating no change was that of Government-County. This belies the significance of the over all effect of the government's activities, particularly those of the country, on downtown Norristown. The true significance of that story was told in earlier chapters. One entry has its own story to tell, however—a story that highlights not just the plight of Norristown but other parts of the United States. One of the two Government-County entries in 1978 appeared at 113 East Main Street. In 1951, that had been the address of the Egolf Furniture Store, famous for its antique and expensive furniture. After Gus Egolf's heirs sold it in 1956, the building had been unable to keep the same renter for any length of time. It finally found a long-lasting tenant in 1974 when it was it was leased by the Montgomery County Methadone Center.

From 1951 to 1978, 17 of the 25 categories registered a net loss. Auto Sales disappeared after 1951. Transportation dropped from three to one by 1953, reflecting the decline in local trolley service. Government-State entries disappeared after 1957. Two categories—School and Manufacturing—were peripheral to a commercial center heavily based on retail sales and service. The (for profit) entries in the School category, which never had much impact on the area, went from three in 1951 to two in 1978. There were two Manufacturing entries in 1951, and never more than that thereafter, with only one listed in 1978. That one, however, was the Continental Baking Company at Main Street's far western end—something good, at least, that had remained unchanged from the first directory to the last: the aroma of fresh-baked bread that greeted the early arrivals to downtown Norristown, whether in 1951 or 1978.

Hotels had ceased to be a major presence on Main Street before 1951, through four still existed at the time. Of those, only the Valley Forge Hotel was of any consequence. Actually, the Valley Forge Hotel was of *considerable* consequence in downtown Norristown, but not in its supposed role as a hotel. By 1975, it had been torn down. The other hotels had disappeared even earlier and also been demolished. Only one new hotel appeared: the Krupps Hotel at 226 West Main Street, which cropped up, along with a bar of the same name, in the 1960 directory. The bar occupied the ground floor, and the hotel the upper floors.

Other categories had an importance beyond what was hinted at by their small numbers. Main Street had three theaters in 1951, all three—the Garrick and the Grand in particular, but also the Norris—with their best days already behind them. Only the Norris survived past 1978, although its original ownership had sold it to a national chain, and its physical condition had sadly deteriorated. It was later torn down and replaced by a McDonald's. Only a small segment of its magnificent art deco exterior survived the wrecking ball, to end up in Florida.

Auto Service stations suffered from the steadily increasing tension between the urban grid and the automobile during the study period. The four service stations listed on downtown Main Street in 1951 saw several name changes, and had steadily dropped in number, finishing at one in 1978, at 220 West Main Street.

Company Offices may not have been central to a largely retail business community, but Main Street had possessed 17 of them in 1951, which turned out to be the category's peak; it was followed by an uneven but steady decline that left only seven company offices listed in 1978.

Financial Service summarized a heterodox group, and included a few quasi-banking organizations. Most were some form of consumer credit company. While you might assume that the fortunes of these companies was closely tied to that of the retail businesses that often occupied the first floors of their addresses, the numbers don't bear that out. While both retail categories began an irreversible decline after 1953, the Financial Service category steadily increased its net numbers until it peaked at 21 in 1962. Thereafter it declined more slowly than did either retail category before undergoing a late collapse, from 13 in 1974 to three in 1978.

Food Service was arguably the most volatile category in terms of individual entries and exits, which is not surprising since restaurants are risky ventures at any time and in any location. Ownership changes allowed two 1951 entries, Gus's Steak Shop at 239 East Main Street and Montgomery Lunch at 145 West Main Street (the home of the "Texas Hot Weiner"), to survive in their original locations. The Blue Jay Restaurant at 22 West Main Street disappeared after 1962 and was replaced by Julius's Hofbrau House, by 1978 already a Norristown meeting place. Nonetheless, the long-term arc of this combined category was downward, as measured by the net numbers: 19 Food Service entries in 1951, and just 8 in 1978. The 1951 directory listed nine Grocery Store/Market entries, only two of which survived until 1978, and then under different ownership: the distinctive low-arch roofline of Acme Markets at 210 East Main Street survived as Fiore Super Market, and the smaller Taglieber's Market at 28 West Main Street was listed in 1978 as Rosen's Grocery Store.

In 1951, an array of professionals had offered their services in small offices amid the retail stores of brick and the banks with their striking façades. These included doctors, dentists, optometrists, attorneys, insurance agents, realtors, and a few who dealt in more than one of the above. This Professional Office category fluctuated, peaking at 51 in 1960 before beginning a decline into the late 1970s. The 1977 and 1978 directories actually showed an increase, from 11 in 1974 to 18 in 1978. While the survival or failure of any individual business has not been the focus of this study, it should be mentioned that two optometrists—William Elson and Morris LaDov—and dentist Israel Ross survived the entire period, and were open for business in the 1978 directory, as they had been in the 1951 directory (though Ross moved in the interim). The same cannot be said for the Corson Building, already ancient in 1951. The building survived, and still does to this day), but the last occupant with the last name Corson left after 1972; that was also the last year listing any professional offices at that address. In 1978, the building listed only residents.

The Service-Professional category fluctuated dramatically between 1951 and 1978, but ultimately declined by six entries (43%) from 14 to 8, with a low of two in 1963. The category of Service-Trades, however, showed no such volatility. In 1951, those businesses totaled 26, then 27 in 1953. After that, the net numbers showed an inexorable decline as tailors, barbers and cleaners steadily closed up shop and were not replaced. Only one Service-Trades business was listed in the 1978 directory: Butwin's Washing Machine Repairs, at 242 West Main Street. The barbershops at Main Street's east end, those favorite Italian hangouts, were no more.

The two categories that had for so long been the backbone of Main Street, Retail-Department Store and Retail-Specialty, together numbered 129; in 1951, they represented 43% of the 312 "for profit" businesses in the Main Street survey area.

These pages paid greater individual attention to Main Street's department stores than to the stores of any other category. They had always been the big names, the "anchors" in modern terms, that had drawn the largest numbers of shoppers to downtown, to the benefit of the many smaller retail-specialty stores surrounding them. Main Street had possessed a representative sample of the major national store names in the 1951 directory, including Sears, W. T. Grant, S. S. Kresge, and F. W. Woolworth. Kresge was transitioning between stores, with two open at that time. Yet even these nationally known stores were never as beloved as the locally owned department stores, Yost's, Block's, and Chatlin's. Yost's had been in decline before 1951, but both Block's and Chatlin's continued to dominate. The Retail-Department Store category in 1951 totaled 15, including six other, smaller stores. By 1978 Main Street listed only two department stores. F. W. Woolworth had survived (it finally closed in 1989), as had one of the lower-tier department stores, Martin's, which had so long existed in the literal shadow of Chatlin's.

Sears was the first to depart Main Street and move to the periphery, then Block's, and finally Chatlin's. None were replaced. All three recognized that their Main Street locations did not offer sufficient parking or display space. Sears, as a national chain not influenced by a local perspective, had come to this conclusion early. Block's was slow to realize its predicament, but managed to leave in time to survive elsewhere, at least for a while. Chatlin's waited too long; by the time Morris Chatlin's widow was confronting the awesome task of beginning all over again, Main Street had ceased to be a commercial destination worth visiting.

Retail had been what Main Street was primarily about, and Retail-Specialty stores its mainstay. Main Street had listed 114 such stores in 1951, 37% of the "for profit" businesses in that year. The net number rose to its peak of 122 in 1953, but from that point on the trend was be inexorably downward, numbering just 48 by 1978. This was a net loss of 66 stores, a drop of almost 58% from 1951 to 1978.

A few businesses listed in 1951 survived, although fewer still under the same family ownership. In 1951, Anthony J. Catagnus listed himself as a bookseller at 271 East Main Street. A change in marketing niche apparently served the business well, for the 1978 directory listed a Catagnus Novelty Shop at the same address. In 1978, Bill Glass still sold and repaired bicycles at 200 West Main Street, just as he had in 1951. The Joseph J. Zummo Hardware Company maintained its store at 259 East Main Street, one of the few firms to not only survive but to remain under the same family ownership. By 1978, there were two other Zummo's Hardware Stores, one at Swede Square in East Norriton and one at the Park Ridge Shopping Center in Lower Providence. Zummo's sons Anthony and Paul remained at the Main Street location; Paul ran the retail store while Anthony looked after the business-to-business segment that he had so carefully nurtured. Brother Vincent operated the Swede Square Store, and Charlie operated the Park Ridge location. In the distant future, only the Main Street location would survive. It does so today, run by the third generation of Zummo men, both named Joseph, in accordance with the family tradition.

Main Street's furniture stores demonstrated a singular historical arc during this period. There were 11 furniture stores in the 1951 directory, and only six in 1978. Of these six, however, four—Baer's, Chain-Mar, Norristown Furniture Co., and Staffano's—had survived the whole period. A fifth, Bondi's, moved to Main Street in 1954. There had been comings and goings in the interim, with the newcomers themselves later leaving, or being purchased by this core of survivors, but the survival rate of this category was remarkable.

It is perhaps appropriate to end this "obituary" by discussing one of the newcomers. This business moved into 244 West Main Street, the site of the Castenova grocery store. After that store closed, the location had been only intermittently rented, and in the 1978 directory it was identified as an "adult" bookstore. While that may seem tawdry enough, it was later discovered that the bookstore was merely a front. Though they did sell adult material, the building was used primarily as a temporary storage facility for drug dealers engaged in the long-distance, illicit drug trade. Main Street, Norristown, had been selected by the drug dealers for its out-of-the-way location, despite its apparent nearness to the interstate highways. The criminals figured that Main Street was little more than a ghost town, so they could hide there in plain sight. And they did, for years.[500]

They were right, as these numbers showed. By 1978, downtown was no longer dying. It had flat-lined.

14

So...What Killed Downtown?

At the beginning of this book I repeated the commonly held view that the blame for the death of America's downtowns should be placed directly on the malls—and then suggested that not only was that answer simplistic, but also verging on downright wrong. Downtown Norristown (and many other downtowns across the nation) was not killed by a single wound but by a series of blows—some potentially lethal, others painful but survivable had they been the only trauma involved. No, in the death of the downtown in Norristown, there is no shortage of suspects and, as it turns out, each one shares in the guilt. Before turning to our prime suspect, we should examine the evidence we have unearthed that points to the other two: both local and county government, and the downtown merchants themselves.

Suspect #1: Local and County Government

Both levels of local government in Norristown, county and borough, contributed blows that weakened the downtown. Neither did so out of malice, nor did any holder of elected office at either level wish the downtown ill, or make a conscious effort to injure it. Although there is no doubt that some of the decisions made by both levels of government did indeed harm downtown, in every case there were other considerations—usually legitimate ones—that took precedence. The case against the County Government of Montgomery County lies in the actions it took; the case against Norristown Borough Council lies in declining to act at all. Both action and inaction contributed to the death—with the latter more significant.

County Government

It is clear from the research done for this work that the government of Montgomery County deserves a larger share of the blame for the collapse of downtown Norristown than has been previously understood. This misunderstanding, as well as the amount of damage involved, can largely be attributed to the timing of various decisions and delays. There was no hint then, and no evidence uncovered since, that county's wounding of Main Street was the result of antagonism on the part of the county government, whether personal or group. The county's goal was always clear (efficient, cost-effective county-level government); what was less clear was its intention at any given time whether or not to expand to best reach that goal. The county's actions must be understood within the context of a steadily increasing bureaucracy, largely congruent with that happening throughout the country, as basic assumptions about the responsibilities of government underwent fundamental change.

The county government always maintained that its actions would benefit downtown; whether it actually believed that or not was, of course, immaterial. Its fundamental motives were financial, as it aimed to do the best it could at the lowest cost to taxpayers. The Commissioners of Montgomery County, as good stewards of the public's tax monies, realized in the early 1950s that the value of Main Street real estate, even on its core block, had fallen sufficiently to make expansion onto Main Street affordable. Their cost/benefit calculations thus pointed them in that direction, but those calculations included more than just dollars. Expansion onto Main Street had the additional, non-financial benefit of utilizing one of the borough's primary roads for the arrival and accommodation of the automobiles the new staff members would use to get to work. It is difficult to conceive of the entrance to any large parking garage being built off of Swede Street above Main, or on Airy Street anywhere near the courthouse.

The county's extension onto Main Street had two effects, one measurably significant, and the other significant but not measurable. These two effects were also largely sequential. The county's purchase of its first two buildings on Main Street in 1954 and two others in 1961 removed a total of 40 entries from the city directories. Only five of these were storefronts, but all five storefronts and 35 other entries were thereafter lost to downtown. What followed the county's 1954 purchase was a period of uncertainty over the fate of the buildings. After 1961, that uncertainty included whether any business locations at all would emerge from the project's steadily evolving focus, from county complex to just a simple garage entrance. This uncertainty remained a factor in concerns about downtown Norristown for a remarkable 13 years, from 1954 to 1967, when construction finally began on the new complex. The period of construction that followed lasted until 1971, as noise, debris, and traffic disruption on Main Street extended the county's period of negative impact on Main Street to a full 17 years. This is the type of impact that cannot be measured, but that it was both substantial and negative cannot be disputed.

That impact also arrived at the worst possible time. Downtown was beginning to feel the competition in 1954, first from Logan Square, but steadily more so from the numerous but shopping centers appearing in East and West Norriton. Main Street was still prosperous at this point, but the total inability of the business community to influence the county's decision process and the decade-long specter of empty, decaying buildings in the heart of downtown helped to set the stage for the feeling of apathy and inevitable decline that would gradually envelop downtown Norristown.

Norristown Borough Council

Leonard Friedman, son of Samuel Friedman, operated The New York Store at 14 East Main Street upon his father's death until the store closed in 1991. He was thus the voice of experience when he observed, "I think most of the merchants felt it was the Borough that did them in." He didn't mean Norristown as a whole but the Borough Council. He was making no accusation of deliberate malice, but rather summing up the frustration shared by downtown merchants over decades of discussion and argument with and within Borough Council, with few actions actually undertaken. He did find specific fault with two of the council's few actions: depriving downtown of revenue from parking meters and changing Main Street to one-way. Both of these actions clearly harmed downtown.

Friedman's father had told him that when the meters were first installed in 1940, the Borough Council had promised to commit all revenues from parking meters—both coins and fines—to promote parking downtown. This unprovable but provocative assertion was repeated by others in newspaper articles and editorials on "the parking problem," and served to muddle the already-turbid waters. While such promises were very possibly made, no written understanding to that effect was ever reached. And the Borough Council proved over the decades that even agreements committed to writing were not always enforceable.

Regardless of where the truth lies concerning the supposed 1940 "promise" to dedicate parking meter revenues to downtown improvements, the Borough Council immediately began to direct the revenues to its own general fund. The success of the meters from 1940 through the 1950s led subsequent councils to continue this practice, and the revenue from the meters became an essential component of borough revenues overall. As meter revenue began to fall in the 1960s, so did revenue from taxes paid by downtown merchants, among other sources. Thus, later attempts to redirect even the declining meter revenue toward the downtown and were doomed to failure by the overall deterioration of the borough's financial position.

Friedman was not the only one who believed that the Borough Council's decision to change first DeKalb Street and then Main Street to one-way seriously damaged downtown Norristown. That the two changeovers occurred 13 years apart speaks to both the Borough's consistency of policy and downtown's decline in importance. The delay in converting Main Street to one-way had everything to do with the opposition of Main Street merchants; it was not until their numbers and influence were in serious decline that the conversion was able to proceed without serious contention.

In its two identified acts of commission that harmed downtown Norristown, the Borough Council demonstrated a fundamentally consistent policy sustained over decades. Both these actions were evidence of the council's fundamental priorities, which did not include nurturing downtown. It could be argued that the Borough Council undertook these two actions in good faith, acting in interests of what was best for the borough as a whole rather than just one component, even one as important as downtown. However, as the previous chapters make it clear, the Borough Council rarely made its decisions based on any cool-headed, benevolent, judicious rationale. More often it made its decisions to act based on whether or not that action would raise taxes on the 12 wards. Perhaps it is fortunate, then, that the Borough Council rarely chose to act. Its actions were quite literally both few and far between. Decisions such as those involving parking meters and one-way streets must be viewed in the larger context of Borough Council's much more often repeated—and therefore even more consistent—policy of inaction amid rancor.

Leonard Friedman understood this. More important to him than the Borough Council's two negative actions had been the times council had been requested, even implored to act and had not. The Borough Council spent the 25 years focused on in this book claiming to listen to everyone's concerns and occasionally offering support (provided that support did not include the expenditure of money), but in reality hearing little and doing less. Expenditures were made, primarily for traffic studies, but made grudgingly; more than once support was withdrawn before an actual expenditure could take place. Thus, whereas the case has been made that the county hurt downtown with its actions and delays in executing them, the negative effect of borough government on downtown Norristown derived largely from its failure to do anything at all.

The Borough Council's policy of inaction was not limited to downtown, nor to the other issues that were discussed in these pages. Its equivocations, delays, and lack of positive response to issues are reflective of what may be fairly termed its style of government. The many claimed acts of omission were, in the final analysis, another component of its general approach, and consistent with the policies illustrated by the two acts of commission. The Borough Council's attitude toward Main Street between 1950 and 1975 conforms to the nature of the relationship from the very beginning. Local government's responsibility was to provide a safe, stable community in which individual entrepreneurship could flourish. Downtown Main Street was given extra protection by the police department, because it was obviously the most profitable target for criminals. No thought was given to "municipal planning" during the periods of downtown's growth and dominance; both were the collective result of individuals' actions. The colorful display of Christmas lights over Main Street represented the kind of expenditure the council had always made: charging Main Street's merchants with a portion of the costs, assessed according to their individual frontage.

These policies had deep roots. Pre-WWI Norristown had long been able to boast of being well run and efficient, and prided itself on how effectively local leaders were able to oversee an expanding and prosperous borough on what had always been a part-time (and close to unpaid) basis. Their successors in the rapidly changing world after WWII fancied themselves able to maintain this efficiency and clung tenaciously to this tradition, despite the increasing complexity of the tasks set before them. While some council members occasionally appeared to possess something approaching the necessary grasp of the changing conditions, the council as a whole retained the old traditions of local, "hands off" government. Most of the members were born, schooled, and successful within the Norristown version of local, limited and largely volunteer government. And most of them resisted almost every suggestion that "outsiders"—even those knowledgeable in their administrative fields, whose ideas and concerns deserved attention and careful consideration—should be given even the smallest amount of power or influence. Time and again the Borough Council rejected assistance and money from outside government sources, unwilling to concede even the least amount of autonomy or accept any degree of outsider oversight. This rejection of outside direction was not always a bad thing, but that is far from an endorsement of the Borough Council's general inaction.

After the mid-1960s, and certainly by the 1970s, both the actions and the inactions of the Borough Council were being driven more and more by new circumstances rather than old traditions. The circumstances were many, but their common effect was to steadily decrease the revenue from taxes, fees, and such special items as parking meters upon which the borough government depended. The borough's overall financial situation had deteriorated to such a point by the mid-1970s that such financial support as the Borough Council rendered—largely through the condemning of properties—to downtown's last attempt at a parking garage should be viewed as surprising. By that time it was clear to the council that it could not possibly afford to commit to even the *possibility* of expending tax revenues if, for example, the proposed garage failed to meet its occupancy expectations. By the time the Borough Council belatedly admitted that they needed to take action to arrest downtown's decline, it was in no position to make a financial contribution. For downtown, the change in motivation was irrelevant; the policy remained consistent, and in the face of a brand new phase of the history of retailing in America, utterly inadequate.

The Borough Council's contribution to the decline of downtown—and to that of Norristown itself—went beyond either acts of commission or policies of benign neglect. One aspect of the Borough Council's behavior cannot be explained by either tradition or changing circumstances. During the period discussed herein, the Borough Council managed to repeatedly project an image not just of inaction, but of quarrelsome futility. It would decide one thing, and then reconsider its decision; it waffled back and forth for months on even such minor issues as parking meter rates. Throughout all its members evidenced public displays of anger, bad manners, and unpleasant behavior, even on the record—which more than hinted at the complex personal feuds that simmered constantly beneath the surface. This was an intangible contribution to be sure, but the growing evidence of apathy and feelings that "nothing ever gets done in Norristown" among the electorate is unmistakable. The conduct of the Borough Council bears much responsibility for this.

This responsibility cannot be attributed to any deep attachment to American business/government traditions. It was, ultimately, personal and a part of Norristown's peculiar character, tinged with a veneer of partisan party politics. The relationships among the members of the Borough Council largely replicated on a personal level the much broader ethnic and religious divisions and prejudices that had long characterized Norristown.

The Norristown Borough Council consistently argued that its general policy of inaction toward downtown was one of fairness in the collection and distribution of revenue, with the good of the many placed above the good of the one. Yet this same Borough Council, practiced, as its predecessors had always practiced, a very different approach within its component electoral wards. One example of this approach relevant here was the time-honored practice of "exonerating" parking tickets at the sole request of a member. This deference of the group to an individual member, although obviously detrimental to borough revenue, continued even as the financial strings began to tighten. That such a ritual was often followed not too long thereafter by discussions of how to raise more revenue, without any apparent recognition of the irony, speaks to the deep-rooted localism of Norristown government administration. This particular version of looking after one specific component ahead of the community as a whole lay at the core of local government, and always had. All successful Norristown municipal politicians looked after their wards first and foremost. With that as a conceptual starting point, looking after the good of the whole community could easily be viewed as looking after the good of someone else's ward, and too often it was.

When reviewing the dreary and repetitious record of the Borough Council, the tendency is to focus on individuals, with Paul Santangelo standing out among a cast of forceful personalities. No one familiar with the facts can underestimate the effect that these strong personalities—armed with the security of assured reelection in their wards—had on the nature and results of Borough Council deliberations. Yet research firmly argued that it was necessary to look deeper than just personalities, and to seek answers in both the structure of borough government and, ultimately, in the residents of Norristown themselves.

In the final analysis, of course, the Norristown Borough Council was an elected governmental body, with its members subject to periodic approval by the voters. This fact must ultimately figure in any judgment of the responsibility that the Borough Council actually bore for the decline of downtown. During the 25-year period focused on in this book, the Norristown Borough Council by any standard failed to adapt to the unprecedented changes taking place all around it. The deliberations of the council were well reported in the *Times Herald*, and the residents of Norristown had every reason to be well aware of the persistent shortcomings of their municipal government. During those 25 years, the residents—the voters—of Norristown had the opportunity to change half of the personnel in the Borough Council every two years; each ward could change its representative every four years. Elections are the final arbiters of the public will; in exercising their will, the voters of Norristown reflected a consistency that largely accounts for the consistency of their elected officials. This consistency was reflected in the tendency of some wards to return the same representative time and time again, with Paul Santangelo the outstanding example. Whether that consistency was the result of apathy, lack of critical thinking, misinformation, or fear could be the subject of its own book.

Norristown's residents also had two opportunities to fundamentally change the form of government that so many of them rightly saw as quarrelsome and incompetent, and they would have had a third opportunity in 1959 had more of them signed the petition to place structural change on the ballot. The voters of Norristown, however, decisively spurned both opportunities to improve the situation. Given the frequent opportunities to make piecemeal change and the two opportunities for fundamental change, it is possible to glean the collective attitude of the residents of Norristown during the period of this study: a staunch conservatism, particularly as regards taxes.

This examination of downtown took place during a period of considerable turnover among the residents of Norristown. The broad financial effect of this turnover was to steadily lower borough revenues. This in turn further squeezed those long-time residents who found themselves called upon to shoulder more and more of a tax burden that was delivering less and less to them. We term their collective response "conservative," but its overwhelming motivation was economic and its overwhelming result a blind opposition to higher taxes, or such devices as new fees that were tax increases by another name. This was a fundamental, and unshakeable, reason for their rejections of governmental change. This financially driven conservatism was a constant during the period of this study, and for many years afterward.

Paul Santangelo's last ward election, in November 1991, exemplifies the durability of this obsession. By 1991, Santangelo was 91 years old, and close to blind and deaf. His presence at council meetings had become a local joke, spread by taped coverage of council meetings on cable, which revealed to a broader audience the extent of his boorish, obstreperous behavior, which physical infirmities had only made worse. He lost in the 1991 general election to Democrat Ervin E. Jones by 231 votes, receiving 632 votes to 863 for Jones (this was for the seat in what was by now the Fourth Ward, due to governmental changes). Post-election analysis of this epic defeat virtually ignored his age and infirmities. Ervin Jones attributed Paul's defeat to a cause even more fundamental than Paul Santangelo himself: "He made a mistake when he voted to raise the trash fee." The Borough Council, faced with still-overwhelming budget issues, had the previous August narrowly approved a $160 annual fee per household for trash collection. The fact that Santangelo supported such an action should be ample evidence that Norristown's financial problems had not improved in the period following the 1975 budget crisis. The charging of a fee for what had previously been paid for by their taxes was a tax increase, and the voters of Norristown realized it. Santangelo, together with another council member with 25 years of experience who had also reluctantly supported the trash fee, was defeated.

Thus when all other considerations are included, the decisive factor was the Norristown voters' visceral hatred of taxes. To indict the Norristown Borough Council for its considered policy of inaction toward downtown Norristown is then, in a very real sense, to indict much of modern-day America. While the residents of Norristown may not have had the government they deserved, they did have the form of government they wanted, whether it served them well or not.

This work makes offers no final judgment on the responsibility of Norristown's government for the borough's decline. Any judgments offered would need to be viewed, too, in the light of the evidence from the decades after 1975. Norristown's overall decline continued well after that year, if indeed it has yet ended. During that time, Norristown did alter its structure of government, then altered it again, to little discernible effect. Perhaps the question is not so much why Norristown declined, but why it continued to do so when other boroughs of similar size and in similar circumstances rebounded. Regardless, the government of the Borough of Norristown cannot be assigned primary blame for the collapse of downtown Norristown. It was shortsighted, rent by divisions, and largely ineffective, and must shoulder partial responsibility for what took place. But the evidence collected here clearly shows that the blame must be shared and fundamental causality directed elsewhere.

Suspect #2: The Downtown Merchants

The efforts of Main Street's merchants during the period of this study deserve considerable praise, more for their persistence than for their success, as the problems they confronted were manifestly wider than downtown Norristown. Yet if we are to find the Norristown Borough Council guilty—with mitigating factors—of clinging to old traditions in the face of manifestly changing circumstances, we must turn the same scrutiny on the merchants. When we do, we find a very similar result.

Downtown's customer base had always been not only borough residents but also those who lived in central Montgomery County. The downtown location had for close to a century a virtual monopoly on retail commerce within this broad marketing area. Downtown Norristown was, and forever had been, the area's only major location for stores and services offering more than day-to-day items. This broader market led to downtown Norristown's growth and regional dominance, and holding onto that regional market was necessary for its continued dominance. After the war, while the population increase brought unprecedented numbers of people into the area, it also brought a transportation revolution, with a new dominant player: the automobile. This had enormous consequences for downtown Norristown, all of them bad.

The unprecedented growth of the population in the greater Norristown area effectively meant that downtown Norristown needed only to secure the patronage of a relatively small percentage of these new shoppers to continue its traditional role of retail center for the central Montgomery area. Statistics demonstrating the continuance of this tradition could be found in the *Times Herald* during the 1950s, but virtually disappeared during the 1960s. The evidence of the city directories demonstrates that the number of downtown businesses declined while the population of the surrounding area was burgeoning. The overall conclusion is clear: downtown Norristown failed to attract even a small percentage of the area's many new shoppers, while simultaneously losing more and more of its borough-based shoppers.

An examination of those alternative shopping locations follows, but first we must focus on the downtown merchant community itself. The downtown merchants were a varied group, but the most common shortcoming was that of limited vision. Over the course of decades prior to WWII, when the customers would be delivered quite close to their very doorstep, downtown Norristown's merchant community became locked into a range of vision largely focused within the basic parameters of downtown itself. Downtown's merchants had paid careful attention to minute changes in the item and price offerings up and down Main Street, but historically had never needed to look far beyond their own boundaries for either competition or ideas. WWII brought a period where more outreach had to take place, but such efforts largely ceased after the war.

This limited vision resulted in downtown Norristown looking after itself first. The Main Street–centered business community's relationship to the smaller West Marshall Street merchant community was limited; the concept of cooperation did not extend beyond setting common operating hours during holidays. Virtually no evidence of efforts toward joint policies for marketing or physical improvements ever surfaced. An observer with today's perspective would quickly realize that the downtown and the

West Marshall Street centers together would fit easily into the footprint of the King of Prussia Mall, with room to spare. Today customers routinely walk farther to get from their cars to the mall stores than anyone who had parked anywhere in downtown Norristown. They also walk farther along the mall's pedestrian "streets" than the entire distance covered by Main Street. Looking back, we can see this, but the merchants of downtown Norristown after 1950 had no such vision.

The only proposal to appear during the period of this study that reflected a wider vision was the idea for a joint parking lot spanning Stony Creek, which at least would connect West Main Street and West Marshall Street. The idea came not from the merchants of either center, but from the *Times Herald*. Nothing was heard about this idea after it was first introduced; the *Times Herald* did not repeat the proposal later. This specific proposal should not itself be overemphasized. It had virtually no lifespan, and may have been a non-starter for good reasons not mentioned in public. Nevertheless, it is important that this was the only proposal to be publicly offered to downtown Norristown that shows signs of progressive thinking, any imagination about what might be happening beyond the individual retail communities themselves. The commercial threat to downtown Norristown that materialized after WWII appeared *all* around the borough, but the responses to counter this threat were limited by the narrow vision that had come to blinker downtown merchants.

This narrow vision not only precluded any substantial effort to join with anyone or anything beyond downtown's limits, but was also the underlying cause of such debacles as the Pigeon-Hole Garage. Many potential sites had been discussed during the years leading up to this one productive effort to build a parking garage. The one that was chosen was too small for its intended purpose, a fact known from the very beginning. Its sole advantage was the crucial one: it was centrally located. A parking garage there would favor neither end of Main Street, and would most directly aid Main Street's core block east of the Public Square. To downtown's parochial-thinking merchants, this outweighed the size advantage of other potential sites, particularly on the western end of Main Street, which was already experiencing serious decline. Technology seemed to offer the solution: lifts to place each automobile into a "pigeon-hole." Convinced that the small lot on Lafayette Street could shelter enough vehicles to earn a profit, the downtown merchants collectively gambled on an untried technology to solve a proven problem. It was a colossal failure. Every subsequent attempt to solve the parking problem would be met with a reminder of this expensive, demoralizing debacle. The argument in the early 1970s over whether a garage proposed for the second block of East Main Street was too distant from the county government complex serves as a coda to this point: If this distance was under question, how much support for the garage could be found on West Main Street, even farther away?

A comparison is required at this point to put the efforts of the downtown merchants in perspective. Had the "Pigeon Hole" Garage actually worked to its full expectation, it could have accommodated approximately 240 automobiles. Across the river at the as-yet-unopened King of Prussia Plaza, graders and asphalt layers were preparing the ground for lots to accommodate 6,000 cars. By the time the Plaza actually opened in 1963, that number had risen to 9,000. This leads to a most unsettling question: would *any* single garage, either the "Pigeon-Hole" or the later one planned to replace the Humane Fire Company on Main Street, have made any real difference?

Suspect #3: Shopping Centers and Malls

The *Polk City Directories* testify that Main Street's decline began in the middle 1950s. By the time the King of Prussia Plaza opened in 1963, Main Street had been in a steady and accelerating decline for years. Norristown's commercial supremacy had already been weakened by the combined effects of Logan Square at the borough's north end and by shopping centers in surrounding townships. The malls that opened in King of Prussia in 1963 and Plymouth Meeting in 1966 undeniably posed a threat that was exponentially greater than that which downtown had already been failing to confront, with predictable results. Main Street in Norristown was located almost exactly between the King of Prussia Plaza and the Plymouth Meeting Mall, each at their respective intersections of limited-access highways. Together their effect was devastating, but their contribution to the decline of Main Street was to greatly accelerate a process by then already well under way.

The focus on the two retail giants as causes of Norristown's decline has obscured both the earlier contribution of the smaller but numerous shopping centers—and some individual large stores—that had begun to appear around Norristown, as well as their later contribution. This group collectively was responsible for wounding Main Street long before the opening of the King of Prussia Plaza. Whether or not these wounds would of themselves have brought about the death of downtown was made moot by the phenomenon of the malls. These centers largely continued to prosper, however, and continued to negatively affect downtown Norristown.

One result of the research for this work was the revelation of the previously overlooked role of the Logan Square Shopping Center. It played a much larger part in the story of the early decline of downtown Norristown than is commonly acknowledged. The opening of Logan Square was a seminal event in the commercial history of Norristown during the second half of the 20th century. Joseph and Harry Butera were among the first to recognize downtown's shortcomings in the era of the automobile and to act on them. Their creation provided the two elements downtown Norristown never could: space to expand and replace the old with the new, and most of all, space for parking. It was not their intention to contribute to harm Main Street, of course. They merely wanted to give Norristown shoppers what they could not get downtown: *free, ample parking.*

Logan Square was the first local competition to downtown from a planned shopping center. By attracting a Sears store, it quickly established itself as a force to be reckoned with, and became Norristown's third shopping area within a very short time. As Main Street declined, Logan Square grew, and within 20 years of its founding its sales volume had eclipsed that of downtown Norristown entirely. By 1969, the county planning commission estimated its gross sales at twice that of the entire central business district.

That success, of course, is made all the more poignant in light of the fact that Logan Square never fulfilled its promise. For all its advantages, Logan Square shares with Main Street the problem outlined in the 1969 Comprehensive Plan: a dependence on narrow, increasingly inadequate local highways to deliver a sufficient number of customers. It thus began to suffer downtown's problem: too many attractive alternatives within a short drive by automobile. Though Logan Square too suffered a slow decline, losing its Sears store and gradually slipping into irrelevancy, its legacy in the post-WWII history of Norristown deserves to be better known.

Not the Butler—the Chauffeur

This examination of the suspects in the death of downtown Norristown makes it clear that while each contributed, none was the primary cause. While three (four, if you separate county and borough government) suspects had a hand in killing the downtown, only shopping centers and malls seem more culpable than the others and might be credited with delivering the actual death blow. Yet there is another, more comprehensive and fundamental suspect for the death of downtown. The malls, the local shopping centers, and the problems with which both county and borough government had to grapple all had one fundamental reason for their appearance: the automobile.

"The automobile" as employed here is, of course, a metaphor for a far-reaching event in U.S. history, the embrace by the population of a means of *individual* transport in the automobile, and by business of the truck for almost equally selective use. This technological change had its roots in the late 19th century and several decades of growth and development in the 20th century before WWII. After the war, and certainly by the 1950s, that embrace quickly accelerated to the point where it has been called "American's love affair with the automobile."

The finding of "death by automobile" is consistent with this work's underlying thesis, which is that transportation was *always* the primary determining factor in Norristown's economic conditions. The fact that this latest change in the dominant mode of transportation had results diametrically opposite from those that had preceded it only reinforces that thesis. Early modes of transportation fed Norristown and made it healthier and stronger; the eventual reliance on and preference for the automobile starved it and led to its painful and inexorable decline. The land that became "The Town of Norris" lay athwart the primary—if primitive—transportation routes of the period prior to the Industrial Revolution, the Schuylkill River and two roadways that themselves had been Indian trails. While dependent upon them, the town grew only slowly, but the railroad brought prosperity to Norristown. Norristown's period of growth and establishment of regional commercial dominance was fueled by the railroad, and the nature of its internal growth was largely determined by the actions of the two primary railroads to reach Norristown.

Then came the automobile. More importantly, the automobile came to a location, Norristown, almost fully laid out to accommodate first the rivers and then the railroad, and built out to accommodate the prosperity the railroad had brought. Earlier internal challenges notwithstanding, the automobile reduced downtown Norristown's problems to a single and seemingly insurmountable problem: a lack of space. "The Philadelphia Plan," which so well suited the Town of Norris and was modified fairly successfully to accommodate the railroads in the nineteenth century, did not serve Norristown well in the mid-20th century.

By then Norristown had developed into a mid-sized example of the classic American downtown centered on Main Street, with brick buildings standing shoulder to shoulder and to the very edge of the sidewalk. A century of growth and prosperity virtually filled the downtown area with such buildings. It did not leave much room for through traffic or parking. The automobile required much greater space to transport an individual shopper into Norristown than had the rails and trolleys, and the increasing numbers of shoppers and their cars quickly became more than the ancient road system could accommodate. The result was the traffic jam.

The widespread adoption of the automobile quickly cost downtown Norristown the monopoly position it had heretofore enjoyed, and after 1950 the spread of local shopping alternatives began to eat away at its dominant position. In a period of greatly increasing local population, Main Street began to lose businesses at a steadily increasing pace. Although the greater Norristown area was growing dramatically, those new residents were not braving the traffic congestion and lack of parking to shop downtown but going elsewhere to more accessible shopping centers on the periphery. At the same time, downtown was losing much of its traditional customer base in the borough for the same reasons. At first the damage to downtown would be felt only as a series of small cuts, none individually fatal, but over time with more wounds inflicted, the downtown was left weakened and bleeding.

This left downtown Norristown unable to fend off for long the full frontal attack made possible by the eastern extension of the Pennsylvania Turnpike to its temporary terminus at King of Prussia, in Upper Merion Township just south of Norristown, across the Schuylkill River. The westernmost section of what would become the Schuylkill Expressway, complete but unused, greeted the turnpike upon its arrival; the opening of the expressway's eastern sections in the succeeding years created at King of Prussia a thoroughly modern version of an ancient process, as the land immediately adjacent to an intersection of two major transportation routes increased greatly in value and underwent "development." This particular example differed in that the two transportation routes had not grown over time, but had suddenly appeared close to full-grown, but the result was a development of the land around their intersection at a greatly accelerated rate.

The superhighways could and did deliver an enormous volume of automobiles to the King of Prussia area. Their intersection in what was almost entirely farmland provided sufficient space to build on a scale that existing downtowns could not begin to match. Manufacturing businesses were drawn there by the availability of land to build large facilities, and by the superhighways' ability to deliver a sufficient number of employees, even from quite far away. Office complexes were likewise seduced. Large department stores located there could draw customers from a marketing area beyond even the wildest imaginings of businesses in years previous. And all these commercial locations could offer what downtown Norristown could not: *free, ample parking.*

This was the blow that mortally wounded Main Street. This completed the fundamental change in Norristown's relationship to the automobile that local shopping centers had begun. The automobile begat the system of limited-access highways, which begat the local suburban shopping center, which begat the regional shopping mall. The automobile not only destroyed downtown as a commercial location, it destroyed the traditional shopping culture that developed there. Long-time Norristown residents who began to frequent the malls would have seen the difference immediately—a difference that had nothing to do with new buildings and displays. They had many more stores from which to choose, and many more products than had ever been available on Main Street or in all of downtown.

What they could no longer find, of course, was the individuality—not to mention the authenticity—of what they had grown up with downtown. Gone was the community connection. While the Norristown Poultry Market's offerings of live chickens killed and plucked before the customer's eyes may have had no future at any location, at no mall would shoppers find the equivalent of Main Street's ethnic-tinged individuality. No one swept the patch of mall tiles in front of Sears, then leaned on the broom to tell passing shoppers about the great deal in aisle four. Shoppers at the mall were not greeted by name as they entered the cavernous stores.

Malls usually featured one or more well-known stores, but they were known solely from their advertising, not the collective memory of the local population. No mall restaurant would, during hunting season, feature venison from deer shot by the business owner/proprietor. There were often, in fact, no owner/proprietors on site, none personally known to you (or your parents), who might even live on your block. No teenager could pick up a purchase without paying because the store owner knew the parents could be trusted. Mall stores lacked the personal relationships that had led them to employ several members of a family as each came of age. The proprietors of mall stores might have been local, but they were not owners, only managers. Shopping on Main Street had been a communal experience, one that had been shared across the generations, with major changes in the goods and services, but very little in the social experience itself. Decades later, shopping malls may very well be in the process of creating their own communal experiences, or they may not. The future of shopping is uncertain, but the past is gone forever.

Main Street, Norristown, Pennsylvania, physically survived, in a shrunken and shriveled form. But the lifestyle of the middle-sized American urban area that it had exemplified did not. That lifestyle was not well served in Norristown by either local businesses or local government, which may have been the case elsewhere across the United States. Yet the death of Main Street and the shopping culture it exemplified cannot be ascribed to individuals, local business or political organizations. All were powerless before the change wrought by the public acceptance of the automobile.

Had the death of downtown Norristown been a singular event, or had its cause been clearly attributable to another singular event, the fact of its death would have little sig-

255

nificance beyond the local. Yet Norristown was not alone; its downtown merchants were participants in a social and economic change that swept America after WWII, as going shopping changed from going downtown to going to the mall.

That change was powered by the automobile.

So who killed downtown? Ultimately, we have to admit the truth. We did it. We killed the downtown. We did it by falling in love with our cars, and with everything they came to represent for us: independence, possibilities, expanded horizons, status.

It is this identification of "the automobile"—or, our so-called love affair with our cars—as the root cause of Norristown's decline that makes its lesson broadly applicable to mid-sized towns, boroughs, and cities across this land...those other hometowns that watched their traditional downtowns suffer and die during the 1950s and afterward. The facts of each case vary: the names of the stores, the local legends in the commercial community, the ethnicity and religion of the broader community, the route numbers, and much more. The list of suspects will be similar, however, often with municipal government at its head. Many localities had better municipal leadership, but some may have had worse. The lesson of downtown Norristown is to look deeper than the local specifics, and to not settle for causality at just the local level.

There is a fundamental incompatibility between the automobile and the compact urban grid. This is a disturbing conclusion, but the passage of time since the period when this book began as a study has continued to produce evidence of this incompatibility. The same issues that Norristown began to grapple with in the 1940s still bedevil many of America's urban grids today. Highways have been built, and highways have been removed; streets have been widened, and streets have been narrowed; the traffic jams are no smaller. Parking meters have been added and have been subtracted; new technology even allows them to require different amounts at different times. Modern versions of the "pigeon-hole" garage have reappeared in our cities. Still, drivers circle the blocks, looking for empty spaces, or they double park. The drama produced by the "solutions" to such basic contradictions as providing curbside parking spaces while also expediting traffic during "rush hour" is still being played out in virtually every American city today. Not one issue the automobile bequeathed to Norristown early on has been satisfactorily resolved within any urban grid on the American landscape, despite the passage of more than half a century, and despite the many billions of dollars expended by all levels of American government since the Pennsylvania Turnpike reached King of Prussia in 1950. The message of the fundamental incompatibility of the automobile and the urban grid is clear, and supported by decades of experience. Unfortunately, the message remains as unacceptable now as it was when Norristown waged its futile struggle.

The solution to Norristown's parking problem turned out to be rather simple: remove the reason for people to go downtown at all. Free, ample parking finally arrived. All it took was to mortally wound the downtown.

References

Alderfer, E. Gordon. *The Montgomery County Story*. Norristown, PA: The Commissioners of Montgomery County, 1951.
Anonymous. "An Old Map of Norristown." HSMC *Sketches* 1 (1895): 405–408.
Anonymous. "Schuylkill Navigation Company." HSMC *Sketches* 4 (1910): 353.
Anonymous. "Schuylkill Canal Navigator." HSMC *Sketches* 4 (1910): 354–361.
Anonymous. "Notes and Documents on the Sesquicentennial of Norristown as a Borough 1812–1962." *HSMC Bulletin* 13, no. 2.
Anonymous. "Opening of the Philadelphia and Norristown Rail Road." *HSMC Bulletin* 17, no. 4 (Spring 1971).
Anonymous. (manuscript contributed by Joseph Shrawder), "The Old Schuylkill Canal," *HSMC Bulletin* 19, no. 2 (Spring 1974): 112–126.
Bauman, John F. "Expressways, Public Housing and Renewal: A Blueprint for Postwar Philadelphia, 1945–1960." *Pennsylvania History* 57 (January 1990): 44–65.
Bean, Theodore W., ed. *History of Montgomery County, Pennsylvania*. Philadelphia: Everts & Peck, 1884. Two volumes; reprinted by the Historical Society of Montgomery County.
Beck, Harry R. "Norristown, Pennsylvania: 1900-1909." PhD diss., University of Pennsylvania, 1956.
Bernstein, Peter L. *Wedding of the Waters: The Erie Canal and the Making of a Great Nation*. New York: W. W. Norton & Company, 2005.
Bruce-Briggs, Barry. *The War Against the Automobile*. New York: E. P. Dutton, 1977.
Bryan, Kirke. "Books on Montgomery County." *HSMC Bulletin* 2, no. 4 (1941): 297–311.
Buck, William J. *History of Montgomery County Within the Schuylkill Valley*. Norristown, PA: E. L. Acker, 1859. As reprinted in *Atlases of Montgomery County, Pennsylvania*. Evansville, IN: Unigraphic, Inc., 1976.
Butera, Harry. *The Memoirs of Harry Butera*. (unpublished)
Carlson, Robert E. "The Pennsylvania Improvement Society and Its Promotion of Canals and Railroads, 1824–1826." *Pennsylvania History* 31, no. 3 (June 1964): 295–310.
Corson, S. Cameron. "Old Roads of Norristown." HSMC *Sketches* 7 (1925): 93–105.
Davidson, Janet F., and Sweeney, Michael S. *On the Move: Transportation and the American Story*. Washington, DC: National Geographic, 2003.
Douglas, George H. *All Aboard! The Railroad in American Life*. New York: Marlowe & Company, 1992.
Dubrow, Michael G. "The College of Philadelphia and the Politics of Revolution, 1755–1779." In *A Pennsylvania Album: Undergraduate Essays on the 250th Anniversary*, edited by Richard Slator Dunn and Mark Frazier Lloyd, 7–12. Philadelphia: Trustees of the University of Pennsylvania, 1990.
Ellis, Joseph J. *His Excellency George Washington*. New York: Vintage Books, 2004.
Faris, John T. *Old Roads Out of Philadelphia*. 2nd ed. Philadelphia and London: J. B. Lippincott Company, 1917.
———. *Old Trails and Roads in Penn's Land*. Philadelphia and London: J. B. Lippincott Company, 1927.

Feather, Augustus G. *The Political Hand-Book of Montgomery County.* Philadelphia: Globe Press Bureau, 1899.

Fisher, Daniel. "Norristown as it was in 1814 and 1815." HSMC *Sketches* 5 (1915): 115–141.

———. "Norristown 65 Years Ago." HSMC *Sketches* 5 (1915): 142–147.

Fisher, Joseph A. *The Reading's Heritage.* New York: The Newcomen Society in North America, 1958.

Fisher, Sidney George. *William Penn: A Biography.* Philadelphia and London: J. B. Lippincott Company, 1932.

Fogelson, Robert M. *Downtown: Its Rise and Fall, 1880–1950.* New Haven, CT: Yale University Press, 2001.

Fornance, Joseph. "The Montgomery County Courthouse in 1850." HSMC *Sketches* 5 (1915): 92–106.

Garreau, Joel. *Edge City; Life on the New Frontier.* New York: Doubleday, 1991.

Gegenheimer, Albert Frank. *William Smith: Educator and Churchman, 1727–1803.* Philadelphia: University of Pennsylvania Press, 1943.

Gibbons, Edward S. "The Building of the Schuylkill Navigation System, 1815–1828." *Pennsylvania History* 57, no. 1 (January 1990): 13–43.

Goddard, Stephen B. *Getting There: The Epic Struggle Between Road and Rail in the American Century.* New York: Basic Books, 1994.

Goldstein, Sidney. "Patterns of Internal Migration, Norristown, Pennsylvania, 1900–1950." (research paper, Department of Sociology, University of Pennsylvania, 1953).

Graham, John W. *William Penn: Founder of Pennsylvania.* London: Headley Bros., 1916.

Goldstein, Sidney, ed. *The Norristown Study: An Experiment in Interdisciplinary Research Training.* Philadelphia: University of Pennsylvania Press, 1961.

Harley, Herbert. *The Town on Three Hills.* (unpublished manuscript in the collections of the Historical Society of Montgomery County, Norristown, PA.)

Harlow, Alvin F. *The Road of the Century: The Story of the New York Central.* New York: Creative Age Press, 1947.

Harmon, George M., ed. *Transportation: The Nation's Lifelines.* Washington, DC: Industrial College of the Armed Forces, 1968.

Heysham, Theodore. *Norristown, 1812–1912.* Norristown: Norristown Herald, 1913.

Hocker, Edward W. "Montgomery County History." HSMC *Bulletin* 12, nos. 1, 2, 3, and 4 (Fall, 1959–Spring 1961).

———. "Chronicles of Montgomery County, 1784–1934." Series published in the Norristown *Times Herald* beginning September 10, 1934; complete series collected into a scrapbook housed in the collections of the Historical Society of Montgomery County, Norristown, PA.

———. *History of Montgomery County.* (unpublished manuscript; housed in the collections of the Historical Society of Montgomery County, Norristown, PA.)

Holstein, G. W. "Swedes' Ford and Surroundings." HSMC *Sketches* 4 (1910): 73–77.

Hull, William I. *William Penn: A Topical Biography.* London: Oxford University Press, 1937.

Ianni, Francis A. J. "The Acculturation of Italo-Americans in Norristown, Pennsylvania, 1900–1950." (research paper, Department of Sociology, University of Pennsylvania, 1958).

Jacobs, Jane. *The Death and Life of Great American Cities.* New York: Random House, 1961.

Jackson, Kenneth T. *Crabgrass Frontier: The Suburbanization of the United States.* New York and Oxford: Oxford University Press, 1985.

Johnson, Steven. *Emergence: The Connected Lives of Ants, Brains, Cities and Software.* New York: Touchstone Books, 2001.

Kirkland Edward Chase. *Men, Cities and Transportation: A Study in New England History.* Cambridge, MA: Harvard University Press, 1948.

Kriebel, H. W. *A Brief History of Montgomery County Pennsylvania.* Norristown: The School Directors' Association, 1923.

Kunstler, James Howard. *The Geography of Nowhere: The Rise and Decline of America's Man-Made Landscape.* New York: Simon & Schuster, 1993.

Larson, John Lauritz. *Internal Improvement: National Public Works and the Promise of Popular Government in the Early United States.* Chapel Hill, NC: University of North Carolina Press, 2001.

Leavitt, Helen. *Superhighway–Superhoax.* New York: Doubleday & Company, 1970.

Ling, Peter J. *America and the Automobile: Technology, Reform and Social Change.* Manchester, England, and New York: Manchester University Press, 1990.

McDonough, Richard A. *The History of the Freedom Valley: Norristown.* Valley Forge, PA: America Responds With Love, 2007.

McShane, Clay. *Down the Asphalt Path: The Automobile and the American City.* New York: Columbia University Press, 1994.

Mowbray, A. Q. *Road to Ruin.* Philadelphia and New York: J. B. Lippincott Company, 1968.

Nolan, J. Bennett. *The Schuylkill.* New Brunswick, NJ: Rutgers University Press, 1951.

Owen, Wilfred, and Dearing, Charles L. *Toll Roads and the Problem of Highway Modernization.* Washington, DC: The Brookings Institution, 1951.

Parsons, William T. "Isaac Norris the Councillor, Master of Norriton Manor." *HSMC Bulletin* 19, no. 1 (Fall 1973): 5–33.

———. "Notes and Documents on the Sesquicentennial of Norristown as a Borough, 1812–1962." *HSMC Bulletin* 13, no. 2: 128–160.

Patterson, Samuel D., ed. *An Act to Erect Norristown Into a Borough and the Several Supplements Passed thereto: Together with the By-Laws and Ordinances Passed by the Town Council.* Norristown, PA: S. D. Patterson, 1833.

Peare, Catherine Owens. *William Penn: A Biography.* Philadelphia and New York: J. B. Lippincott Company, 1957.

The Pennsylvanian. "Opening of the Philadelphia and Norristown Rail Road (August 18, 1835)." Reprinted in HSMC *Bulletin* 17:282–286.

Pennypacker, Samuel W. "The University of Pennsylvania in its Relations to the State of Pennsylvania." *The Pennsylvania Magazine of History and Biography* 15 (1891).

———. *The Autobiography of a Pennsylvanian: Volume 3.* Philadelphia: John C. Winston Co., 1918.

Rae, John B. *The Road and the Car in American Life.* Cambridge, MA: MIT Press, 1971.

Raitz, Karl, ed. *The National Road.* Baltimore and London: Johns Hopkins University Press, 1996.

Rambo, Charles Norris. "The Town of Norris." (public address delivered on Historical Day, May 10, 1912; signed copy in Norristown box "Anniversary Books" of the Historical Society of Montgomery County library.)

Reader, John. *Cities.* New York: Atlantic Monthly Press, 2004.

Reed, Willoughby H. "The Thompson Family and the Jeffersonville Inn." HSMC *Sketches* 1 (1895): 348–393.

Roberts, Victor J. "First Five Blocks of DeKalb Street." *HSMC Bulletin* 19, no. 3 (Fall 1974): 216–229.

Rose, Mark H. *Interstate: Express Highway Politics 1941–1956.* Lawrence, KS: Regents Press of Kansas, 1979.

Sanderlin, Walter S. "The Expanding Horizons of the Schuylkill Navigation Company, 1815–1870." *Pennsylvania History* 36, no. 2 (April 1969).

Seely, Bruce E. *Building the American Highway System: Engineers as Policy Makers.* Philadelphia: Temple University Press, 1987.

Sharlin, Harold I. *Technological Change and Its Effects in Norristown, Pennsylvania, 1900–1956*. Philadelphia: University of Pennsylvania, 1958.

Schrack, David. "Norriton Township." HSMC *Sketches* 1 (1895): 122–133.

Schuyler, David. "Prologue to Urban Renewal: The Problem of Downtown Lancaster, 1945–1960." *Pennsylvania History* 61, no. 1 (January 1994).

Schwartz, Joel. "To Every Man's Door: Railroads and the Use of Streets in Jacksonian Philadelphia." *The Pennsylvania Magazine of History and Biography* 128, no. 9 (January 2004).

Shearer, Henry K. "The Economic Effects of the Original Section of the Pennsylvania Turnpike on Adjacent Areas." PhD diss., University of Pennsylvania, 1955.

Soltow, James H. *Manufacturing in Norristown, Pennsylvania, in the Twentieth Century*. Philadelphia: University of Pennsylvania, 1954.

Smith, Edwin F. "Early Roads, Canals and Railroads in Pennsylvania." HSMC *Sketches* 4 (1910): 337–362.

Smyth, S. Gordon. "Matson's Ford." HSMC *Sketches* 4 (1910): 62–72.

Soltow, James H. "The Small City Industrialist, 1900–1950: A Case Study of Norristown, Pennsylvania." *The Business History Review* 32, no. 1 (Spring 1958).

Sweinhart, Frederick C. "The Turnpikes of Pennsylvania: Precursors of Good Roads in America." *HSMC Bulletin* 9, no. 4 (April 1955): 254–62.

Taylor, George Rogers. *The Transportation Revolution 1815–1860*. New York: Holt, Rinehart and Winston, 1951.

Toll, Jean Barth, and Schwager, Michael J., eds. *Montgomery County: The Second Hundred Years*. Norristown: Montgomery County Federation of Historical Societies, 1983.

Toole, Robert C. *Mass Communications, Norristown: Pennsylvania, 1900–1950*. Philadelphia: University of Pennsylvania, 1954.

Wallace, Paul A. *Indian Paths of Pennsylvania*. Harrisburg: The Pennsylvania Historical and Museum Commission, 1965.

Wanger, George F. P. "Pottstown's Efforts to Become a County Seat." HSMC *Sketches* 3 (1905): 367–384.

Wanger, Irving P. "The Forming of Montgomery County." HSMC *Sketches* 4:45–61.

Wharton, Robert Richard. *A Study of the Subjective Class System as Described by a Random Sample of Respondents in Norristown, Pennsylvania*. Philadelphia: University of Pennsylvania, 1961.

Zelinsky, Wilbur. "The Pennsylvania Town: An Overdue Geographical Account." *Geographical Review* 67 (1977).

Norristown Municipal Government Publications

Surviving records for the period of this study:

Council Journal

No. 12: 2/19/1935–12/29/1943; No. 13: 1/1944–12/1951; No. 14: 1/1952–2/1955; No. 15: 1/1956–12/1961; MISSING: No. 16: 1/1962–12/1965; No. 17: 1/3/1966–12/30/1968; No. 18: 1/7/1969–12/28/1970; No. 19: 1/5/1971–12/28/1973; No. 20: 1/7/1974–12/30/1976

Ordinances

No. 6: 1/5/1942–12/30/1947; No. 7: 1/1948–12/1951; No. 8: 1/7/1952–1/25/1957; No. 9: 2/5/1957–12/31/1964; No. 10: 1/1/1965–12/31/ 1971

Resolutions

No. 1: 12/6/1966–12/30/1976

Committees of the Borough of Norristown

No. 7: 1940–1941; MISSING: Nos. 8 and 9, 1942–1945; No. 10: 1946–1947; No. 11: 1948–1949; No. 12: 1950–1951; No. 13: 1952–1953; No. 14: 1954–1955; No. 15: 1956–1957; No. 16: 1958–1959; No. 17: 1960–1961; No. 18: 1962–1964; No. 19: 1965–1966; No. 20: 1967–1968; No. 21: 1969; No. 22: 1970–1971; No. 23: 1972; No. 24: 1973–1974; No. 25: 1975–1976

Collections of the Historical Society of Montgomery County

Borough of Norristown. *The Borough of Norristown, Pennsylvania 1932 Report.* HSMC files, Norristown Box: "Histories & Borough Info"

———. *Norristown: Philadelphia's Most Home-Like Suburb.* Norristown, PA: R. L. P. Reifsneider, 1905. HSMC files, Norristown Box: "Anniversary Books"

———. *Official Record of the One Hundred Twenty-Fifth Anniversary Celebration of the Borough of Norristown Pennsylvania, September Twelfth to Eighteenth, Nineteen Hundred Thirty-Seven.* HSMC files, Norristown Box: "Anniversary Books"

———. *Sesquicentennial, 1812–1962; Norristown, Pennsylvania, May 4 to 12, 1962, Souvenir Program.* HSMC files, Norristown Box: "Anniversary Books"

Montgomery County Planning Commission. *Comprehensive Plan Report for Norristown Borough–1965, Vol. I.* HSMC files, Norristown Box: "Renewal"

———. *Comprehensive Plan Report for Norristown Borough–1965, Vol. II.* HSMC files, Norristown Box: "Histories & Borough Info"

———. *Comprehensive Plan Report for Norristown Borough–1965, Vol. IV.* HSMC files, Norristown Box: "Histories & Borough Info"

———. *Comprehensive Plan Report for Norristown Borough–1968, Vol. IV.* HSMC files, Norristown Box: "Histories & Borough Info"

———. *Comprehensive Plan 1969, Norristown Borough, Montgomery County, Pennsylvania.* HSMC files, Norristown Box "Renewal"

———. "Summary and Analysis of the Norristown Borough Resident Questionnaire." October, 1966. HSMC files, Norristown Box: "Maps, Misc. Organizations"

Redevelopment Authority of the County of Montgomery, PA. *Redevelopment Proposal: Saw Mill Run Urban Renewal Plan, Norristown, Pennsylvania.* September 1966. HSMC files, Norristown Box: "Renewal"

David M. Walker Associates, Inc., Consultants, prepared for the Montgomery County Redevelopment Authority. *GNRP Interim Report: Norristown, Vol. I: Existing Conditions, Analysis and Preliminary Recommendations.* 1969. HSMC files, no file number.

———. *GNRP Interim Report: Norristown, Vol. II: Market Analysis, Housing Demand and Summary Conclusions.* 1970. HSMC files, no file number.

———. *Norristown General Neighborhood Renewal Program Interim Report Two. Market Analysis, Housing Demand and Summary Conclusions.* February 1970. HSMC files, no file number.

The Greater Norristown Corporation. *1979: The First Steps: Annual Report.* October 1979. HSMC files, Norristown Box: "Renewal"

———. *1980: The First Year: Annual Report.* April 1980. HSMC files, Norristown Box: "Renewal"

Interviews Conducted

John Ashton
Robert Butera
Francis (Frank) Caiola
John Carty
Frank (Hank Cisco) Ciaccio
John (Jack) Coll
Alice Davenport
The Honorable Horace A. Davenport
William DeAngelis
Margaret Dellasanti
Mary Ellen DiGregorio
Frances Zummo Doyle
Mary Early
Lawrence Friedman
William Giambrone
Ned Offner
Kenneth Randall
Richard H. Schmoyer
Donald Shapiro
Joseph Verunni
Karen Wolfe
Florence "Johnny" Young
Rory Zummo

Index

Endnotes

PART I

Chapter 1

1 Sidney Goldstein, ed., *The Norristown Study: An Experiment in Interdisciplinary Research Training* (Philadelphia: University of Pennsylvania Press, 1961), 4.
2 *Norristown Study*, 31.
3 Jean Barth Toll and Michael J. Schwager, eds., *Montgomery County: The Second Hundred Years* (Norristown: Montgomery County Federation of Historical Societies, 1983), 463.
4 Jane Jacobs, *The Death and Life of Great American Cities* (New York: Random House, 1961), 16.
5 J. Bennett Nolan, *The Schuylkill* (New Brunswick, NJ: Rutgers University Press, 1951), 5.
6 Nolan, *Schuylkill*, 10.
7 Edward W. Hocker, *History of Montgomery County* (unpublished manuscript), 3; Theodore Heysham, *Norristown, 1812–1912* (Norristown: Norristown Herald, 1913), 24.
8 Hocker manuscript, 3.
9 Hocker, "Chronicles of Montgomery County, 1784–1934," in Norristown *Times Herald* 9/2/1960.
10 William I. Hull, *William Penn: A Topical Biography* (London: Oxford University Press, 1937), 54.
11 John T. Faris, *Old Roads Out of Philadelphia* (Philadelphia and London: J. B. Lippincott Company, second edition, 1917).
12 E. Gordon Alderfer, *The Montgomery County Story* (Norristown: The Commissioners of Montgomery County, 1951), 930.
13 Heysham, 20.
14 H. W. Kriebel, *A Brief History of Montgomery County, Pennsylvania* (Norristown: The School Directors' Association, 1923), 130; Heysham, 25.
15 See Alderfer, Kriebel and Heysham.
16 Hocker manuscript, 796; Alderfer, 35.
17 Heysham, 26.
18 Theodore W. Bean, ed., *History of Montgomery County, Pennsylvania* (Philadelphia: Everts & Peck, HSMC, 1884), vol. II, 123.
19 Hocker manuscript, 140.
20 For the details of this process, see Samuel W. Pennypacker, "The University of Pennsylvania in its Relations to the State of Pennsylvania," *The Pennsylvania Magazine of History and Biography* XV (1891): 96.
21 Alderfer, 146.
22 Hocker manuscript, 136.
23 Irving P. Wanger, "The Forming of Montgomery County," HSMC *Sketches* 4, 55.
24 William J. Buck, *History of Montgomery County Within the Schuylkill Valley* (Norristown, PA: E. L. Acker, 1859). As reprinted in *Atlases of Montgomery County, Pennsylvania*, (Evansville, IN: Unigraphic, Inc., 1976), 89.
25 Hocker manuscript, 139; Alderfer, 146-48.
26 Montgomery County, Pennsylvania, Deed Book #2, Indenture #390, 463–464.
27 Wanger, 56–57.
28 Hocker, *TH*, 5/12/1958.
29 Deed Book #2, Indenture #390, page 463–464.
30 Pennypacker, 96.
31 Deed Book #2, Indenture #390, page 463–64.
32 Albert Frank Gegenheimer, *William Smith, Educator and Churchman, 1727–1803*, (Philadelphia: University of Pennsylvania Press, 1943), 80–87.

33 Michael G. Dubrow, "The College of Philadelphia and the Politics of Revolution," in *A Pennsylvania Album: Undergraduate Essays on the 250th Anniversary* (Philadelphia: Trustees of the University of Pennsylvania, 1990), 10–11.

Chapter 2
34 Hocker manuscript, 3; Heysham, 24.
35 Wilbur Zelinsky, "The Pennsylvania Town: An Overdue Geographical Account," *Geographical Review* 67 (1977).
36 Hocker, *TH*, 7/18/1955.
37 Hocker manuscript, 799.
38 Hocker manuscript, 801.
39 Buck, 20.
40 Hocker, *TH*, 5/18/1959; manuscript, 799–801.
41 Hocker, *TH*, 1/15/1937.
42 Hocker manuscript, 801; *TH* 1/12/1962.
43 Hocker manuscript, 801–803.
44 Hocker manuscript, 802; Alderfer, 165–166.
45 Hocker, *TH* 1/29/1937; *TH* 1/15/1962.
46 Alderfer, 97.
47 Frederick C. Sweinhart, "The Turnpikes of Pennsylvania: Precursors of Good Roads in America." *HSMC Bulletin* 9, no. 4 (April 1955): 257.
48 Heysham, 49.
49 Hocker, *TH*, 7/22/1955.
50 Hocker, *TH*, 8/6/1947.
51 Hocker manuscript, 853.
52 Alderfer, 172.
53 Edward S. Gibbons, "The Building of the Schuylkill Navigation System, 1815–1828." *Pennsylvania History* 57, no. 1 (1990): 24–32.
54 Hocker, *TH*, 2/17/1961.
55 Hocker, *TH*, 4/21/1954.
56 *Norristown Herald*, 2/23/1831.
57 George H. Douglas, *All Aboard! The Railroad in American Life* (New York: Marlowe & Company, 1992), 24–25; Sweinhart, 258.
58 *Norristown Register*, as quoted in Bean, *History*, 331.
59 Hocker, *TH*, 5/21/1971; 14.
60 Hocker, *TH*, 2/7/1951; 12/28/1953; 4/2/1956.
61 Alderfer, 174.
62 George Rogers Taylor, *The Transportation Revolution 1815–1860* (New York: Holt, Rinehart and Winston, 1951), 100.
63 Toll and Schwager, 1310.
64 Alderfer, 211; Hocker, *TH*, 5/21/1971, 14.
65 *TH*, 7/30/1934.
66 Hocker, *TH*, 8/1/1955.
67 Alvin F. Harlow, *The Road of the Century: The Story of the New York Central* (New York: Creative Age Press, 1947), 319–335.
68 Toll and Schwager, 392, 475; *TH*, 9/15/1958.

Chapter 3
69 Alderfer, 166.
70 Hocker manuscript, 807-808.
71 Victor J. Roberts, "First Five Blocks of DeKalb Street," *HSMC Bulletin* XIX, no. 3 (1974), 219; Hocker manuscript, 808.
72 Samuel D. Patterson, ed., *An Act to Erect Norristown into a Borough…and Ordinances Passed by the Town Council* (Norristown, 1833), 3–6.
73 Patterson, 24–25.

[74] Heysham, map facing page 39.
[75] Herbert Harley, *The Town on Three Hills* (unpublished manuscript).
[76] Roberts, 219; Hocker manuscript, 808.
[77] Hocker manuscript, 808.
[78] Kriebel, 142–43.
[79] Toll and Schwager, vol. II, 900.
[80] Hocker, *TH*, 4/6/1959.
[81] Toll and Schwager, vol. I, 455, 462–65.
[82] Hocker, *TH* 11/19/1951.
[83] Hocker, *TH*, 1/15/1962.
[84] *TH*, 5/3/1962, 73.
[85] *TH*, 8/19/1966, 8.
[86] *Norristown Register*, 12/14/1925.
[87] *Norristown Study*, 39; *TH* 6/5/1963, 1, 32.
[88] Hocker, *TH*, 10/24/1958.
[89] *TH* 11/16/1957; Hocker, *TH*, 1/20/1958; Alderfer, 123.
[90] Toll and Schwager, 1281.
[91] B.E. Block obituary, *TH*, 11/20/1956; *TH*, 9/9/1959.
[92] Samuel W. Pennypacker, *Autobiography of a Pennsylvanian, Volume 3* (Philadelphia: John C. Winston Co., 1918), 162.
[93] *TH*, 3/19/1957.
[94] *TH* 8/15/1958; Lawrence Friedman interview.
[95] Information on Joseph Zummo and family was obtained through interviews with Rory Zummo and Fran Doyle, granddaughters of Joseph.
[96] Hocker, *TH*, 8/11/1954.
[97] Hocker manuscript, 863; *TH*, 2/23/1962; 5/3/1962.
[98] Hocker manuscript, 863; *TH*, 2/23/1962; 5/3/1962.
[99] Hocker, *TH*, 2/5/1960.
[100] *TH*, 11/22/1963, 12.
[101] Heysham, 23–24.
[102] *TH*, 4/2/1937.
[103] *TH*, 4/3/1937.
[104] Hocker, *TH*, 9/12/1956.
[105] *Norristown Herald*, 5/11/1912.
[106] *TH*, 4/3/1937.

Chapter 4
[107] Hocker, *TH*, 4/13/1953.
[108] Hocker, *TH*, 7/7/1947; 5/8/1961.
[109] Toll and Schwager, 475.
[110] Alderfer, 91.
[111] *Herald*, 7/24/1899; 9/4/1899.
[112] Alderfer, 215.
[113] *Herald*, 7/17/1899.
[114] *TH*, 5/3/1962.
[115] *TH*, 12/21/1961; "Town Talk" column.
[116] *Norristown Register*, 8/22/1927.
[117] Hocker manuscript, 853.
[118] Hocker, *TH*, 8/1/1955; 4/2/1956; *TH*, 11/11/1925.
[119] Toll and Schwager, 1283–1284.
[120] *TH*, 3/11/1925.
[121] *TH*, 10/19/1922; 8/15/1958; Friedman interview.
[122] *TH*, 9/30/1948.
[123] *TH* 8/29/1924; Hocker, *TH*, 2/5/1960.
[124] Ciaccio, Zummo interviews.

[125] *Herald*, 11/1/1927; *Herald*, 10/5/1928; *TH*, 9/9/1959.
[126] *TH*, 1/26/1925.
[127] *TH*, 6/5/1963, 1, 32; *Norristown Study*, 39.
[128] *TH*, 6/25/1931; Hocker, *TH*, 5/24/1946.
[129] *TH*, 8/15/1924; 3/21/1928; 11/16/1957; 10/24/1958.
[130] Hocker, *TH*, 10/17/1949.
[131] Promotional pamphlet, HSMC stacks, Norristown Borough box.
[132] Hocker, *TH*, 10/17/1949.
[133] Hocker, *TH*, 10/17/1949.
[134] *TH*, 12/9/1925.
[135] Promotional pamphlet, HSMC stacks, Norristown Borough box.
[136] Hocker, *TH*, 10/17/1949.
[137] *TH*, 8/15/1924.
[138] *TH*, 1/18/1928; 1, 18.
[139] *TH*, 1/16/1929, 1, 2.
[140] *Norristown Study*, 35.
[141] *Norristown Study*, 242.
[142] Verunni interview.
[143] Randall interview.
[144] Florence Johnson Young interview.
[145] Davenport interview.
[146] *Norristown Study*, 31–34
[147] *Norristown Study*, 31.
[148] Early interview.
[149] *TH*, 8/8/1933.
[150] *TH*, 12/18/1933.
[151] *TH*, 1/21/1935.
[152] *TH*, 6/3/1935.
[153] Friedman interview.
[154] *TH*, 9/30/1947.
[155] Zummo, Doyle interviews.
[156] *TH*, 1/21/1931, 1, 2.
[157] *TH*, 1/19/1933, 1, 19.
[158] *TH*, 1/17/1934, 1, 15.
[159] *TH*, 1/16/1935, 1.
[160] *TH*, 1/21/1937, 1.
[161] *TH*, 2/2/1938, 1.
[162] *TH*, 2/2/1939, 1.
[163] *TH*, 1/18/1940, 1.
[164] *TH*, 1/16/1941, 1.
[165] Randall, Early interviews.
[166] *TH*, 5/8/1930.
[167] *TH*, 12/22/1930.
[168] Frances Zummo Doyle interview.
[169] DeAngelis interview.
[170] *TH*, 5/18/1937.
[171] *TH*, 5/27/1937.
[172] *TH*, 9/11/, 9/14, 9/16, 9/18/1937.
[173] *Register*, 1/2/1931.
[174] *TH*, 11/14/1931.
[175] *TH*, 4/21/1959.
[176] Toll and Schwager, 392.
[177] *TH*, 12/12/1931.
[178] *TH*, 12/19/1932; 7/30/1934.
[179] *TH*, 8/18/1934.

[180] Hocker, *TH*, 4/2/1956.
[181] "Town Talk" column, *TH* 12/21/1961.
[182] Borough of Norristown *Ordinances* 4.
[183] *Council Journal* 12, January 2, 1940, 279.
[184] *TH*, 2/6/1940, 1, 2.
[185] *Council Journal* 12, 2/6/1940, 286.
[186] *TH*, 2/7/1940, 1, 5.
[187] *TH*, 5/20/1940.
[188] *TH*, 12/30/1941 year end article; 1/11/1946, 1.
[189] *TH*, 1/15/1943, 1; 1/19/1943, 1.
[190] Early interview.
[191] Young interview.
[192] Doyle, Zummo interviews.
[193] *TH*, 1/21/1943, 1, 4.
[194] *TH*, 1/17/1946, 1, 4.

Chapter 5

[195] *TH*, 9/5/1945, 6.
[196] *TH*, 6/11/1946, 10.
[197] *TH*, 11/6/1947, 1, 3.
[198] *TH*, 1/16/1947, 1.
[199] *TH*, 11/16/1948, 1, 18.
[200] *Council Journal* 13, 4/5/1949, 299; Ordinance no. 827, *Ordinances* 7, 4/5/1949, 140–41.
[201] *TH*, 4/19/1949, 1.
[202] Karl Raitz, ed., *The National Road* (Baltimore and London: The Johns Hopkins University Press, 1996), 217, 221, 312–315.
[203] *TH*, 12/5/1945, 1.
[204] *TH*, 11/30/1945, 1.
[205] *TH*, 1/2/1946.
[206] *TH*, 6/18/19446, 10.
[207] *TH*, 1/20/1949, 1, 32.
[208] *TH*, 10/6/1949, 1, 2.
[209] *TH*, 1/18/1949, 1.
[210] *TH*, 1/29/1949, 1, 2.
[211] *TH*, 8/5/1949, 1.
[212] *TH*, 9/13/1950, 1, 2.
[213] *TH*, 7/3/1951, 1, 3.
[214] *TH*, 7/3/1951, 1, 3.
[215] John F. Bauman, "Expressways, Public Housing and Renewal: A Blueprint for Postwar Philadelphia, 1945-1960," in *Pennsylvania History* 57, no. 1 (1990): 52.
[216] Bruce E. Seely, *Building the American Highway System; Engineers as Policy Makers* (Philadelphia: Temple University Press, 1987).
[217] *TH*, 12/5/1949.
[218] *TH*, 8/26/1949.
[219] *TH*, 10/21/1949.
[220] *TH*, 3/25/1950.

Chapter 6

[221] *Norristown Study*, 227.
[222] *Norristown Study*, 35.
[223] William DeAngelis interview.
[224] Florence Johnson "Johnny" Young interview.
[225] Young interview
[226] Young interview.
[227] Ciaccio interview

[228] The Honorable Horace A. Davenport interview.
[229] Alice Davenport interview.
[230] Leonard Friedman interview
[231] Harry Butera, *The Memoirs of Harry Butera* (unpublished manuscript).
[232] Butera manuscript, 45.
[233] Robert Butera interview.
[234] Butera manuscript, 45.
[235] Butera interview.
[236] Butera interview
[237] Butera, DeAngelis interviews.
[238] *TH*, 1/10/1995.
[239] Butera interview.
[240] Offner interview.
[241] Butera interview.
[242] *TH*, 4/7/1972, 1, 4.
[243] Giambrone interview.
[244] Butera, DeAngelis interviews.
[245] *TH*, 4/9/1959, 11.
[246] DeAngelis interview.
[247] *TH*, 11/20/1965, 1, 3.
[248] DeAngelis interview.

Chapter 7

[249] *Norristown Study*, 31.
[250] *TH*, 11/3/1951, 1.
[251] Randall interview.
[252] Giambrone, Ciaccio interviews.
[253] Offner, Randall, Early interviews.
[254] Ciaccio interview.
[255] Young, Early interviews.
[256] Ciaccio interview.
[257] John Carty interview.
[258] Ciaccio interview,
[259] Early interview.
[260] Early, Wolfe interviews.
[261] Ciaccio interview.
[262] DeAngelis, Davenport interviews.
[263] Young, Ciaccio interviews.
[264] Ciaccio interview.
[265] Ciaccio interview.
[266] Ciaccio interview.
[267] Carty interview.
[268] Ciaccio interview.
[269] Ciaccio interview.
[270] Offner interview.
[271] John Ashton interview.
[272] George Gazonas, correspondence with the author.
[273] Ciaccio interview.
[274] Ciaccio interview.
[275] Offner, Ciaccio interviews.
[276] Ciaccio, Offner, DeAngelis, Randall interviews.
[277] Offner interview.
[278] Ciaccio interview.
[279] Ciaccio, DeAngelis, Davenport, Young interviews.
[280] Giambrone interview.

281 Frances Zummo Doyle, interview

282 Verunni interview

283 Donald Shapiro interview.

284 Friedman interview.

285 Friedman interview.

286 Butera interview

287 Ciaccio interview.

288 Rory Zummo interview.

289 Friedman interview.

290 Aristotle Gazonas, written communication with the author.

291 Ciaccio interview.

292 Ciaccio interview.

293 Verunni interview.

294 Rory Zummo interview

295 Fran Doyle interview.

296 Ciaccio interview.

297 Ned Offner, personal communication

298 *TH*, 10/25/1957, 1, 3; Ciaccio interview.

299 Ciaccio interview.

300 Ciaccio interview.

301 Ciaccio interview.

302 Ciaccio interview.

PART II

Chapter 8

303 Offner interview.

304 *TH*, 7/30/1950, 1.

305 DeAngelis interview.

306 DeAngelis, Offner interviews.

307 Harry Butera, in the *TH*, 1/6/1950, 1, 3.

308 Butera interview.

309 *Council Journal* 13, 1/24/1950, 354.

310 *Committees*, No. 12, 2, 3.

311 *Council Journal* 13, 3/7/1950, 368.

312 *Council Journal* 13, 4/4/1950, 375; *Ordinances* 7, 4/4/1950, 370–71.

313 *TH*, 8/12/1954, 1, 3.

314 *TH*, 10/14/1954, 1, 11.

315 Ciaccio interview.

316 *Council Journal* 15, 4/2/1957, no page #.

317 *TH*, 4/3/1957, 1, 3.

318 Verunni interview.

319 Early interview.

320 Norristown Chamber of Commerce.

321 Henry K. Shearer, *The Economic Effects of the Original Section of the Pennsylvania Turnpike on Adjacent Areas*, (Philadelphia: University of Pennsylvania, 1955).

322 *TH*, 6/18/1958.

323 Paul Koons, to the author.

324 *TH*, 1/9/1960, 10.

325 *Montgomery Newspapers*, 11/13/1956.

326 *TH*, 7/24/1954, 1, 2.

327 *Norristown Study*, 309–10.

Chapter 9

328 *TH*, 8/12/1952, 1, 14.
329 *TH*, 7/10/1956, 1.
330 *TH*, 6/30/1955, 1.
331 Resolution no. 1011, 4/17/1952, *Ordinances* 8, 49
332 DeAngelis interview.
333 Butera interview.
334 *TH*, 4/10/1952, 1, 34.
335 *TH*, 2/3/1956, 1, 2.
336 *TH*, 11/20/1952, 1, 3.
337 Hocker, *TH*, 8/23/1954, 11.
338 *TH*, 1/20/1954, 1, 3.
339 *TH*, 2/10/1954, 1, 20.
340 *TH*, 1/20/1954, 1, 3.
341 *TH*, 7/22/1954, 1, 3.
342 *TH*, 7/22/1954, 1, 3.
343 *TH*, 10/10/1971, 1, 3.
344 *TH*, 10/10/1961, 1, 3.
345 *TH*, 7/19/1955, 1, 3.
346 *TH*, 11/30/2002; quote is from his son, James J. Bondi.
347 *TH*, 3/5/1957, 1, 24.
348 *TH*, 5/9/1958, 1, 3.
349 In the custom of the times, the disease was not mentioned. The information comes from Rory Zummo interview.
350 *TH*, 7/5/1958, 1, 3.
351 *TH*, 6/25/1959, 1.
352 *TH*, 9/24/1959, 18.
353 Ciaccio, Early, Wolfe interviews.
354 *TH*, 1/19/1961, 2.
355 *TH*, 1/16/1958, 1, 3.
356 *TH*, 1/18/1962, 1, 4.
357 *TH*, 7/28/1954, 10.

Chapter 10

358 *Council Journal* 15, 8/9/1961, no page #.
359 *Council Journal* 15, 9/5/1961, no page #.
360 Ordinance no. 967, 10/10/1951, *Ordinances* 7, 367; *Council Journal* 13, 10/10/1951, 502.
361 Resolution no. 973, 12/4/1951, *Ordinances* 7, 381; Resolution no. 974, 12/4/1951, *Ordinances* 7, 382.
362 Resolution no. 1000, 3/4/1952, *Ordinances* 7, 34; Resolution no. 1001, 3/4/1952, *Ordinances* 7, 35.
363 Ordinance no. 1047, 11/10/1952, *Ordinances* 8, 95–96.
364 *TH*, 9/21/1956, 1, 3.
365 *TH*, 9/21/1956, 1, 3.
366 *Council Journal* 14, 12/17/1953, no page #; Ordinance no. 1097, 12/17/1953; *Ordinances* 8, no page #.
367 Ordinance no. 1097, 12/17/1953; *Ordinances* 8, no page #.
368 *Council Journal* 14, July 12, 1953, no page #; *TH*, 7/15/1953, 1, 18.
369 *Council Journal* 14, August 4, 1953, no page #; *TH*, 8/5/1953, 1, 3.
370 Charles Kelly, to the author.
371 *Council Journal* 14, 11/3/1954, no page #; *TH*, 11/4/1954, 1, 2.
372 *Council Journal* 15, 3/5/1957, no page #.
373 *Council Journal* 15, 3/3/1959, no page #.

[374] *Council Journal* 15, 4/7/1959, no page #; Ordinance no. 1419, 3/3/1959, *Ordinances* 9, no page #.
[375] *Council Journal* 15, 9/2/1958, no page #.
[376] *Council Journal* 15, 11/5/1958, no page #.
[377] *TH*, 1/22/1959, 1, 3.
[378] *TH*, 5/4/1960, 1.
[379] *TH*, 6/12/1961, 1, 3.
[380] *TH*, 6/13/1961, 1.
[381] *TH*, 12/21/1962, 1, 18.
[382] *TH*, 12/21/1962, 1, 18.

Chapter 11
[383] *Council Journal* 15, April 5, 1960, no page #; *TH*, 4/6/1960, 1.
[384] *TH*, 5/14/1962, 1, 24.
[385] *TH*, 5/3/1962, 1, 20.
[386] DeAngelis, Davenport interviews
[387] *TH*, 7/29/1954, 1, 3.
[388] *TH*, 8/8/1953, 1
[389] Ciaccio interview.

PART III

Chapter 12
[390] *TH*, 5/3/1962, 3.
[391] MCPC, "Comprehensive Plan—1965, Vol. IV," HSMC files, Norristown Box: "Renewal," IX–59.
[392] MCPC Comprehensive Plan—1965, vol. IV, IX–61.
[393] MCPC Comprehensive Plan—1965, Vol. I, II–35.
[394] MCPC Comprehensive Plan—1965, Vol. II, xiv.
[395] *TH*, 11/29/1966, 1, 4.
[396] *TH*, 1/30/1969, 1.
[397] David M. Walker Associates Inc., *GNRP, Interim Report: Norristown, Vol. II: Existing Conditions, Analysis and Preliminary Recommendations. (1970)*, 33–35.
[398] Walker, *GNRP, Interim Report, vol. II* (December 1969), section II, no page #.
[399] Walker, *GNRP, Interim Report, vol. II* (December 1969), section II, no page #.
[400] Walker, *GNRP, Interim Report, vol. II* (December 1969), section II, no page #.
[401] Walker, *GNRP, Interim Report, vol. II* (December 1969), section II, no page #.
[402] Walker, *GNRP, Interim Report, vol. II* (December 1969), section II, no page #.
[403] *Comprehensive Plan 1969, Norristown Borough, Montgomery County Pennsylvania.* HSMC files, Norristown Box: "Renewal," no page #.
[404] *Council Journal* 18, 7/7/1970, no page #.
[405] DeAngelis interview.
[406] *TH*, 7/10/1963, 1, 3.
[407] *TH*, 11/19/1964, 18.
[408] Jack Coll interview.
[409] Doyle interview.
[410] Early interview.
[411] *TH*, 3/4/1968, 1, 7.
[412] *TH*, 5/21/1968, 5.
[413] *TH*, 11/8/1968, 1, 3.
[414] Walker, *GNRP, Interim Report, vol. II* (February 1970), 22.
[415] Walker, "Estimated Sales Structure of Major Shopping Centers and Other Areas of Retail Activity Forming Part of the Retail Market Surrounding Norristown, Pennsylvania, 1968/9 (Annual Sales, $000)"; *GNRP, Interim Report, vol. II,* 12–13.
[416] *TH*, 5/21/1968, 4.

[417] *TH*, 1/24/1969, 1, 2.
[418] *TH*, 1/29/1970, 1, 2.
[419] *TH*, 4/24/1964, 1, 4.
[420] *TH*, 4/24/1964, 1, 4.
[421] Friedman, Dellasanti interviews.
[422] Butera interview.
[423] Butera interview.
[424] *TH*, 3/15/1963, 1, 6.
[425] *TH*, 7/23/1965, 1, 6.
[426] *TH*, 7/24/1965, 8.
[427] *TH*, 2/2/1965, 10.
[428] *TH*, 7/22/1954, 14.
[429] *TH*, 7/8/1964, 1, 40.
[430] *TH*, 7/20/1964, 10.
[431] *TH*, 7/24/1964, 1, 14.
[432] *TH*, 11/13/1964, 1, 3.
[433] *TH*, 9/29/1965, 1, 12.
[434] *Council Journal* 17, 12/6/1966, no page #.
[435] *TH*, 12/7/1966, 1, 34.
[436] *TH*, 12/12/1966, 18.
[437] *TH*, 4/27/1967, 1, 46.
[438] *TH*, 11/8/1963, 1, 14.
[439] *TH*, 6/12/1964, 3.
[440] *TH*, 1/17/1967, 5.
[441] *TH*, 1/16/1968, 6, 1/14/1969, 17.
[442] *TH*, 7/1/1963, 1, 24.
[443] *TH*, 2/7/1963, 18.
[444] *TH*, 8/16/1965, 9.
[445] *TH*, 5/2/1966.

Chapter 13
[446] Ciaccio interview.
[447] Doyle interview.
[448] *TH*, 7/28/1970, 1, 5.
[449] Doyle interview.
[450] *TH*, 5/17/1972, 1.
[451] *TH*, 4/27/1970, 1.
[452] *TH*, 11/8/1971, 16.
[453] *TH*, 1/14/1972, 9.
[454] Wolfe interview.
[455] Richard H. Schmoyer interview.
[456] *TH*, 12/2/1972, 1.
[457] Giambrone interview.
[458] *TH*, 2/17/1971, 2.
[459] Giambrone interview.
[460] *TH*, 2/12/1972, 3.
[461] *TH*, 6/21/1971, 1, 10.
[462] *TH*, 6/19/1971, 1, 12.
[463] Toll and Schwager, 459; Caiola interview.
[464] Caiola interview.
[465] Caiola interview.
[466] *Council Journal* 19, 11/9/1971, no page #.
[467] *Council Journal* 19, 3/7/1972, no page #; *TH*, 2/3/1973, 1, 13.
[468] *Council Journal* 18, 7/27/1970, no page #.
[469] *Council Journal* 18, 7/27/1970, no page #.

470 *Council Journal* 19, 1/14/1971, no page #.
471 "Report and Recommendations of the Norristown Charter Commission," April 2, 1971. HSMC files, Norristown "Renewal" box.
472 Charter Commission Report; *TH,* 4/3/1971, 1, 3.
473 *TH,* 6/9/1971, 1, 3.
474 Caiola interview.
475 *Council Journal* 19, 12/7/1971, no page #; *TH* 12/8/1971, 1, 13.
476 *Council Journal* 19, 12/29/1971, no page #.
477 *Council Journal* 19, 2/1/1972, no page #; *TH,* 2/2/1972, 1, 8.
478 *TH,* 7/6/1973, 1, 34
479 *TH,* 1/19/1970, 1.
480 *TH,* 4/3/1970, 14
481 *TH,* 11/27/1970, 1, 8.
482 *Committees* 22, 5/10/1971, no page #.
483 *Council Journal* 19, 11/9/1971, no page #.
484 *TH,* 4/21/1972, 1.
485 *TH,* 4/26/1972, 4.
486 *Committees* 24, 5/21/1973, no page #.
487 *Council Journal* 19, 12/28/1973, no page #.
488 *Committees* 24, 4/4/1974 no page #.
489 *TH,* 4/5/1974, 1, 22.
490 *Council Journal* 20, 5/7/1974, no page #.
491 *TH,* 7/11/1974, 1, 30.
492 *Council Journal* 20, 4/2/1974, no page #.
493 Giambrone interview.
494 *TH,* 2/22/1974, 1, 11.
495 *TH,* 7/24/1974, 1, 6.
496 Butera interview.
497 Wolfe interview.
498 *TH,* 9/23/1975, 2.
499 The net numbers also do not reflect any fluctuation in the net totals that may have occurred during that span of years. In the case of Government-County, this was significant; of Bank, less so; both were discussed in the narrative.
500 Schmoyer interview.

CPSIA information can be obtained
at www.ICGtesting.com
Printed in the USA
BVHW041309040520
579166BV00012B/453

9 780615 722221